Clashing Views in

Business Ethics and Society

TWELFTH EDITION

Selected, Edited, and with Introductions by

Lisa H. Newton
Fairfield University

Elaine E. Englehardt
Utah Valley University

Michael S. Pritchard
Western Michigan

McGraw Hill

Connect
Learn
Succeed™

TAKING SIDES: CLASHING VIEWS IN BUSINESS ETHICS AND SOCIETY, TWELFTH EDITION

Published by McGraw-Hill, a business unit of The McGraw-Hill Companies, Inc., 1221 Avenue of the Americas, New York, NY 10020. Copyright © 2012 by The McGraw-Hill Companies, Inc. All rights reserved. Previous edition(s) © 2010, 2008, and 2006. Printed in the United States of America. No part of this publication may be reproduced or distributed in any form or by any means, or stored in a database or retrieval system, without the prior written consent of The McGraw-Hill Companies, Inc., including, but not limited to, in any network or other electronic storage or transmission, or broadcast for distance learning.

Some ancillaries, including electronic and print components, may not be available to customers outside the United States.

Taking Sides® is a registered trademark of the McGraw-Hill Companies, Inc.
Taking Sides is published by the **Contemporary Learning Series** group within the McGraw-Hill Higher Education division.

1 2 3 4 5 6 7 8 9 0 DOC/DOC 1 0 9 8 7 6 5 4 3 2 1

MHID: 0-07-352735-1
ISBN: 978-0-07-352735-2
ISSN: 95-8385

Managing Editor: *Larry Loeppke*
Senior Developmental Editor: *Jade Benedict*
Senior Permissions Coordinator: *DeAnna Dausener*
Senior Marketing Communications Specialist: *Mary Klein*
Marketing Specialist: *Alice Link*
Project Manager: *Erin Melloy*
Design Coordinator: *Brenda A. Rolwes*
Cover Graphics: *Rick D. Noel*
Buyer: *Nicole Baumgartner*
Media Project Manager: *Sridevi Palani*

Compositor: MPS Limited, a Macmillan Company
Cover Image: © Getty Images RF

www.mhhe.com

Editors/Academic Advisory Board

Members of the Academic Advisory Board are instrumental in the final selection of articles for each edition of TAKING SIDES. Their review of articles for content, level, and appropriateness provides critical direction to the editors and staff. We think that you will find their careful consideration well reflected in this volume.

TAKING SIDES: Clashing Views in BUSINESS ETHICS AND SOCIETY
Twelfth Edition

EDITORS

Lisa H. Newton
Fairfield University

Elaine E. Englehardt
Utah Valley University

Michael S. Pritchard
Western Michigan

ACADEMIC ADVISORY BOARD MEMBERS

Preface

*The principle by which we naturally either approve or disapprove of our own
conduct, seems to be altogether the same with that by which we exercise the
like judgments concerning the conduct of other people. We either approve or
disapprove of the conduct of another man according as we feel that, when
we bring his case home to ourselves [i.e. when we imagine ourselves into his
situation], we either can or cannot entirely sympathize with the sentiments
and motives which directed it. And, in the same manner, we either approve
or disapprove of our own conduct, according as we feel that, when we place
ourselves in the situation of another man, and view it, as it were, with his
eyes and from his station, we either can or cannot entirely enter into and sympathize with the sentiments and motives which influenced it. We can never
survey our own sentiments and motives, we can never form any judgment concerning them, unless we remove ourselves, as it was, from our natural station,
and endeavor to view them as at a certain distance from us. But we can do
this in no other way than by endeavoring to view them with the eyes of other
people, or as other people are likely to view them.*

(Adam Smith, *The Theory of Moral Sentiments,*
in Raphael, vol. 2, p. 226).[1]

This volume is the twelfth edition of *Taking Sides: Clashing Views in Business
Ethics and Society*, and is edited by Lisa H. Newton, Elaine E. Englehardt, and
Michael S. Pritchard. It contains 40 sections, presented in a pro and con format,
that debate a total of 20 different controversial issues in business ethics. In this
book we ask you, the reader to examine the accepted practices of business in the
light of justice, rights, dignity, and human needs. As Smith notes in the preceding
paragraph, we ask you to consider what moral imperatives and values should be at
work for you and for others. Specifically we ask this in the light of business
practices.

This method of presenting opposing views on an issue grows out of the
ancient learning method of dialogue. Two assumptions lead us to seek the truth
in a dialogue between opposed positions. The first assumption is that the Truth
is really available to us, and that it is important for us to find it. The second is
that no one of us has the entire truth, or truth with a capital T. The way to reach
the truth is to form our initial opinions on a subject and give voice to them in
oral and written form. These opinions must pass the test of public discussion in
that it presents information in a sensible manner. Then we let others with differing opinions reply, and while they are doing so, we listen carefully. The truth
that comes into being in the public space of dialogue—literally, the space

---

[1]Adam Smith, in D.D. Raphael and A.L. Macfie, eds., *The Theory of Moral Sentiments* (Oxford,
1976).

between the two disputants—becomes part of our opinions on other related matters. We now have more informed opinions, and they are reliably based on the reasoning that emerged in the course of airing those views.

Each issue in this volume has an issue *introduction* that sets the stage for the debate as it is argued in the YES and NO selections. Each issue concludes with a *postscript* that makes some final observations and points the way to other questions related to the issue. The introductions and postscripts do not preempt what is the reader's specific task: to achieve a critical and informed view of the issue at stake. In reading an issue and forming your own opinion, you should not feel confined to adopt one or the other of the positions presented. There are positions in between the given views, or totally outside them, and the *suggestions for further reading* that appear in each issue postscript should help you to continue your study of the subject. At the back of the book is a listing of all the *contributors to this volume*, for further information on the varied backgrounds of the writers represented in this book.

Changes to this edition   This edition represents a change in editors and a substantial revision. Lisa H. Newton continues as the lead editor. We thank Maureen M. Ford for the work she has completed in past editions. Elaine E. Englehardt and Michael S. Pritchard join Lisa H. Newton in presenting four new issues and nine new writings. These issues include: Can Individual Virtue Survive Corporate Pressure? (Issue 4); Are the Risks of Derivatives Manageable? (Issue 5); Should Price Gouging be Regulated? (Issue 9); Are Sweatshops an Inhumane Business Practice? (Issue 18). We have changed an author on a favorite issue: Is Increasing Profits the Only Social Responsibility of Business? by including an interesting view by Michael Porter and Mark Kramer (Issue 3).

A word to the instructor   *Taking Sides: Clashing Views in Business Ethics and Society* is only one title in the *Taking Sides* series. If you are interested in seeing the table of contents for any other titles, please visit the *Taking Sides* Web site at http://www.mhhe.com/cls. You may also consult the *Taking Sides* correlation chart.

Acknowledgments   We thank our families for their support, patience, caring, and spunk. Thanks also to colleagues Matt Holland, Caitlin Anderson, and Danielle. A special tribute to Millie and Kirk.

Lisa H. Newton
Fairfield University

Elaine E. Englehardt
Utah Valley University

Michael S. Pritchard
Western Michigan University

Contents In Brief

Contents

If we will but leave self-interested people to seek their own advantage, Adam Smith (1723–1790) argues, the result, unintended by any one of them, will be the greater advantage of all. No government interference is necessary to protect the general welfare. Leave people to their own self-interested devices, Karl Marx (1818–1883) and Friedrich Engels (1820–1895) reply, and those who by luck and inheritance own the means of production will rapidly reduce everyone else to virtual slavery. The few may be fabulously happy, but all others will live in misery.

Johnson and Kwak argue that risk always has been and always will be a vital ingredient in the making of profits. They explain that when imprudent risks are taken whether in life or in business, the consequences can be harmful for many, not just the risk taker. The consequences of bad risks do not change their views on the value of risk in business. Eichengreen believes that economists have overrated risk as the essential feature for a successful business. He believes much of the economic collapse of 2008 was caused by inappropriate risks that perhaps economic theories sanctioned, but should have never been practiced.

Friedman argues that businesses have neither the right nor the ability to fool around with social responsibility as distinct from profit-making. They serve employees and customers best when they do their work with maximum efficiency. The only restrictions on the pursuit of profit that Friedman accepts are the requirements of law and "the rules of the game" ("open and free competition without deception or fraud"). Porter and Kramer ask that the purpose of the corporation be redefined as one of shared value, which brings the needs and interests of society and business together. By enhancing the needs of society, the supply and demands within business will stabilize for new generations.

Joining the long-standing debate on the possibility of free choice and moral agency in the business world, Quincy Lee Centennial Professor of Business and Philosophy at the University of Texas in Austin Robert C. Solomon argues that whatever the structures, the individual's choice is free, and therefore his character or virtue is of the utmost importance in creating a good moral tone in the life of a business. Stuart Professor of Philosophy at Princeton University Gilbert Harman employs determinist arguments to conclude that no individual can of his own free choice make a difference in a group enterprise.

Eric Krell finds that one of the major corporate goals of the human resource office is to build true corporate ethics. He believes this can be done with a code of ethics, through performance reviews, and with ethics audits. Through this process, employees' good and corporate good can become the same. Greg Young and David Hasler believe that strengthening the role of ethical and reputational capital has been given the short shrift within corporations. It may be that one day ethics audits and ethics codes could be essential in building capital. However, they state that until management understands that poor ethics make for poor profits, business practices will continue to ignore the place of an ethics core within their organization.

Jeremy Snyder contends that price gouging conflicts with the goal of equitable access to goods essential to a minimally flourishing human life. Efficient provision of essential goods is not sufficient to prevent serious inequities. Regulations are needed for equitable access. Matt Zwolinski argues that price gouging can be morally permissible, even though this does not mean that price gougers are morally virtuous. Considerations of the availability of institutional alternatives and distributive justice may render price gouging morally acceptable. In any case, regulations cannot be expected to resolve the moral issues more satisfactorily than the market itself.

UNIT 3   HUMAN RESOURCES: THE CORPORATION AND EMPLOYEES   173

Issue 10.   Does Blowing the Whistle Violate Company Loyalty?   174

Philosopher Sissela Bok asserts that although blowing the whistle is often justified, it does involve dissent, accusation, and a breach of loyalty to the employer. Robert A. Larmer argues, on the contrary, that putting a stop to illegal or unethical company activities may be the highest type of loyalty an employee can display.

Issue 11.   Is Employer Monitoring of Employee Social Media Justified?   192

Brian Elzweig and Donna K. Peeples write that although an employer does need to be respectful of their employees' privacy, they also have the responsibility to avoid negligent hiring and negligent retention. They find that the monitoring of an employee's, or a potential employee's, social media is a viable way to avoid these potentially serious problems. This is not to say that an employer's monitoring of social media should be without limits. Special care should be taken in respect to state privacy laws regarding expected privacy and laws regarding the protection of employees outside of company time. Eric Krell recognizes the importance of employee privacy and believes that it must be safeguarded. To appropriately do so, he believes that a concrete, written plan needs to be drafted, and often reevaluated, in coordination with each company's human resource department and a VP of employee security. This will ensure not only a uniform policy throughout the company, but will disclose to the employees if and in what ways their social media will be monitored.

Roger Lowenstein explains that often businesses decide to walk away from enterprises that aren't sound investments. He uses this analogy to conclude that it is acceptable for homeowners to walk away from their home investment when the value of the home is much less than the overall loan on the home. Rick Moran explains that just because businesses walk away from poor investments doesn't mean that Americans should also lack ethics. He encourages home buyers to remain true to their ethical obligations with their housing investment even though the economic costs can be high.

The consumer's interest in knowing where his food comes from does not necessarily have to do with the chemical and nutritional properties of the food. Kosher pastrami, for instance, is identical to the nonkosher product, and dolphin-safe tuna is still tuna. But we have a real and important interest in knowing the processes by which our foods arrived on the table, Bereano argues, and the demand for a label for bioengineered foods is entirely legitimate. Levitt points out that as far as the law is concerned, only the nutritional traits and characteristics of foods are subject to safety assessment. Labeling has been required only where health risks exist, or where there is danger that a product's marketing claims may mislead the consumer as to the food's characteristics. Breeding techniques have never been subject to labeling, nor should genetic engineering techniques.

UNIT 5   GLOBAL OBJECTIVES   293

In the absence of accepted enforcement agencies, there is little probability that any multinational corporation will suffer for violation of rules restricting business for the sake of the common good. Since any business that tried to conform to moral rules in the absence of enforcement would unjustifiably cease to be competitive, it must be the case, Velasquez argues, that moral strictures are not binding on such companies. Velasquez's logic is impressive, replies Fleming, but conditions on the ground in the multinational corporation are not as he describes. Real corporations tend to deal with long-term customers and suppliers in the goldfish bowl of international media exposure and must adhere to moral standards or lose business.

Philosophers Arnold and Bowie argue that managers of multinational enterprises have a duty to ensure that workers in their supply chains are treated with dignity and respect, which includes paying a living wage to those who work in factories with which they contract. Sollars and Englander contend that this work is needed for the very survival of individuals, and the multinational enterprises are not participating directly in the coercion of the workers in sweatshops.

Schulman holds that the human genome is a different business enterprise than other patent applications. The genome stands for essential building blocks of the human species and as such questions of ethics and human dignity should be studied. Lever explains that the U.S. Patent Office has issued thousands of patents on genes and believes the legality of this is established. She also believes the moral concerns have been answered on patents, mainly because the genes have been isolated and altered significantly and are part of a scientific bank of genes for overall research.

Red Cavaney, president and chief executive officer of the American Petroleum Institute, argues that recent revolutionary advances in technology will yield sufficient quantities of available oil for the foreseeable future. James Howard Kunstler contends that the peak of oil production, Hubbert's Peak, was itself the important turning point in our species' relationship to petroleum. Unless strong conservation measures are put in place, the new scarcity will destroy much that we have come to expect in our lives.

Correlation Guide

The *Taking Sides* series presents current issues in a debate-style format designed to stimulate student interest and develop critical-thinking skills. Each issue is thoughtfully framed with an issue summary, an issue introduction, and a postscript. The pro and con essays—selected for their liveliness and substance—represent the arguments of leading scholars and commentators in their fields.

Taking Sides: Clashing Views in Business Ethics and Society, 12/e is an easy-to-use reader that presents issues on important topics such as *green technology, CEO compensation,* and *price gouging.* For more information on *Taking Sides* and other *McGraw-Hill Contemporary Learning Series* titles, visit www.mhhe.com/cls.

This convenient guide matches the issues in **Taking Sides: Business Ethics and Society, 12/e** with the corresponding chapters in three of our best-selling McGraw-Hill Ethics textbooks by DesJardins, Hosmer and Ghillyer.

Taking Sides: Business Ethics and Society, 12/e	An Introduction to Business Ethics, 4/e by DesJardins	The Ethics of Management, 7/e by Hosmer	Business Ethics Now, 3/e by Ghillyer
Issue 1. Can Capitalism Lead to Human Happiness?	**Chapter 1:** Why Study Ethics?	**Chapter 6:** How Can a Business Organization Be Made Moral?	**Chapter 1:** Understanding Ethics
Issue 2. Is Risk the Best Theory for Capitalism?	**Chapter 2:** Ethical Theory and Business	**Chapter 2:** Moral Analysis and Economic Outcomes	**Chapter 2:** Defining Business Ethics
Issue 3. Is Increasing Profits the Only Social Responsibility of Business?	**Chapter 3:** Corporate Social Responsibility?	**Chapter 6:** How Can a Business Organization Be Made Moral?	**Chapter 4:** Corporate Social Responsibility
Issue 4. Can Individual Virtue Survive Corporate Pressure?	**Chapter 7:** Ethical Responsibilities in the Workplace?	**Chapter 1:** The Nature of Moral Problems in Management	**Chapter 5:** Corporate Governance
Issue 5. Can Ethics Codes Build "True" Corporate Ethics?	**Chapter 7:** Ethical Responsibilities in the Workplace?	**Chapter 3:** Moral Analysis and Legal Requirements	**Chapter 3:** Organizational Ethics
Issue 6. Was the Financial Industry Responsible for the Economic Meltdown of 2008?	**Chapter 2:** Ethical Theory and Business	**Chapter 3:** Moral Analysis and Legal Requirements	**Chapter 5:** Corporate Governance **Chapter 6:** The Role of Government
Issue 7. Should the Government Be Responsible to Bailout Financial Institutions to Avert an Economic Disaster?	**Chapter 4:** Corporate Culture, Governance, and Ethical Leadership	**Chapter 3:** Moral Analysis and Legal Requirements	**Chapter 6:** The Role of Government

(Continued)

Taking Sides: Business Ethics and Society, 12/e	An Introduction to Business Ethics, 4/e by DesJardins	The Ethics of Management, 7/e by Hosmer	Business Ethics Now, 3/e by Ghillyer
Issue 8. Are the Risks of Derivatives Manageable?	**Chapter 7:** Ethical Responsibilities in the Workplace?	**Chapter 2:** Moral Analysis and Economic Outcomes	**Chapter 5:** Corporate Governance
Issue 9. Should Price Gouging Be Regulated?	**Chapter 3:** Corporate Social Responsibility? **Chapter 4:** Corporate Culture, Governance, and Ethical Leadership **Chapter 8:** Marketing Ethics: Product Safety, Pricing, and Suppliers	**Chapter 2:** Moral Analysis and Economic Outcomes	**Chapter 5:** Corporate Governance
Issue 10. Does Blowing the Whistle Violate Company Loyalty?	**Chapter 7:** Ethical Responsibilities in the Workplace?	**Chapter 1:** The Nature of Moral Problems in Management **Chapter 4:** Moral Analysis and Ethical Duties	**Chapter 7:** Blowing the Whistle
Issue 11. Is Employer Monitoring of Employee Social Media Justified?	**Chapter 6:** Moral Rights in the Workplace	**Chapter 3:** Moral Analysis and Legal Requirements	**Chapter 8:** Ethics and Technology
Issue 12. Is "Employment-at-Will" Good Social Policy?	**Chapter 6:** Moral Rights in the Workplace	**Chapter 4:** Moral Analysis and Ethical Duties	**Chapter 5:** Corporate Governance
Issue 13. Is CEO Compensation Justified by Performance?	**Chapter 4:** Corporate Culture, Governance, and Ethical Leadership	**Chapter 4:** Moral Analysis and Ethical Duties	**Chapter 5:** Corporate Governance
Issue 14. Should Advertising Directed at Children be Restricted?	**Chapter 9:** Marketing Ethics: Advertising and Target Marketing	**Chapter 3:** Moral Analysis and Legal Requirements **Chapter 4:** Moral Analysis and Ethical Duties	**Chapter 4:** Corporate Social Responsibility
Issue 15. Should Homeowners Employ Strategic Default Options with Mortgages?	**Chapter 9:** Marketing Ethics: Advertising and Target Marketing	**Chapter 2:** Moral Analysis and Economic Outcomes	**Chapter 10:** Making it Stick: Doing What's Right in a Competitive Market
Issue 16. Should We Require Labeling for Genetically Modified Food?	**Chapter 9:** Marketing Ethics: Advertising and Target Marketing	**Chapter 4:** Moral Analysis and Ethical Duties	**Chapter 8:** Ethics and Technology
Issue 17. Are Multinational Corporations Free from Moral Obligation?	**Chapter 12:** International Business and Globalization	**Chapter 6:** How Can a Business Organization Be Made Moral?	**Chapter 9:** Ethics and Globalization
Issue 18. Are Sweatshops an Inhumane Business Practice?	**Chapter 12:** International Business and Globalization	**Chapter 6:** How Can a Business Organization Be Made Moral?	**Chapter 9:** Ethics and Globalization
Issue 19. Should Patenting Genes Be Understood as Unethical?	**Chapter 10:** Business' Environmental Responsibilities	**Chapter 4:** Moral Analysis and Ethical Duties	**Chapter 8:** Ethics and Technology
Issue 20. Should the World Continue to Rely on Oil as a Major Source of Energy?	**Chapter 10:** Business' Environmental Responsibilities **Chapter 12:** International Business and Globalization	**Chapter 4:** Moral Analysis and Ethical Duties	**Chapter 9:** Ethics and Globalization

Introduction

An Essay on the Background of Business Ethics: Ethics, Economics, Law, and the Corporation

Philosophy is a conversation; philosophical ethics is a conversation about conduct, the doing of good and the avoiding of evil. Business ethics is a conversation about right and wrong conduct in the business world. This book is aimed at an audience of students who expect to pursue careers in business, who know that there are knotty ethical problems out there, and who want a chance to confront them ahead of time. The method of confronting them is an invitation to join in a debate, a contest of contrary facts and conflicting values in many of the major issues of the millennium. This introductory essay, in effect a short text on the major components of business theory, should make it easier to join in the argument. Managing ethical policy problems in a company takes a wide background—in ethics, economics, law, and the social sciences—that the book cannot hope to provide. But since some background assumptions in these fields are relevant to several of the problems we take on, we will sketch out very briefly the major understandings that control them. There is ultimately no substitute for thorough study of the rules of the game and years of experience and practice, but an overview of the playing field may at least make it easier for a novice to understand the object and limitations of the standard plays.

Business ethics was generally known as the world's most famous oxymoron (a term that contradicts itself into impossibility) until the last thirty years. Then came the alarming newspaper headlines. Foreign bribes, scandals on Wall Street, exploding cars, conflicts over whistleblowers and civil rights in the workplace suddenly came into the headlines and would not go away. Now we know that value questions are never absent from business decisions, and that moral responsibility is the first requirement of a manager in any business. Out of all this has emerged a general consensus that a thorough grounding in ethical reasoning is essential preparation for a career in business.

This book will not supply the substance of a course in ethics. For that you are directed to any of several excellent texts in business ethics (see the suggested readings at the end of this essay), or to any general text in ethics. *Taking Sides* teaches ethics from the issue upward, rather than from the principle downward. You will, however, come upon much of the terminology of ethical reasoning in the course of considering these cases.

Economics: the Capitalist Background

Capitalism as we know it is the product of the thought of Adam Smith (1723–1790), a Scottish philosopher and economist, and a small number of his European contemporaries. The fundamental "capitalist act" is the *voluntary exchange:* Two adults, of sound mind and clear purposes, meet in the marketplace, to which each repairs in order to satisfy some felt need. They discover that each has that which will satisfy the other's need—the housewife needs flour, the miller needs cash—and they exchange, at a price such that the exchange furthers the interest of each. The *marginal utility* to the participant in the free market of the thing acquired must exceed that of the thing traded, or else why would he make the deal? So each party to the voluntary exchange walks away from it richer.

Adding to the value of the exchange is the *competition* of dealers and buyers; because there are many purveyors of each good, the customer is not forced to pay exorbitant prices for things needed (it is a sad fact of economics that to the starving man, the marginal value of a loaf of bread is very large, and a single merchant could become unjustly rich). Conversely, competition among the customers (typified by an auction) makes sure that the available goods end in the hands of those to whom they are worth the most. So at the end of the market day, not only does everyone go home richer (in real terms) than when he came—the voluntariness of the exchange ensures that—but also, as rich as he could possibly be, since he had available all possible options of goods or services to buy and all possible purchasers of his goods or services for sale.

Sellers and buyers win the competition through *efficiency*, through producing the best quality goods at the lowest possible price, or through allotting their scarce resources toward the most valuable of the choices presented to them. It is to the advantage of all participants in the market, then, to strive for efficiency, that is, to keep the cost of goods for sale as low as possible while keeping the quality as high as possible. Adam Smith's most memorable accomplishment was to recognize that the general effect of all this self-interested scrambling would be to make the most possible goods of the best possible quality available at the lowest possible price. Meanwhile, sellers and buyers alike must keep an eye on the market as a whole, adjusting production and purchasing to take advantage of fluctuations in *supply and demand*. Short supply will make goods more valuable, raising the price, and that will bring more suppliers into the market, whose competition will lower the price, to just above the cost of manufacture for the most efficient producers. Increased demand for any reason will have the same effect. Should supply exceed demand, the price will fall to a point where the goods will be bought. Putting this all together, Smith realized that in a system of free enterprise, you have demonstrably the best possible chance of finding for sale what you want, in good quantity and quality, at a reasonable price. Forget benevolent monarchs ordering things for our good, he suggested; in this system we are led as by an *"invisible hand"* to serve the common good even as we think we are being selfish.

Adam Smith's theory of economic enterprise and the "wealth of nations" emerged in the Natural Law tradition of the eighteenth century. As was the fashion for that period, Smith presented his conclusions as a series of iron laws: the Law of Supply and Demand that links supply, demand, and price; the law that links efficiency with success; and ultimately, the laws that link the absolute freedom of the market with the absolute growth of the wealth of the free market country.

To these laws were added others, specifying the conditions under which business enterprise would be conducted in capitalist countries. The laws of *population* of Thomas Malthus (1766–1834) concluded that the supply of human beings would always reach the limits of its food supply, ensuring that the bulk of humanity would always live at the subsistence level. Since Smith had already proved that employers will purchase labor at the lowest possible price, it was a one-step derivation for David Ricardo (1772–1823) to conclude that workers' *wages* would never exceed the subsistence level, no matter how prosperous industrial enterprise should become. From these capitalist theorists alone proceeded the nineteenth-century assumption that society would inevitably divide into two classes, a tiny minority of fabulous wealth and a vast majority of subsistence-level workers.

The Marxian Critique

For Western political philosophy, history emerged as a significant factor in our understanding with the work of the nineteenth-century philosopher G. W. F. Hegel (1770–1831), who traced the history of the Western world as an ordered series of ideal forms, evolving one from another in logical sequence toward an ideal future. A young German student of Hegel's, Karl Marx (1818–1883), concluded from his study of economics that Hegel had to be wrong: The phases of history were ruled not by ideas, but by the *material conditions* of life, and their evolution one from another came about as the ruling class of each age generated its own revolutionary overthrow.

Marx's theory, especially as it applies to the evolution of capitalism, is enormously complex; for the purposes of this unit, it can be summarized simply. According to Marx, the *ruling class* in every age is the group that *owns the means of production* of the age's product. Through the seventeenth century, the product was almost exclusively agricultural, and the means of production was almost exclusively agricultural land: Landowners were the aristocrats and rulers. With the coming of commerce and industry, the owners of the factories joined the ruling class and eventually dominated it. It was in the nature of such capital-intensive industry to concentrate within itself more capital: Its greater efficiency would, as Adam Smith had proved, drive all smaller labor-intensive industry out of business, and its enormous income would be put to work as more capital, expanding the domain of the factory and the machine indefinitely (at the expense of the cottage and the human being). Thus would the wealth of society concentrate in fewer and fewer hands, as the owners of the factories expanded their enterprises without limit into mighty industrial empires, dominated by machines and by the greed of their owners.

Meanwhile, all this wealth was being produced by a new class of workers, the unskilled factory workers. Taken from the ranks of the obsolete peasantry, artisans and craftsmen, this new working class, the "proletariat," expanded in numbers with the gigantic mills, whose "hands" they were. Work on the assembly line demanded no education or skills, so the workers could never make themselves valuable enough to command a living wage on the open market. They survived as a vast underclass, interchangeable with the unemployed workers (recently displaced by more machines) who gathered around the factory gates looking for jobs, *their* jobs. As Ricardo had demonstrated, they could never bargain for any wage above the subsistence level—just enough to keep them alive. As capitalism and its factories expanded, the entire population, excepting only the wealthy capitalist families, sank into this hopeless pauperized class.

So Marx took from Ricardo the vision of ultimate division of Western society under capitalism: into a tiny group of fabulously wealthy capitalists and a huge mass of paupers, mostly factory workers. The minority would keep the majority in strict control by its hired thugs (the state: the army and the police), control rendered easier by thought control (the schools and the churches). The purpose of the "ideology" taught by the schools and the churches—the value structure of capitalism—was to show both classes that the capitalists had a right to their wealth (through the sham of liberty, free enterprise, and the utilitarian benefits of the free market) and a perfect right to govern everyone else (through the sham of democracy and equal justice). Thus the capitalists could enjoy their wealth in good conscience and the poor would understand their moral obligation to accept the oppression of the ruling class with good cheer.

Marx foresaw, and in his writings attempted to help bring about, the disillusionment of the workers: There will come a point when they will suddenly ask, *why* should we accept oppression all our lives? and the search for answers to this question will show them the history of their situation, expose the falsehood of the ideology and the false consciousness of those who believe it, show them their own strength, and lead them directly to the solution that will usher in the new age of socialism—the revolutionary overthrow of the capitalist regime. Why, after all, should they not undertake such a revolution? People are restrained from violence against oppression only by the prospect of losing something valuable, and the industrialized workers of the world had nothing to lose but their chains.

As feudalism had been swept away, then, by the "iron broom" of the French Revolution, so capitalism would be swept away by the revolt of the masses, the irresistible uprising of the vast majority of the people against the tiny minority of industrial overlords and their terrified minions—the armed forces, the state, and the church. After the first rebellions, Marx foresaw no lengthy problem of divided loyalties in the industrialized countries of the world. Once the scales had fallen from their eyes, the working-class hirelings of army and police would quickly turn their guns on their masters, and join their natural allies in the proletariat in the task of creating the new world.

After the revolution, Marx predicted, there would be a temporary "dictatorship of the proletariat," during which the last vestiges of capitalism would be eradicated and the authority to run the industrial establishment returned to the workers of each industry. Once the economy had been decentralized, to turn each factory into an industrial commune run by its own workers and each landed estate into an agricultural commune run by its farmers, the state as such would simply wither away. Some central authority would certainly continue to exist, to coordinate and facilitate the exchange of goods within the country (one imagines a giant computer, taking note of where goods are demanded, where goods are available, and where the railroad cars are, to take the goods from one place to the other). But with no ruling class to serve, no oppression to carry out, there will be no need of state to rule *people;* what is left will be confined to the administration of *things.*

Even as he wrote, just in time for the Revolution of 1848, Marx expected the end of capitalism as a system. Not that capitalism was evil in itself; Marx did not presume to make moral judgments on history. Indeed, capitalism was necessary as an economic system, to concentrate the wealth of the country into the industries of the modern age. So capitalism had a respectable past, and would still be necessary, for a while, in the developing countries, to launch their industries. But that task completed, it had no further role in history, and the longer it stayed around, the more the workers would suffer and the more violent the revolution would be when it came. The sooner the revolution, the better; the future belonged to communism.

As the collapse of the Communist governments in Eastern Europe demonstrates, if demonstration were needed, the course of history has not proceeded quite as Marx predicted in 1848. In fairness, it might be pointed out that no other prophets of the time had any more luck with prognostication; the twentieth century took all of us by surprise. But there is much in Marx's analysis which is rock solid, possibly for reasons, especially ethical reasons, that he himself would have rejected. In any case, since Marx wrote, all participants in the debate on the nature and future of capitalism have had to respond to his judgments and predictions.

Law: Recovering for Damages Sustained

Life is full of misfortune. Ordinarily, if you suffer misfortune, you must put up with it, and find the resources to deal with it. If your misfortune is my fault, however, the law may step in and make me pay for those damages, one way or another. Through the *criminal law,* the public steps in and demands punishment for an offense that is serious enough to outrage public feeling and endanger public welfare. If I knock you on the head and take your wallet, the police will find me, restore your wallet to you, and imprison or otherwise punish me for the crime. Strictly speaking, you should recover from me not only your wallet, but the money to sew up your head and damages for the fright and insult. But the average street criminal does not have the money to make full restitution to his victims; in fact, you'll be lucky to get your wallet back.

Through the *civil law,* if I do you damage through some action of mine, you may take me to civil court and ask a judge (and jury) to determine whether I have damaged you, if so by how much, and how I should pay you back for that damage. There are a number of forms of action under which you may make your claim; the most common for business purposes are *contract* and *torts.* If you and I agree to (or "contract for") some undertaking, and I back out on it, after you have relied on our agreement to commit your resources to the undertaking, you have a right to recover what you have lost. In torts, if I simply injure you in some way, hurting you in health, life or limb, or destroying your property, I have done you a wrong ("tort," in French), and I must pay for the damage I have done. How much I will have to pay will depend (as the jury will determine) on (1) the amount of the damage that has been caused, (2) the extent to which I knew or should have known that my action or neglect to act would cause damage (my *culpability*), and (3) the extent to which *you* contributed to the damage, beyond whatever I did (*contributory negligence*).

In the debates that follow, one (on the Pinto automobile) has to do with suits at law alleging *negligence,* a tort, on the part of a company, in that it made and put up for sale a product known to be defective, and that the defect injured its users. To establish negligence, civil or criminal, four elements must be demonstrated: First, there must have been a *duty:* The party accused of negligence must have had a preexisting duty to the plaintiff. Second, there must have been a *breach,* or failure to fulfill, that duty. Third, the plaintiff must have suffered an *injury.* And fourth, the breach of the duty must have been the *proximate cause* of the injury, the thing that actually brought it about. Where negligence is alleged in a product liability case, it must be established that the manufacturer had a duty to make a product that could not do certain sorts of harm; that the duty was breached, the harm caused, that nothing else was to blame, and that the manufacturer therefore must compensate the victim for the damage done.

There are very similar allegations in other cases here, even when no lawsuit is at issue. In all of these cases one set of claims amounts to an accusation of deliberately damaging innocent consumers, placing them in harm's way for the sake of profit; the other set counters that the company did not know and could not have known that the product was dangerous, and/or that the freely chosen behavior of the consumers contributed in some way to the damage that was done, so the company cannot be held totally responsible. In all cases, *risk* and *responsibility* are the central issues: When a small car explodes and burns when hit by a much larger van, to what extent is the company responsible for the flimsiness of the car and to what extent did the consumer assume the risk of that happening when she bought a small, economical car? (And whatever happened to the responsibility of the driver of the van?) Should companies be ultimately responsible for any harm that comes from the use of the products they so profitably marketed and sold? Or should consumers be content to bear the responsibility for risks they have freely accepted? Our ambivalence on this question as a society mirrors, and proceeds from, the ambivalence of the individual at the two poles of materialization of risk: When we are in a hurry, short of cash, or in need of a cigarette, then risky behavior looks to us to be our right, and we are resentful of the busybodies who would always be having us play it safe and wear our rubbers when it rains. But when the risk materializes—when the accident or the disease happens—the perception of that risk (and the direction of that resentment) change drastically. From the perspective of the hospital bed, it is crystal clear that the behavior was not worth the risk, that we never realized the behavior was risky, that we would never have engaged in the behavior if we had known how risky it was, that we should have been warned about the risks, and that it was someone's duty to warn us. In that instantaneous change of perspective, three elements of negligence come into view: duty, breach, and injury. No wonder product liability suits are so common.

Yet the suit is a relatively recent phenomenon because of a peculiarity in the law. Until the twentieth century, a judge faced with a consumer who had been injured by a product (physically or financially) had to apply the principle of *caveat emptor*—Let the Buyer Beware—and could ask the seller to pay damages only to the original buyer, and only if the exact defect in the product could be proved. For example, a defective kerosene lamp might explode and burn five people, but the exact defect (broken seam or shoddy wick) had to be brought into court or the case would be thrown out. In addition, the buyer could sue only the seller, not the manufacturer or designer, for the right to collect damages rested on the law of *contract*, not torts, and upon the warrant of merchantability implied in the contractual relationship between buyer and seller. The cause of the action was understood to be a breach in that contract.

There matters stood until 1916, when an American judge allowed a buyer to sue the manufacturer of a product. A Mr. MacPherson had been injured when his car collapsed under him due to a defect in the wood used to build one of the wheels, and MacPherson went to court against the Buick Motor Company. The judge reasoned that the action was in torts, specifically negligence, and not in contract, for a manufacturer is under a duty to make carefully any product that could be expected to endanger life, and this duty existed irrespective of any contract. So if MacPherson, or any future user of the product, was injured because the product was badly made, he could collect damages even if he had never dealt with the manufacturer in any way.

In the 1960s the automobile was still center stage in the arguments over the duties of manufacturers. Ralph Nader's book *Unsafe at Any Speed* (1966) spearheaded the consumer rights movement with its scathing attack on General Motors and its exposé of the dangerous design of the Corvair. In response to the consumer activism resulting from that movement, Congress passed the Consumer Product Safety Act in 1972 and empowered the Consumer Product Safety Commission, an independent federal agency, to set safety standards, require warning labels, and order recalls of hazardous products. When three girls died in a Ford Pinto in 1978, the foundations of consumer rights against careless manufacturers were well established. What is new in the Ford Motor Company case is the allegation of *criminal* negligence—in effect, criminal homicide.

At present, product liability suits are major uncharted reefs in the navigational plans of American business. If a number of people die in a fire in a hotel, for instance, their families will often sue not only the hotel, for culpable negligence, but the manufacturers of the furniture that burned, alleging that it should have been fire-retardant; the manufacturers of the cushions on the furniture, alleging that they gave off toxic fumes in the fire; and the manufacturers of the chemicals that went into those cushions, alleging that there was no warning to the consumers on the toxicity of those chemicals in fire conditions. The settlements that can be obtained are used to finance the suit, and the law firm that is managing it, for the years that it will take to exhaust all the appeals. This phenomenon of unlimited litigation is relatively new on the American scene, and we are not quite sure how to respond to it.

The Corporation

The human being is a social animal. We exist in the herd, and depend for our lives on the cooperation of those around us. Who are they? Our anthropologists tell us that originally we traveled in extended families, then settled down into villages of intensely interlocked groups of families. With the advent of the modern era, we have found our identities in family, village, church, and nation. Yet in the great transformation of the obligations of the Western world (see Henry Maine [1822–1888], *From Status to Contract*), we have abandoned the old family-oriented care systems and thrown ourselves upon the mercy of secondary organizations: club, corporation, and State. The French sociologist Emil Durkheim (1858–1917) suggested (in his classic work, *Suicide*) that following the collapse of the family and the church, the corporation would be the association, in the future, that would supply the social support that every individual needs to maintain the moral life.

Can the corporation do that? Or is the corporation merely the organization that implements Adam Smith's self-interested pursuit of the dollar, with no purpose but to maximize return on investment to the investors while protecting them from unlimited liability? The issue of "meaningful work" raises this question in particularly direct form. On the other hand, once formed, and having become a major community figure and employer, does the corporation have a right to exist that transcends at least the immediate pursuit of money? The issue of "hostile takeovers" sends us back to the purpose and foundation of business enterprise in America. Let us review: When an entrepreneur gets a bright idea for how to make money, he secures the capital he will need to run the business from investors (venture capitalists), uses that capital to buy the land, buildings, and machinery he will need to see it through, hires the labor needed to do the work, and goes into production. As the income from the enterprise comes in, he pays the suppliers of raw materials, pays the workers, pays the taxes, rent, mortgages, and utility bills, keeps some for himself (salary), and then divides up the rest of the income ("profit") among the investors (probably including himself) in proportion to the capital they invested. Motives of all parties are presupposed: The entrepreneur wants money, the laborers want money, so do the landlords, and so, of course, do the investors, who are the shareholders in the company. The investors thought that this enterprise would yield them a higher return on their capital than any other investment available to them at the time; that's why they invested. Meanwhile, this is a free country, and people can move around. If the worker sees a better job, he'll take it; if the landlord can rent for more, he'll terminate the lease; and if the investors see a better place to put their capital, they'll move it. The determiner of the flow of capital is the rate of return, no more and no less. "Loyalty to the company," faithfulness to the corporation for the sake of the association itself, is not on anyone's agenda—not on the worker's, certainly not on the landlord's, and *most* certainly not on the shareholder's.

The shareholders are represented by a board of directors elected by them to see that the company is run efficiently—that is, that costs are kept down and income up, to yield the highest possible return. The board of directors hires management—the cadre of corporate officers headed by the president/chief executive officer to do the actual running of the company. The corporate officers thus stand in a *quasi-fiduciary* relationship to the shareholders; that is, they are forbidden by the understandings on which the corporation is founded to do anything at all except that which will protect and enhance the interests of the shareholders. That goes for all the normal business decisions made by the management; even the decision not to break the law can be seen as a prudent estimate of the financial costs of lawbreaking.

Yet our dealings with the business world, as citizens and as consumers, have always turned on recognition and support of the huge, reliable corporations in established industries: not just coal and steel, which had certain natural limitations built into their consumption of natural resources, but the automobile companies, the airlines, the consumer products companies, even the banks. Companies had "reputations," "integrity," cultivated (and bought and sold) "good will," consumers cooperated with the companies that catered to them in developing "brand loyalty." And, most importantly, those working in business cooperated with their employers in developing "company loyalty," which became a part of their lives as loyalty to one's tribe or nation was part of the lives of their ancestors. Is the company that sought our loyalty—and got it—just a scrap of paper, to disappear as soon as return on investment falls below the nearest competition? What part do we want our corporations to play in our associative life? If we want them to be any more than profit maximizers for the investors, what sorts of protections would we have to offer them, and what sorts of limitations should we put on their not-for-profit activities?

Current Issues

Business ethics ultimately rests on a base of political philosophy, economics, and philosophical ethics. As these underlying fields change, new topics and approaches will surface in business ethics. For example, "hostile takeovers" did not take place very often in the regulatory climate that obtained prior to the Reagan administration. The change in political philosophy introduced by his administration resulted in new business practices, which resulted in new ethical problems. Also, the work of John Rawls, a professor of philosophy at Harvard, profoundly influenced our understandings of distributive justice, and therefore our understanding of acceptable economic distribution in the society. The work currently being done in "postmodern" philosophy will change the way we see human beings generally, and hence the activity of business.

No single work can cover all the issues of ethical practice in business in all their range and particularity, especially since, as above, we are dealing with a moving target. Our task here is much more limited. The purpose of this book is just to allow you to grapple with some of the ethical issues of current business practice in the safety of the classroom, before they come up on the job where human rights and careers are at stake and legal action looms outside the boardroom, or factory, door. We think that rational consideration of these issues now will help you prepare for a lifetime of the types of problems that naturally arise in a complex and pluralistic society. You will find here no dogmas, no settled solutions to memorize. These problems do not have preset answers, but require, as Whitehead insisted, that you use your mind, to balance the values in conflict and to work out acceptable policies in each issue. To do business ethics, you must learn to think critically, to look beyond short-term advantage and traditional ways of doing things, to become an innovator. The exercise provided by these debates should help you in this learning.

There is no doubt that businesspersons think that ethics is important. Sometimes the reasons why they think ethics is important have to do only with the long-run profitability of business enterprise. Greater employee honesty and diligence will improve the bottom line, strict attention to environmental and employee health laws is necessary to preserve the company from expensive lawsuits and fines. But ethics goes well beyond profitability, to the lives that we live and the persons we want to be. What the bottom line has taught us is that the working day is not apart from life. We must bring the same integrity and care to the contexts of factory and office that we are used to showing at home and among our friends. The third imperative of business ethics is to make of your business life an opportunity to become, and remain, the person that you know you ought to be—and as far you can, to extend that opportunity to others.

We attempt, in this book, to present in good, debatable form some of the issues that raise the big questions—of justice, of rights, of the common good—in order to build bridges between the workaday world of employment and the ageless world of morality. If you will enter into these dialogues with an open mind, a willingness to have it changed, and a determination to master the skills of critical thinking that will enable you to make responsible decisions in difficult situations, you may be able to help build the bridges for the new ethical issues that will emerge in the century to come. At the least, that is our hope.

Suggested Readings for the Ethics Background for Business Ethics

Beauchamp, Tom L., and Norman E. Bowie. *Ethical Theory and Business*. 8th ed. Englewood Cliffs, NJ: Prentice Hall, 2008.

DeGeorge, Richard T. *Business Ethics*. 7th ed. Englewood Cliffs, NJ: Prentice Hall, 2009.

Donaldson, Thomas, and Patricia H. Werhane. *Ethical Issues in Business: A Philosophical Approach*. 8th ed. Englewood Cliffs, NJ: Prentice Hall, 2007.

Goodpaster, Kenneth, Laura Nash, and Henri-Claude de Bettignies. *Business Ethics: Policies and Persons*. 4th ed. New York: McGraw-Hill, 2005.

Hoffman, W. Michael, and Jennifer Mills Moore. *Business Ethics: Readings and Cases in Corporate Morality*. 4th ed. New York: McGraw-Hill, 2001.

Newton, Lisa H. *Permission to Steal*. Hoboken, NJ: John Wiley and Sons, Inc., 2007.

Pritchard, Michael S. *Professional Integrity: Thinking Ethically*. Lawrence, KS: University of Kansas Press, 2006.

Schmidt, David P., and Lisa H Newton. *Wake-Up Calls: Classic Cases in Business Ethics*. Florence, KY: Cengage, 2003.

Shaw, William, and Vincent Barry. *Moral Issues in Business*. 11th ed. Belmont, CA: Wadsworth, 2009.

Velasquez, Manuel. *Business Ethics: Concepts and Cases*. 6th ed. Englewood Cliffs, NJ: Prentice Hall, 2006.

Internet References . . .

Business Ethics Resources on WWW

Sponsored by the Centre for Applied Ethics, site of business ethics resources links to corporate codes of ethics, business ethics institutions and organizations, and online papers and publications, as well as other elements.

http://www.ethics.ubc.ca/

International Business Ethics Institute

The International Business Ethics Institute offers professional services to organizations interested in implementing, expanding, or modifying business ethics and corporate responsibility programs. Its mission is to foster global business practices that promote equitable economic development, resource sustainability, and democratic forms of government.

http://www.business-ethics.org/

Capitalism and the Corporation

*G*iven *the behavior of the highest officials of the most profitable enterprises in the country in recent years, we might wonder if there is such a thing as ethical business! Where are moral standards to be found in the business enterprise—in the actions of the managers? In the policies, internal and external, of the corporation? Or in the capitalist system itself? How can business itself be encouraged to adopt higher ethical standards than we have seen in operation recently?*

- Can Capitalism Lead to Human Happiness?
- Is Risk the Best Theory for Capitalism?
- Is Increasing Profits the Only Social Responsibility of Business?
- Can Individual Virtue Survive Corporate Pressure?
- Can Ethics Codes Build "True" Corporate Ethics?

ISSUE 1

Can Capitalism Lead to Human Happiness?

YES: Adam Smith, from *An Inquiry Into the Nature and Causes of the Wealth of Nations,* vols. 1 and 2b (1869)

NO: Karl Marx and Friedrich Engels, from *The Communist Manifesto* (1848)

ISSUE SUMMARY

YES: If we will but leave self-interested people to seek their own advantage, Adam Smith (1723–1790) argues, the result, unintended by any one of them, will be the greater advantage of all. No government interference is necessary to protect the general welfare.

NO: Leave people to their own self-interested devices, Karl Marx (1818–1883) and Friedrich Engels (1820–1895) reply, and those who by luck and inheritance own the means of production will rapidly reduce everyone else to virtual slavery. The few may be fabulously happy, but all others will live in misery.

T he confrontation of capitalism and communism dominated the twentieth century. In these selections we have the classic defense of the free market and its most powerful opposition. The rationale of capitalism portrays it as an unintended coordination of self-interested actions into the production of the greatest welfare of the whole. The argument is elegant and powerful: As a natural result of free competition in a free market, quality will improve and prices will decline without limit, thereby raising the real standard of living of every buyer. To protect themselves in competition, sellers will be forced to innovate, discover new products and new markets, thereby raising the real wealth of the society as a whole. Products improve without limit, wealth increases without limit, and society prospers.

But how fares the Common Man—the "least advantaged" members of society, as John Rawls would characterize them? Not very well. Only when free competition *fails*, because the economy is expanding so rapidly that it runs out of labor, can the working man's wages rise in a free market. For the most efficient factory will be the one that hires its workers at lowest cost, and if all industry is accomplished by essentially unskilled labor, and every worker can therefore be replaced by any other, there is no reason to pay any worker beyond the subsistence wage. Fortunately for the capitalist, according to the theory, such a market imbalance—too few workers and therefore "artificially" high wages—will rapidly disappear, as greater prosperity causes more of the working-class babies to survive to adulthood and enter into the workforce. Smith and eighteenth-century economists Thomas Malthus and David Ricardo were in agreement: As the society as a whole approaches maximum efficiency, all except the capitalists, the owners, approach the subsistence level of survival. So all the accumulated "wealth" of the nation actually ends up in the hands only of the employers, the factory owners, who enjoy the low prices of bread themselves, and save the money they would have to spend to keep their workers alive if the bread were more expensive. Another way of putting that point: Adam Smith was absolutely correct if he is taken to be describing capital *formation;* but when it comes to the *distribution* of the wealth the free market has created, his mechanisms have no way of ensuring justice.

This is where Karl Marx comes in. He focuses not on the making of the wealth—Adam Smith is quite correct on how wealth is created and accumulated. Instead he asks how the wealth is distributed—who gets it, and gets to enjoy it, when it has been generated by the capitalist process. There is no reason under Heaven that all that money has to languish in the bank accounts of the super-rich, or decorate their houses and their poodles. The welfare of the nation as a whole would be vastly increased if it could be shared systematically with the workers, to allow them to join their employers as consumers of the manufactured goods of the society. Lord John Maynard Keynes would later point out that such distribution would be an enormous spur to the economy; Marx was more concerned that it would be a great gain in justice.

Yes, but if the controllers of the wealth, the capitalists, are required to share it with the workers who produced it, will they not lose motivation to put that money at risk in such productive enterprises? This is one of the empirical questions that surround the issue of social justice in a free market society, often arising when CEO salaries are under discussion. It may seem counterintuitive that CEOs whose salary is reduced from $46.2 million per annum to $24.3 million per annum would suffer a serious loss of incentive to keep working, but that has been argued. Other questions concern entitlement—are not those who control the capital entitled to the entire return on it?—the justice of combination (Adam Smith also had to deal with unions), and the relative importance of liberty and equality as political values. Other questions concern the possibility of "pure" capitalist endeavors. Adam Smith's arguments surely work for small factories and farms, where no producer is big enough to influence the market. These were the only business enterprises he knew. But does it apply to technology-created monopolies and oligopolies? And does it contemplate speculating millions of dollars in foreign currency? Keep in mind, as you read these selections, that the controversy is not bounded by the historical understandings of Marx and his opponents, but goes to the core of our notions of entitlement, social welfare, and justice.

YES

Adam Smith

An Inquiry Into the Nature and Causes of the Wealth of Nations

Of the Division of Labour

The greatest improvement in the productive powers of labour, and the greater part of the skill, dexterity, and judgment with which it is anywhere directed or applied, seem to have been the effect of the division of labour.

The effects of the division of labour, in the general business of society, will be more easily understood by considering in what manner it operates in some particular manufactures. It is commonly supposed to be carried furthest in some very trifling ones; not perhaps that it really is carried further in them than in others of more importance: but in those trifling manufactures which are destined to supply the small wants of but a small number of people, the whole number of workmen must necessarily be small; and those employed in every different branch of the work can often be collected into the same workhouse, and placed at once under the view of the spectator. In those great manufactures, on the contrary, which are destined to supply the great wants of the great body of the people, every different branch of the work employs so great a number of workmen, that it is impossible to collect them all into the same workhouse. We can seldom see more, at one time, than those employed in one single branch. Though in such manufactures, therefore, the work may really be divided into a much greater number of parts than in those of a more trifling nature, the division is not near so obvious, and has accordingly been much less observed.

To take an example, therefore, from a very trifling manufacture, but one in which the division of labour has been very often taken notice of, the trade of the pin-maker; a workman not educated to this business (which the division of labour has rendered a distinct trade), nor acquainted with the use of the machinery employed in it (to the invention of which the same division of labour has probably given occasion), could scarce, perhaps, with his utmost industry, make one pin in a day, and certainly could not make twenty. But in the way in which this business is now carried on, not only the whole work is a peculiar trade, but it is divided into a number of branches, of which the greater part are likewise peculiar trades. One man draws out the wire, another straights it, a third cuts it, a fourth points it, a fifth grinds it at the top for receiving the head; to make the head requires two or three distinct operations; to put it on is a peculiar business, to whiten the pins is another; it is even a trade by itself

From Adam Smith, *An Inquiry Into the Nature and Causes of the Wealth of Nations,* vols. 1 and 2b (1869). Notes omitted.

to put them into the paper; and the important business of making a pin is, in this manner, divided into about eighteen distinct operations, which in some manufactories are all performed by distinct hands, though in others the same man will sometimes perform two or three of them. I have seen a small manufactory of this kind where ten men only were employed, and where some of them consequently performed two or three distinct operations. But though they were very poor, and therefore but indifferently accommodated with the necessary machinery, they could, when they exerted themselves, make among them about twelve pounds of pins in a day. There are in a pound upwards of four thousand pins of a middling size. Those ten persons, therefore, could make among them upwards of forty-eight thousand pins in a day. Each person, therefore, making a tenth part of forty-eight thousand pins, might be considered as making four thousand eight hundred pins in a day. But if they had all wrought separately and independently, and without any of them having been educated to this peculiar business, they certainly could not each of them have made twenty, perhaps not one pin in a day; that is, certainly, not the two hundred and fortieth, perhaps not the four thousand eight hundredth part of what they are at present capable of performing, in consequence of a proper division and combination of their different operations. . . .

This great increase of the quantity of work, which, in consequence of the division of labour, the same number of people are capable of performing, is owing to three different circumstances: first, to the increase of dexterity in every particular workman; secondly, to the saving of the time which is commonly lost in passing from one species of work to another; and lastly, to the invention of a great number of machines which facilitate and abridge labour, and enable one man to do the work of many. . . .

It is the great multiplication of the productions of all the different arts, in consequence of the division of labour, which occasions, in a well-governed society, that universal opulence which extends itself to the lowest ranks of the people. Every workman has a great quantity of his own work to dispose of beyond what he himself has occasion for: and every other workman being exactly in the same situation, he is enabled to exchange a great quantity of his own goods for a great quantity, or, what comes to the same thing, for the price of a great quantity of theirs. He supplies them abundantly with what they have occasion for, and they accommodate him as amply with what he has occasion for, and a general plenty diffuses itself through all the different ranks of the society.

Observe the accommodation of the most common artificer or day-labourer in a civilised and thriving country, and you will perceive that the number of people of whose industry a part, though but a small part, has been employed in procuring him this accommodation exceeds all computation. The woollen coat, for example, which covers the day-labourer, as coarse and rough as it may appear, is the produce of the joint labour of a great multitude of workmen. The shepherd, the sorter of the wool, the wool-comber or carder, the dyer, the scribbler, the spinner, the weaver, the fuller, the dresser, with many others, must all join their different arts in order to complete even this homely production. How many merchants and carriers, besides, must have been employed in transporting the materials from some of those workmen to others who often live in a very distant part of the country! How much commerce and navigation in particular, how many ship-builders, sailors, sail-makers, rope-makers, must have been employed in order to bring together the different drugs made use of by the dyer, which often come from the remotest corners of the world! What a variety of labour too is necessary in order to produce the tools of the meanest of those workmen! To say nothing of such complicated machines as the ship of the sailor, the mill of the fuller, or even the loom of the weaver, let us consider only what a variety of labour is requisite in order to form that very simple machine, the shears with which the shepherd clips the wool. The miner, the builder of the furnace for smelting the ore, the feller of the timber, the burner of the charcoal to be made use of in the smelting-house, the brickmaker, the bricklayer, the workmen who attend the furnace, the millwright, the forger, the smith, must all of them join their different arts in order to produce them. Were we to examine, in the same manner, all the different parts of his dress and household furniture, the coarse linen shirt which he wears next his skin, the shoes which cover his feet, the bed which he lies on, and all the different parts which compose it, the kitchen-grate at which he prepares his victuals, the coals which he makes use of for that purpose, dug from the bowels of the earth, and brought to him perhaps by a long sea and a long land carriage, all the other utensils of his kitchen, all the furniture of his table, the knives and forks, the earthen or pewter plates upon which he serves up and divides his victuals, the different hands employed in preparing his bread and his beer, the glass window which lets in the heat and the light and keeps out the wind and the rain, with all the knowledge and art requisite for preparing that beautiful and happy invention, without which these northern parts of the world could scarce have afforded a very comfortable habitation, together with the tools of all the different workmen employed in producing those different conveniences; if we examine, I say, all these things, and consider what a variety of labour is employed about each of them, we shall be sensible that without the assistance and co-operation of many thousands, the very meanest person in a civilised country could not be provided, even according to, what we very falsely imagine, the easy and simple manner in which he is commonly accommodated. Compared, indeed, with the more extravagant luxury of the great, his accommodation must no doubt appear extremely simple and easy; and yet it may be true, perhaps, that the accommodation of an European prince does not always so much exceed that of an industrious and frugal peasant, as the accommodation of the latter exceeds that of many an African king, the absolute master of the lives and liberties of ten thousand naked savages.

Of the Principle Which Gives Occasion to the Division of Labour

This division of labour, from which so many advantages are derived, is not originally the effect of any human wisdom, which foresees and intends that general opulence to which it gives occasion. It is the necessary, though very slow and gradual consequence of a certain propensity in human nature which has in view no such extensive utility; the propensity to truck, barter, and exchange one thing for another.

Whether this propensity be one of those original principles in human nature, of which no further account can be given; or whether, as seems more probable, it be the necessary consequence of the faculties of reason and speech, it belongs not to our present subject to inquire. It is common to all men, and to be found in no other race of animals, which seem to know neither this nor any other species of contracts. . . . But man has almost constant occasion for the help of his brethren, and it is in vain for him to expect it from their benevolence only. He will be more likely to prevail if he can interest their self-love in his favour, and show them that it is for their own advantage to do for him what he requires of them. Whoever offers to another a bargain of any kind, proposes to do this. Give me that which I want, and you shall have this which you want, is the meaning of every such offer; and it is in this manner that we obtain from one another the far greater part of those good offices which we stand in need of. It is not from the benevolence of the butcher, the brewer, or the baker, that we expect our dinner, but from their regard to their own interest. We address ourselves, not to their humanity but to their self-love, and never talk to them of our own necessities but of their advantages. Nobody but a beggar chooses to depend chiefly upon the benevolence of his fellow-citizens. Even a beggar does not depend upon it entirely. The charity of well-disposed people, indeed, supplies him with the whole fund of his subsistence. But though this principle ultimately provides him with all the necessaries of life which he has occasion for, it neither does nor can provide him with them as he has occasion for them. The greater part of his occasional wants are supplied in the same manner as those of other people, by treaty, by barter, and by purchase. With the money which one man gives him he purchases food. The old clothes which another bestows upon him he exchanges for other old clothes which suit him better, or for lodging, or for food, or for money, with which he can buy either food, clothes, or lodging, as he has occasion.

. . . Each animal is still obliged to support and defend itself, separately and independently, and derives no sort of advantage from that variety of talents with which nature has distinguished its fellows. Among men, on the contrary, the most dissimilar geniuses are of use to one another; the different produces of their respective talents, by the general disposition to truck, barter, and exchange, being brought, as it were, into a common stock, where every man may purchase whatever part of the produce of other men's talents he has occasion for. . . .

Of Restraints Upon the Importation From Foreign Countries of Such Goods as Can Be Produced at Home

. . . The general industry of the society never can exceed what the capital of the society can employ. As the number of workmen that can be kept in employment by any particular person must bear a certain proportion to his capital, so the number of those that can be continually employed by all the members of a great society, must bear a certain proportion to the whole capital of that society, and never can exceed that proportion. No regulation of commerce can increase the quantity of industry in any society beyond what its capital can maintain. It can only divert a part of it into a direction into which it might not otherwise have gone; and it is by no means certain that this artificial direction is likely to be more advantageous to the society than that into which it would have gone of its own accord.

Every individual is continually exerting himself to find out the most advantageous employment for whatever capital he can demand. It is his own advantage, indeed, and not that of the society, which he has in view. But the study of his own advantage naturally, or rather necessarily, leads him to prefer that employment which is most advantageous to the society.

First, every individual endeavours to employ his capital as near home as he can, and consequently as much as he can in the support of domestic indus-try; provided always that he can thereby obtain the ordinary, or not a great deal less than the ordinary, profits of stock.

Thus, upon equal or nearly equal profits, every wholesale merchant natu-rally prefers the home trade to the foreign trade of consumption, and the for-eign trade of consumption to the carrying trade. In the home trade his capital is never so long out of his sight as it frequently is in the foreign trade of consump-tion. He can know better the character and situation of the persons whom he trusts, and, if he should happen to be deceived, he knows better the laws of the country from which he must seek redress. In the carrying trade, the capital of the merchant is, as it were, divided between two foreign countries, and no part of it is ever necessarily brought home, or placed under his own immediate view and command. The capital which an Amsterdam merchant employs in carry-ing corn from Konigsberg to Lisbon, and fruit and wine from Lisbon to Konigs-berg, must generally be the one half of it at Konigsberg and the other half at Lisbon. No part of it need ever come to Amsterdam. The natural residence of such a merchant should either be at Konigsberg or Lisbon, and it can only be some very particular circumstance which can make him prefer the residence of Amsterdam. The uneasiness, however, which he feels at being separated so far from his capital, generally determines him to bring part both of the Konigsberg goods which he destines for the market of Lisbon, and of the Lisbon goods which he destines for that of Konigsberg, to Amsterdam; and though this nec-essarily subjects him to a double charge of loading and unloading, as well as to the payment of some duties and customs, yet for the sake of having some part of his capital always under his own view and command, he willingly submits to this extraordinary charge; and it is in this manner that every country which has any considerable share of the carrying trade, becomes always the empo-rium, or general market, for the goods of all the different countries whose trade it carries on. The merchant, in order to save a second loading and unloading, endeavours always to sell in the home market as much of the goods of all those different countries as he can, and thus, so far as he can, to convert his carrying trade into a foreign trade of consumption. A merchant, in the same manner, who is engaged in the foreign trade of consumption, when he collects goods for foreign markets, will always be glad, upon equal or nearly equal profits, to sell as great a part of them at home as he can. He saves himself the risk and trouble of exportation, when, so far as he can, he thus converts his foreign trade of consumption into a home trade. Home is in this manner the centre, if I may say so, round which the capitals of the inhabitants of every country are continually circulating, and towards which they are always tending, though by particular causes they may sometimes be driven off and repelled from it towards more distant employments. But a capital employed in the home trade, it has already been shown, necessarily puts into motion a greater quantity of domestic industry, and gives revenue and employment to a greater number of the inhabitants of the country, than an equal capital employed in the foreign trade of consumption; and one employed in the foreign trade of consumption has the same advantage over an equal capital employed in the carrying trade. Upon equal, or only nearly equal profits, therefore, every individual naturally inclines to employ his capital in the manner in which it is likely to afford the greatest support to domestic industry, and to give revenue and employment to the greatest number of people of his own country.

Secondly, every individual who employs his capital in the support of domestic industry, necessarily endeavours so to direct that industry, that its produce may be of the greatest possible value.

The produce of industry is what it adds to the subject or materials upon which it is employed. In proportion as the value of this produce is great or small, so will likewise be the profits of the employer. But it is only for the sake of profit that any man employs a capital in the support of industry; and he will always, therefore, endeavour to employ it in the support of that industry of which the produce is likely to be of the greatest value, or to exchange for the greatest quantity either of money or of other goods.

But the annual revenue of every society is always precisely equal to the exchangeable value of the whole annual produce of its industry, or rather is precisely the same thing with that exchangeable value. As every individual, therefore, endeavours as much as he can both to employ his capital in the support of domestic industry, and so to direct that industry that its produce may be of the greatest value, every individual necessarily labours to render the annual revenue of the society as great as he can. He generally, indeed, neither intends to promote the public interest, nor knows how much he is promoting it. By preferring the support of domestic to that of foreign industry, he intends only his own security; and by directing that industry in such a manner as its produce may be of the greatest value, he intends only his own gain, and he is in this, as in many other cases, led by an invisible hand to promote an end which was no part of his intention. Nor is it always the worse for the society that it was no part of it. By pursuing his own interest he frequently promotes that of the society more effectually than when he really intends to promote it. I have never known much good done by those who affected to trade for the public good. It is an affectation, indeed, not very common among merchants, and very few words need be employed in dissuading them from it.

What is the species of domestic industry which his capital can employ, and of which the produce is likely to be of the greatest value, every individual, it is evident, can, in his local situation, judge much better than any statesman or lawgiver can do for him. The statesman, who should attempt to direct private people in what manner they ought to employ their capitals, would not only load himself with a most unnecessary attention, but assume an authority which could safely be trusted, not only to no single person, but to no council or senate whatever, and which would nowhere be so dangerous as in the hands of a man who had folly and presumption enough to fancy himself fit to exercise it.

To give the monopoly of the home market to the produce of domestic industry, in any particular art or manufacture, is in some measure to direct private people in what manner they ought to employ their capitals, and must, in almost all cases, be either a useless or a hurtful regulation. If the produce of domestic can be brought there as cheap as that of foreign industry, the regulation is evidently useless. If it cannot, it must generally be hurtful. It is the maxim of every prudent master of a family, never to attempt to make at home what it will cost him more to make than to buy. The tailor does not attempt to make his own shoes, but buys them of the shoemaker. The shoemaker does not attempt to make his own clothes, but employs a tailor. The farmer attempts to make neither the one nor the other, but employs those different artificers. All of them find it for their interest to employ their whole industry in a way in which they have some advantage over their neighbours, and to purchase with a part of its produce, or, what is the same thing, with the price of a part of it, whatever else they have occasion for.

What is prudence in the conduct of every private family, can scarce be folly in that of a great kingdom. If a foreign country can supply us with a commodity cheaper than we ourselves can make it, better buy it of them with some part of the produce of our own industry, employed in a way in which we have some advantage. The general industry of the country, being always in proportion to the capital which employs it, will not thereby be diminished, no more than that of the above-mentioned artificers, but only left to find out the way in which it can be employed with the greatest advantage. It is certainly not employed to the greatest advantage, when it is thus directed towards an object which it can buy cheaper than it can make. The value of its annual produce is certainly more or less diminished, when it is thus turned away from producing commodities evidently of more value than the commodity which it is directed to produce. According to the supposition, that commodity could be purchased from foreign countries cheaper than it can be made at home. It could, therefore, have been purchased with a part only of the commodities, or, what is the same thing, with a part only of the price of the commodities, which the industry employed by an equal capital would have produced at home, had it been left to follow its natural course. The industry of the country, therefore, is thus turned away from a more to a less advantageous employment, and the exchangeable value of its annual produce, instead of being increased, according to the intention of the lawgiver, must necessarily be diminished by every such regulation.

By means of such regulations, indeed, a particular manufacture may sometimes be acquired sooner than it could have been otherwise, and after a certain time may be made at home as cheap or cheaper than in the foreign country. But though the industry of the society may be thus carried with advantage into a particular channel sooner than it could have been otherwise, it will by no means follow that the sum total, either of its industry or of its revenue, can ever be augmented by any such regulation. The industry of the society can augment only in proportion as its capital augments, and its capital can augment only in proportion to what can be gradually saved out of its revenue. But the immediate effect of every such regulation is to diminish its revenue, and what diminishes its revenue is certainly not very likely to augment its capital faster than it would have augmented of its own accord, had both capital and industry been left to find out their natural employments.

Though for want of such regulations the society should never acquire the proposed manufacture, it would not, upon that account, necessarily be the poorer in any one period of its duration. In every period of its duration its whole capital and industry might still have been employed, though upon different objects, in the manner that was most advantageous at the time. In every period its revenue might have been the greatest which its capital could afford, and both capital and revenue might have been augmented with the greatest possible rapidity.

The natural advantages which one country has over another in producing particular commodities are sometimes so great, that it is acknowledged by all the world to be in vain to struggle with them. By means of glasses, hot-beds, and hot-walls, very good grapes can be raised in Scotland, and very good wine too can be made of them, at about thirty times the expense for which at least equally good can be brought from foreign countries. Would it be a reasonable law to prohibit the importation of all foreign wines, merely to encourage the making of claret and burgundy in Scotland? But if there would be a manifest absurdity in turning towards any employment thirty times more of the capital and industry of the country than would be necessary to purchase from foreign countries an equal quantity of the commodities wanted, there must be an absurdity, though not altogether so glaring, yet exactly of the same kind, in turning towards any such employment a thirtieth or even a three-hundredth part more of either. Whether the advantages which one country has over another be natural or acquired, is in this respect of no consequence. As long as the one country has those advantages and the other wants them, it will always be more advantageous for the latter rather to buy of the former than to make. It is an acquired advantage only which one artificer has over his neighbour who exercises another trade; and yet they both find it more advantageous to buy of one another than to make what does not belong to their particular trades.

Manifesto of the Communist Party

A spectre is haunting Europe—the spectre of Communism. All the powers of old Europe have entered into a holy alliance to exorcise this spectre; Pope and Czar, Metternich and Guizot, French Radicals and German police-spies.

Where is the party in opposition that has not been decried as communistic by its opponents in power? Where the opposition that has not hurled back the branding reproach of Communism, against the more advanced opposition parties, as well as against its reactionary adversaries?

Two things result from this fact.

I. Communism is already acknowledged by all European Powers to be itself a Power.

II. It is high time that Communists should openly, in the face of the whole world, publish their views, their aims, their tendencies, and meet this nursery tale of the Spectre of Communism with a Manifesto of the party itself.

To this end, Communists of various nationalities have assembled in London, and sketched the following manifesto, to be published in the English, French, German, Italian, Flemish and Danish languages.

Bourgeois and Proletarians

The history of all hitherto existing society is the history of class struggles.

Freeman and slave, patrician and plebeian, lord and serf, guild-master and journeyman, in a word; oppressor and oppressed, stood in constant opposition to one another, carried on an uninterrupted, now hidden, now open fight, a fight that each time ended, either in a revolutionary re-constitution of society at large, or in the common ruin of the contending classes.

In the early epochs of history, we find almost everywhere a complicated arrangement of society into various orders, a manifold graduation of social rank. In ancient Rome we have patricians, knights, plebeians, slaves; in the Middle Ages, feudal lords, vassals, guild-masters, journeymen, apprentices, serfs; in almost all of these classes, again, subordinate gradations.

The modern bourgeois society that has sprouted from the ruins of feudal society, has not done away with class antagonisms. It has but established new classes, new conditions of oppression, new forms of struggle in place of the old ones.

Our epoch, the epoch of the bourgeoisie, possesses, however, this distinctive feature; it has simplified the class antagonisms. Society as a whole is

From Karl Marx and Friedrich Engels, *The Communist Manifesto* (1848).

more and more splitting up into two great hostile camps, into two great classes directly facing each other: Bourgeoisie and Proletariat.

From the serfs of the Middle Ages sprang the chartered burghers of the earliest towns. From these burgesses the first elements of the bourgeoisie were developed.

The discovery of America, the rounding of the Cape, opened up fresh ground for the rising bourgeoisie. The East-Indian and Chinese markets, the colonization of America, trade with the colonies, the increase in the means of exchange in commodities, generally, gave to commerce, to navigation, to industry, an impulse never before known, and thereby, to the revolutionary element in the tottering feudal society, a rapid development.

The feudal system of industry, under which industrial production was monopolized by closed guilds, now no longer sufficed for the growing wants of the new markets. The manufacturing system took its place. The guild-masters were pushed on one side by the manufacturing middle-class; division of labor between the different corporate guilds vanished in the face of division of labor in each single workshop.

Meantime the markets kept ever growing, the demand, ever rising. Even manufacturing no longer sufficed. Thereupon, steam and machinery revolutionized industrial production. The place of manufacture was taken by the giant, Modern Industry, the place of the industrial middle-class, by industrial millionaires, the leaders of whole industrial armies, the modern bourgeoisie.

Modern Industry has established the world-market, for which the discovery of America paved the way. This market has given an immense development to commerce, to navigation, to communication by land. This development has, in its turn, reacted on the extension of industry; and in proportion as industry, commerce, navigation, railways extended in the same proportion the bourgeoisie developed, increased its capital, and pushed into the background every class handed down from the Middle Ages.

We see, therefore, how the modern bourgeoisie is itself the product of a long course of development, of a series of revolutions in the modes of production and of exchange.

Each step in the development of the bourgeoisie was accompanied by a corresponding political advance of that class. An oppressed class under the sway of the feudal nobility, an armed and self-governing association in the medieval commune, here independent urban republic (as in Italy and Germany), there taxable "third estate" of the monarchy (as in France), afterwards, in the period of manufacturing proper, serving either the semi-feudal or the absolute monarchy as a counterpoise against the nobility, and in fact, cornerstone of the great monarchies in general, the bourgeoisie has at last, since the establishment of Modern Industry and of the world-market, conquered for itself, in a modern representative State, exclusive political sway. The executive of the modern State is but a committee for managing the common affairs of the whole bourgeoisie.

The bourgeoisie, historically, has played a most revolutionary part.

The bourgeoisie, wherever it has got the upper hand, has put an end to all feudal, patriarchal, idyllic relations. It has pitilessly torn asunder the motley feudal ties that bound man to his "natural superiors," and has left remaining no other nexus between man and man than naked self-interest, than callous "cash payment." It has drowned the most heavenly ecstasies of religious fervor, of chivalrous enthusiasm, of philistine sentimentalism, in the icy water of egotistical calculation. It has resolved personal worth into exchange value, and in place of the numberless indefeasible chartered freedoms, has set up that single, unconscionable freedom—Free Trade. In one word, for exploitation, veiled by religious and political illusions, it has substituted naked, shameless, direct, brutal exploitation.

The bourgeoisie has stripped of its halo every occupation hitherto honored and looked up to with reverent awe. It has converted the physician, the lawyer, the priest, the poet, the man of science, into its paid wage-laborers.

The bourgeoisie has torn away from the family its sentimental veil, and has reduced the family relation to a mere money relation.

The bourgeoisie has disclosed how it came to pass that the brutal display of vigor in the Middle Ages, which Reactionists so much admire, found its fitting complement in the most slothful indolence. It has been the first to show what man's activity can bring about. It has accomplished wonders far surpassing Egyptian pyramids, Roman aqueducts, and Gothic cathedrals; it has conducted expeditions that put in the shade all former Exoduses of nations and crusades.

The bourgeoisie cannot exist without constantly revolutionizing the instruments of production, and thereby the relations of production, and with them the whole relations of society. Conservation of the old modes of production in unaltered form, was, on the contrary, the first condition of existence for all earlier industrial classes. Constant revolutionizing of production, uninterrupted disturbance of all social conditions, everlasting uncertainty and agitation distinguish the bourgeois epoch from all earlier ones. All fixed, fast-frozen relations, with their train of ancient and venerable prejudices and opinions, are swept away, all newly-formed ones become antiquated before they can ossify. All that is solid melts into air, all that is holy is profaned, and man is at last compelled to face with sober senses, his real conditions of life, and his relations with his kind.

The need of a constantly expanding market for its products chases the bourgeoisie over the whole surface of the globe. It must nestle everywhere, settle everywhere, establish connections everywhere.

The bourgeoisie has through its exploitation of the world-market given a cosmopolitan character to production and consumption in every country. To the great chagrin of Reactionists, it has drawn from under the feet of industry the national ground on which it stood. All old-established national industries have been destroyed or are daily being destroyed. They are dislodged by new industries, whose introduction becomes a life and death question for all civilized nations, by industries that no longer work up indigenous raw material, but raw material drawn from the remotest zones; industries whose products are consumed, not only at home, but in every quarter of the globe. In place of the old wants, satisfied by the productions of the country, we find new wants, requiring for their satisfaction the products of distant lands and climes. In place of the old local and national seclusion and self-sufficiency, we have intercourse in every direction, universal inter-dependence of nations. And as in material, so also in intellectual production. The intellectual creations of individual nations become common property. National one-sidedness and narrow-mindedness become more and more impossible, and from the numerous national and local literatures there arises a world-literature.

The bourgeoisie, by the rapid improvement of all instruments of production, by the immensely facilitated means of communication, draws all, even the most barbarian, nations into civilization. The cheap prices of its commodities are the heavy artillery with which it batters down all Chinese walls, with which it forces the barbarians' intensely obstinate hatred of foreigners to capitulate. It compels all nations, on pain of extinction, to adopt the bourgeois mode of production; it compels them to introduce what it calls civilization into their midst, i.e., to become bourgeois themselves. In a word, it creates a world after its own image.

The bourgeoisie has subjected the country to the rule of the towns. It has created enormous cities, has greatly increased the urban population as compared with the rural, and has thus rescued a considerable part of the population from the idiocy of rural life. Just as it has made the country dependent on the towns, so it has made barbarian and semibarbarian countries dependent on the civilized ones, nations of peasants on nations of bourgeois, the East on the West.

The bourgeoisie keeps more and more doing away with the scattered state of the population, of the means of production, and of property. It has agglomerated population, centralized means of production, and has concentrated property in a few hands. The necessary consequence of this was political centralization. Independent, or but loosely connected provinces, with separate interests, laws, governments and systems of taxation, became lumped together in one nation, with one government, one code of laws, one national class-interest, one frontier and one customs-tariff.

The bourgeoisie, during its rule of scarce one hundred years, has created more massive and more colossal productive forces than have all preceding generations together. Subjection of Nature's forces to man, machinery, application of chemistry to industry and agriculture, steam-navigation, railways, electric telegraphs, clearing of whole continents for cultivation, canalization of rivers, whole populations conjured out of the ground—what earlier century had even a presentiment that such productive forces slumbered in the lap of social labor?

We see then: the means of production and of exchange on whose foundations the bourgeoisie built itself up, were generated in feudal society. At a certain stage in the development of these means of production and of exchange, the conditions under which feudal society produced and exchanged, the feudal organization of agriculture and manufacturing industry, in one word, the feudal relations of property became no longer compatible with the already developed productive forces; they became so many fetters. They had to be burst asunder; they were burst asunder.

Into their places stepped free competition, accompanied by a social and political constitution adapted to it, and by the economical and political sway of the bourgeois class.

A similar movement is going on before our own eyes. Modern bourgeois society with its relations of production, of exchange and of property, a society that has conjured up such gigantic means of production and of exchange, is like the sorcerer, who is no longer able to control the powers of the nether world whom he has called up by his spells. For many a decade past the history of industry and commerce is but the history of the revolt of modern productive forces against modern conditions of production, against the property relations that are the condition for the existence of the bourgeoisie and of its rule. It is enough to mention the commercial crises that by their periodical return put on trial, each time more threateningly, the existence of the entire bourgeois society. In these crises a great part not only of the existing products, but also of the previously created productive forces, are periodically destroyed. In these crises there breaks out an epidemic that, in all earlier epochs, would have seemed an absurdity—the epidemic of overproduction. Society suddenly finds itself put back into a state of momentary barbarism; it appears as if a famine, a universal war of devastation had cut off the supply of every means of subsistence; industry and commerce seem to be destroyed; and why? Because there is too much civilization, too much means of subsistence, too much industry, too much commerce. The productive forces at the disposal of society no longer tend to further the development of the conditions of bourgeois property; on the contrary, they have become too powerful for these conditions, by which they are fettered, and so soon as they overcome these fetters, they bring disorder into the whole of bourgeois society, endangering the existence of bourgeois property. The conditions of bourgeois society are too narrow to comprise the wealth created by them. And how does the bourgeoisie get over these crises? On the one hand by enforced destruction of a mass of productive forces; on the other, by the conquest of new markets, and by the more thorough exploitation of the old ones. That is to say, by paving the way for more extensive and more destructive crises, and by diminishing the means whereby crises are prevented.

The weapons with which the bourgeoisie felled feudalism to the ground are now turned against the bourgeoisie itself.

But not only has the bourgeoisie forged the weapons that bring death to itself; it has also called into existence the men who are to wield those weapons—the modern working-class—the proletarians.

In proportion as the bourgeoisie, i.e., capital, is developed, in the same proportion is the proletariat, the modern working-class, developed, a class of laborers, who live only so long as they find work, and who find work only so long as their labor increases capital. These laborers, who must sell themselves piecemeal, are a commodity, like every other article of commerce, and are consequently exposed to all the vicissitudes of competition, to all the fluctuations of the market.

Owing to the extensive use of machinery and to division of labor, the work of the proletarians has lost all individual character, and, consequently, all charm for the workman. He becomes an appendage of the machine, and it is only the most simple, most monotonous, and most easily acquired knack that is required of him. Hence, the cost of production of a workman is restricted, almost entirely, to the means of subsistence that he requires for his maintenance, and for the propagation of his race. But the price of a commodity, and also of labor, is equal to its cost of production. In proportion, therefore, as the repulsiveness of the work increases, the wage decreases. Nay more, in proportion as the use of machinery and division of labor increases, in the same proportion the burden of toil also increases, whether by prolongation of the working hours, by increase of the work enacted in a given time, or by increased speed of the machinery, etc.

Modern Industry has converted the little workshop of the patriarchal master into the great factory of the industrial capitalist. Masses of laborers, crowded into the factory, are organized like soldiers. As privates of the industrial army they are placed under the command of a perfect hierarchy of officers and sergeants. Not only are they the slaves of the bourgeois class, and of the bourgeois State, they are daily and hourly enslaved by the machine, by the over-looker, and, above all, by the individual bourgeois manufacturer himself. The more openly this despotism proclaims gain to be its end and aim, the more petty, the more hateful and the more embittering it is.

The less the skill and exertion or strength implied in manual labor, in other words, the more modern industry becomes developed, the more is the labor of men superseded by that of women. Differences of age and sex have no longer any distinctive social validity for the working class. All are instruments of labor, more or less expensive to use, according to their age and sex.

No sooner is the exploitation of the laborer by the manufacturer so far at an end, that he receives his wages in cash, than he is set upon by the other portions of the bourgeoisie, the landlord, the shopkeeper, the pawnbroker, etc.

The low strata of the middle class—the small trades-people, shopkeepers, and retired tradesmen generally, the handicraftsmen and peasants—all these sink gradually into the proletariat, partly because their diminutive capital does not suffice for the scale on which Modern Industry is carried on, and is swamped in the competition with the large capitalists, partly because their specialized skill is rendered worthless by new methods of production. Thus the proletariat is recruited from all classes of the population.

The proletariat goes through various stages of development. With its birth begins its struggle with the bourgeoisie. At first the contest is carried on by individual laborers, then by the workpeople of a factory, then by the operatives of one trade, in one locality, against the individual bourgeois who directly exploits them. They direct their attacks not against the bourgeois conditions of production, but against the instruments of production themselves; they destroy imported wares that compete with their labor, they smash to pieces machinery, they set factories ablaze, they seek to restore by force the vanished status of the workman of the Middle Ages.

At this stage the laborers still form an incoherent mass scattered over the whole country, and broken up by their mutual competition. If anywhere they unite to form more compact bodies, this is not yet the consequence of their own active union, but of the union of bourgeoisie, which class, in order to attain its own political ends, is compelled to set the whole proletariat in motion, and is moreover yet, for a time, able to do so. At this stage, therefore, the proletarians do not fight their enemies, but the enemies of their enemies, the remnants of absolute monarchy, the landowners, the non-industrial bourgeoisie, the petty bourgeoisie. Thus the whole historical movement is concentrated in the hands of the bourgeoisie; every victory so obtained is a victory for the bourgeoisie.

But with the development of industry the proletariat not only increases in number, it becomes concentrated in great masses, its strength grows, and it feels that strength more. The various interests and conditions of life within the ranks of the proletariat are more and more equalized, in proportion as machinery obliterates all distinction of labor, and nearly everywhere reduces wages to the same low level. The growing competition among the bourgeoisie, and the resulting commercial crises, make the wages of the worker ever more fluctuating. The unceasing improvement of machinery, ever more rapidly developing, makes their livelihood more and more precarious, the collisions between individual workmen and individual bourgeois take more and more the character of collision between two classes. Thereupon the workers begin to form combinations (Trades Unions) against the bourgeoisie; they club together in order to keep up the rate of wages; they found permanent associations in order to make provision beforehand for these occasional revolts. Here and there the contest breaks out into riots.

Now and then the workers are victorious, but only for a time. The real fruits of their battles lie, not in the immediate result, but in the ever expanding union of the workers. This union is helped on by the improved means of communication that are created by modern industry, and that place the workers of different localities in contact with one another. It was just this contact that was needed to centralize the numerous local struggles, all of the same character, into one national struggle between classes. But every class struggle is a political struggle. And that union, to attain which the burghers of the Middle Ages, with their miserable highways, required centuries, the modern proletarians, thanks to railways, achieve in a few years.

This organization of the proletarians into a class, and consequently into a political party, is continually being upset again by the competition between the workers themselves. But it ever rises up again, stronger, firmer, mightier. It compels legislative recognition of particular interests of the workers, by taking advantage of the divisions among the bourgeoisie itself. Thus the ten-hour bill in England was carried.

Altogether collisions between the classes of the old society further, in many ways, the course of development of the proletariat. The bourgeoisie finds itself involved in a constant battle. At first with the aristocracy; later on, with those portions of the bourgeoisie itself, whose interests have become antagonistic to the progress of industry; at all times, with the bourgeoisie of foreign countries. In all these battles it sees itself compelled to appeal to the proletariat, to ask for its help, and thus, to drag it into the political arena. The bourgeoisie itself, therefore, supplies the proletariat with its own elements of political and general education, in other words, it furnishes the proletariat with weapons for fighting the bourgeoisie.

Further, as we have already seen, entire sections of the ruling classes are, by the advance of industry, precipitated into the proletariat, or are at least threatened in their conditions of existence. These also supply the proletariat with fresh elements of enlightenment and progress.

Finally, in times when the class-struggle nears the decisive hour, the process of dissolution going on within the ruling class, in fact, within the whole range of old society, assumes such a violent, glaring character, that a small section of the ruling class cuts itself adrift, and joins the revolutionary class, the class that holds the future in its hands. Just as, therefore, at an earlier period, a section of the nobility went over to the bourgeoisie, so now a portion of the bourgeoisie goes over to the proletariat, and in particular, a portion of the bourgeois ideologists, who have raised themselves to the level of comprehending theoretically the historical movements as a whole.

Of all the classes that stand face to face with the bourgeoisie today, the proletariat alone is a really revolutionary class. The other classes decay and finally disappear in the face of Modern Industry; the proletariat is its special and essential product. . . .

In the conditions of the proletariat, those of old society at large are already virtually swamped. The proletarian is without property; his relation to his wife and children has no longer anything in common with the bourgeois family-relations; modern industrial labor, modern subjugation to capital, the same in England as in France, in America as in Germany, has stripped him of every trace of national character. Law, morality, religion, are to him so many bourgeois prejudices, behind which lurk in ambush just as many bourgeois interests.

All the preceding classes that got the upper hand, sought to fortify their already acquired status by subjecting society at large to their conditions of appropriation. The proletarians cannot become masters of the productive forces of society, except by abolishing their own previous mode of appropriation, and thereby also every other previous mode of appropriation. They have nothing of their own to secure and to fortify; their mission is to destroy all previous securities for, and insurances of, individual property.

All previous historical movements were movements of minorities, or in the interests of minorities. The proletarian movement is the self-conscious, independent movement of the immense majority, in the interest of the immense majority. The proletariat, the lowest stratum of our present society, cannot stir, cannot raise itself up, without the whole superincumbent strata of official society being sprung into the air.

Though not in substance, yet in form, the struggle of the proletariat with the bourgeoisie is at first a national struggle. The proletariat of each country must, of course, first of all settle matters with its own bourgeoisie.

In depicting the most general phases of the development of the proletariat, we traced the more or less veiled civil war, raging within existing society, up to the point where that war breaks out into open revolution, and where the violent overthrow of the bourgeoisie lays the foundation for the sway of the proletariat.

Hitherto, every form of society has been based, as we have already seen, on the antagonism of oppressing and oppressed classes. But in order to oppress a class, certain conditions must be assured to it under which it can, at least, continue its slavish existence. The serf, in the period of serfdom, raised himself to membership in the commune, just as the petty bourgeois, under the yoke of feudal absolutism, managed to develop into a bourgeois.

The modern laborer, on the contrary, instead of rising with the progress of industry, sinks deeper and deeper below the conditions of existence of his own class. He becomes a pauper, and pauperism develops more rapidly than population and wealth. And here it becomes evident that the bourgeoisie is unfit any longer to be the ruling class in society, and to impose its conditions of existence upon society as an over-riding law. It is unfit to rule, because it is incompetent to assure an existence to its slave within his slavery, because it cannot help letting him sink into such a state that it has to feed him, instead of being fed by him. Society can no longer live under this bourgeoisie, in other words, its existence is no longer compatible with society.

The essential condition for the existence, and for the sway of the bourgeois class, is the formation and augmentation of capital; the condition for capital is wage-labor. Wage-labor rests exclusively on competition between the laborers. The advance of industry, whose involuntary promoter is the bourgeoisie, replaces the isolation of the laborers, due to competition, by their revolutionary combination, due to association. The development of Modern Industry, therefore, cuts from under its feet the very foundation on which the bourgeoisie produces and appropriates products. What the bourgeoisie therefore produces, above all, are its own grave-diggers. Its fall and the victory of the proletariat are equally inevitable.

POSTSCRIPT

Can Capitalism Lead to Human Happiness?

As a society, Americans have always prized liberty over equality. We have always believed what we thought followed from Smith—that the wealth of the society as a whole was the only legitimate goal of economic enterprise as a whole, and that distribution for the sake of equity, or charity, was a side issue, best left to churches and private charity. We Americans have resisted any attempts at socializing such basic needs as medicine, communications (the telephone companies), and economic security for the old, young, and infirm. We have always enjoyed characterizing our business system as one where, as far as your personal income is concerned, "the sky's the limit." We point to the failures of "socialism" in England and Sweden, and cite with particular satisfaction the fall of communism in Eastern Europe and Russia.

We have built some safety nets: Social Security, Medicare and Medicaid, Aid to Dependent Children, and the like. But these and all the other elements of the welfare system have become a major problem and political issue for both parties. People in that system complain about its failure to provide adequately for those in the most need, babies and the infirm elderly. Meanwhile, conservative members of Congress complain that even these modest subsidies are costing the taxpayer too much, and recent modifications to these programs have put firm time limits on our ability to access them.

Why should subsidies to the poor bother us so? We provide price supports to farmers, corporate welfare (bailouts) to businesses, subsidized water and grazing land at public expense to ranchers and farmers, and access to minerals on public land for miners. We have allowed even foreign companies to come into the national forests, to mine and forest for their own profit, even when they leave tailings and barren land for us as taxpayers to clean up and restore. Why, it might be asked, should we subsidize the rich in our tender public compassion, while resenting the poor?

In most of the redistributive activities of the economy, we see the very visible hands of the CEOs and the Wall Street analysts. Where, in all of this, is the Invisible Hand of Adam Smith? Or does the whole arrogant parade of conspicuous billionaires force us to consider the alternatives to Adam Smith? Was Marx's political philosophy persuasive? Should we work to redistribute the productive assets of the country? The last two decades of economic reform have seen a steady redistribution in the other direction, as the richest persons in the country absorb more and more of the wealth and income, as the poorest get poorer. How can this be right?

21

Suggested Reading

For more information on this subject the following readings may be of help:

Robert L. Heilbroner, *The Worldly Philosophers,* 7th ed. (New York: Touchstone, 1999).

Karl Marx, *The Communist Manifesto* (New York: Penguin Classics, 2002).

Donald McCloskey, "Bourgeois Virtue," *American Scholar* 63 (1994).

David Schweickart, *Against Capitalism* (Cambridge: Cambridge University Press, 1993).

Adam Smith, *The Wealth of Nations,* Selected Edition (Oxford University Press, 2008).

ISSUE 2

Is Risk the Best Theory for Capitalism?

YES: **Simon Johnson and James Kwak,** from "The New World of Financial Risk," *Financial Executive* (January/February 2009).

NO: **Barry Eichengreen,** from "The Last Temptation of Risk," *The National Interest* (May/June 2009), pp. 8–14

ISSUE SUMMARY

YES: Johnson and Kwak argue that risk always has been and always will be a vital ingredient in the making of profits. They explain that when imprudent risks are taken whether in life or in business, the consequences can be harmful for many, not just the risk taker. The consequences of bad risks do not change their views on the value of risk in business.

NO: Eichengreen believes that economists have overrated risk as the essential feature for a successful business. He believes much of the economic collapse of 2008 was caused by inappropriate risks that perhaps economic theories sanctioned, but should have never been practiced.

Uncertainties underlie many business decisions in a variety of corporations. Sometimes the risk involves taking on a new product or business line, or assessing if regulators allow a corporation to buy out a firm's biggest competitor. Risk can also focus on ethical challenges that could compromise one of the critical operating assumptions of a corporation. Johnson and Kwak argue that risk diversification and management are part of the central pillars of finance and investment, and have been since the ancient days of civilization. They posit that underestimating risk led to the current global economic crisis. Some of the problems in the crisis involved managers who were unqualified to measure the sophisticated risks that their investment firms were facing. Risk is often seen as critical to the mission of an organization. They state that some of the financial derivatives employed during the crisis merely did damage while others caused destruction. However, they believe that risk is needed in a healthy business and it can be managed through perhaps diversifying lines of business or setting aside risk capital or other reserves. Johnson and Kwak expect that government and industry regulations may provide greater transparency and better methods for identifying and managing systematic risk. However, they also believe these may be many years in the making. Their advice for companies is to continue to prepare for significant booms and busts in the market and manage their cash flow accordingly. Financial risk, they contend, is the best way of doing business, but businesses should carefully work through the implications of risks they undertake.

Barry Eichengreen believes that risk strategies should be replaced by theories of economics based on statistics. He posits that the current economic downturn was the result of financial decision makers relying on "cherry-picking" risk theories that supported their risk measures. He asks where the business schools and "intellectual agenda setters" were when the economic crisis was building. His answer is that often the theories of risk that are modeled don't work when the economy is in crisis. "Value at Risk" was one of these models. Business students were asked to help corporations determine daily financial risks. The theory sounded workable, but it wasn't. Risk and return could not be reduced to a "set of equations specified by an MBA and solved by a machine." He further explains that some of the major problems in the current economic scandal have to do with conflicts of interest, self-dealing, and other ethical misdeeds. As an example, he cites risk taking that awards generous bonuses and severance packages for handsome returns today. However, he notes that now the shareholders are holding the "worthless paper" based on this theory of risk. Eichengreen believes that economics must now be based on empirical evidence in economics. Real-world observation will be driving risk. Risk theories won't be driving the market.

YES

**Simon Johnson and
James Kwak**

The New World of Financial Risk

Risk is an ever-present condition of human endeavor and of all financial and business activity. Businesspeople have been struggling to manage risk for millennia. Insurance contracts date back to multiple ancient civilizations. Contract and tort law developed, in part, as mechanisms for allocating risk. Risk diversification and risk management are among the central pillars of modern finance and investment.

Of course, risk is not all bad. "Nothing ventured, nothing gained" is an ancient principle that was only formalized by modern finance theory. Innovation is necessarily risky; at the very least, there is the risk of wasting time. Developing new products, entering new markets, acquiring companies—these are all risky yet potentially profitable projects.

What is bad, however, is underestimating risk or assuming that you have mastered it. Both of these factors contributed to the current global economic crisis.

The main causes of the crisis are well known, although there are debates about their relative importance. The following will focus on the underestimation or mismanagement of risk.

Risk in the Financial Crisis

The most common place to look for excessive risk is leverage. When it collapsed, Lehman Brothers Holdings Inc. had a leverage ratio above 30; its assets were worth more than 30 times its capital. However, simply blaming leverage is not strictly accurate.

First, high leverage is not necessarily risky; it depends on what is done with the borrowed money. For example, borrowing a little money to bet on one number on the roulette wheel is riskier than borrowing a lot of money to invest in Treasury bonds.

Second, insolvency is not what killed Lehman, at least not directly. Lehman fell victim to a modern-day bank run, in which financial institutions declined to renew their short-term funding.

For whatever reason (and solvency fears played a part), market participants started worrying that Lehman might not be able to pay off its creditors, and therefore, tried to pull their money out first; as a result, their fears became self-fulfilling.

The precipitating cause of Lehman's failure was not leverage, but liquidity risk—which no one was prepared for. The Lehman bankruptcy itself, and the resulting settlement of hundreds of billions of dollars of credit-default swaps on Lehman debt, did not plunge other large banks into bankruptcy. However, it forced the Reserve Fund to break the buck, freezing money markets.

In addition, seeing a major bank vanish awakened all financial institutions to the reality of counterparty risk—the chance that your counterparty might not be there when needed to close a trade—which was the single biggest reason for the American International Group Inc. bailout.

AIG was a major trader in credit-default swaps (CDS)—contracts to insure bonds or bond-like securities against default—As the subprime crisis deepened and the likelihood of default increased, AIG's potential obligations increased. When the bond rating agencies downgraded AIG, investors with a CDS contract with AIG started wondering if the firm could pay, and those with CDS contracts with other third parties started wondering if they were dependent on AIG.

As a result, everyone lost confidence in everyone else.

Governments have responded to the financial crisis by taking on risk from financial institutions. Since March, the Federal Reserve allowed investment banks to borrow from the Fed using a wide range of collateral.

The effective nationalization of Fannie Mae and Freddie Mac transferred their assets to the government balance sheet. The Federal Deposit Insurance Corp. has guaranteed new debt issued by banks, and the Citigroup Inc. bailout guaranteed assets on Citi's balance sheet.

The basic principle is sound: the U.S. government, with its unmatched ability to raise (or create) money, can absorb far more risk than any bank. However, risk does not simply go away when it is nationalized. CDS spreads on U.S. sovereign (U.S. Treasury) debt had climbed from 6 basis points at the end of April to almost 40 basis points in November.

The problem is much more pronounced for other nations. Obviously, Iceland could not afford to bail out its overgrown banking sector. But even Eurozone countries—such as Greece and Ireland, where CDS spreads climbed past 200 basis points in November—are increasingly seen as default risks.

As investors pull their money from emerging markets and invest it in "safe" countries, we are seeing a resurgence of currency risk. Capital flight causes emerging market currencies to fall, making it harder for companies and governments to pay off debts in foreign currencies.

For example, in Hungary, some households that took mortgages in Japanese yen—hoping to take advantage of lower interest rates—have seen their payments skyrocket. Russia has used up 20 percent of its foreign currency reserves trying to support its currency. Investors in the carry trade (borrowing yen at low rates and investing it elsewhere at high rates) were burned as the yen appreciated rapidly.

We may even see a resurgence of political risk. Financial crises and recessions can trigger unpleasant political consequences. In addition to old-fashioned protectionism, domestic governments may decide to favor their citizens over foreign creditors, for example by canceling foreign debt. Argentina took a small step toward suspending the rule of law in nationalizing its private pension system and there may be more to come.

Systematic Underestimation of Risk

During the "great moderation" of the last 20 years, many market participants systematically underestimated the risks, forgetting the basic principle that higher returns entail higher risk. One explanation for this phenomenon is psychological: the longer we go without a major crisis, the more confident we become that a crisis can be avoided, and the less wary we become—until a crisis erupts.

While this may be true, there are more specific explanations as well. There are existing mechanisms for managing risk. One of them is bond rating agencies. Moody's, Standard & Poor's, Fitch, and others rate bonds by their creditworthiness, traditionally using fundamental analysis. Many investors trusted the rating agencies to render accurate judgments about the likelihood of default.

However, rating agencies made many dubious calls in the past several years, particularly with collateralized-debt obligations (CDO) and other structured products. While conflict of interest may have been a factor, the skills and manpower of the agencies were overwhelmed by the number and complexity of new securities; the system could not cope with the demands put upon it.

Another source of overconfidence was the new science of risk management. In the late-20th century, mathematical finance and the massive growth in computing power put sophisticated quantitative models in the hands of professional investors. The vast sums of money to be made contributed to the trend.

Much of this quantitative firepower was dedicated to taming risk. The risk of each asset was measured, using its price volatility, and correlations between assets were calculated to determine how exogenous shocks would ripple through an entire portfolio. Quantitative models estimated the likelihood of specific events, such as credit defaults. Monte Carlo simulations tested the robustness of trading strategies under a wide range of conditions.

These models helped make investment banks feel secure in taking on high leverage. The modern "value-at-risk" models were both more scientific than traditional approaches and more attractive, since they tended to require less capital. The 2004 Basel Capital II Accord even recommended allowing banks to use their own internal models for determining capital requirements.

The result was that as hedge funds began collapsing in 2007, analysts would say these events could only happen every "10,000 years"—a clear indication that their models were faulty. One problem was basing statistical models on a data set that only covered a limited period.

Because housing prices had not declined by 15 percent during that period, the models found it extremely unlikely that housing prices could decline by

15 percent, and on those assumptions CDOs backed by mortgages were unlikely to default. When housing prices did, indeed, decline by 15 percent, of course, all bets were off.

Securitization was another tool to manage risk. By pooling and then subdividing assets, it spread the risk across a large number of investors. However, securitization contributed to a decline in underwriting standards, because lenders no longer had to bear the risks of their decisions alone. This is not the fault of securitization itself: investors still should have been assessing the risks of the securities they were buying. But this clearly did not happen.

Also, securitization made it possible to create securities that were even more risky than the underlying assets; there are CDO tranches that will be completely worthless if the default rate on the underlying loans reaches only 10 percent.

Modern risk management also brought new forms of hedging. Futures contracts and derivatives are nothing new. But the invention of the interest-rate swap in the 1980s and the CDS in the 1990s created new ways to hedge fixed-income securities.

Credit-default swaps can help investors who do not want to bear the risk of a default. But when used to create "risk-free" assets with higher yields than U.S. Treasuries, clearly someone is underestimating the risk. And we saw the consequences with AIG: instead of dissipating risk, CDS concentrated risk among major financial institutions that had unbalanced positions.

The cumulative result was the emergence of a new degree of systemic risk. Financial institutions discovered unexpected risks that threatened to spread through the entire system via collapsing institutions, falling asset values, volatile exchange rates and fear.

Against this backdrop, the U.S. and other wealthy nations stepped forward with an unprecedented combination of financial weapons, including new liquidity measures, guarantees for many types of assets, and bank recapitalization.

The New Order of Financial Risk

Late last year, there was still no assurance that these measures would work. While the series of bank recapitalizations appeared to stem the panic, the deep recession that has begun has compounded the difficulties faced by banks.

Not only subprime mortgages are falling in value, but banks are now expected to take writedowns on auto loans, credit cards, prime mortgages, commercial mortgages, mortgage-backed securities and corporate debt. In this context, the initial round of recapitalization is unlikely to be enough, at least for some banks. Citigroup has already needed a fresh bailout. Other banks may need one as well.

However, it is highly unlikely that the government will let the largest banks fail. The authors expect continued equity injections, as necessary, although the terms may change: the government may begin taking common shares, and will probably also insist on a suspension of dividend payments, as it tries to force banks to use their money for lending to a beleaguered real economy. As more and more money is needed for the systematically important banks, Treasury may have to let some smaller banks fail rather than devoting capital to them.

The new presidential administration will fundamentally rethink the way financial institutions are regulated. One key item on the agenda will be better management of risk across the financial system. This will require better ways of identifying where the risk is, which means more transparency.

There will almost certainly be increased disclosure requirements for off-balance-sheet exposures such as structured investment vehicles. Credit-default swaps will be traded on exchanges.

There will be some measure of disclosure required for hedge funds, because of suspicions that their trading strategies may be contributing to volatility and concerns that forced liquidations by hedge funds are driving down asset prices. As long as hedge-fund positions remain invisible, it will be difficult to accurately assess the systemic risks of the financial sector.

There will be a restructuring of regulatory roles, with a likely reduction in the number of regulators, clarification of their relationships and increase in their power to monitor institutions and take action when necessary.

Financial institutions will also change the way they do business. After the crisis has passed, they will go back to taking bigger risks in pursuit of higher yields and profits, as surely as day follows night. But underwriting standards—not only for home mortgages but also for business lending of all types—will remain tight for years.

Bond rating agencies, newly chastened and increasingly regulated, will err on the side of conservatism, increasing the price of debt. Risk managers will gain more power but will also come under greater scrutiny from CEOs and boards of directors.

Quantitative models will not go away, but will be tested against a broader range of possible scenarios; indeed, simply entering in the data from the current crisis would make those models more robust.

CDS spreads will be higher, and dealers will be more careful to have balanced positions. Liquidity risk and counterparty risk are likely to become more explicit considerations in dealings between financial institutions; increased transparency may become a prerequisite simply to do business.

Implications for Nonfinancial Companies

Currently, nonfinancial firms are grappling with the worst recession in decades. For many, demand for credit is falling due to lower customer demand; for those that need credit, supply has fallen sharply, as banks focus on their own survival.

Now may be a good time to look for new banking relationships, as not all banks have suffered equally, depending on their asset portfolios. While all companies are affected by the credit crunch, the divide between the most highly rated companies and everyone else has widened greatly.

In the short term, many companies will simply have to adapt to doing business with less credit. The U.S. is experiencing a type of crisis that until recently has only been seen in emerging markets, where the usual outcome is that the real economy has to adapt to a world of limited credit.

To be sure, the U.S. is not an emerging market, and the Federal Reserve has signaled that it will do everything in its power to keep credit flowing—even buying commercial paper directly from companies.

But the situation will not return to normal for several quarters. And with equity prices depressed, few companies are likely to want to raise money by issuing more shares.

Longer term, new regulations and somewhat more conservative behavior by financial institutions should create a more transparent and healthier financial system. However, it will also create higher costs for businesses.

One consequence of the widespread underestimation of risk was that investors were willing to lend money cheaply, and businesses were one of the major beneficiaries. Debt will likely remain more expensive than during the boom, and equity will be expensive until prices recover, which could take years.

Businesses will also need diversified funding strategies. Just like a bank, real-economy businesses do not want to be caught without access to short-term funding. Issuing debt for longer durations at higher cost may be necessary to protect against a possible contraction in credit from a jittery financial sector.

Also, like banks, businesses will need sophisticated risk-management models that can forecast the firm's financial position under a variety of scenarios. For multinational companies, these models must take into account the global volatility of this year, including sudden currency swings and rapid changes in fortune of individual countries.

The collapse of the leveraged-loan market has forced private-equity firms onto the sidelines, cutting off oxygen to the mergers and acquisitions market and eliminating another factor propping up equity prices.

In the short term, this means that more companies will end up in bankruptcy as opposed to being rolled up in larger companies' consolidation strategies. However, it also means that cash-rich companies with secure sources of funding may be able to acquire targets cheaply. Right now potential acquirers are probably waiting for equity values to fall even further before going shopping. But as in all downturns, there are opportunities for the survivors to become stronger.

Finally, large companies in any industry should recognize that they are unable to fully control risk-taking by their own employees. The costs of such behavior have been most vividly illustrated in financial institutions such as BNP Paribas, which lost billions of euros due to bets by Jérome Kerviel. But any organization with significant financial positions runs a similar risk.

Recent news reports have highlighted local governments or government agencies that took risky bets involving synthetic CDO or interest-rate swaps in an effort to gain higher yields on their excess cash. In all likelihood, the same took place in the private sector as well, where it is more difficult for journalists to dig up.

In any case, companies must ensure that their financial managers have the necessary skills and that sufficient internal controls are in place.

The Future

The fall of the Berlin Wall and the end of the Cold War raised hopes for a new era of international peace and stability. Those hopes were dimmed by 9/11 and the Afghanistan and Iraq Wars. Similarly, the "great moderation" of the 1990s and early 2000s raised hopes that the vagaries of the business cycle had been tamed and that risk had been brought under control.

Those hopes have now been definitively dashed.

Perhaps the most general conclusion one can draw is that risk cannot be simply engineered out of the system.

Some interpreted the relatively mild business cycles of the period from 1982 to 2007 as a sign of fundamental changes in the economy or of improvements in central bank monetary policies. Instead, it may have simply reflected ordinary statistical variation.

While new regulation may provide greater transparency and improved mechanisms for identifying and managing systemic risk, it will likely be many years in the making, and may be significantly undermined or re-purposed by the financial institutions and their elected representatives themselves.

In the meantime, and perhaps indefinitely, companies should expect significant booms and busts and take action to manage their investments and cash flow accordingly.

The one consolation is that the turbulence of 2008 may provide the impetus for a stronger, safer financial system, and may also teach businesses in all industries how to navigate the rapids of financial risk better. If so, it could inaugurate a new chapter in the long history of economic growth.

Barry Eichengreen

 **NO**

The Last Temptation of Risk

The Great Credit Crisis has cast into doubt much of what we thought we knew about economics. We thought that monetary policy had tamed the business cycle. We thought that because changes in central-bank policies had delivered low and stable inflation, the volatility of the pre-1985 years had been consigned to the dustbin of history; they had given way to the quaintly dubbed "Great Moderation." We thought that financial institutions and markets had come to be self-regulating—that investors could be left largely if not wholly to their own devices. Above all we thought that we had learned how to prevent the kind of financial calamity that struck the world in 1929.

We now know that much of what we thought was true was not. The Great Moderation was an illusion. Monetary policies focusing on low inflation to the exclusion of other considerations (not least excesses in financial markets) can allow dangerous vulnerabilities to build up. Relying on institutional investors to self-regulate is the economic equivalent of letting children decide their own diets. As a result we are now in for an economic and financial downturn that will rival the Great Depression before it is over.

The question is how we could have been so misguided. One interpretation, understandably popular given our current plight, is that the basic economic theory informing the actions of central bankers and regulators was fatally flawed. The only course left is to throw it out and start over. But another view, considerably closer to the truth, is that the problem lay not so much with the poverty of the underlying theory as with selective reading of it—a selective reading shaped by the social milieu. That social milieu encouraged financial decision makers to cherry-pick the theories that supported excessive risk taking. It discouraged whistle-blowing, not just by risk-management officers in large financial institutions, but also by the economists whose scholarship provided intellectual justification for the financial institutions' decisions. The consequence was that scholarship that warned of potential disaster was ignored. And the result was global economic calamity on a scale not seen for four generations.

❧

So where were the intellectual agenda setters when the crisis was building? Why did they fail to see this train wreck coming? More than that, why did they consort actively with the financial sector in setting the stage for the collapse?

For economists in business schools the answer is straightforward. Business schools see themselves as suppliers of inputs to business. Just as General Motors provides its suppliers with specifications for the cold-rolled sheet it needs for fabricating auto bodies, J. P. Morgan makes clear the kind of financial engineers it requires, and business schools deem to provide. In the wake of the 1987 stock-market crash, Morgan's chairman, Dennis Weatherstone, started calling for a daily "4:15 Report" summarizing how much his firm would lose if tomorrow turned out to be a bad day. His counterparts at other firms then adopted the practice. Soon after, business schools jumped to supply graduates to write those reports. Value at Risk, as that number and the process for calculating it came to be known, quickly gained a place in the business-school curriculum.

The desire for up-to-date information on the risks of doing business was admirable. Less admirable was the belief that those risks could be reduced to a single number which could then be estimated on the basis of a set of math-ematical equations fitted to a few data points. Much as former–GM CEO Alfred Sloan once sought to transform automobile production from a craft to an engi-neering problem, Weatherstone and his colleagues encouraged the belief that risk and return could be reduced to a set of equations specified by an MBA and solved by a machine.

Getting the machine to spit out a headline number for Value at Risk was straightforward. But deciding what to put into the model was another matter. The art of gauging Value at Risk required imagining the severity of the shocks to which the portfolio might be subjected. It required knowing what new vari-ables to add in response to financial innovation and unfolding events. Doing this right required a thoughtful and creative practitioner. Value at Risk, like dynamite, can be a powerful tool when in the right hands. Placed in the wrong hands—well, you know.

These simple models should have been regarded as no more than starting points for serious thinking. Instead, those responsible for making key deci-sions, institutional investors and their regulators alike, took them literally. This reflected the seductive appeal of elegant theory. Reducing risk to a single number encouraged the belief that it could be mastered. It also made it easier to leave early for that weekend in the Hamptons.

Now, of course, we know that the gulf between assumption and reality was too wide to be bridged. These models were worse than unrealistic. They were weapons of economic mass destruction.

For some years those who relied on these artificial constructs were not caught out. Episodes of high volatility, like the 1987 stock-market crash, still loomed large in the data set to which the model was fit. They served to high-light the potential for big shocks and cautioned against aggressive investment strategies. Since financial innovation was gradual, models estimated on his-torical data remained reasonable representations of the balance of risks.

⋅⊰◉⊱⋅

With time, however, memories of the 1987 crash faded. In the data used by the financial engineers, the crash became only one observation among many generated in the course of the Great Moderation. There were echoes, like the all-but-failure of the hedge fund Long-Term Capital Management in 1998. (Over four months the company lost $4.6 billion and had to be saved through a bailout orchestrated by the Federal Reserve Bank of New York.) But these warning signs were muffled by comparison. This encouraged the misplaced belief that the same central-bank policies that had reduced the volatility of inflation had magically, perhaps through transference, also reduced the volatility of financial markets. It encouraged the belief that mastery of the remaining risk made more aggressive investment strategies permissible. It made it possible, for example, to employ more leverage—to make use of more borrowed money—without putting more value at risk.

Meanwhile, deregulation was on the march. Memories of the 1930s disaster that had prompted the adoption of restrictions like the Glass-Steagall Act, which separated commercial and investment banking, faded with the passage of time. This tilted the political balance toward those who, for ideological reasons, favored permissive regulation. Meanwhile, financial institutions, in principle prohibited from pursuing certain lines of business, found ways around those restrictions, encouraging the view that strict regulation was futile. With the elimination of regulatory ceilings on the interest rates that could be paid to depositors, commercial banks had to compete for funding by offering higher rates, which in turn pressured them to adopt riskier lending and investment policies in order to pay the bill. With the entry of low-cost brokerages and the elimination of fixed commissions on stock trades, broker-dealers like Bear Stearns, which had previously earned a comfy living off of such commissions, now felt compelled to enter riskier lines of business.

But where the accelerating pace of change should have prompted more caution, the routinization of risk management encouraged precisely the opposite. The idea that risk management had been reduced to a mere engineering problem seduced business in general, and financial businesses in particular, into believing that it was safe to use more leverage and to invest in more volatile assets.

Of course, risk officers could have pointed out that the models had been fit to data for a period of unprecedented low volatility. They could have pointed out that models designed to predict losses on securities backed by residential mortgages were estimated on data only for years when housing prices were rising and foreclosures were essentially unknown. They could have emphasized the high degree of uncertainty surrounding their estimates. But they knew on which side their bread was buttered. Senior management strongly preferred to take on additional risk, since if the dice came up seven they stood to receive megabonuses, whereas if they rolled snake eyes the worst they could expect was a golden parachute. If an investment strategy that promised high returns today threatened to jeopardize the viability of the enterprise tomorrow, then this was someone else's problem. For a junior risk officer to warn the members of the investment committee that they were taking undue risk would have dimmed his chances of promotion. And so on up the ladder.

~⊙~

Why corporate risk officers did not sound the alarm bells is thus clear enough. But where were the business-school professors while these events were unfolding? Answer: they were writing textbooks about Value at Risk. (Truth in advertising requires me to acknowledge that the leading such book is by a professor at the University of California.) Business schools are rated by business publications and compete for students on the basis of their record of placing graduates. With banks hiring graduates educated in Value at Risk, business schools had an obvious incentive to supply the same.

But what of doctoral programs in economics (like the one in which I teach)? The top PhD-granting departments only rarely send their graduates to positions in banking or business—most go on to other universities. But their faculties do not object to the occasional high-paying consulting gig. They don't mind serving as the entertainment at beachside and ski-slope retreats hosted by investment banks for their important clients.

Generous speaker's fees were thus available to those prepared to drink the Kool-Aid. Not everyone indulged. But there was nonetheless a subconscious tendency to embrace the arguments of one's more "successful" colleagues in a discipline where money, in this case earned through speaking engagements and consultancies, is the common denominator of success.

Those who predicted the housing slump eventually became famous, of course. Princeton University Press now takes out space ads in general-interest publications prominently displaying the sober visage of Yale University economics professor Robert Shiller, the maven of the housing crash. Not every academic scribbler can expect this kind of attention from his publisher. But such fame comes only after the fact. The more housing prices rose and the longer predictions of their decline looked to be wrong, the lonelier the intellectual nonconformists became. Sociologists may be more familiar than economists with the psychic costs of nonconformity. But because there is a strong external demand for economists' services, they may experience even-stronger economic incentives than their colleagues in other disciplines to conform to the industry-held view. They can thus incur even-greater costs—economic and also psychic—from falling out of step.

Why belabor these points? Because it was not that economic theory had nothing to say about the kinds of structural weaknesses and conflicts of interest that paved the way to our current catastrophe. In fact, large swaths of modern economic theory focus squarely on the kind of generic problems that created our current mess. The problem was not an inability to imagine that conflicts of interest, self-dealing and herd behavior could arise, but a peculiar failure to apply those insights to the real world.

Take for example agency theory, whose point of departure is the observation that shareholders find it difficult to monitor managers, who have an incentive to make decisions that translate into large end-of-current-year bonuses but not necessarily into the long-term health of the enterprise. Risk taking that produces handsome returns today but ends in bankruptcy tomorrow may be perfectly congenial to CEOs who receive generous bonuses and severance packages but not to shareholders who end up holding worthless paper. This work had long pointed to compensation practices in the financial sector as encouraging short-termism and excessive risk taking and heightening conflicts of interest. The failure to heed such warnings is all the more striking given that agency theory is hardly an obscure corner of economics. A Nobel Prize for work on this topic was awarded to Leonid Hurwicz, Eric Maskin and Roger Myerson in 2007. (So much for the idea that it is only the financial engineers who are recognized by the Nobel Committee.)

Then there is information economics. It is a fact of life that borrowers know more than lenders about their willingness and capacity to repay. Who could know better what motivation lurks in the mind of the borrower and what opportunities he truly possesses? Taking this observation as its starting point, research in information economics has long emphasized the existence of adverse selection in financial markets—when interest rates rise, only borrowers with high-risk projects offering some chance of generating the high returns needed to service and repay loans will be willing to borrow. Indeed, if higher interest rates mean riskier borrowers, there may be no interest rate high enough to compensate the lender for the risk that the borrower may default. In that case lending and borrowing may collapse.

These models also show how borrowers have an incentive to take on more risk when using other people's money or if they expect to be bailed out when things go wrong. In the wake of recent financial rescues, the name for this problem, "moral hazard," will be familiar to even the casual newspaper reader. Again this is hardly an obscure corner of economics: George Akerlof, Michael Spence and Joseph Stiglitz were awarded the Nobel Prize for their work on it in 2001. Here again the potential problems of an inadequately regulated financial system would have been quite clear had anyone bothered to look.

Finally there is behavioral economics and its applications, including behavioral finance. Behavioral economics focuses on how cognition, emotion, and other psychological and social factors affect economic and financial decision making. Behavioral economists depart from the simpleminded benchmark that all investors take optimal decisions on the basis of all available information. Instead they acknowledge that decision making is not easy. They acknowledge that many decisions are taken using rules of thumb, which are often formed on the basis of social convention. They analyze how, to pick an example not entirely at random, decision making can be affected by the psychic costs of nonconformity.

It is easy to see how this small step in the direction of realism can transform one's view of financial markets. It can explain herd behavior, where everyone follows the crowd, giving rise to bubbles, panics and crashes. Economists have succeeded in building elegant mathematical models of decision making under these conditions and in showing how such behavior can give rise to extreme instability. It should not be a surprise that people like the aforementioned George Akerlof and Robert Shiller are among the leaders in this field.

Moreover, what is true of investors can also be true of regulators, for whom information is similarly costly to acquire and who will similarly be tempted to follow convention—even when that convention allows excessive risk taking by the regulated. Indeed, these theories suggest that the attitudes of regulators may be infected not merely by the practices and attitudes of their fellow regulators, but also by those of the regulated. Economists now even have a name for this particular version of the intellectual fox-in-the-henhouse syndrome: cognitive regulatory capture.

And what is true of investors and regulators, introspection suggests, can also be true of academics. When it is costly to acquire and assimilate information about how reality diverges from the assumptions underlying popular economic models, it will be tempting to ignore those divergences. When convention within the discipline is to assume efficient markets, there will be psychic costs if one attempts to buck the trend. Scholars, in other words, are no more immune than regulators to the problem of cognitive capture.

What got us into this mess, in other words, were not the limits of scholarly imagination. It was not the failure or inability of economists to model conflicts of interest, incentives to take excessive risk and information problems that can give rise to bubbles, panics and crises. It was not that economists failed to recognize the role of social and psychological factors in decision making or that they lacked the tools needed to draw out the implications. In fact, these observations and others had been imaginatively elaborated by contributors to the literatures on agency theory, information economics and behavioral finance. Rather, the problem was a partial and blinkered reading of that literature. The consumers of economic theory, not surprisingly, tended to pick and choose those elements of that rich literature that best supported their self-serving actions. Equally reprehensibly, the producers of that theory, benefiting in ways both pecuniary and psychic, showed disturbingly little tendency to object. It is in this light that we must understand how it was that the vast majority of the economics profession remained so blissfully silent and indeed unaware of the risk of financial disaster.

With the pressure of social conformity being so powerful, are we economists doomed to repeat past mistakes? Will we forever follow the latest intellectual fad and fashion, swinging wildly—much like investors whose behavior we seek to model—from irrational exuberance to excessive despair about the operation of markets? Isn't our outlook simply too erratic and advice therefore too unreliable to be trusted as a guide for policy?

Maybe so. But amid the pervading sense of gloom and doom, there is at least one reason for hope. The last ten years have seen a quiet revolution in the practice of economics. For years theorists held the intellectual high ground. With their mastery of sophisticated mathematics, they were the high-prestige members of the profession. The methods of empirical economists seeking to analyze real data were rudimentary by comparison. As recently as the 1970s, doing a statistical analysis meant entering data on punch cards, submitting them at the university computing center, going out for dinner and returning some hours later to see if the program had successfully run. (I speak from experience.) The typical empirical analysis in economics utilized a few dozen, or at most a few hundred, observations transcribed by hand. It is not surprising that the theoretically inclined looked down, fondly if a bit condescendingly, on their more empirically oriented colleagues or that the theorists ruled the intellectual roost.

But the IT revolution has altered the lay of the intellectual land. Now every graduate student has a laptop computer with more memory than that decades-old university computing center. And she knows what to do with it. Just like the typical twelve-year-old knows more than her parents about how to download data from the internet, for graduate students in economics, unlike their instructors, importing data from cyberspace is second nature. They can grab data on grocery-store spending generated by the club cards issued by supermarket chains and combine it with information on temperature by zip code to see how the weather affects sales of beer. Their next step, of course, is to download securities prices from Bloomberg and see how blue skies and rain affect the behavior of financial markets. Finding that stock markets are more likely to rise on sunny days is not exactly reassuring for believers in the efficient-markets hypothesis.

The data sets used in empirical economics today are enormous, with observations running into the millions. Some of this work is admittedly self-indulgent, with researchers seeking to top one another in applying the largest data set to the smallest problem. But now it is on the empirical side where the capacity to do high-quality research is expanding most dramatically, be the topic beer sales or asset pricing. And, revealingly, it is now empirically oriented graduate students who are the hot property when top doctoral programs seek to hire new faculty.

Not surprisingly, the best students have responded. The top young economists are, increasingly, empirically oriented. They are concerned not with theoretical flights of fancy but with the facts on the ground. To the extent that their work is rooted concretely in observation of the real world, it is less likely to sway with the latest fad and fashion. Or so one hopes.

The late twentieth century was the heyday of deductive economics. Talented and facile theorists set the intellectual agenda. Their very facility enabled them to build models with virtually any implication, which meant that policy makers could pick and choose at their convenience. Theory turned out to be too malleable, in other words, to provide reliable guidance for policy.

In contrast, the twenty-first century will be the age of inductive economics, when empiricists hold sway and advice is grounded in concrete observation of markets and their inhabitants. Work in economics, including the abstract model building in which theorists engage, will be guided more powerfully by this real-world observation. It is about time.

Should this reassure us that we can avoid another crisis? Alas, there is no such certainty. The only way of being certain that one will not fall down the stairs is to not get out of bed. But at least economists, having observed the history of accidents, will no longer recommend removing the handrail.

POSTSCRIPT

Is Risk the Best Theory for Capitalism?

Risk profile in an institution can drive strategic business. Sometimes these risk profiles can distort specific risk decisions. Risk and reward are often seen as hand-in-glove mechanisms for a business. If a manager distorts a risk, it may be some time before principal shareholders see that the risks are being gamed. Eichengreen states that often mismanagement of the risks takes place under a wider business theory. He warns that risk is a complicated business factor that must be empirically guided and then allowed to be theory based. For Johnson and Kwak, it would be wise to take advantage of those institutions who have miscalculated risk. They find these firms may be up for a takeover because of their unethical or unwise risk decisions. They contend that risk will always drive the market. The institutions that use risk properly will be able to take advantage of the firms that base risk on greedy miscalculations.

Suggested Readings

Simon Heffer, "If We Take Away All the Risk, Then Capitalism is Finished," *The Daily Telegraph,* London ed. (September 19, 2007) p. 20.

Jessica Ramierez, et al. "Stop Saving Now!" (Cover story). *Newsweek* (vol. 153, no. 12, 2009), pp. 26–29.

Rex A. McKenzie, "Casino Capitalism with Derivatives: Fragility and Instability in Contemporary Finance." *Review of Radical Political Economics* (vol. 43, no. 2, 2011), pp. 198–215.

ISSUE 3

Is Increasing Profits the Only Social Responsibility of Business?

YES: Milton Friedman, from "The Social Responsibility of Business Is to Increase its Profits," *New York Times Magazine* (September 13, 1970).

NO: Michael E. Porter and Mark R. Kramer, from "Creating Shared Value: How to Reinvent Capitalism—and Unleash a Wave of Innovation and Growth," *Harvard Business Review* (January/February 2011), pp. 63–70

ISSUE SUMMARY

YES: Friedman argues that businesses have neither the right nor the ability to fool around with social responsibility as distinct from profit-making. They serve employees and customers best when they do their work with maximum efficiency. The only restrictions on the pursuit of profit that Friedman accepts are the requirements of law and "the rules of the game" ("open and free competition without deception or fraud").

NO: Porter and Kramer ask that the purpose of the corporation be redefined as one of shared value, which brings the needs and interests of society and business together. By enhancing the needs of society, the supply and demands within business will stabilize for new generations.

In 1972, Milton Friedman declared that corporations practicing social responsibility are victims of "pure and unadulterated socialism." His stance is that business has no conscience; rather that business is concerned with profit, and not with promoting desirable social ends. Specifically, Friedman explains that a business does not have a responsibility to provide employment, eliminate discrimination, or avoid pollution. He believes that businesses who do believe they have social responsibilities are "unwitting puppets of the intellectual forces that have been undermining the basis of a free society these past decades." Friedman holds that a corporation is merely an artificial person and in this sense may have artificial responsibilities. He holds firmly that even in this vague sense, "business as a whole cannot be said to have responsibilities."

This theory of Friedman was recently challenged by a 2010 Supreme Court finding (*Citizens United v. FEC*), which allows that corporations as persons can contribute to political candidates. Friedman, however, is basing his theory on business profits going directly to the stockholders and states that a corporate executive is an employee of the owners of the business. He contends that businesses practicing social responsibility are guilty of taxation without representation. He explains that the corporate executive is spending someone else's money if corporate funds are given to a charity or social cause. He admits that individuals within the corporation may spend their own funds on charity.

Friedman states it is a serious misuse of funds to contribute corporate funds to charity or social causes because the executive is "imposing taxes on the one hand, and deciding how the tax proceeds shall be spent, on the other." He further states that people need to be responsible for their own actions, and not allow others to exploit them for selfish or unselfish purposes.

Porter and Kramer explain that the more business assists in society's problems, the more business is blamed for causing them. They find the root cause of this concern is that often businesses and others look at optimizing short-term financial performance—in a bubble—rather than looking at the longer-term successes that can occur when businesses understand their role in society. They ask that a "shared value" approach be tried that involves creating economic value in a way that "also creates value for society by addressing its needs and challenges." These authors believe that business and society should not be pitted against each other as Friedman suggests. Rather the two can create values that can drive innovation and productivity growth in the economy. They also believe that in a sense capitalism needs to be reshaped in a way that helps rather than distances society. They explain that "societal needs, not just conventional economic costs, build supportive industry clusters at the company's locations." Their approach holds that the competitiveness of a company and the health of the communities around it are closely intertwined.

YES

Milton Friedman

The Social Responsibility of Business Is to Increase Its Profits

When I hear businessmen speak eloquently about the "social responsibilities of business in a free-enterprise system," I am reminded of the wonderful line about the Frenchman who discovered at the age of 70 that he had been speaking prose all his life. The businessmen believe that they are defending free enterprise when they declaim that business is not concerned "merely" with profit but also with promoting desirable "social" ends; that business has a "social conscience" and takes seriously its responsibilities for providing employment, eliminating discrimination, avoiding pollution and whatever else may be the catchwords of the contemporary crop of reformers. In fact they are—or would be if they or anyone else took them seriously—preaching pure and unadulterated socialism. Businessmen who talk this way are unwitting puppets of the intellectual forces that have been undermining the basis of a free society these past decades.

The discussions of the "social responsibilities of business" are notable for their analytical looseness and lack of rigor. What does it mean to say that "business" has responsibilities? Only people can have responsibilities. A corporation is an artificial person and in this sense may have artificial responsibilities, but "business" as a whole cannot be said to have responsibilities, even in this vague sense. The first step toward clarity in examining the doctrine of the social responsibility of business is to ask precisely what it implies for whom.

Presumably, the individuals who are to be responsible are businessmen, which means individual proprietors or corporate executives. Most of the discussion of social responsibility is directed at corporations, so in what follows I shall mostly neglect the individual proprietors and speak of corporate executives.

In a free-enterprise, private-property system, a corporate executive is an employee of the owners of the business. He has direct responsibility to his employers. That responsibility is to conduct the business in accordance with their desires, which generally will be to make as much money as possible while conforming to the basic rules of the society, both those embodied in law and those embodied in ethical custom. Of course, in some cases his employers may have a different objective. A group of persons might establish a corporation for an eleemosynary purpose—for example, a hospital or a school. The manager of such a corporation will not have money profit as his objective but the rendering of certain services.

In either case, the key point is that, in his capacity as a corporate executive, the manager is the agent of the individuals who own the corporation or establish the eleemosynary institution, and his primary responsibility is to them.

Needless to say, this does not mean that it is easy to judge how well he is performing his task. But at least the criterion of performance is straightforward, and the persons among whom a voluntary contractual arrangement exists are clearly defined.

Of course, the corporate executive is also a person in his own right. As a person, he may have many other responsibilities that he recognizes or assumes voluntarily—to his family, his conscience, his feelings of charity, his church, his clubs, his city, his country. He may feel impelled by these responsibilities to devote part of his income to causes he regards as worthy, to refuse to work for particular corporations, even to leave his job, for example, to join his country's armed forces. If we wish, we may refer to some of these responsibilities as "social responsibilities." But in these respects he is acting as a principal, not an agent; he is spending his own money or time or energy, not the money of his employers or the time or energy he has contracted to devote to their purposes. If these are "social responsibilities," they are the social responsibilities of individuals, not of business.

What does it mean to say that the corporate executive has a "social responsibility" in his capacity as businessman? If this statement is not pure rhetoric, it must mean that he is to act in some way that is not in the interest of his employers. For example, that he is to refrain from increasing the price of the product in order to contribute to the social objective of preventing inflation, even though a price increase would be in the best interests of the corporation. Or that he is to make expenditures on reducing pollution beyond the amount that is in the best interests of the corporation or that is required by law in order to contribute to the social objective of improving the environment. Or that, at the expense of corporate profits, he is to hire "hard-core" unemployed instead of better qualified available workmen to contribute to the social objective of reducing poverty.

In each of these cases, the corporate executive would be spending someone else's money for a general social interest. Insofar as his actions in accord with his "social responsibility" reduce returns to stockholders, he is spending their money. Insofar as his actions raise the price to customers, he is spending the customers' money. Insofar as his actions lower the wages of some employees, he is spending their money.

The stockholders or the customers or the employees could separately spend their own money on the particular action if they wished to do so. The executive is exercising a distinct "social responsibility," rather than serving as an agent of the stockholders or the customers or the employees, only if he spends the money in a different way than they would have spent it.

But if he does this, he is in effect imposing taxes, on the one hand, and deciding how the tax proceeds shall be spent, on the other.

This process raises political questions on two levels: principle and consequences. On the level of political principle, the imposition of taxes and the expenditure of tax proceeds are governmental functions. We have established elaborate constitutional, parliamentary and judicial provisions to control these functions, to assure that taxes are imposed so far as possible in accordance with the preferences and desires of the public—after all, "taxation without representation" was one of the battle cries of the American Revolution. We have a system of checks and balances to separate the legislative function of imposing taxes and enacting expenditures from the executive function of collecting taxes and administering expenditure programs and from the judicial function of mediating disputes and interpreting the law.

Here the businessman—self-selected or appointed directly or indirectly by stockholders—is to be simultaneously legislator, executive and jurist. He is to decide whom to tax by how much and for what purpose, and he is to spend the proceeds—all this guided only by general exhortations from on high to restrain inflation, improve the environment, fight poverty and so on and on.

The whole justification for permitting the corporate executive to be selected by the stockholders is that the executive is an agent serving the interests of his principal. This justification disappears when the corporate executive imposes taxes and spends the proceeds for "social" purposes. He becomes in effect a public employee, a civil servant, even though he remains in name an employee of a private enterprise. On grounds of political principle, it is intolerable that such civil servants—insofar as their actions in the name of social responsibility are real and not just window dressing—should be selected as they are now. If they are to be civil servants, then they must be selected through a political process. If they are to impose taxes and make expenditures to foster "social" objectives, then political machinery must be set up to make the assessment of taxes and to determine through a political process the objectives to be served.

This is the basic reason why the doctrine of "social responsibility" involves the acceptance of the socialist view that political mechanisms, not market mechanisms, are the appropriate way to determine the allocation of scarce resources to alternative uses.

On the grounds of consequences, can the corporate executive in fact discharge his alleged "social responsibilities"? On the other hand, suppose he could get away with spending the stockholders' or customers' or employees' money. How is he to know how to spend it? He is told that he must contribute to fighting inflation. How is he to know what action of his will contribute to that end? He is presumably an expert in running his company—in producing a product or selling it or financing it. But nothing about his selection makes him an expert on inflation. Will his holding down the price of his product reduce inflationary pressure? Or, by leaving more spending power in the hands of his customers, simply divert it elsewhere? Or, by forcing him to produce less because of the lower price, will it simply contribute to shortages? Even if he could answer these questions, how much cost is he justified in imposing on his stockholders, customers and employees for this social purpose? What is his appropriate share and what is the appropriate share of others?

And, whether he wants to or not, can he get away with spending his stockholders', customers' or employees' money? Will not the stockholders fire him? (Either the present ones or those who take over when his actions in the name of social responsibility have reduced the corporation's profits and the price of its stock.) His customers and his employees can desert him for other producers and employers less scrupulous in exercising their social responsibilities.

This facet of "social responsibility" doctrine is brought into sharp relief when the doctrine is used to justify wage restraint by trade unions. The conflict of interest is naked and clear when union officials are asked to subordinate the interest of their members to some more general purpose. If the union officials try to enforce wage restraint, the consequence is likely to be wildcat strikes, rank-and-file revolts and the emergence of strong competitors for their jobs. We thus have the ironic phenomenon that union leaders—at least in the U.S.—have objected to Government interference with the market far more consistently and courageously than have business leaders.

The difficulty of exercising "social responsibility" illustrates, of course, the great virtue of private competitive enterprise—it forces people to be responsible for their own actions and makes it difficult for them to "exploit" other people for either selfish or unselfish purposes. They can do good—but only at their own expense.

Many a reader who has followed the argument this far may be tempted to remonstrate that it is all well and good to speak of government's having the responsibility to impose taxes and determine expenditures for such "social" purposes as controlling pollution or training the hard-core unemployed, but that the problems are too urgent to wait on the slow course of political processes, that the exercise of social responsibility by businessmen is a quicker and surer way to solve pressing current problems.

Aside from the question of fact—I share Adam Smith's skepticism about the benefits that can be expected from "those who affect to trade for the public good"—this argument must be rejected on grounds of principle. What it amounts to is an assertion that those who favor the taxes and expenditures in question have failed to persuade a majority of their fellow citizens to be of like mind and that they are seeking to attain by undemocratic procedures what they cannot attain by democratic procedures. In a free society, it is hard for "evil" people to do "evil," especially since one man's good is another's evil.

I have, for simplicity, concentrated on the special case of the corporate executive, except only for the brief digression on trade unions. But precisely the same argument applies to the newer phenomenon of calling upon stockholders to require corporations to exercise social responsibility (the recent G.M. crusade for example). In most of these cases, what is in effect involved is some stockholders trying to get other stockholders (or customers or employees) to contribute against their will to "social" causes favored by the activists. Insofar as they succeed, they are again imposing taxes and spending the proceeds.

The situation of the individual proprietor is somewhat different. If he acts to reduce the returns of his enterprise in order to exercise his "social responsibility," he is spending his own money, not someone else's. If he wishes to spend his money on such purposes, that is his right, and I cannot see that there is any objection to his doing so. In the process, he, too, may impose costs on employees and customers. However, because he is far less likely than a large corporation or union to have monopolistic power, any such side effects will tend to be minor.

Of course, in practice the doctrine of social responsibility is frequently a cloak for actions that are justified on other grounds rather than a reason for those actions.

To illustrate, it may well be in the long-run interest of a corporation that is a major employer in a small community to devote resources to providing amenities to that community or to improving its government. That may make it easier to attract desirable employees, it may reduce the wage bill or lessen losses from pilferage and sabotage or have other worthwhile effects. Or it may be that, given the laws about the deductibility of corporate charitable contributions, the stockholders can contribute more to charities they favor by having the corporation make the gift than by doing it themselves, since they can in that way contribute an amount that would otherwise have been paid as corporate taxes.

In each of these—and many similar—cases, there is a strong temptation to rationalize these actions as an exercise of "social responsibility." In the present climate of opinion, with its widespread aversion to "capitalism," "profits," the "soulless corporation" and so on, this is one way for a corporation to generate goodwill as a by-product of expenditures that are entirely justified in its own self-interest.

It would be inconsistent of me to call on corporate executives to refrain from this hypocritical window-dressing because it harms the foundations of a free society. That would be to call on them to exercise a "social responsibility"! If our institutions, and the attitudes of the public make it in their self-interest to cloak their actions in this way, I cannot summon much indignation to denounce them. At the same time, I can express admiration for those individual proprietors or owners of closely held corporations or stockholders of more broadly held corporations who disdain such tactics as approaching fraud.

Whether blameworthy or not, the use of the cloak of social responsibility, and the nonsense spoken in its name by influential and prestigious businessmen, does clearly harm the foundations of a free society. I have been impressed time and again by the schizophrenic character of many businessmen. They are capable of being extremely far-sighted and clearheaded in matters that are internal to their businesses. They are incredibly short-sighted and muddle-headed in matters that are outside their businesses but affect the possible survival of business in general. This short-sightedness is strikingly exemplified in the calls from many businessmen for wage and price guidelines or controls or income policies. There is nothing that could do more in a brief period to destroy a market system and replace it by a centrally controlled system than effective governmental control of prices and wages.

The short-sightedness is also exemplified in speeches by businessmen on social responsibility. This may gain them kudos in the short run. But it helps to strengthen the already too prevalent view that the pursuit of profits is wicked and immoral and must be curbed and controlled by external forces. Once this view is adopted, the external forces that curb the market will not be the social consciences, however highly developed, of the pontificating executives; it will be the iron fist of government bureaucrats. Here, as with price and wage controls, businessmen seem to me to reveal a suicidal impulse.

The political principle that underlies the market mechanism is unanimity. In an ideal free market resting on private property, no individual can coerce any other, all cooperation is voluntary, all parties to such cooperation benefit or they need not participate. There are no values, no "social" responsibilities in any sense other than the shared values and responsibilities of individuals. Society is a collection of individuals and of the various groups they voluntarily form.

The political principle that underlies the political mechanism is conformity. The individual must serve a more general social interest—whether that be determined by a church or a dictator or a majority. The individual may have a vote and say in what is to be done, but if he is overruled, he must conform. It is appropriate for some to require others to contribute to a general social purpose whether they wish to or not.

Unfortunately, unanimity is not always feasible. There are some respects in which conformity appears unavoidable, so I do not see how one can avoid the use of the political mechanism altogether.

But the doctrine of "social responsibility" taken seriously would extend the scope of the political mechanism to every human activity. It does not differ in philosophy from the most explicitly collectivist doctrine. It differs only by professing to believe that collectivist ends can be attained without collectivist means. That is why, in my book *Capitalism and Freedom*, I have called it a "fundamentally subversive doctrine" in a free society, and have said that in such a society, "there is one and only one social responsibility of business—to use its resources and engage in activities designed to increase its profits so long as it stays within the rules of the game, which is to say, engages in open and free competition without deception or fraud."

Michael E. Porter and
Mark R. Kramer

 **NO**

Creating Shared Value: How to Reinvent Capitalism—and Unleash a Wave of Innovation and Growth

Capitalism is under siege. . . . Diminished trust in business is causing political leaders to set policies that sap economic growth. . . . Business is caught in a vicious circle. . . . The purpose of the corporation must be redefined around CREATING SHARED VALUE.

The Capitalist System is under siege. In recent years business increasingly has been viewed as a major cause of social, environmental, and economic problems. Companies are widely perceived to be prospering at the expense of the broader community.

Even worse, the more business has begun to embrace corporate responsibility, the more it has been blamed for society's failures. The legitimacy of business has fallen to levels not seen in recent history. This diminished trust in business leads political leaders to set policies that undermine competitiveness and sap economic growth. Business is caught in a vicious circle.

A big part of the problem lies with companies themselves, which remain trapped in an outdated approach to value creation that has emerged over the past few decades. They continue to view value creation narrowly, optimizing short-term financial performance in a bubble while missing the most important customer needs and ignoring the broader influences that determine their longer-term success. How else could companies overlook the wellbeing of their customers, the depletion of natural resources vital to their businesses, the viability of key suppliers, or the economic distress of the communities in which they produce and sell? How else could companies think that simply shifting activities to locations with ever lower wages was a sustainable "solution" to competitive challenges? Government and civil society have often exacerbated the problem by attempting to address social weaknesses at the expense of business. The presumed trade-offs between economic efficiency and social progress have been institutionalized in decades of policy choices.

Companies must take the lead in bringing business and society back together. The recognition is there among sophisticated business and thought leaders, and promising elements of a new model are emerging. Yet we still lack

From *Harvard Business Review*, January/February 2011, pp. 63–70. Copyright © 2011 by Harvard Business School Publishing. Reprinted by permission.

an overall framework for guiding these efforts, and most companies remain stuck in a "social responsibility" mind-set in which societal issues are at the periphery, not the core.

The solution lies in the principle of shared value, which involves creating economic value in a way that also creates value for society by addressing its needs and challenges. Businesses must reconnect company success with social progress. Shared value is not social responsibility, philanthropy, or even sustainability, but a new way to achieve economic success. It is not on the margin of what companies do but at the center. We believe that it can give rise to the next major transformation of business thinking.

A growing number of companies known for their hard-nosed approach to business—such as GE, Google, IBM, Intel, Johnson & Johnson, Nestlé, Unilever, and Wal-Mart—have already embarked on important efforts to create shared value by reconceiving the intersection between society and corporate performance. Yet our recognition of the transformative power of shared value is still in its genesis. Realizing it will require leaders and managers to develop new skills and knowledge—such as a far deeper appreciation of societal needs, a greater understanding of the true bases of company productivity, and the ability to collaborate across profit/nonprofit boundaries. And government must learn how to regulate in ways that enable shared value rather than work against it.

Capitalism is an unparalleled vehicle for meeting human needs, improving efficiency, creating jobs, and building wealth. But a narrow conception of capitalism has prevented business from harnessing its full potential to meet society's broader challenges. The opportunities have been there all along but have been overlooked. Businesses acting as businesses, not as charitable donors, are the most powerful force for addressing the pressing issues we face. The moment for a new conception of capitalism is now; society's needs are large and growing, while customers, employees, and a new generation of young people are asking business to step up.

The purpose of the corporation must be redefined as creating shared value, not just profit per se. This will drive the next wave of innovation and productivity growth in the global economy. It will also reshape capitalism and its relationship to society. Perhaps most important of all, learning how to create shared value is our best chance to legitimize business again.

Moving Beyond Trade-Offs

Business and society have been pitted against each other for too long. That is in part because economists have legitimized the idea that to provide societal benefits, companies must temper their economic success. In neoclassical thinking, a requirement for social improvement—such as safety or hiring the disabled—imposes a constraint on the corporation. Adding a constraint to a firm that is already maximizing profits, says the theory, will inevitably raise costs and reduce those profits.

A related concept, with the same conclusion, is the notion of externalities. Externalities arise when firms create social costs that they do not have to bear, such as pollution. Thus, society must impose taxes, regulations, and penalties so that firms "internalize" these externalities—a belief influencing many government policy decisions.

This perspective has also shaped the strategies of firms themselves, which have largely excluded social and environmental considerations from their economic thinking. Firms have taken the broader context in which they do business as a given and resisted regulatory standards as invariably contrary to their interests. Solving social problems has been ceded to governments and to NGOs. Corporate responsibility programs—a reaction to external pressure—have emerged largely to improve firms' reputations and are treated as a necessary expense. Anything more is seen by many as an irresponsible use of shareholders' money. Governments, for their part, have often regulated in a way that makes shared value more difficult to achieve. Implicitly, each side has assumed that the other is an obstacle to pursuing its goals and acted accordingly.

The concept of shared value, in contrast, recognizes that societal needs, not just conventional economic needs, define markets. It also recognizes that social harms or weaknesses frequently create internal costs for firms—such as wasted energy or raw materials, costly accidents, and the need for remedial training to compensate for inadequacies in education. And addressing societal harms and constraints does not necessarily raise costs for firms, because they can innovate through using new technologies, operating methods, and management approaches—and as a result, increase their productivity and expand their markets.

Shared value, then, is not about personal values. Nor is it about "sharing" the value already created by firms—a redistribution approach. Instead, it is about expanding the total pool of economic and social value. A good example of this difference in perspective is the fair trade movement in purchasing. Fair trade aims to increase the proportion of revenue that goes to poor farmers by paying them higher prices for the same crops. Though this may be a noble sentiment, fair trade is mostly about redistribution rather than expanding the overall amount of value created. A shared value perspective, instead, focuses on improving growing techniques and strengthening the local cluster of supporting suppliers and other institutions in order to increase farmers' efficiency, yields, product quality, and sustainability. This leads to a bigger pie of revenue and profits that benefits both farmers and the companies that buy from them. Early studies of cocoa farmers in the Côte d'Ivoire, for instance, suggest that while fair trade can increase farmers' incomes by 10% to 20%, shared value investments can raise their incomes by more than 300%. Initial investment and time may be required to implement new procurement practices and develop the supporting cluster, but the return will be greater economic value and broader strategic benefits for all participants.

The Roots of Shared Value

At a very basic level, the competitiveness of a company and the health of the communities around it are closely intertwined. A business needs a successful community, not only to create demand for its products but also to provide critical public assets and a supportive environment. A community needs successful businesses to provide jobs and wealth creation opportunities for its citizens. This interdependence means that public policies that undermine the productivity and competitiveness of businesses are self-defeating, especially in a global economy where facilities and jobs can easily move elsewhere. NGOs and governments have not always appreciated this connection.

In the old, narrow view of capitalism, business contributes to society by making a profit, which supports employment, wages, purchases, investments, and taxes. Conducting business as usual is sufficient social benefit. A firm is largely a self-contained entity, and social or community issues fall outside its proper scope. (This is the argument advanced persuasively by Milton Friedman in his critique of the whole notion of corporate social responsibility.)

This perspective has permeated management thinking for the past two decades. Firms focused on enticing consumers to buy more and more of their products. Facing growing competition and shorter-term performance pressures from shareholders, managers resorted to waves of restructuring, personnel reductions, and relocation to lower-cost regions, while leveraging balance sheets to return capital to investors. The results were often commoditization, price competition, little true innovation, slow organic growth, and no clear competitive advantage.

In this kind of competition, the communities in which companies operate perceive little benefit even as profits rise. Instead, they perceive that profits come at their expense, an impression that has become even stronger in the current economic recovery, in which rising earnings have done little to offset high unemployment, local business distress, and severe pressures on community services.

It was not always this way. The best companies once took on a broad range of roles in meeting the needs of workers, communities, and supporting businesses. As other social institutions appeared on the scene, however, these roles fell away or were delegated. Shortening investor time horizons began to narrow thinking about appropriate investments. As the vertically integrated firm gave way to greater reliance on outside vendors, outsourcing and offshoring weakened the connection between firms and their communities. As firms moved disparate activities to more and more locations, they often lost touch with any location. Indeed, many companies no longer recognize a home—but see themselves as "global" companies.

These transformations drove major progress in economic efficiency. However, something profoundly important was lost in the process, as more -fundamental opportunities for value creation were missed. The scope of strategic thinking contracted.

Strategy theory holds that to be successful, a company must create a distinctive value proposition that meets the needs of a chosen set of customers. The firm gains competitive advantage from how it configures the value chain, or the set of activities involved in creating, producing, selling, delivering, and supporting its products or services. For decades businesspeople have studied positioning and the best ways to design activities and integrate them. However, companies have overlooked opportunities to meet fundamental societal needs and misunderstood how societal harms and weaknesses affect value chains. Our field of vision has simply been too narrow.

In understanding the business environment, managers have focused most of their attention on the industry, or the particular business in which the firm competes. This is because industry structure has a decisive impact on a firm's profitability. What has been missed, however, is the profound effect that location can have on productivity and innovation. Companies have failed to grasp the importance of the broader business environment surrounding their major operations.

How Shared Value Is Created

Companies can create economic value by creating societal value. There are three distinct ways to do this: by reconceiving products and markets, redefining productivity in the value chain, and building supportive industry clusters at the company's locations. Each of these is part of the virtuous circle of shared value; improving value in one area gives rise to opportunities in the others.

The concept of shared value resets the boundaries of capitalism. By better connecting companies' success with societal improvement, it opens up many ways to serve new needs, gain efficiency, create differentiation, and expand markets.

The ability to create shared value applies equally to advanced economies and developing countries, though the specific opportunities will differ. The opportunities will also differ markedly across industries and companies—but every company has them. And their range and scope is far broader than has been recognized. [The idea of shared value was initially explored in a December 2006 HBR article by Michael E. Porter and Mark R. Kramer, "Strategy and Society: The Link Between Competitive Advantage and Corporate Social Responsibility."]

Reconceiving Products and Markets

Society's needs are huge—health, better housing, improved nutrition, help for the aging, greater financial security, less environmental damage. Arguably, they are the greatest unmet needs in the global economy. In business we have spent decades learning how to parse and manufacture demand while missing the most important demand of all. Too many companies have lost sight of that most basic of questions: Is our product good for our customers? Or for our customers' customers?

In advanced economies, demand for products and services that meet societal needs is rapidly growing. Food companies that traditionally concentrated on taste and quantity to drive more and more consumption are refocusing on the fundamental need for better nutrition. Intel and IBM are both devising ways to help utilities harness digital intelligence in order to economize on power usage. Wells Fargo has developed a line of products and tools that help customers budget, manage credit, and pay down debt. Sales of GE's Ecomagination products reached $18 billion in 2009—the size of a Fortune

150 company. GE now predicts that revenues of Ecomagination products will grow at twice the rate of total company revenues over the next five years.

In these and many other ways, whole new avenues for innovation open up, and shared value is created. Society's gains are even greater, because businesses will often be far more effective than governments and nonprofits are at marketing that motivates customers to embrace products and services that create societal benefits, like healthier food or environmentally friendly products.

Equal or greater opportunities arise from serving disadvantaged communities and developing countries. Though societal needs are even more pressing there, these communities have not been recognized as viable markets. Today attention is riveted on India, China, and increasingly, Brazil, which offer firms the prospect of reaching billions of new customers at the bottom of the pyramid—a notion persuasively articulated by C.K. Prahalad. Yet these countries have always had huge needs, as do many developing countries.

Similar opportunities await in nontraditional communities in advanced countries. We have learned, for example, that poor urban areas are America's most underserved market; their substantial concentrated purchasing power has often been overlooked. (See the research of the Initiative for a Competitive Inner City, at icic.org.)

The societal benefits of providing appropriate products to lower-income and disadvantaged consumers can be profound, while the profits for companies can be substantial. For example, low-priced cell phones that provide mobile banking services are helping the poor save money securely and transforming the ability of small farmers to produce and market their crops. In Kenya, Vodafone's M-PESA mobile banking service signed up 10 million customers in three years; the funds it handles now represent 11% of that country's GDP. In India, Thomson Reuters has developed a promising monthly service for farmers who earn an average of $2,000 a year. For a fee of $5 a quarter, it provides weather and crop-pricing information and agricultural advice. The service reaches an estimated 2 million farmers, and early research indicates that it has helped increase the incomes of more than 60% of them—in some cases even tripling incomes. As capitalism begins to work in poorer communities, new opportunities for economic development and social progress increase exponentially.

For a company, the starting point for creating this kind of shared value is to identify all the societal needs, benefits, and harms that are or could be embodied in the firm's products. The opportunities are not static; they change constantly as technology evolves, economies develop, and societal priorities shift. An ongoing exploration of societal needs will lead companies to discover new opportunities for differentiation and repositioning in traditional markets, and to recognize the potential of new markets they previously overlooked.

Meeting needs in underserved markets often requires redesigned products or different distribution methods. These requirements can trigger fundamental innovations that also have application in traditional markets. Microfinance, for example, was invented to serve unmet financing needs in developing countries. Now it is growing rapidly in the United States, where it is filling an important gap that was unrecognized.

Redefining Productivity in the Value Chain

A company's value chain inevitably affects—and is affected by—numerous societal issues, such as natural resource and water use, health and safety, working conditions, and equal treatment in the workplace. Opportunities to create shared value arise because societal problems can create economic costs in the firm's value chain. Many so-called externalities actually inflict internal costs on the firm, even in the absence of regulation or resource taxes. Excess packaging of products and greenhouse gases are not just costly to the environment but costly to the business. Wal-Mart, for example, was able to address both issues by reducing its packaging and rerouting its trucks to cut 100 million miles from its delivery routes in 2009, saving $200 million even as it shipped more products. Innovation in disposing of plastic used in stores has saved millions in lower disposal costs to landfills.

The new thinking reveals that the congruence between societal progress and productivity in the value chain is far greater than traditionally believed (see the exhibit "The Connection Between Competitive Advantage and Social Issues"). The synergy increases when firms approach societal issues from a shared value perspective and invent new ways of operating to address them. So far, however, few companies have reaped the full productivity benefits in areas such as health, safety, environmental performance, and employee retention and capability.

But there are unmistakable signs of change. Efforts to minimize pollution were once thought to inevitably increase business costs—and to occur only because of regulation and taxes. Today there is a growing consensus that major improvements in environmental performance can often be achieved with better technology at nominal incremental cost and can even yield net cost savings through enhanced resource utilization, process efficiency, and quality.

In each of the areas in the exhibit, a deeper understanding of productivity and a growing awareness of the fallacy of short-term cost reductions (which often actually lower productivity or make it unsustainable) are giving rise to new approaches. The following are some of the most important ways in which shared value thinking is transforming the value chain, which are not independent but often mutually reinforcing. Efforts in these and other areas are still works in process, whose implications will be felt for years to come.

Energy Use and Logistics

The use of energy throughout the value chain is being reexamined, whether it be in processes, transportation, buildings, supply chains, distribution channels, or support services. Triggered by energy price spikes and a new awareness of opportunities for energy efficiency, this reexamination was under way even before carbon emissions became a global focus. The result has been striking improvements in energy utilization through better technology, recycling, cogeneration, and numerous other practices—all of which create shared value.

We are learning that shipping is expensive, not just because of energy costs and emissions but because it adds time, complexity, inventory costs, and management costs. Logistical systems are beginning to be redesigned to reduce shipping distances, streamline handling, improve vehicle routing, and the like. All of these steps create shared value. The British retailer Marks & Spencer's ambitious overhaul of its supply chain, for example, which involves steps as simple as stopping the purchase of supplies from one hemisphere to ship to another, is expected to save the retailer £175 million annually by fiscal 2016, while hugely reducing carbon emissions. In the process of reexamining logistics, thinking about outsourcing and location will also be revised (as we will discuss below).

Resource Use

Heightened environmental awareness and advances in technology are catalyzing new approaches in areas such as utilization of water, raw materials, and packaging, as well as expanding recycling and reuse. The opportunities apply to all resources, not just those that have been identified by environmentalists. Better resource utilization—enabled by improving technology—will permeate all parts of the value chain and will spread to suppliers and channels. Landfills will fill more slowly.

For example, Coca-Cola has already reduced its worldwide water consumption by 9% from a 2004 baseline—nearly halfway to its goal of a 20% reduction by 2012. Dow Chemical managed to reduce consumption of fresh water at its largest production site by one billion gallons—enough water to supply nearly 40,000 people in the U.S. for a year—resulting in savings of $4 million. The demand for water-saving technology has allowed India's Jain Irrigation, a leading global manufacturer of complete drip irrigation systems for water conservation, to achieve a 41% compound annual growth rate in revenue over the past five years.

Procurement

The traditional playbook calls for companies to commoditize and exert maximum bargaining power on suppliers to drive down prices—even when purchasing from small businesses or subsistence-level farmers. More recently, firms have been rapidly outsourcing to suppliers in lower-wage locations.

Today some companies are beginning to understand that marginalized suppliers cannot remain productive or sustain, much less improve, their quality. By increasing access to inputs, sharing technology, and providing financing, companies can improve supplier quality and productivity while ensuring access to growing volume. Improving productivity will often trump lower prices. As suppliers get stronger, their environmental impact often falls dramatically, which further improves their efficiency. Shared value is created.

A good example of such new procurement thinking can be found at Nespresso, one of Nestlé's fastest-growing divisions, which has enjoyed annual growth of 30% since 2000. Nespresso combines a sophisticated espresso machine with single-cup aluminum capsules containing ground coffees from around the world. Offering quality and convenience, Nespresso has expanded the market for premium coffee.

Obtaining a reliable supply of specialized coffees is extremely challenging, however. Most coffees are grown by small farmers in impoverished rural areas of Africa and Latin America, who are trapped in a cycle of low productivity, poor quality, and environmental degradation that limits production volume. To address these issues, Nestlé redesigned procurement. It worked intensively with its growers, providing advice on farming practices, guaranteeing bank loans, and helping secure inputs such as plant stock, pesticides, and fertilizers. Nestlé established local facilities to measure the quality of the coffee at the point of purchase, which allowed it to pay a premium for better beans directly to the growers and thus improve their incentives. Greater yield per hectare and higher production quality increased growers' incomes, and the environmental impact of farms shrank. Meanwhile, Nestlé's reliable supply of good coffee grew significantly. Shared value was created.

Embedded in the Nestlé example is a far broader insight, which is the advantage of buying from capable local suppliers. Outsourcing to other locations and countries creates transaction costs and inefficiencies that can offset lower wage and input costs. Capable local suppliers help firms avoid these costs and can reduce cycle time, increase flexibility, foster faster learning, and enable innovation. Buying local includes not only local companies but also local units of national or international companies. When firms buy locally, their suppliers can get stronger, increase their profits, hire more people, and pay better wages—all of which will benefit other businesses in the community. Shared value is created.

Distribution

Companies are beginning to reexamine distribution practices from a shared value perspective. As iTunes, Kindle, and Google Scholar (which offers texts of scholarly literature online) demonstrate, profitable new distribution models can also dramatically reduce paper and plastic usage. Similarly, microfinance has created a cost-efficient new model of distributing financial services to small businesses.

Opportunities for new distribution models can be even greater in nontraditional markets. For example, Hindustan Unilever is creating a new direct-to-home distribution system, run by underprivileged female entrepreneurs, in Indian villages of fewer than 2,000 people. Unilever provides microcredit and training and now has more than 45,000 entrepreneurs covering some 100,000 villages across 15 Indian states. Project Shakti, as this distribution system is called, benefits communities not only by giving women skills that often double their household income but also by reducing the spread of communicable diseases through increased access to hygiene products. This is a good example of how the unique ability of business to market to hard-to-reach consumers can benefit society by getting life-altering products into the hands of people that need them. Project Shakti now accounts for 5% of Unilever's total revenues in India and has extended the company's reach into rural areas and built its brand in media-dark regions, creating major economic value for the company.

Employee Productivity

The focus on holding down wage levels, reducing benefits, and offshoring is beginning to give way to an awareness of the positive effects that a living wage, safety, wellness, training, and opportunities for advancement for employees have on productivity. Many companies, for example, traditionally sought to minimize the cost of "expensive" employee health care coverage or even eliminate health coverage altogether. Today leading companies have learned that because of lost workdays and diminished employee productivity, poor health costs them more than health benefits do. Take Johnson & Johnson. By helping employees stop smoking (a two-thirds reduction in the past 15 years) and implementing numerous other wellness programs, the company has saved $250 million on health care costs, a return of $2.71 for every dollar spent on wellness from 2002 to 2008. Moreover, Johnson & Johnson has benefited from a more present and productive workforce. If labor unions focused more on shared value, too, these kinds of employee approaches would spread even faster.

Location

Business thinking has embraced the myth that location no longer matters, because logistics are inexpensive, information flows rapidly, and markets are global. The cheaper the location, then, the better. Concern about the local communities in which a company operates has faded.

That oversimplified thinking is now being challenged, partly by the rising costs of energy and carbon emissions but also by a greater recognition of the productivity cost of highly dispersed production systems and the hidden costs of distant procurement discussed earlier. Wal-Mart, for example, is increasingly sourcing produce for its food sections from local farms near its warehouses. It has discovered that the savings on transportation costs and the ability to restock in smaller quantities more than offset the lower prices of industrial farms farther away. Nestlé is establishing smaller plants closer to its markets and stepping up efforts to maximize the use of locally available materials.

The calculus of locating activities in developing countries is also changing. Olam International, a leading cashew producer, traditionally shipped its nuts from Africa to Asia for processing at facilities staffed by productive Asian workers. But by opening local processing plants and training workers in Tanzania, Mozambique, Nigeria, and Côte d'Ivoire, Olam has cut processing and shipping costs by as much as 25%—not to mention, greatly reduced carbon emissions. In making this move, Olam also built preferred relationships with local farmers. And it has provided direct employment to 17,000 people—95% of whom are women—and indirect employment to an equal number of people, in rural areas where jobs otherwise were not available.

These trends may well lead companies to remake their value chains by moving some activities closer to home and having fewer major production locations. Until now, many companies have thought that being global meant moving production to locations with the lowest labor costs and designing their supply chains to achieve the most immediate impact on expenses. In reality, the strongest international competitors will often be those that can establish deeper roots in important communities. Companies that can embrace this new locational thinking will create shared value.

AS THESE examples illustrate, reimagining value chains from the perspective of shared value will offer significant new ways to innovate and unlock new economic value that most businesses have missed.

POSTSCRIPT

Is Increasing Profits the Only Social Responsibility of Business?

Social organizations often find success in terms of funds expended, benefits achieved, or other economic models. Porter and Kramer state that shared value includes policies and operating practices that enhance the competitiveness of a company while at the same time moving forward the economic and social conditions of the communities around the company. Friedman would find their view unacceptable in that economic growth should be merely for the corporation without taking into account any social factors. Friedman would contend that business contributes to society by creating a profit, which supports investments, taxes, and employment. The shared value approach explains that businesses can reconceive products and markets, redefine productivity in the value chain, and build supportive industry clusters at the company's locations.

Suggested Readings

Geoffrey P. Lantos, "The Boundaries of Strategic Corporate Social Responsibility," *Journal of Consumer Marketing* (vol. 18, no. 7, 2001).

Joshua D. Margolis and James P. Walsh. "Misery Loves Companies: Rethinking Social Initiatives by Business," *Administrative Science Quarterly* (vol. 48, no. 2, June 2003).

Lance Moir, "What Do We Mean by Corporate Social Responsibility?" *Corporate Governance* (vol. 1, no. 2, 2001).

John Mackey and T. J. Rodgers, "Rethinking the Social Responsibility of Business," *Reason* (October 2005).

Milton Friedman, "A Friedman Doctrine: The Social Responsibility of Business is to Increase Its Profits," *The New York Times Magazine* (September 13, 1970).

ISSUE 4

Can Individual Virtue Survive Corporate Pressure?

YES: Robert C. Solomon, from "Victims of Circumstances? A Defense of Virtue Ethics in Business," *Business Ethics Quarterly* (January 2003)

NO: Gilbert Harman, from "No Character or Personality," *Business Ethics Quarterly* (January 2003)

ISSUE SUMMARY

YES: Joining the long-standing debate on the possibility of free choice and moral agency in the business world, Quincy Lee Centennial Professor of Business and Philosophy at the University of Texas in Austin Robert C. Solomon argues that whatever the structures, the individual's choice is free, and therefore his character or virtue is of the utmost importance in creating a good moral tone in the life of a business.

NO: Stuart Professor of Philosophy at Princeton University Gilbert Harman employs determinist arguments to conclude that no individual can of his own free choice make a difference in a group enterprise.

We have long recognized that the world looks very different from internal and external perspectives.

From the inside, the choices people make are very clearly *their* choices. They wrestle with their fear, they encourage their generosity, they praise themselves for farsightedness and blame themselves for carelessness and haste—and at the end, they choose. "Character" is that foundation in right living that strengthens or enables people to make the right choices by prevailing against the external pressures to make the wrong choices. For example, an athlete is strengthened or enabled to win a contest because he has disciplined himself to exercise regularly.

From the outside, observers can easily explain one's choices by references to the external circumstances and incentives. One may protest that the observers know nothing of one's internal processes, but the standard response is, whatever you may have thought of the situation, given the circumstances, you had no choice but to do what you did.

Philosophically, one notes the difference in perspectives as "free will versus determinism," originally a dispute over whether actions are caused by free choice or by circumstances. Since the philosopher David Hume (1711–1776) explored the subject, we have learned to adopt a more sophisticated analysis of the dispute. One can conclude that, generally, all human actions are determined not just by external circumstances but also by the entire history and upbringing of the agent. One can also conclude that all human actions are free in that the agent, in choosing, builds creatively on that history and upbringing to adapt to the external circumstances.

Robert C. Solomon and Gilbert Harman address a more limited question: If agents (presumably employees in a corporation) are clearly people of good education, sound upbringing, and good character, can one expect that they will act rightly, no matter what external circumstances business life throws at them? Does virtue play a role in the conduct of business? In light of the recent scandals, Enron and all the others, the question becomes very serious indeed.

Certain experiments in social psychology, as mentioned in the selections, suggest that it does not. The Milgram experiments comprised a series of studies of human behavior conducted in several locations in New England, beginning in 1964. Dr. Stanley Milgram invited volunteers from the communities to participate in a "learning" experiment. The purpose, he explained to them, was to find out if negative reinforcement (punishment) speeded up learning of a simple task. Volunteers were directed to man a menacing board of "electrical shock administration" buttons, with one labeled "danger!" The volunteers drew lots to see who would be "student" and who "teacher." As the "teacher," they would administer shocks to the "student." Each time the "student" made a mistake, a higher level of shock would be administered, resulting in the "students" crying out in pain at the higher levels. If a "student" made enough mistakes, the instructions called for the "teacher" to press the "danger!" button; when that happened, there was only an ominous silence from the "student."

Of course the whole thing was a hoax. The lots the volunteers drew were all labeled "teacher." The "student" was an actor employed by Milgram, and the board was a phony. The question Milgram was really trying to answer concerned obedience to authority: Would a normal adult, who knew that it was wrong to inflict pain on another human being and who was given no pressure but the instructions of someone in a white coat, obediently inflict what he had every reason to believe was serious and possibly lethal injury on an innocent stranger? The answer was—an alarming percent of the time—yes, he would.

What does one mean by "character"? Is character supposed to produce virtuous behavior automatically, even when the situation is completely staged and artificial? Is there still room for virtue among the fierce pressures of the business world?

Ask yourself, as you read these selections, just how prepared you are to meet demanding situations as an employee or as a citizen. Is your community of faith or ethics strong enough to enable you to do the right thing in a situation that frightens or constricts you? How would you teach new employees in a company to do the right thing in a difficult situation?

YES

Robert C. Solomon

Victims of Circumstances?
A Defense of Virtue
Ethics in Business

Abstract: Should the responsibilities of business managers be understood independently of the social circumstances and "market forces" that surround them, or (in accord with empiricism and the social sciences) are agents and their choices shaped by their circumstances, free only insofar as they act in accordance with antecedently established dispositions, their "character"? Virtue ethics, of which I consider myself a proponent, shares with empiricism this emphasis on character as well as an affinity with the social sciences. But recent criticisms of both empiricist and virtue ethical accounts of character deny even this apparent compromise between agency and environment. Here is an account of character that emphasizes dynamic interaction both in the formation and in the interplay between personal agency and responsibility on the one hand and social pressures and the environment on the other.

Business ethics is a child of ethics, and business ethics, like its parents, is vulnerable to the same threats and challenges visited on its elders. For many years, one such threat (or rather, a family of threats) has challenged moral philosophy, and it is time it was brought out in the open in business ethics as well. It is a threat that is sometimes identified by way of the philosophical term, "determinism," and though its status in the philosophy of science and theory of knowledge is by no means settled, it has nevertheless wreaked havoc on ethics. If there is determinism, so the argument goes, there can be no agency, properly speaking, and thus no moral responsibility. But determinism admits of at least two interpretations in ethics. The first is determination by "external" circumstances, including pressure or coercion by other people. The second is determination within the person, in particular, by his or her *character*. In the former case, but arguably not in the latter, there is thought to be a problem ascribing moral responsibility.[1]

The argument can be readily extended to business ethics. Versions of the argument have been put forward with regard to corporations, for instance, in the now perennial arguments whether corporations can be or cannot be

From *Business Ethics Quarterly*, January 1, 2003, pp. 43–62. Copyright © 2003 by *Business Ethics Quarterly*. Reprinted by permission of The Philosophy Documentation Center, publisher of *Business Ethics Quarterly*. References omitted.

held responsible.[2] One familiar line of argument holds that only individuals, not corporations, can be held responsible for their actions. But then corporate executives like to excuse their actions by reference to "market forces" that render them helpless, mere victims of economic circumstances, and everyone who works in the corporation similarly excuses their bad behavior by reference to those who set their agenda and policies. They are mere "victims of circumstances." They thus betray their utter lack of leadership. Moreover, it doesn't take a whole lot of research to show that people in corporations tend to behave in conformity with the people and expectations that surround them, even when what they are told to do violates their "personal morality." What (outside of the corporation) might count as "character" tends to be more of an obstacle than a boon to corporate success for many people. What seems to count as "character" in the corporation is a disposition to please others, obey superiors, follow others, and avoid personal responsibility.

In general philosophy, [Immanuel] Kant tried desperately to separate determinism and moral responsibility, defending determinism in the domain of science and "Nature" but preserving agency and responsibility in the domain of ethics. "I have found it necessary to limit knowledge to make room for faith," as he put in one of his most concise but rather misleading *bon mots*. Other philosophers were not so bold. They were willing to accept determinism (even if conjoined with skeptical doubts) and somehow fit agency and responsibility into its domain. David Hume and John Stuart Mill, the two most illustrious empiricist promoters of this strategy, suggested that an act is free (and an agent responsible) if it "flows from the person's character,"[3] where "character" stood for a reasonably stable set of established character traits that were both morally significant and served as the antecedent causal conditions demanded by determinism. Adam Smith, Hume's best friend and the father of not only modern economics but of business ethics too, agreed with this thesis. It was a good solution. It saved the notions of agency and responsibility, it was very much in line with our ordinary intuitions about people's behavior, and it did not try to challenge the scientific establishment. So, too, a major movement in business ethics, of which I consider myself a card-carrying member, is "virtue ethics," which takes the concept of character (and with it the related notions of virtue and integrity) to be central to the idea of being a good person in business. Among the many virtues of virtue ethics in business, one might think, is that, as in Hume and Mill, it would seem to keep at bay the threat of situational ("external") determinism.

Such a solution seems particularly appropriate for business ethics because the concept of character fills the void between institutional behaviorism ("organizational behavior") and an overblown emphasis on free will and personal autonomy that remains oblivious to context, the reality of office work, and the force of peer and corporate pressures. It provides a locus for responsibility without sacrificing the findings of "management science." But I have mixed feelings about the empiricist solution. On the one hand, it seems to me too weak. It does not account (or try to account) for actions "out of character," heroic or saintly or vicious and shockingly greedy behavior, which could not have been predicted of (or even by) the subject. And it does not (as Aristotle does) rigorously hold a person responsible for the formation of his or her character. Aristotle makes it quite clear that a wicked person is responsible for his or her character not because he or she could *now* alter it but because he or she could have and should have acted differently early on and established very different habits and states of character. The corporate bully, the greedy entrepreneur, and the office snitch all would seem to be responsible for not only what they do but who they are, according to Aristotle's tough criterion.

On the other hand, however, the empiricist solution overstates the case for character. (This is what some psychologists, and Gilbert Harman, refer to as the "attribution error.") The empiricists make it sound as if character is something both settled and "robust" (the target of much of the recent psychological literature). Character consists of such traits as honesty and trustworthiness that are more or less resistant to social or interpersonal pressures. But character is never fully formed and settled. It is always vulnerable to circumstances and trauma. People change, and they are malleable. They respond in interesting and sometimes immediate ways to their environment, their peers and pressures from above. Put into an unusual, pressured, or troubled environment, many people will act "out of character," sometimes in heroic but more often in disappointing and sometimes shocking ways. In the corporate setting, in particular, people joke about "leaving their integrity at the office door" and act with sometimes shocking obedience to orders and policies that they personally find unethical and even downright revolting.

These worries can be taken care of with an adequate retooling of the notion of character and its place in ethics, and this is what I will try to do here. But my real worry is that in the effort to correct the excesses of the empiricist emphasis on character, the baby is being thrown out with the bath toys. In recent work by Gilbert Harman and John Doris, in particular, the very notion of character is being thrown into question.[4] Indeed, Harman suggests that "there may be no such thing." Doris entitles his book, tellingly, *Lack of Character*. Both Harman and Doris argue at considerable length that a great deal of what we take as "character" is in fact (and demonstrably) due to specific social settings that reinforce virtuous conduct. To mention two often-used examples, clergy act like clergy not because of character but because they surround themselves with other clergy who expect them to act like clergy. So, too, criminals act like criminals not because of character but because they hang out with other criminals who expect them to act like criminals. Harman argues vehemently against what he calls the illusion of "a robust sense of character." Doris argues, at book length, a very detailed and remarkably nuanced account of virtue and responsibility without character. The conclusion of both authors is that virtue ethics, construed in terms of character, is at best a mistake, and at worst a vicious political maneuver.

It is worth saying a word about this "vicious political maneuver" that is the political target of Harman's and Doris's arguments. I share in their concern, and I, too, would want to argue against those who, on the basis of an absurd notion of character, expect people to "pick themselves up by their own bootstraps," blaming the poor, for instance, for their own impoverishment and thus ignoring social and political (not to mention medical and racial) disadvantages that are certainly not their fault. I, too, reject such a notion of character, but I am not willing to dispense with the very notions of character and the virtues in order to do this.

So, too, in business ethics, there is a good reason to be suspicious of a notion of character that is supposed to stand up to overwhelming pressures without peer or institutional support. I would take Harman's and Doris's arguments as a good reason to insist on sound ethical policies and rigorous ethical enforcement in corporations and in the business community more generally, thus maximizing the likelihood that people will conform to the right kinds of corporate expectations. Nevertheless, something extremely important can get lost in the face of that otherwise quite reasonable and desirable demand. It is the idea that a person can, and should, resist those pressures, even at considerable cost to oneself, depending on the severity of the situation and circumstances. That is the very basis on which virtue ethics has proven to be so appealing to people in business. It is the hope that they can, and sometimes will, resist or even rise up against pressures and policies that they find to be unethical.

So whatever my worries, I find myself a staunch defender of character and the indispensability of talk about character in both ethics and business ethics.[5] To quote my friend and colleague Ed Hartman, "the difference between Peter Hempel [one of the most wonderful human beings we ever met] and Richard Nixon is not just a matter of environment." In both everyday life and in business, there are people we trust, and there are people we do not, often on the basis of a substantial history of disappointments and betrayal. And we trust or distrust those people in much the same circumstances and under much the same conditions. To be sure, character is vulnerable to environment but it is also a bulwark *against* environment. Character supplies that familiar and sometimes uncomfortable or even uncanny resistance to untoward pressures that violate our "principles" or morally disgust us or are damaging to our "integrity." It is character and not God or the Superego that produces that nagging inner voice called "conscience." (It has been suggested that conscience produces character rather than the other way around, but apart from religious predilections there seems to be little sound philosophical argument or empirical research to defend this.) One person refuses to obey a directive to short-change his customers while another refuses to cheat on her expense account despite the fact that everyone around her is doing so. It is character that makes the difference, though not, to be sure, *all* the difference.

Some of my concern with this issue is personal. Like most conscientious people, I worry about my integrity and character, what sorts of temptations and threats I could and would withstand. I feel ashamed (or worse) when I give into those temptations and humiliated when I succumb to (at least some of) those threats. I am occasionally even proud about those temptations and threats I have withstood. Philosophically ("existentially"), I worry about how we view ourselves when the balance of accounts is shifted over to causal and statistical explanations of behavior instead of a continuing emphasis on character, agency, and responsibility. Will that give almost everyone an excuse for almost everything?[6] . . .

The "New Empiricism" Virtue Ethics and Empirical Science

Harman and Doris attack virtue ethics in general and the concept of character in particular on the grounds that they do not survive experimental findings in the past few decades. Exhibit number one for both of them is the infamous Stanley Milgram experiments in which people with supposedly good character performed the most despicable acts when encouraged to do so by an authority (the experimenter). But though empirical research in social psychology can on occasion shock us, surprise us, annoy us, and sometimes burst our illusions, it all gets weighed and accounted for, whether well or badly, in terms of our ordinary folk psychology observations and the ordinary concepts of belief, desire, emotion, character, and interpersonal influences, interactions, and institutions. There are no Copernican revolutions and no Michelson-Morley experiments. The Milgram and other experiments such as those by [J. M.] Darley and [C. D.] Batson that play a central role in Doris's and Harman's arguments get rationalized and explained in all sorts of ways, but none of them in violation of the basic forms of psychological explanation that Aristotle would have found perfectly familiar.[7] Of course, there remains a debate about the relative influence of "external" (environmental) and "inner" factors (character), but the debate, whichever way it goes, remains within the framework of folk psychology and our ordinary psychological concepts.

We might be disturbed, for example, that so many subjects followed the instructions of an authority figure to the point of (what they thought was) the torturing of another human being, but the various explanations in terms of "obedience to authority" or the unusual circumstances of the experiment (how often are most of us told to punish anyone?) do nothing to challenge our ordinary moral intuitions. It just reminds us of something we'd rather not remember, that ordinary people sometimes act very badly in group and institutional situations. This should come as no surprise to those of us who do corporate and organizational ethics. . . .

I have long been an advocate of cooperation between moral philosophy and the social sciences in business ethics. I think that the more we know about how people actually behave in corporations, the richer and more informed our moral judgments and, more important, our decisions will be. In particular, it is very instructive to learn how people will behave in extraordinary circumstances, those in which our ordinary moral intuitions do *not* give us a clue. All of us have asked, say, with regard to the Nazi disease in Germany in the Thirties, how we would have behaved; or how we would behave, think, and feel if we worked for a tobacco company. But even in an ordinary corporation (which is not the same as a university in which there is at least the illusion of individual autonomy and "academic freedom"), the question of "obedience to authority" comes front and center.

Thus an experiment like the Milgram experiment is shocking precisely because it does not seem to presuppose any extraordinary context. Milgram's experiment, which would certainly be prohibited today, has to do with subjects inflicting potentially lethal shocks to victim-learners (in fact the experimenter's accomplices). Even when the victim-learners pleaded for them to stop, the majority of subjects continued to apply the shocks when ordered to do so by the authorities (the experimenters). One could easily imagine this "experiment" being confirmed in any corporation.[8] But I find the use of such research to undermine the notion of character not at all convincing.[9] Harman, for example, argues that

> Empirical studies designed to test whether people behave differently in ways that might reflect their having different character traits have failed to find relevant differences. It is true that studies of this sort are very difficult to carry out and there have been few such studies. Nevertheless, the existing studies have had negative results. Since it is possible to explain our ordinary belief in character traits as deriving from certain illusions, we must conclude that there is no empirical basis for the existence of character traits.[10]

But in addition to leaping from "very few studies" that are "difficult to carry out" to the conclusion that there is "no empirical basis for the existence of character traits," the whole weight of the argument comes to depend on the *possibility* of explaining our ordinary belief in character traits as "deriving from certain illusions." But what would such an explanation consist of? What illusions are we talking about? And what is our "ordinary belief in character"? I will argue that it does not require the "robust" notion attacked by Harman. . . .

What Is a Virtue and Whence Character?

Harman does a nice job of delimiting the ordinary notions of virtue and character, namely those that are most relevant to business ethics. He distinguishes character from various psychological disorders (schizophrenia, mania, depression). More dubiously, he distinguishes character from "innate aspects of temperament such as shyness or being a happy or sad person."[11] Kant, oddly enough, quite correctly insists that being happy (though an "inclination") can be a virtue, as it makes us more inclined to do our duty. But Harman is not just attacking the virtues. He is after character traits in general. Shyness, for example, is a non-moral example of a character trait. Harman considers this a prime example of "false attribution." But I think Jean-Paul Sartre has his eye on something very important when he refers to the citing of such a character trait as "bad faith," namely, where we point to a causal syndrome where we should be talking about decisions and the cultivation (in a very strong sense) of character.[12] There is a certain element of such Sartrianism (an insistence on existential choices rather than robust character) in Harman's argument (with which I quite agree), but this is a very different set of reasons for questioning or qualifying the concepts of character and the virtues.[13]. . .

In the ordinary conceptions of character traits and virtues, Harman and Doris tell us, people differ in their possession of such traits and virtues. People are different, and these differences explain their differences in behavior.

Harman: "We ordinarily suppose that a person's character traits *help* to explain at least some of the things the person does" (italics mine). But, he says, "the fact that people regularly behave in different ways does not establish that they have different character traits. The difference *may* be due to their different situations rather than differences in their characters" (italics mine). But notice that there is no consistency whatever between insisting that a person's character traits *help* to explain their behavior and insisting that a difference in behavior *may* be due to the different situations in which two people find themselves. So, too, Doris's objection to globalism is that people (in experimental situations) fail to display the consistency and stability that explanations in terms of character require. But again, the short-term experiments that he cites do not undermine our more ordinary long-term judgments about personal propensities and dispositions. At best, they force us to face some hard truths about ourselves and consider other propensities and dispositions that may not be virtuous at all.

In our "ordinary conception" two people (one honest, one dishonest) in the same situation (discovering a lost wallet in the street, encountering a person in apparent desperate need, being ordered by an experimenter to "keep on punishing") will very probably act differently. But any philosopher worthy of his or her debating trophies will quickly point out that no two situations are sufficiently similar to make that case. It is only a very thin description of "the situation" (the experimental set-up) that makes it seem so. Subjects come from different backgrounds and different social classes. They are different genders. They may as a consequence have very different senses of the situation. I would not join Joel Feinberg in claiming that those students who do not stop for a stranger in need (in Darley and Batson's much-discussed "Good Samaritan" experiment) have a "character flaw," but neither would I conclude (with Doris) that their behavior is largely "situational."[14] The student's way of seeing and being in the situation may be very different, and this, of course, is just what Aristotle says about character. It is, first of all, a kind of perception, based on good up-bringing. Thus I think Harman is being a bit disingenuous when he argues that "they must be disposed to act differently in the same circumstances (as they perceive those circumstances)." The question of character begins with how they perceive those circumstances.

. . . Corporate managers and employees feel obliged and committed to act in conformity with corporate pressures and policies even when they are questionable or unethical, and they learn to rationalize accordingly. The question is, does any of this imply that we should give up or give in on character? Or should we say that character is both cultivated and maintained through the dynamic interaction of individuals and groups in their environment and they in turn develop those virtues (and vices) that in turn motivate them to remain in the situations in which their virtues are supported, reinforced, and not threatened?

In Milgram's famous "shocking people" experiment in the early 1960s (just as America was getting more deeply involved in the morass of Vietnam), the experimental data were indeed shocking, even to Milgram and his colleagues who expected no such result. In the social context of the times, questions about obedience to authority (left over from the Nuremberg trials not so many years before) had a special poignancy, especially in the face of the soon to be challenged American "innocence" of the time. It was very upsetting to find that good, solid, ordinary middle-class people could be ordered (but not coerced) to act so brutally (whether or not they had severe misgivings about their behavior at the time—a matter of no small importance here). The facts of the experiment are beyond dispute. But what the experiment means remains highly controversial, and it does not deserve the central place in the attack on character that it is now receiving. Doris claims that "Milgram's experiments show how apparently non-coercive situational factors may induce destructive behavior despite the apparent presence of contrary evaluative and dispositional structures." Accordingly, he "gives us reason to question the robustness of dispositions implicated in compassion-relevant moral behavior."[15]

Well, no. The disposition (virtue) that is most prominent and robust in this very contrived and unusual situation, the one that virtually all of the subjects had been brought up with and practiced everyday since childhood, was doing what they were told by those in authority. Compassion, by contrast, is a virtue more often praised than practiced, except on specially designated occasions (giving to the neediest at Christmas time) or stretching the term to include such common courtesies as restraining one's criticism of an unprepared student or letting the other car go first at a four-way intersection. (I would argue that such examples betray a lack of understanding of what compassion is.) Most often, people display compassion by "feeling sorry for" those much worse off than they, a very small expenditure of effort even when it is sincere. It seems to me that what the Milgram experiment shows—and what subsequent events in Vietnam made all too painfully obvious—was that despite our high moral opinions of ourselves and our conformist chorus singing about what independent individuals we all are, Americans, like Germans before them, are capable of beastly behavior in circumstances where their *practiced* virtues are forced to confront an unusual situation in which unpracticed efforts are required. In the Milgram experiment as in Vietnam, American subjects and soldiers were compelled by their own practiced dispositions to follow orders even in the face of consequences that were intolerable. Obedience may not always be a virtue. . . .

In discussions of Vietnam, those who were not there (especially politicians) like to talk about the virtue of courage as the defining trait of the American forces. What they ignore, of course, is the very nature of the war. In several important memoirs by soldiers who served there, Bill Broyles and Tim O'Brien, it becomes clear that courage was just about the last thing on most of the soldiers minds.[16] They were terrified of losing legs and arms. They were moved by camaraderie and a sense of mutual obligation. (The virtue-name "loyalty" misses the mark.) The only discussion of courage in O'Brien's book has to do with a single heroic figure, a Captain Johansen whom he likens to Hector in Homer's *Iliad*. But this one character is exemplary in precisely the fact that he alone talked about and exemplified true courage. But the absence of courage (which is not to imply anything like cowardice on the part of the American troops) had a great deal to do with the nature of this particular war. It lacked any sense of purpose or progress. It lacked any sense of meaning for most of the men. And so, in that moral vacuum, all that was left for most soldiers was the worry about their own physical integrity and their keen sense of responsibility for each other. The atrocities at My Lai and Thanh Phong followed as a matter of course. There was no context in which either character or courage could be exercised.

Which brings us back to the misgivings and feelings of discomfort experienced by some (not all) of the subjects and the "grunts" in Vietnam. Feelings of compassion (and other moral sentiments) may not be definitive in motivating behavior, especially if one has not faced anything like the awful situation in which the subjects and soldiers found themselves. But it does not follow that there is nothing more for virtue ethics to say about such cases. Experiments such as Milgram's are no longer allowed on college campuses, and for good reason. The feelings provoked in the subjects were too painful, and often with lasting damage.[17] And this is nothing, of course, compared to the posttraumatic experiences of many of those who served in Vietnam. The robustness of compassion must be measured not simply in terms of whether the subjects refused to continue with the experiment or not (most did) or whether the soldiers continued to do as they were ordered but by how powerful and upsetting the feelings they experienced both during and after the experiment. It is worth noting that there were a few sadists who actually enjoyed cruelty. There were others that were brutalized by the experiment and many who were brutalized by the war. That, it seems to me, should not be discounted. Bosses today are once again being forced to lay off thousands of their managers and employees. (Market forces is the inescapable explanation.) But there is all the difference in the world between those monsters like the infamous Al "Chainsaw" Dunlap who took such evident pride in cross the board cuts and virtual saints such as Aaron Feuerstein who felt so badly about having to lay off workers (after a fire gutted his factory) that he kept them on the payroll until the company got back on its feet.[18]

The Milgram Experiment Revisited: A Model of Corporate Life?

Is corporate life nothing but the vectors of peer pressures, leaving very little or even no room for the personal virtues? Does social psychology show that this is not the case only for corporate grinds but for all of us? Empirically-minded philosophers love to find a single experiment, or perhaps two, that make this case for them, that is, which provide the basis for speculative excursions that go far beyond the (usually rather timid) findings of the social psychologists themselves. Harman's appeal to the two famous experiments by Milgram and by Darley and Batson are illustrative. Doris takes in a much wider swath of the social science literature, but even he is forced to admit, throughout his admirable book, that there are profound reasons for not generalizing from particular experiments to a good deal of "real life."

Regarding the Milgram experiment, Harman (following Ross and Nisbett) rejects as implausible any explanation in terms of a "character defect" and suggests instead the "step-wise character of the shift from relatively unobjectionable behavior to complicity in a pointless, cruel, and dangerous ordeal." I think that this is indeed part of the explanation. Milgram's subjects needed to have their callousness cultivated even as they dutifully obeyed the authorities (like the proverbial frog in slowly boiling water). The subjects could not have been expected to simply shock strangers on command. But where Harman adds that we are tempted to make the "fundamental attribution error" of blaming the subject's destructive obedience on a personal defect, I would say instead that what the Milgram experiment shows is how foolish and tragic the otherwise important virtues of conformity and obedience can be. There is no "personal defect" on display here precisely because what the experiment shows is the consistency and stability of *that* virtue. And the fact that it is (like all virtues) not always a virtue is no argument against its status as part of the core of the explanation of the subjects' behavior. The rest of the explanation involves not just the incremental but also the disorienting nature of the situation. . . .

The other often-used case for "lack of character" is the case of the "good Samaritan," designed by Darley and Batson. Seminary students, on their way to give an assigned lecture (on "the good Samaritan") were forced to confront a person (an accomplice of the experimenter) on their way. Few of them stopped to help. It is no doubt true that the difference between subjects and their willingness to help the (supposed) victim can be partially explained on the basis of such transient variables as the fact that they were "in a hurry." And it is probably true as well (and not at all surprising to those of us who are not pushing "faith-based initiatives" these days) that people who were (or claimed to be) religious or who were about to talk on a religious topic of direct relevance to the experience did not act so differently as they would have supposed. But does it follow that character played no role? I would say that all sorts of character traits, from one's ability to think about time and priorities to one's feelings of anxiety and competence when faced with a (seemingly) suffering human being all come into play. Plus, of course, the sense of responsibility and obligation to arrive at an appointment on time, which once again slips into the background of the interpretation of the experiment and so blinds us to the obvious.

As in the Milgram experiment, how much is the most plausible explanation of the case precisely one that the experimenters simply assume but ignore, namely the character trait or virtue of promptness, the desire to arrive at the designated place on time? It is not lack of character. It is a *conflict* of character traits, one practiced and well-cultivated, the other more often spoken of than put in practice. Theology students have no special claims on compassion. They just tend to talk about it a lot. And as students they have had little opportunity to test and practice their compassion in ways that are not routine. . . .

What is not debatable, it seems to me, is that people present themselves differently, whether or not their presentations accurately represent their virtues and vices (which longer exposure is sure to reveal). I have long argued that the subject of explanation is not just the behavior of an agent but the behavior of an *agent-in-situation* (or some such odd locution). In business ethics, in particular, the behavior in question is the behavior of an *"individual-within-the-organization,"* which is not for a moment to deny that this context may not be the only one of relevance in moral evaluation. Context is essential but it isn't everything. Virtues and vices are important for our explanations of human behavior, but they make sense only in the context of particular situations and cultural surroundings. There is no such thing as courage or generosity in abstraction, but it does not follow that there is no such thing as courage or generosity.

Conclusion: In Defense of Business Virtue Ethics

Virtue ethics has a long pedigree, going back to Plato and Aristotle, Confucius in China, and many other cultures as well as encompassing much of Medieval and modern ethics—including, especially, the ethics of Hume, Adam Smith, and the other "Moral Sentiment Theorists." But we would do well to remind ourselves just why virtue and character have become such large concerns in the world today—in business ethics and in politics in particular. The impetus comes from such disparate sources as the Nuremberg trials and American atrocities in Vietnam, teenage drug use and peer pressure, and the frequently heard rationalization in business and politics that "everyone is doing it." The renewed emphasis on character is an attempt to build a personal bulwark (call it "integrity") against such pressures and rationalizations and (though half-heartedly) to cultivate virtues other than those virtues of unquestioning obedience that proved to be so dominant in the Milgram experiments and in Vietnam atrocities such as My Lai.

. . . If we are to combat intolerance, encourage mutual forgiveness, and facilitate human flourishing in contexts plagued by ethnic hatred, for instance, there is no denying the need for mediating institutions that will create the circumstances in which the virtues can be cultivated. Closer to home, the cultivation of the virtues in much-touted moral education also requires the serious redesign of our educational institutions. And much of the crime and commercial dishonesty in the United States and in the world today is due, no doubt, to the absence of such designs and character-building contexts. (The market, said the late great "Buddhist" economist E. F. Schumaker, "is the institutionalization of non-responsibility."[19]) We need less moralizing and more beneficent social engineering.

I could not agree more with these aims. But the existentialist twist to which Harman alludes (that we *choose* our circumstances) and the postmodern turn encouraged by Doris (that we acknowledge that for the most part our circumstances make us) convince me not that we should eliminate talk of the virtues and character but fully acknowledge both the role of the social sciences (*all* of the social sciences) and stop preaching the virtues without due emphasis upon *both* personal responsibility and the force of circumstances. Like Doris, we should appreciate more such "out of character" heroic and saintly behavior (he mentions Oscar Schindler in particular) and the exigencies of context and circumstances. But we should insist, first and foremost, that people—at any rate, people *like us*—are responsible for what they do, and what they make of themselves.

Notes

1. See, for example, Robert Young, "The Implications of Determinism," in Peter Singer, *A Companion to Ethics* (London: Blackwell, 1991). I am not considering here the post-Freudian complications of determination by way of compulsion or personality disorder.

2. E.g., Kenneth Goodpaster and John B. Matthews, Jr., "Can a Corporation Have a Conscience?" *Harvard Business Review*, Jan–Feb. 1982; John Ladd, "Morality and the Ideal of Rationality in Formal Organizations," *The Monist*, Oct. 1970; Peter A. French, *Collective and Corporate Responsibility* (New York: Columbia University Press, 1984). French, Peter A., "Responsibility and the Moral Role of Corporate Entities," in R. Edward Freeman, ed., *Business as a Humanity (Ruffin Lectures II)* (New York: Oxford, 1994); Peter A. French, "The Corporation as a Moral Person," *American Philosophical Quarterly* 16:3 (1979). Manuel G. Velasquez, *Business Ethics* (Engelwood Cliffs, N.J.: Prentice-Hall, 1982 and further editions).

3. David Hume, *An Enquiry Concerning Human Understanding*, 2nd ed. L. A. Sleby; Biggee, ed. (Clarendon: Oxford University Press, 1902). John Stuart Mill, *A System of Logic* 8th ed. (New York: Harper & Row, 1874). Adam Smith, *Theory of the Moral Sentiments* (London: George Bell, 1880).

4. Gilbert Harman, "Moral Philosophy Meets Social Psychology: Virtue Ethics and the Fundamental Attribution Error," *Proceedings of the Aristotelian Society* 99(1998–99): 315–331. Revised version in Harman, G., *Explaining Value and Other Essays in Moral Philosophy* (Oxford: Clarendon Press, 2000), 165–178. See also, "The Nonexistence of Character Traits," *Proceedings of the Aristotelian Society* 100 (1999–2000): 223–226. John Doris, *Lack of Character: Personality and Moral Behavior* (New York: Cambridge University Press, 2002).

5. Two philosophical defenses of character are Joel Kupperman, "The Indispensability of Character," in *Philosophy*, April 2001, 76(2): 239–250, and Maria Merritt, "Virtue Ethics and Situationist Personality Psychology," in *Ethical Theory and Moral Practice* 3 (2000): 365–383.

6. The fight against the pervasiveness of excuses is something I learned early on from Jean-Paul Sartre and pursue in some detail in my series, *No Excuses: Existentialism and the Meaning of Life* (The Teaching Company, 2000).

7. I would plea for something of an exception in the case of the fascinating flow of neuropsychiatric research of the last thirty or so years, which does indeed go beyond folk psychology, not only in its particular findings but in the very vocabulary and structure of its explanations. Nevertheless, what is so dazzling in much of this research is precisely that way in which neurological anomalies violate our ordinary "folk psychology" explanations. I will limit my references to two. The first is a wonderful series of studies published by Oliver Sachs over the years, including *The Man Who Mistook His Wife for a Hat and Other Clinical Tales* (Touchstone, 1998). The second is the recent research of Antonio Damasio, esp. in *Descartes's Error* (Putnam, 1994).

8. Stanley Milgram, "Behavioral Study of Obedience," *Journal of Abnormal and Social Psychology*, vol. 67, 1963; *Obedience to Authority* (New York: HarperCollins, 1983).

9. I have argued with both Harman and Doris that they have made selective use of social science research. In particular, they have restricted their appeals and references almost entirely to social psychology and have been correspondingly neglectful of counter-arguments in personality theory. The difference in perspective—and consequently the tension—between these two branches of empirical psychology are extremely significant to the argument at hand. See, e.g., Todd F. Heatherton (ed.), Joel Lee Weinberger, (ed.), *Can Personality Change?* [edited book] (Washington, D.C.: American Psychological Association, 1994), xiv, 368. A. Caspi, and B. W Roberts (1999), "Personality Continuity and Change Across the Life Course" in L. A. Pervin and O. P. John (eds.), *Handbook of Personality: Theory an d Research,* 2nd ed., (New York: Guilford), 300–326. Thomas J. Bouchard, Jr., "The Genetics of Personality," [chapter], Kenneth Blum (ed.); Ernest P. Noble, (ed.) et al., *Handbook of Psychiatric Genetics* (Boca Raton, Fla.: CRC Press, Inc. 1997), 273–296.

10. Gilbert Harman, "Moral Philosophy Meets Social Psychology" (web version), 1.

11. But see a similar distinction defended by Ed Hartman, "The Role of Character in Business Ethics," in J. Dienhart, D. Moberg, and R. Duska, *The Next Phase of Business Ethics: Integrating Psychology and Ethics* (Amsterdam: JAI/Elsevier, 2001), 341–354.

12. Jean-Paul Sartre, *Being and Nothingness,* trans. H. Barnes (New York: Philosophical Library, 1956), see for instance 104f.

13. An essay that uses the Milgram experiment to talk about "excuses" is A. Strudler and D. Warren, "Authority, Heuristics, and the Structure of Excuses," in J. Dienhart, D. Moberg, and R. Duska, *The Next Phase of Business Ethics,* 355–375. My own view is that "everybody's doing it" is NO excuse, or at best a mitigating one. See my *No Excuses: Existentialism and the Meaning of Life.* See also the now classic essay by Ron Green, "Everybody's Doing It," in *Business Ethics Quarterly* 1(1): 75–94.

14. J. M. Darley and C. D. Batson, "From Jerusalem to Jericho: A Study of Situational and Disposition Variables in Helping Behavior," *Journal of Personality and Social Psychology* 27, 1973.

15. Doris, 69.

16. William Broyles, Jr. *Brothers in Arms* (New York: Knopf, 1986) and Tim O'Brien, *If I Die in a Combat Zone Box Me Up and Ship Me Home* (New York: Delacorte, 1973). Both books are discussed by Thomas Palaima in "Courage and Prowess Afoot in Homer and in Vietnam" in *Classical and Modem Literature,* 20/3/(2000).

17. See Milgram, *Obedience to Authority.*

18. See my discussion in *A Better Way to think about Business* (Oxford, 1999), 10.

19. E. F. Schumaker, *Small is Beautiful* (Harper and Row, 1973).

References

Blackburn, Simon. 1995. *Essays in Quasi-Realism* (New York: Oxford University Press.

Bouchard, Thomas J., Jr. 1997. "The Genetics of Personality" [chapter]. Kenneth Blum (ed.), Ernest P. Noble, (ed.) et al. *Handbook of Psychiatric* Genetics. BocaRaton, Fla.: CRC Press, Inc., 273–296.

Broyles, William, Jr. 1986. *Brothers in Arms*. New York: Knopf.

Carr, Alfred. Jan.–Feb. 1968. "Is Business Bluffing Ethical?" *Harvard Business Review:* 143–153.

Caspi, A., and B. W. Roberts. 1999. "Personality Continuity and Change Across the Life Course" in *Handbook of Personality: Theory and Research* 2nd ed. L. A. Pervin and O. P. John (eds.). New York: Guilford, 300–326.

Damasio, Antonio. 1994. *Descartes's Error.* New York: Putnam.

Darley, J. M., and C. D. Batson. 1973. "From Jerusalem to Jericho: A Study of Situational and Dispositional Variables in Helping Behavior." *Journal of Personality and Psychology* 27.

Doris, John. 2002. *Lack of Character: Personality and Moral Behavior.* New York: Cambridge University Press.

French, Peter A. 1984. Collective and Corporate Responsibility. New York: Columbia University Press.

———. 1979. "The Corporation as a Moral Person." *American Philosophical Quarterly* 16 (3).

———. "Responsibility and the Moral Role of Corporate Entities." 1994. In *Business as a Humanity (Ruffin Lectures II)*. R. Edward Freeman (ed.). New York: Oxford.

Funder, David C. 2001. "Personality." *Annual Review of Psychology.* 52:197–221.

Goodpaster, Kenneth, and John B. Matthews, Jr. Jan.–Feb. 1982. "Can a Corporation Have a Conscience? *Harvard Business Review.*

Green, Ronald. "Everybody's Doing It." *Business Ethics Quarterly* 1(1): 75–94.

Griffiths, Paul. 1997. *What Emotions Really Are.* Chicago University of Chicago Press. 1998–99.

Harman, Gilbert. 1998–99. "Moral Philosophy Meets Social Psychology: Virtue Ethics and the Fundamental Attribution Error." *Proceedings of the Aristotelian Society* (99): 315–331.

———. 1999–2000. "The Nonexistence of Character Traits." *Proceedings of the Aristotelian Society* (100): 223–226.

———. 2000. *Explaining Value and Other Essays in Moral Philosophy.* Oxford: Clarendon Press, 165–178.

Hartman, Edwin M., ed. 2001. "The Role of Character in Business Ethics." in *The Next Phase of Business Ethics: Integrating Psychology and Ethics.* J. Dienhart, D. Moberg, and R. Duska (eds.). Amsterdam: JAI/Elsevier, 341–354.

Heatherton, Todd F. and Joel Lee Weinberger (eds.). 1994. "Can Personality Change? [edited book]. Washington, D.C.: American Psychological Association, 368.

Hume, David. 1902. *An Enquiry Concerning Human Understanding,* 2nd ed. L. A. Sleby-Biggee (ed.). Clarendon: Oxford University Press.

Kenrick, D. T., and Funder, D. C. 1988. "Profiting from Controversy: Lessons from the Person-Situation Debate." *American Psychologist* (43): 23–34.

Kupperman, Joel. April 2001. "The Indispensability of Character." *Philosophy* 76(2): 239–250.

Ladd, John. Oct. 1970. "Morality and the Ideal of Rationality in Formal Organizations." *The Monist.*

MacIntyre, Alasdair. 1984. *After Virtue*. Notre Dame: Notre Dame University Press.

Merritt, Maria. 2000. "Virtue Ethics and Situationist Personality Psychology." *Ethical Theory and Moral Practice* (3): 365–383.

Milgram, Stanley. 1963. "Behavioral Study of Obedience." *Journal of Abnormal and Social Psychology* 67.

Milgram, Stanley. 1983. *Obedience to Authority*. New York: HarperCollins.

Mill, John Stuart. 1874. *A System of Logic*. 8th ed. New York: Harper & Row.

Nietzsche, Friedrich. 1954. *Thus Spoke Zarathustra*. Trans., Kaufmann. New York:Viking, 207.

Nisbett and Ross. 1980. *Human Inference: Strategies and Shortcomings of Social Judgement*. Englewood Cliffs, N.J.: Prentice-Hall.

O'Brien, Tim. 1973. *If I Die in a Combat Zone Box Me Up and Ship Me Home*. New York: Delacorte.

Palaima, Thomas. 2000. "Courage and Prowess Afoot in Homer and in Vietnam," in *Classical and Modern Literature* 20 (3): 1–22.

Sachs, Oliver. 1998. *The Man Who Mistook His Wife for a Hat and Other Clinical Tales*. New York: Touchstone.

Sartre, Jean-Paul. 1956. *Being and Nothingness*. Trans. H. Barnes. New York: Philosophical Library.

Schumaker, E. F. 1973. *Small is Beautiful*. New York: Harper and Row.

Smith, Adam. 1880. *Theory of the Moral Sentiments*. London: George Bell.

Solomon, Robert C. 1993. *Ethics and Excellence*. New York: Oxford University Press.

———. 1999. *A Better Way to Think about Business*. New York: Oxford University Press.

Strudler, A., and D. Warren. 2001. "Authority, Heuristics, and the Structure of Excuses" in *The Next Phase of Business Ethics*. J. Dienhart, D. Moberg, and R. Duska (eds.), 355–375.

Velasquez, Manuel G. 1982. *Business Ethics*. Engelwood Cliffs, N.J.: Prentice-Hall.

Young, Robert. 1991. "The Implications of Determinism" in *A Companion to Ethics*. Peter Singer (ed.). London Blackwell.

Gilbert Harman

No Character or Personality

Abstract: [Robert] Solomon argues that, although recent research in social psychology has important implications for business ethics, it does not undermine an approach that stresses virtue ethics. However, he underestimates the empirical threat to virtue ethics, and his a priori claim that empirical research cannot overturn our ordinary moral psychology is overstated. His appeal to seemingly obvious differences in character traits between people simply illustrates the fundamental attribution error. His suggestion that the Milgram and Darley and Batson experiments have to do with such character traits as obedience and punctuality cannot help to explain the relevant differences in the way people behave in different situations.

. . . I want to suggest that Solomon underestimates the force of the threat to his version of business virtue ethics and I want to say a bit more about how the evidence from social psychology implies such "fragmentation."

Psychology and Folk Psychology

It is uncontroversial that there is usually a difference between the study of ordinary conceptions of a given phenomenon and the study of the phenomenon itself. We distinguish between folk or common-sense physics, which is studied by certain psychologists, and physics, which is studied by physicists; these are both interesting subjects, but they are different. Similarly, there is a clear difference between the study of conceptions people at a certain time had about witches and witchcraft and the study of what was actually true about people who were taken to be witches and phenomena thought to be witchcraft. We distinguish between the study of how people conceive of God from the study of theology. We distinguish between the study of doctors' views about good medical treatment and an investigation into what sorts of treatment are actually effective. We distinguish interviewers' conceptions of the value of interviewing from whether interviews actually improve selection processes.[1] In the same way, there is a clear conceptual difference between what people generally think about character and personality and what is actually the case; the study of what people think about character and personality (as in "personality theory" or "personality psychology") is part of the study of folk psychology and is not the same as a study of character and personality.

From *Business Ethics Quarterly*, vol. 13, no. 1, January 2003, pp. 87–94. Copyright © 2003 by *Business Ethics Quarterly*. Reprinted by permission of The Philosophy Documentation Center, publisher of *Business Ethics Quarterly*. References omitted.

Surprisingly, Solomon expresses doubts about this sort of difference with respect to the virtues. He says that "there is an easy but wholly misleading analogy with physics." He agrees that "many of our moral intuitions are erroneous or archaic," but insists that "our moral intuitions are not *like* our intuitions in physics. There is no 'matter of fact' independent of our intuitions and attitudes." Furthermore, he says, "*All* psychology, if it is psychology at all, is one or another version of 'folk psychology' ('the only game in town,' according to Jerry Fodor)."

In response, I have to say that, although it has often been argued (e.g., by Dennett, 1981; Fodor, 1987) that psychology has to be belief and desire psychology, I am not familiar with any similar argument that psychology must for that reason also include commitment to character and personality traits. In particular, I do not believe that Fodor has ever made such an argument. Fodor's (1975) "only game in town" is supposed to be a certain sort of computational functionalism involving a "language of thought" with no reference whatsoever to character traits.

Furthermore, whether or not there is a matter of fact about what is right or wrong, it is obvious that many moral judgments presuppose matters of fact. To belabor the point, if I say you were wrong to hit Bob in the nose, I presuppose that in fact you hit Bob in the nose and, if you did not, I am mistaken. Similarly, if I say that you have a certain virtuous character, I presuppose that you have a character. Perhaps, as Solomon believes, it is not a matter of fact whether such a character is virtuous. But it is a matter of fact whether you have the character, and whether there are character traits at all.

In addition to offering these relatively a priori arguments for doubting that social psychology could undermine ordinary conceptions of character and personality traits, Solomon also notes the existence of the field of "personality theory." He has, he says, "long been an advocate of cooperation between moral philosophy and the social sciences in business ethics." But, he says,

> What about that voluminous literature *not* in social psychology but in the (artificially competing) field of personality theory? . . . If we want to play off moral philosophy and virtue ethics against the social sciences, let's make sure that all of the social sciences are represented and not just social psychology.

However, personality theory or personality psychology is in pretty bad institutional shape. Solomon refers to Funder (2001), a bravely upbeat review of the current (utterly dismal) state of personality psychology that nevertheless acknowledges that personality psychology has collapsed as an academic subject. So, Funder revealingly bemoans

> the permanent damage to the infrastructure of personality psychology wreaked by the person-situation debate of the 1970s and 1980s. . . . [O]ne reason for the trend . . . for so much personality research being done by investigators not affiliated with formal programs in personality may be that there are so few formal programs to be affiliated with. The graduate programs in personality psychology that were shrunken beyond recognition or even abolished during the 1970s and 1980s have not been revived. (213)

Why does the critique of virtue ethics appeal to social psychology rather than to personality psychology? Because personality psychology has been concerned with characterizing ordinary folk conceptions of personality. Social psychology is concerned with the accuracy of these conceptions. To the extent that you are interested in the truth and accuracy of claims about character and personality, you need to consult social psychology, not "personality psychology."[2]

What Is the Fundamental Attribution Error?

The librarian carried the old woman's groceries across the street. The receptionist stepped in front of the old man in line. The plumber slipped an extra $50 into his wife's purse. Although you were not asked to make any inferences about any of these characters, chances are that you inferred that the librarian is helpful, the receptionist rude, and the plumber generous. Perhaps because we do not realize the extent to which behavior is shaped by situations, we tend to spontaneously infer such traits from behavior." (Kunda, 1999, 435)

Psychologists refer to this tendency as "correspondence bias" or "the fundamental attribution error." It is a bias toward explanations in terms of corresponding personality traits, the error of ignoring situational factors. The bias seems to be associated with a perceptual tendency to pay more attention to a figure than to its ground, and there appear to be significant cultural differences in the extent to which people are subject to this tendency and to the fundamental attribution error (Nisbett, 1998).

Having once attributed a trait to a given person, an observer has a strong tendency to continue to attribute that trait to the person even in the face of considerable disconfirming evidence, a tendency psychologists sometimes call "confirmation bias," a bias toward noting evidence that is in accord with one's hypothesis and toward disregarding evidence against it.[3]

Even in a world with no individual differences in character traits or personality traits, people would still strongly believe that there were such differences, as long as they were subject to the fundamental attribution error and to confirmation bias. This means that the apparent obviousness of the claim that people differ in such traits (as in Ed Hartman's comparison, endorsed by Solomon, between Hempel and Nixon) is less evidential than one may think. True, it is "obvious" that, some people have different character and personality traits than others. But our finding this fact so obvious is predicted by our tendency to the fundamental attribution error whether or not there are such differences.

Subtle Situational Effects

Minor and seemingly irrelevant differences in the perceived situation sometimes make significant differences to what people do. Doris (2002) discusses several examples.

Imagine a person making a call in a suburban shopping plaza. As the caller leaves the phone booth, along comes Alice, who drops a folder full of papers that scatter in the caller's path. Will the caller stop and help before the only copy of Alice's magnum opus is trampled by the bargain-hungry throngs? . . . [I]n an experiment by Isen and Levin (1972) . . . the paperdropper was an experimental assistant or "confederate." For one group of callers, a dime was planted in the phone's coin return slot; for the other, the slot was empty. [The results are that, of 16 callers who found a dime, 14 helped and 2 did not; of 25 who did not find a dime, 1 helped and 24 did not.] . . . Finding a bit of change is something one would hardly bother to remark on in describing one's day, yet it makes the difference between helping and not. (Doris, 2002, p. 30)

Whether or not a theology student stops to help someone who seems to be having a heart attack may depend on how much of a hurry the student is in to accomplish a comparatively trivial goal (Darley and Batson, 1973). Whether someone in a waiting room will go to the aid of another person who seems to have fallen off a ladder in the next room may depend on whether there is another person in the waiting room who seems unconcerned with the apparent fall (Latane and Darley, 1970).

In the Milgram (1974) experiment, subjects were led by gradual steps to do something they would never have done straight away, namely to administer very severe electrical shocks to another person. The gradualness of the process with no obvious place to stop seems an important part of the explanation why they obeyed a command to shock the other person in that experiment although they would not have done so if directly ordered to give the severe shock at the very beginning.

Similarly, if you are trying not to give into temptation to drink alcohol, to smoke, or to eat caloric food, the best advice is not to try to develop "willpower" or "self-control." Instead, it is best to head the situationist slogan, "People! Places! Things!" Don't go to places where people drink! Do not carry cigarettes or a lighter and avoid people who smoke! Stay out of the kitchen!

Sometimes a person acts well or badly in a seemingly unusual way. Concerning any such case, there is an issue as to what makes the difference that leads to such seemingly unusual behavior. When you perceive or learn about someone you do not know doing such an unusual thing, you have a strong tendency to attribute the behavior to some good or bad trait of the person in question. When you learn that a certain seminary student walked right past someone who seemed to be having a heart attack, actually stepping right over the person, you tend to think of the student as incredibly callous.

The question is what makes the difference that leads to the unusual or surprising behavior. Is it that some theology students are more compassionate than others? Does the Milgram experiment show that almost everyone is basically evil?

Solomon says that certain character traits are relevant in these cases, namely, (1) obedience to (the experimenters') authority and (2) promptness. But relevant to what? Since Solomon thinks that all the experimental subjects had these traits, he does not suppose that these common traits are responsible for the *differences* in helping behavior that were observed. Nor do they account for the difference in obedience between a subject who is commanded to give an intense shock to someone at the very beginning and a subject who starts by giving a little shock and who increases the shock by very small steps.

No one supposes that these two experiments, taken by themselves, show that there are no character traits. What they show is that aspects of a particular situation can be important to how a person acts in ways that ordinary people do not normally appreciate, leading them to attribute certain distinctive actions to an agent's distinctive character rather than to subtle aspects of the situation. In particular, observers [of] some of the events that occur in these experiments are strongly inclined to blame those participants who did not stop to help or who provided intense shocks, thinking that the explanation of these agent's immoral actions lies in their terrible character. But the observers are wrong: that cannot be the explanation.

Near the end of his remarks, Solomon says, "Empirically-minded philosophers love to find a single experiment or perhaps two that . . . provide the basis for speculative excursions which go far beyond the (usually rather timid) findings of the social psychologists themselves." I need to emphasize that the Milgram experiment and others mentioned so far are only a few of the different experiments illustrating subtle effects of situations and the ways in which observers fail to understand those effects, leading observers to make the fundamental attribution error. Furthermore, as I have been insisting, the "speculative excursions" Solomon attributes to Doris and me do not go "far beyond the . . . findings of the social psychologists," but are in fact part of the settled core of the subject of social psychology.

Traits

We must distinguish individual acts of honesty or dishonesty, courage or cowardice, compassion or coldness from the corresponding character traits. The ordinary conception of a character or personality trait is of a relatively broadbased disposition to respond in the relevant way with acts of the corresponding sort. In an important discussion, Merritt (2000) shows that Aristotelian virtue ethics and most contemporary versions of virtue ethics (*but not Hume's theory*) appeal to character traits in this broad sense.

Now, the evidence indicates that people may differ in certain relatively narrow traits but do not have broad and stable dispositions corresponding to the sorts of character and personality traits we normally suppose that people have. Doris's (2002) defense of the fragmentation of character, derided by Solomon, is so widely accepted by social psychologists that a similar account can be found in any introductory textbook in social psychology. This is how Kunda (1999) puts the point:

> Our notion of traits as broad and stable dispositions that manifest themselves to the same extent in a variety of situations cannot hold water. However, this does not mean that there are no enduring and systematic differences among individuals. My intuitions that I am a very different person from my brother or that my children have predictably

different patterns of behavior need not be wrong. Such intuitions may be based on meaningful and stable differences among individuals but not the kind of differences implied by the traditional understanding of traits. . . . [For example,] Carol is extremely extroverted in one-on-one situations, is only moderately extroverted when in small groups, and is not at all extroverted in large groups. She will appear very comfortable and outgoing if you meet with her alone, but will clam up and appear very shy and awkward if you encounter her in a large group setting. Linda has a very different profile. She is extremely extroverted in large groups but not at all extroverted in one-on-one situations. She may appear composed and comfortable when lecturing to a large audience but withdrawn and aloof if you approach her alone. (Kunda, 1999, 443–4)

In conclusion, it appears that we are truly quite consistent in our behavior within each situation, and it is quite appropriate to expect such consistency in others. But we run into trouble when we expect this consistency to extend to other situations as well. Even slight variations in the features of a situation can lead to dramatic shifts in people's behavior. (Kunda, 1999, 499)

Free Will and Responsibility

Solomon worries that in the rejection of the sort of character and personality traits that are accepted in ordinary moral thinking and in his version of virtue ethics,

> something extremely important can get lost. . . . It is the idea that [one] can and should resist [certain] pressures, even at considerable cost to oneself, depending on the severity of the situation and circumstances. That is the very basis on which virtue ethics has proven to be so appealing to people in business.

This is clearly a different issue. Of course, people can and should resist such pressures and we should encourage them to do so. But the point has nothing to do with whether people have character traits. As Solomon would certainly agree, even a person without relevant character traits can and should resist.

Solomon worries about the philosophical consequences of denying the existence of character, because that would be to go "over to causal and statistical explanations of behavior instead of a continuing emphasis on character, agency, and responsibility." But people do not need character traits in order to have agency and responsibility. As Doris (2002, chaps. 7–8) persuasively argues, denying the existence of character traits in no way undermines the notions of agency and of responsibility.

Conclusion

Aristotelian style virtue ethics shares with folk psychology a commitment to broad-based character traits of a sort that people simply do not have. This does not threaten free will and moral responsibility, but it does mean that it is a mistake to base business ethics on that sort of virtue ethics. This leaves open the possibility of Merritt's (2000) Humean style virtue ethics in which virtuous behavior is socially supported and sustained.

Notes

1. For discussion of the well-known "interview illusion," see, e.g., Kunda (1999), 179–89, and references cited there. Interviews are simultaneously very unreliable indicators of later performance and also very vivid. Using interviews adds expensive vivid noise to a decision process. Solomon (who says the Princeton Philosophy Department's practice of not interviewing job candidates is "peculiar") suggests that the point of interviewing is to see how well the candidate will "fit in" with others on the job. The point about expensive vivid noise obviously applies here as well, as is noted in Miller and Cantor (1982), who nevertheless suggest that there is still a point to having a candidate for a teaching position give a talk to members of the hiring department, because these members will almost certainly all have the same impression of the talk, so their decision will tend to be unanimous. (When the Princeton Philosophy Department discussed whether to continue interviewing job candidates, it considered the Miller Cantor point but decided that it did not particularly care about unanimity.)

2. Doris (2002, 67–75) discusses the relation between social psychology and personality psychology in some detail.

3. Confirmation bias is discussed, e.g., in Gilovich (1993), chap. 3.

References

Darely, J. M. 1973. "From Jerusalem to Jericho: A Study of Situational and Dispositional Variables in Helping Behavior." *Journal of Personality and Social Psychology* 27:100–8.

Dennett, D. C. 1981. *Brainstorms: Philosophical Essays on Mind and Psychology.* Cambridge, Mass.: MIT Press.

Doris, J. 2002. *Lack of Character: Personality and Moral Behavior.* New York: Cambridge University Press.

Fodor, J. A. 1975. *The Language of Thought.* New York: Thomas Crowell.

———. 1987. *Psychosemantics: The Problem of Meaning in the Philosophy of Mind.* Cambridge, Mass.: MIT Press.

Funder, D. C. 2001. "Personality." *Annual Review of Psychology* 52: 197–221.

Gilovich, T. 1993. *How We Know What Isn't So: The Fallibility of Human Reason in Everyday Life.* New York: The Free Press.

Harman, G. 1998–99. "Moral Philosophy Meets Social Psychology: Virtue Ethics and the Fundamental Attribution Error." *Proceedings of the Aristotelian Society* 99: 315–31.

———. 1999–2000. "The Nonexistence of Character Traits." *Proceedings of the Aristotelian Society* 100: 223–6.

Isen, A. M., and P. F. Levin. 1972. "Effect of Feeling Good on Helping: Cookies and Kindness." *Journal of Personality and Social Psychology* 21: 384–8.

Kunda, Z. 1999. *Social Cognition: Making Sense of People.* Cambridge, Mass.: MIT Press.

Latané, B., and J. M. Darley. 1970. *The Unresponsive Bystander: Why Doesn't He Help?* New York: Appleton-Century-Crofts.

Merritt, M. 2000. "Virtue Ethics and Situationist Personality Psychology." *Ethical Theory and Moral Practice* 3: 365–83.

Milgram, S. 1974. *Obedience to Authority.* New York: Harper and Row.

Miller, G. A., and N. Cantor. 1982. Review of *Human Inference: Strategies and Shortcomings of Social Judgement.* In *Social Cognition* 1: 83–93.

Nisbett, R. 1998. "Essence and Accident." In *Attribution and Social Interaction: The Legacy of Edward E. Jones,* ed. J. M. Darley and J. Cooper. Washington, D.C.: American Psychological Association.

Solomon, R. 2003. "Victims of Circumstances? A Defense of Virtue Ethics in Business." *Business Ethics Quarterly* 13(1): 43–62.

POSTSCRIPT

Can Individual Virtue Survive Corporate Pressure?

This issue draws on the background of classic behavioral experiments, well known in the field of social psychology. One is often required to master portions of a scientific field in order to understand a question confronting the business world. For example, to understand the Pinto case (Issue 13) one may well have to know a bit of automotive engineering. To understand the dispute over the labeling of genetically modified organisms (Issue 14), one may have to learn how genes can be inserted into reproductive material of plants. Increasingly, business is about information and scientific knowledge, and the corporate officer is expected to be knowledgeable about the fields that interface his or her company's business.

Suggested Readings

John Dalla Costa, *The Ethical Imperative: Why Moral Leadership is Good Business,* (Reading, MA: Perseus Books, 1998).

Kevin T. Jackson, *Building Reputational Capital,* (New York: Oxford University Press, 2004).

Joel Lefkowitz, *Ethics and Values in Industrial-Organizational Psychology,* (Mahwah, NJ: Lawrence Erlbaum Associates, 2003).

Ronald R. Sims, *Ethics and Corporate Social Responsibility: Why Giants Fall,* (Westport, CT.: Praeger, 2003).

Robert C. Solomon, *A Better Way to Think About Business,* (New York: Oxford, 1999).

ISSUE 5

Can Ethics Codes Build "True" Corporate Ethics?

YES: Eric Krell, from "How to Conduct an Ethics Audit: An Ethics Audit Can Reveal Gaps in Your Ethics Policies and Practices," *HR Magazine* (April 2010), pp. 48–51.

NO: Greg Young and David S. Hasler, from "Managing Reputational Risks: Using Risk Management for Business Ethics and Reputational Capital," *Strategic Finance* (November 2010), pp. 37–46

ISSUE SUMMARY

YES: Eric Krell finds that one of the major corporate goals of the human resource office is to build true corporate ethics. He believes this can be done with a code of ethics, through performance reviews, and with ethics audits. Through this process, employees' good and corporate good can become the same.

NO: Greg Young and David Hasler believe that strengthening the role of ethical and reputational capital has been given the short shrift within corporations. It may be that one day ethics audits and ethics codes could be essential in building capital. However, they state that until management understands that poor ethics make for poor profits, business practices will continue to ignore the place of an ethics core within their organization.

$\mathbf{S}$ince the collapse of Enron early in the current century, corporate ethics has taken a much more prominent position of importance. In Congress, new legislation was adopted to promote corporate integrity, such as the Sarbanes–Oxley Act, which states that publicly traded companies must disclose whether they have a code of ethics to deter wrongdoing. The 2010 Dodd–Frank Wall Street Reform and Consumer Protection Act has also given many corporations an added incentive to create a culture of ethics in their individual places of business.

One of newer procedures that corporations have begun to implement is to conduct what is called an "Ethics Audit." As its name suggests, a third party is given the task of performing detailed inspections to determine whether employees are adhering to a clearly stated set of ethical codes. According to

Eric Krell, these "Ethics Audits have been implemented in significant numbers." The Ethics Resource Center's 2009 National Business Ethics Survey notes that on-the-job misconduct is down, whistle-blowing is up, and ethical organizational cultures are stronger. Krell finds the audits helpful, and also stresses that management in human resources should set the overall ethical tone for the company. Human resources managers have the ability to go over performance reviews and determine if problems are developing or being allowed to slide. An outside firm or consultant could also be hired to conduct the ethics audit. Krell explains the more frequent the audits, the more the company will know if its policies and procedures are being practiced in an ethical manner. Krell further explains that the firm must explain a clear and concise code of conduct and strong definitions of ethical behavior. He contends that the risk of neglecting ethics audits can be dangerous, because when unethical conduct is allowed it will affect the stakeholders including suppliers, customers, and the overall community. Unethical behavior has an immediate effect on the overall organization. He believes that ethics audits can stop problems before they have a chance to grow.

Despite these trends of improved ethical communication in corporate cultures, Greg Young and David Hasler suggest that this is simply not enough. They maintain what is needed is an understanding by CEOs and company owners that "unethical conduct puts reputational capital—and economic value—at risk." In other words, there is an inherent economic value in having a strong reputation for ethical conduct in the world, as well as goodwill from stakeholders such as employees, customers, and local citizens. Young and Hasler argue that what has prevented CEOs and company owners from adopting this view in the past are two obstacles: "anticipating reputational risks and . . . quantifying reputational capital."

Young and Hasler recommend implementing a new system called *Enterprise Risk Management,* or ERM. This system incorporates such Western philosophical principles as personal virtue, distributive justice, and economic efficiency into a measurable format. By assigning dollar values to the inherent risks in public reputation and willingness to cooperate from stakeholders, the economic value of ethical decisions can be measured strictly in dollars and cents.

In short, Young and Hasler believe that ERM is needed for companies to have a true incentive for acting ethically. If CEOs can be persuaded to believe that ethical misdeeds are hurting their bottom line, then they will do what it takes to rectify their company's behavior. They argue that ERM provides ample evidence that "lapses in business ethics can lead to enterprise costs, damaged relationships . . . that significantly harm financial performance."

YES

Eric Krell

How to Conduct an Ethics Audit: An Ethics Audit can Reveal Gaps in Your Ethics Policies and Practices

When it comes to corporate ethics, bad news is good news. According to the Ethics Resource Center's 2009 National Business Ethics Survey, on-the-job misconduct is down, whistle-blowing is up, and ethical organizational cultures are stronger. Despite these trends, there may be no better time for human resource managers to conduct or participate in ethics-related audits.

Setting the Tone

Several legal developments in recent years have placed newfound focus on how companies behave. An example is the Sarbanes-Oxky Act, with its emphasis on "tone at the top" and its requirement that publicly traded companies disclose whether they have a code of ethics to deter wrongdoing. The Federal Acquisition Regulation and the Federal Sentencing Guidelines also have a significant impact on organizations' ethics policies and practices by requiring or providing incentives to encourage businesses of all kinds and sizes to adopt codes of conduct, train their employees on these codes, and create effective audit and reporting mechanisms.

HR professionals play a crucial role in shaping corporate ethical codes, policies and procedures and then communicating and teaching that information to the workforce. In many companies, the top HR manager either serves as the de facto chief ethics and compliance officer or works with the person in that role to manage ethics and compliance programs. Apart from the chief executive officer, there may be no more important ethical role model in the organization than an HR manager.

"Employees watch HR like hawks, and they should," says Phillip Daniels, SPHR, HR manager for Montgomery College in Rockville, Md. "If HR managers mess up, how can we expect employees to adhere to the ethical standards that we're promoting? As HR managers, we essentially need to serve as the poster children for ethical behavior."

HR managers who thrive as ethical role models almost always play central roles in conducting ethics-related audits, notes Marjorie Doyle, principal of ethics consulting firm Marjorie Doyle & Associates in Landenberg, Pa., and a member of the Advisory Board of Directors for the Society of Corporate Compliance and Ethics. As a former chief corporate ethics and compliance officer, "I spent a lot of time with HR," she says.

HR managers are "trying to get people to do the right thing. They also tend to manage the annual performance review process and operate the communications network within the company, both of which are crucial to ethics audits," Doyle says. "They have a feel for whether certain behaviors are as ethical as they need to be."

Daniels agrees. "As an HR manager, you have to be out there listening and identifying potential problems," he says. "Not every unethical behavior or practice exerts a direct financial impact, but we should be looking for those issues because doing so can help improve the organization."

Laying the Groundwork

Ethics audits ensure that behaviors an organization espouses in its code of conduct and policies and procedures exist in practice and that behavior forbidden in these documents does not occur.

The risk of neglecting ethics audits can be severe. After its ethics-related implosion, Enron became well-known for the fact that the framed values statements in conference rooms were at odds with employees' behavior on trading floors. And, more-immediate problems potentially exist for companies that do not conduct ethics audits: "Employees' faith in the organization can deteriorate," says Art Crane, SPHR, president of HR advisory firm Capstone Services in Sherman, Conn. "Morale can decline. A company sets a dangerous precedent by letting something that violates its ethics policy slide."

The danger can spread to other stakeholders, including customers, suppliers and community members. "If word gets out that you are not an ethical organization, you run the risk of losing business," Crane notes.

Conducting an ethics audit requires a team effort as well as a clear definition of ethical behavior. While many larger companies staff a chief ethics and compliance officer position, that individual is not solely responsible for each employee's behavior.

For this reason, Conway, Ark.-based Nabholz Construction Co. has an ethics committee consisting of top legal, finance, HR and operational executives. "We want to have diverse skills on the committee and to make sure all of our geographies are represented," says Andrea Woods, SPHR, vice president and corporate counsel for the private company with about 850 employees.

Nabholz Construction's ethics committee takes responsibility for monitoring and investigating ethics hotline calls and e-mails. The hotline system is managed by a third-party provider, an arrangement that Woods says strengthens objectivity and independence. The committee conducts ethics audits as part of an annual internal audit process. In addition, a divisional controller, an HR employee and Woods conduct spot ethics audits on the recommendation of the committee.

The frequency Woods describes—annual audits on all ethics-related areas and spot ethics audits on an as-needed basis in response to risk assessments—

jibes with what ethics consultants recommend. Depending on company size and auditing resources, Crane notes, some companies may audit their entire ethics programs only once every two years. However, the occurrence of a major organizational realignment may necessitate more frequent ethics audits in its wake.

Whether or not corporate leaders seek outside help on ethics audits depends on the nature and magnitude of the issues. "If the issue involves something very important to the company, it helps to get an outside perspective and the impartial judgment that a third party provides," Crane says. "If the company conducts the audit internally and outside stakeholders are paying close attention to the issue, it can be more difficult to say, 'Yes, we audited our ethics internally and everything is just fine.' That may be received as a matter of the fox guarding the henhouse."

Making It Tangible

Regardless of whether ethics audits are woven into internal audit processes, performed internally in response to changing risk profiles or conducted by an external auditor, the question is "What are you auditing against?" says Mark Snyderman, senior knowledge leader at LRN, a company that helps businesses develop ethical corporate cultures.

The answer requires a distinction between two disciplines frequently lumped together in corporate America: ethics and compliance.

Ethics refers to the amorphous area of behavior. Compliance refers to adherence to legal regulations. A company may be fully compliant yet still engage in unethical practices. While that may seem like a clear distinction on paper, it becomes muddled in a global business environment.

"There are many countries around the world that don't have antitrust laws," says Snyderman, who previously served as chief ethics and compliance officer and assistant general counsel for Coca-Cola. "A company could in theory engage in price fixing in those countries. From an ethical standpoint, however, I would recommend that every company take the position, 'We are not going to do that.'"

Compliance audits compare internal behaviors to external regulations. Ethics audits compare internal behaviors to internal guidelines on behavior— guidelines that exist in corporate codes of conduct and ethics-related policies and procedures. Of course, some compliance problems may stem from ethical lapses; others may arise from process or operational bugs. That's why many business leaders conduct ethical audits in tandem with financial or operational audits.

"Your code of conduct—some companies call it a code of ethics— represents your central document," Snyderman says. "This document should be generated from the company's values."

The code should be translated into specific guidance within policies and procedures. "You don't need to start out with the 10 commandments and 500 related rules, but you do need to have something specific to audit against," Doyle says. For example, what does an ethical violation related to bribery or conflict of interest look like? "Be very descriptive in your policies and procedures about what these things mean," she recommends. Also, have managers and employees establish performance goals related to ethics and compliance so employees can be evaluated against those objectives.

Doyle says greater specificity in ethics-related policies and procedures paves the way for ethics-related performance objectives and metrics. These metrics help enable more-tangible ethics audits. "One of the most difficult challenges is making this highfalutin-sounding concept of ethics actually become very granular," she adds.

Filling the HR Role

An ethics audit resembles a financial or operational audit. It involves interviews with employees and managers, reviews of records and other information, and, sometimes, observations of processes and practices.

The most common ethics audits, Snyderman and Crane report, examine conflicts of interest, access to company information, bidding and award practices, giving and receiving gifts, and employee discrimination issues.

Snyderman describes the actual audits as time-consuming and based on checklists. They involve a team that typically consists of an HR professional, an internal auditor, legal managers, and an ethics and compliance manager. The team visits an area of the organization to conduct research in response to a specific incident or as part of an ongoing auditing cycle.

The primary mission is to compare ethics guidelines with actual behaviors, but team members also look for other issues that may need to be addressed through communications, training or subsequent audits.

The team clearly identifies who will be interviewed and what information and observations are required. "Generally, the HR person on the team knows people in the department and will introduce the team," Doyle says.

HR professionals also play a pivotal role in responding to ethical or legal issues or violations that the audit identifies, whether the response takes the form of disciplining an employee, conveying educational material about the topic to a larger audience or integrating the topic into training. If the ethics audit concerns employment issues, HR typically takes a lead role in conducting the audit, Snyderman reports.

During her previous work as a chief ethics and compliance officer for DuPont and VetcoGray, Doyle says, HR managers were her "main partners," ones she worked with to incorporate ethics-related measures into annual performance reviews. At VetcoGray, now a General Electric oil and gas business, for example, she teamed with HR managers to tie 20 percent of employees' base salaries and 20 percent of bonus compensation to specific ethics performance measures.

"If there is an ethics and compliance officer in the company and they have not contacted the HR manager, the HR manager should knock on that person's door, sit down and talk about how your jobs are very much intertwined," Doyle advises.

Greg Young and
David S. Hasler

Managing Reputational Risks: Using Risk Management for Business Ethics and Reputational Capital

Lapses in business ethics can lead to enterprise costs, damaged relationships with key stakeholders, and lost opportunities that significantly harm financial performance. Conversely, an enterprise's reputation for ethical conduct can be a crucial asset for achieving its strategic and financial objectives. It's surprising, therefore, that the role of ethics and reputational capital are the least developed aspects of enterprise risk management (ERM).

The *Enterprise Risk Management—Integrated Framework* and guidelines from the Committee of Sponsoring Organizations of the Treadway Commission (COSO) are fast becoming standards for best practices in organizations (www .coso.org/guidance.htm).While there are many varieties of ERM in practice today, all recognize that ethical values underlie a firm's ability to accomplish enterprise objectives. Yet much of the current discussion about ethics focuses on corporate culture, conduct, and compliance in a post-Enron world of the Sarbanes-Oxley Act (SOX) and corporate sentencing guidelines. Though important, these dimensions don't directly examine the value of ethics as an asset to build trust in important business relationships. As a consequence, most people's understanding of best practices to manage business ethics is limited.

Here we explore stakeholders' perceptions of ethics in order to bring reputational capital more clearly to the forefront of ERM. We do so by extending the ERM paradigm to identify and assess risks to reputational capital. First, we suggest a process to identify the scope of ethical principles and behaviors that are most appropriate for building reputational capital by illustrating this process with the *IMA Statement of Ethical Professional Practice*. Second, we account for differences in enterprise context that systematically narrow the focus of ethics governance. Third, we describe a framework that integrates ethics with the COSO ERM components to elicit stakeholders' assessments of enterprise reputational capital.

What's at Stake?

The foundational role of ethics in ERM isn't surprising. Business misconduct can lead to direct costs of legal fees, monetary fines, sanctions, and operational recovery. Given a choice in partnering, stakeholders—relationship partners

From *Strategic Finance*, November 2010, pp. 37–46. Copyright © 2010 by Institute of Management Accountants—IMA. Reprinted by permission via Copyright Clearance Center.

such as employees, customers, suppliers, community groups, and owners—
are likely to prefer a relationship with an enterprise that has a reputation for
integrity. For the enterprise, a reputation for poor ethics can lead to costs of
replacing lost partners or going it alone. Labor, operating, and overhead costs
may increase if the enterprise is perceived to be so unprincipled in its conduct
toward employees that its recruiting and retention of skilled personnel are at
risk. Similarly, purchasing, logistics, and overhead costs may increase if suppliers judge the enterprise to be unfair or dishonest.

In our post-Enron/WorldCom/Tyco era, reputations of large, publicly
traded companies (for better or worse) are likely to be broadly known. Public
reaction to notorious lapses in business ethics has increased worldwide legislative, regulatory, judicial, and media demands for visibility into corporate
governance of business ethics. In this context, an enterprise reputation that
fosters goodwill has economic value. Unethical conduct puts reputational
capital—and economic value—at risk.

Traditionally, the practice of ethics management has focused on corporate ethical values within the organization and sequential activities to prevent,
detect, report, and respond to misconduct. But this focus on misconduct limits
people's understanding of ethics as a form of reputational capital that has value
in important business relationships. Moreover, the focus on misconduct makes
it difficult to integrate traditional ethics programs within the ERM framework.

Given such a consequential role for ethics and the momentum of ERM in
current business practice, it's surprising that ethics isn't more developed in the
ERM discussion. As George L. Head wrote in expert commentary for the International Risk Management Institute in February 2005 (see www.irmi.com/expert/
articles/2005/head02.aspx), "[T]he fields of ethics and risk management need each
other. Good risk management and good ethics are, and need to be, linked . . .
[but] I have used the word 'ethics' in print probably less than 100 times."

Two important obstacles to extending ERM to ethics have been the difficulties in anticipating reputational risks and in quantifying reputational capital. We seek to overcome these difficulties with a structured process to elicit
stakeholder judgments about a company's commitment to principled ethical
behavior in their relationship.

Building on ethical responsibilities to stakeholders is increasingly recognized as a best practice in organizational ethics programs, but so far this
approach hasn't been integrated with risk management. Importantly, quantifying stakeholder assessments lends itself to aggregation for an overall perspective on enterprise-level risk to reputational capital. Let's now look at a process
that identifies the scope of ethical principles and behaviors most appropriate
for building reputational capital.

Identifying Ethics and Behaviors for Reputational Capital

To illustrate a structured approach, we'll draw on principles from the *IMA
Statement of Ethical Professional Practice,* which you can find at www.imanet
.org/PDFs/Statement%20of%20Ethics_web.pdf, mapping them to the ethical

content on which trustworthy reputations are built and describing enterprise behavior that embodies that content in stakeholder relationships: *"The fundamental principles in the* IMA *Statement of Ethical Professional Practice are Honesty, Fairness, Objectivity, and Responsibility. Members shall act in accordance with these principles and shall encourage others within their organizations to adhere to them."*

In Table 1 we juxtapose these fundamental IMA principles—honesty, fairness, objectivity, and responsibility—with concise descriptions of their associated ethical principles from Western philosophy—personal virtue, legal compliance, economic efficiency, distributive justice, and procedural justice. The table shows the explicit one-to-one relationship between the first three IMA principles and the principles of personal virtue, legal compliance, and economic efficiency. Interestingly, there are two philosophical flavors of fairness to discuss with stakeholders—fairness in enterprise outcomes and fairness in enterprise decision procedures (see Table 1, bottom two rows).

The value of reputational capital is a function of benefits gained and costs avoided because of stakeholders' willingness to cooperate in order to accomplish enterprise goals. As reputational capital increases, the enterprise can better leverage stakeholder relationships to increase its own productivity. [The] enterprise has ethical principles at its core that drive its behavior in relationships, stakeholder perceptions of the enterprise can be elicited in the structure of the ERM framework, and the enterprise-stakeholder relationship is the locus where a company earns reputational capital and the stakeholder grants it. The relationship is where stakeholders interact with the enterprise and detect the integrity with which enterprise behavior fits with its stated values. Reputation is the stakeholders' perception of patterns in these interactions and behaviors.

We describe a method to prompt stakeholders to identify and quantify their perspective on an enterprise's reputational capital. This method integrates the ethical principles described in Table 1 with the eight ERM components of the COSO framework. This structure elicits a comprehensive dialogue with stakeholders about the drivers of and risks to reputational capital in the enterprise-stakeholder relationship. The comprehensiveness of this approach is a particularly valuable aid to risk management when ethical principles aren't uniformly prominent within the enterprise.

Before we detail the integrated structure, we first describe the strategic context that influences management to be more attentive to some ethical principles and stakeholders and less attentive to others. In these situations, the comprehensive structure provided by integrating the ethical principles with the COSO framework guides risk managers to elicit stakeholder descriptions of enterprise reputational risk that might otherwise be overlooked.

The relative prominence of the ethical principles in the internal environment may vary from one enterprise to another. The unique context of an organization is likely to influence management to give more attention to some principles over others. Understanding the distinctive content of different ethical principles, therefore, gives insight into the basis for an enterprise's reputation with stakeholders. For example, the principles most prominent to the managers of a small corporation selling to a more powerful customer, such as

Table 1

Ethical Principles and Enterprise Behavor:
Drivers of Reputational Capital in Enterprise-Stakeholder Relationships

IMA Principle of Ethical Professional Practice	Ethical Principles from Western Philosophy	Stakeholders' Perception of Enterprise Behavior in Relationship
Honesty	**Personal Virtue:** Act with the intention of causing pride and avoiding shame; take responsibility to nurture trustworthy relationships with honesty and integrity.	(a) Trustworthy, honest, cooperative, and deserving esteem. (b) Every level of the enterprise (i.e., each component of COSO ERM framework) nurtures relationship with stakeholder.
Responsibility	**Legal Compliance:** A responsible member of society does not violate laws enacted by legitimate legislative, regulatory, or judicial processes and nurtures relationships when legal institutions are just emerging or transitioning from one form to another.	Obeys established legal institutions governing the enterprise's operations; develops relationships to govern operations where legal institutions are not well-established.
Objectivity	**Economic Efficiency:** Act with the intention of achieving best possible profits without harrning others, subject to market and legal constraints. Inform business relationships with objective information regarding product features, prices, and activity costs.	(a) Access to useful, unbiased information on product features, prices, and activity costs; (b) Does no harm to free markets, public safety, and environment while pursuing its own profit; (c) Alert to best profit-making opportunities.
Fairness (in outcomes)	**Distributive Justice:** Share value-added with stakeholders; form and sustain business relationships by showing fairness in care and respect for the needs of others; take responsibility to produce outcomes stakeholders prefer and find beneficial.	Fair in prices, costs, and activities to support stakeholders' preferences.
Fairness (in process)	**Procedural Justice:** Give stakeholders fair access to have their voice heard in your decision making so their interests are protected even if they disagree with a decision outcome.	Gives fair access to participate in activities and decisions.

a vendor selling to Walmart, may differ from those values most prominent to the managers of a large retailer sourcing from weaker suppliers, such as The Body Shop's relationships with small villages and women-led cooperatives in emerging economies.

Two important dimensions in an enterprise's strategic context—its ownership structure and its bargaining power in stakeholder relationships—may cause its managers to view some ethical principles as more prominent than others in daily operations and decision making.

Publicly owned companies in the U.S. are subject to significant legal and fiduciary obligations and securities regulations, such as SOX. In this context, the legal compliance and economic efficiency principles are heavily weighted in the relationships of publicly owned enterprises with government and shareholders. It follows that ethics management in publicly owned corporations will prominently feature these two principles.

Privately owned enterprises, on the other hand, are relatively free of compliance requirements from SOX, the Securities & Exchange Commission (SEC), and shareholder lawsuits. Coming to the fore of management's attention instead are partners, customers, and suppliers, whose interests need to be represented fairly in organizational decision making. Accordingly, we expect justice principles will be prominent in stakeholder relationships with privately owned enterprises. When transactions, relationships, and contracts become increasingly complex but not tightly regulated by law, it becomes more difficult to anticipate all possible situations and contingencies that may arise. In this situation, stakeholders are likely to value opportunities to voice their preferences in the enterprise procedures and decision making—the definition of procedural justice.

In another context, an enterprise whose bargaining power isn't strong enough to compel agreements with its stakeholders may induce them to cooperate by calling attention to its reputation for fair distribution of added value. An enterprise culture with visibly prominent distributive justice principles is likely to attract and sustain critical relationships even when the enterprise lacks compelling power.

For example, a privately held Internet grocer in the New York area adds value for customers by offering quality "farm-fresh" food with the convenience of online shopping and home delivery. New customers were its biggest source of revenue, and, to attract them, the company offered discounts on large orders. Revenues were rising, but profits were falling as customers dropped the service after using their discounts. In addition, the business wasn't dominant in its local area, so customers had other grocery choices. In this context, we expect this online grocer would improve relationships with its customers by emphasizing its reputation for fair distribution of added value. Earlier, we described fairness in outcomes as a form of the distributive-justice ethical principle and expressed the stakeholders' perspective as *"Fair in prices, costs, and activities to support stakeholders' preferences"* (see Table 1). In the case of the online grocer, customer behavior indicated that pricing for new customers was perceived as fair, but the quality of grocer activities supporting convenience and food quality wasn't supporting the preferences of existing customers. To solve this problem, management shifted emphasis by substantially increasing investment in customer service and stopping promotional discounts for new customers. After two years of this approach, the bulk of revenue comes from repeat customers, and the company had its first profitable year (see the August 11 and August 17, 2010, issues of *The New York Times* to read articles about FreshDirect).

. . . Take, for example, small biotechnology firms that often partner with other businesses for complementary strengths that reduce the time to bring new drugs to market. Those small firms less willing to give up a larger portion of the added value are less likely to partner with large, powerful multinationals. Instead, they seek more accommodating partners, such as those from emerging economies, to form relationships in which the relative power is more comparable and the fairness of outcomes more closely defined by a distributive justice principle. One interesting example of this is the new drug discovery partnerships between small Western companies and Indian companies (see the November 25, 2006, issue of *India Business Insight*). Conversely, the opportunity to choose from among many small but equally acceptable potential partners in an honest and free market gives large multinationals the ability to negotiate and enforce more self-interested outcomes.

For publicly owned companies with relatively high power in stakeholder relationships, . . . we expect a reputation for economic efficiency and legal compliance to be the larger contributors toward forming and sustaining important relationships critical to achieving enterprise objectives.

For example, many leading mortgage lenders recently announced plans to exit the subprime segment of the residential mortgage market because of increased regulatory constraints and reduced prospects for profitability. Two months earlier, more than 100 California consumer groups had written an open letter to six of these lenders, asking them to declare a temporary moratorium on foreclosures for all mortgages issued with inappropriate pricing, such as those increasingly threatening the subprime market. While press reports appeared about both the consumer groups' letter and the lenders' decision, no press report linked the two events in any way. We aren't suggesting lenders willfully ignored the consumer advocacy voice, but note that the attention of reasonable managers in large public enterprises is a finite resource that's compelled to focus on legal compliance and economic incentives.

In the United States today, legal and regulatory oversight is extremely rigorous in publicly traded markets for equity capital. Generally, an enterprise whose reputation is that of an efficient wealth creator will tend to have access to more financial resources to achieve its objectives. Conversely, substantial financial obstacles arise for firms known to disregard legal requirements or ignore the economic conclusions from an objective analysis of demand, pricing, and costs.

Of course, privately owned businesses must comply with legal requirements as well as cover their operating costs and costs of capital, but they usually don't have the same level of governmental oversight and legal responsibility to owners as public enterprises do. Accordingly, . . . for privately owned companies with relatively low power in stakeholder relationships, we expect a reputation for distributive justice and procedural justice to be the larger contributors toward forming and sustaining important relationships critical to achieving enterprise objectives. It follows that ethics management in these companies will prominently feature these two fairness-based principles.

As enterprise power increases in comparison to its stakeholders' power, such as when it brings unique strength to its relationships, then the enterprise will be able to sustain relationships while keeping more monetary or economic benefit for itself and distributing less to its stakeholders. While stakeholders may not have all their preferences satisfied in this distribution, they are likely to continue their cooperation as long as they have fair access to voice their concerns, protect their interests, and participate in a cordial enterprise decision-making process. For example, small, privately owned retailers don't have resources to pay employees comparably to workers at larger competitors. Yet many small business owners report they attract and retain outstanding employees by offering a greater role in decision making in a more cordial, family-like atmosphere. Accordingly, . . . for privately owned companies with relatively high power in stakeholder relationships, such as in the employer-employee relationship, we expect a reputation for procedural justice will be the largest contributor toward forming and sustaining important stakeholder relationships.

Risk Management Approach to Reputational Capital

Managing risks to reputational capital requires a sustained dialogue with stakeholders. As Carly Fiorina, former CEO of Hewlett-Packard, recently told an audience at the MIT Sloan School of Management, "[G]ood ethics and good judgment are what must drive business behavior. . . . Employees and customers always know what's wrong." Good ERM practice also means being alert to opportunities. "The corporate reputation is valuable," Jack F. Ward, executive-in-residence at Georgia State University's Southern Institute for Business and Professional Ethics, said at the 2007 Ethics and Governance Conference of the Association to Advance Collegiate Schools of Business. "Avoid a poor ethical climate. . . . Talk to buyers, suppliers, and community groups."

The ERM approach to reputational capital is a process that uses ethical principles as descriptors of enterprise relationships with stakeholders and structures stakeholders' assessments of reputational risks and consequences. We'll now apply the ethical principles to the eight components in the COSO *Enterprise Risk Management—Integrated Framework* to structure dialogue with stakeholders (see Table 2 for a summary).

No matter the context of their governance or negotiating power, all business reputations rely on the fundamental integrity of their personnel to be trustworthy, honest, and cooperative. We capture this in the personal virtue dimension of enterprise reputation, and we ask the stakeholder to score the enterprise on a 1 to 10 scale, where 1 is the lowest and 10 is the highest, according to their perception of the relationship. For the first ERM component, internal environment, the respondent is directed to "Score the enterprise on the extent to which you believe the following characteristics accurately describe it—trustworthy, honesty, cooperative, integrity." (See Table 3.) Dialogue with stakeholders also may elicit the reasons underlying the scores and examples to support their perception of the extent to which principles are applied to action. Table 3 also lists questions to elicit scores for these ERM components: objective setting, control activities, information and communication, and monitoring. Companies may use them to start a dialogue with the stakeholder respondents, and, in the course of this dialogue, additional questions and useful information to assess risk to reputational capital may arise.

We now turn our attention to ERM components three, four, and five: event identification, risk assessment, and risk response. With these components, we group actions into labeled sets according to the significance of their consequences, analyze the likelihood that risks will occur, estimate the impact on enterprise performance if a risk event does occur, and develop a set of actions to mitigate negative consequences. As the middle columns of Table 2 show, the risk manager elicits from the stakeholder a description of future events that, if they were to occur, would change the scores in the stakeholder's earlier responses (columns 1, 2, 6, 7, 8). Then, for each event, the stakeholder estimates the likelihood or probability that it will occur in the forthcoming period. The risk manager then asks the stakeholder to reconsider his or her scores in each cell of columns 1, 2, 6, 7, and 8 with the assumption that each risk event does occur and to estimate the event's consequences in terms of costs and benefits for the enterprise-stakeholder relationship.

Finally, for the events with the greatest expected consequences (i.e., likelihood times benefits, net of costs), the risk manager asks the stakeholder to consider the alternative enterprise responses—avoid the risk, accept it, reduce it, or share it with another party, such as with accommodation from the stakeholder group—and to make a judgment about the likely consequences of each for the relationship.

After completing these tasks for the personal virtue row of the table, the risk manager continues to elicit the stakeholder perceptions for the other ethical principles of legal compliance, economic efficiency, distributive justice, and procedural justice. As discussed earlier, we expect that the risk manager will detect systematic differences in the prominence of ethical principles that arise because of the incentives found in the enterprise. Ownership structures—private or public—and enterprise power relative to the stakeholder (who prevails in bargaining) matter. The table key for Table 2 reminds risk managers to be alert to the full scope of ethical principles that drive stakeholders' judgments and incorporate this broader set in their approach to business ethics excellence.

A Structured Approach Toward Business Ethics Excellence

A risk-management approach to reputational capital becomes truly strategic when it provides:

- Credible and persuasive assurance to senior management—and to the board of directors to whom they are responsible—that the organization is on track to accomplish objectives,
- Reliable monitoring and reporting systems, and
- Activities operating in conformance with the organization's principles.

Shakespeare reminds us in *Hamlet,* however, that "there is nothing either good or bad, but thinking makes it so." Modern business managers may think

Table 2

Risk Management of Reputational Capital

ERM Framework to Elicit Stakeholder Description of Enterprise

	#1 Internal Environment	#2 Objective Setting	#3 Event Identification
PERSONAL VIRTUE (a) Trustworthy, honest, cooperative, and deserving esteem. (b) Every enterprise level in COSO ERM framework nurtures relationship with stakeholder.			(A) Stakeholder describes future events that, if they were to occur, would change the scores in cells of other columns.
LEGAL COMPLIANCE Obeys established legal institutions governing the enterprise's operations; develops relationships to govern operations where legal institutions are not well-established.			(B) For each event described in (A), stakeholder estimates the likelihood that it will occur in the forthcoming period.
ECONOMIC EFFICIENCY (a) Access to useful, unbiased information on product features, prices, and activity costs; (b) Does no harm to free markets, public safety, and environment while pursuing its own profit; (c) Alert to best profit-making opportunities.			
DISTRIBUTIVE JUSTICE Fair in prices, costs, and activities to support stakeholders' preferences.			
PROCEDURAL JUSTICE Fair access to participate in activities and decisions.			

Table Key

Business ethics programs typically focus on **Personal Virtue** but need to manage reputational capital in ERM framework.	High power and public enterprises likely focus on **Legal Compliance** and **Economic Efficiency** principles of business ethics but may need to manage risks to broader reputational capital.

Reputational Capital and Risk

#4 Risk Assessment	#5 Risk Response	#6 Control Activities	#7 Information & Communication	#8 Monitoring
Assume each event described in Column #3 occurs. (A) What is the new score in each cell of the other columns? (B) Stakeholder estimates the event's consequences (e.g., costs and benefits) for the enterprise.	For each event described in Column #3(A), consider these alternative enterprise responses: avoid the risk, accept it, reduce it, or share it with another party, such as with insurance or with accommodation from your stakeholder group. Make a judgment about each possible alternative response: Is it likely to make scores and consequences prompted in Column #4 better or worse?			

Business ethics programs need to do more to assess reputational capital as guided in ERM Components #3–5.	Low power and private enterprises likely focus on **Distributive Justice** and **Procedural Justice** principles of business ethics but may need to manage risks to broader reputational capital.

differently about the appropriate mix of ethical principles given their organizational context and may have diverse stakeholders whose thinking plays significant roles in determining the value and risks to reputational capital.

Obstacles to managing risks to reputational capital include difficulties in identifying and quantifying ethics-based metrics. Further, an enterprise's self-assessment may tend to be inward looking, so the organization may not

Table 3

ERM Components Drive Elicitation Dialogue with Stakeholders

#1: INTERNAL ENVIRONMENT	Score the enterprise on the extent to which you believe the following characteristics accurately describe it—trustworthy, honesty, cooperative, integrity.
#2: OBJECTIVE SETTING	Score the enterprise on the extent to which you believe its targets and objectives for the coming period are likely to (a. improve; b. hurt) its relationship with your group.
#6: CONTROL ACTIVITIES	Score the enterprise on the extent to which you believe its policies and procedures ensure it operates in a manner likely to (a. improve; b. hurt) its relationship with your group.
#7: INFORMATION & COMMUNICATION	Score the enterprise on the extent to which you believe its manner of collecting, using, and sharing information is likely to (a. improve; b. hurt) its relationship with your group.
#8: MONITORING	Score the enterprise on the extent to which you believe its manner of detecting violations of operating standards is likely to (a. improve; b. hurt) its relationship with your group.

learn about risks to relationships from the perspective of important stakeholders. Companies can identify and quantify these risks by asking stakeholders how they would assess them if they applied ethical principles to the COSO ERM framework. Accordingly, we suggest more discussion to develop a structured ERM approach toward business ethics excellence that's focused on building reputational capital.

We began this discussion by describing a stakeholder approach to integrating ethics with the components of COSO's ERM framework. We proposed a diagnostic tool to identify the prominent ethical principles embedded in critical relationships and the enterprise context, and we extended the ERM framework to elicit stakeholder assessments of reputational capital. These assessments may identify the expected value of negative consequences, such as direct damages of fines and penalties, cleanup costs including legal and remedial correctives, and costs from damaged relationships with important stakeholders such as customers, employees, suppliers, communities, and government. Positive consequences may include avoiding these negatives, of course, but also may include the expected value of benefits from profit-making activities made feasible by more cooperative and more durable relationships.

We call on ethics managers to use this ERM approach to identify and quantify risks to reputational capital and apply best practices for assuring senior management that the ethical foundations supporting enterprise objectives are well managed.

POSTSCRIPT

Can Ethics Codes Build "True" Corporate Ethics?

Many experts, however, would argue that correctly performed Ethics Audits are still the most effective way for establishing honesty in company cultures. They argue that in nearly every location where Ethics Audits have been consistently performed, there have been significant improvements. They contend that the rules do their job as long as they are enforced. By creating detailed rules that everyone must follow, and by performing audits regularly, a culture is created where the rules are respected. This in turn leads to an increased comfort in whistle-blowing as well as other mechanisms that prevent ethical breaches. Finally, by employing federal regulations and incentives for those who meet guidelines, it becomes extremely difficult, if not impossible, for a well-regulated company to break the rules.

Suggested Readings

"The Good, the Bad, and Their Corporate Code of Ethics: Enron, Sarbanes-Oxley, and the Problems with Legislating Good Behavior." *Harvard Law Review* (vol. 116, no. 7, 2003), p. 2123.

Amey Stone, "Putting Teeth in Corporate Ethics Codes." *Businessweek Online* (2004).

Ethan B. Kapstein, "The Corporate Ethics Crusades." *Foreign Affairs* (vol. 80, no. 5, 2001), pp. 105–119.

Internet References . . .

STAT-USA/Internet

This site, a service of the U.S. Department of Commerce, provides one-stop Internet browsing for business, trade, and economic information. It contains daily economic news, frequently requested statistical releases, information on export and international trade, domestic economic news and statistical series, and databases.

http://www.stat-usa.gov/stat-usa.html

PhRMA: America's Pharmaceutical Companies

PhRMA membership represents approximately 100 U.S. pharmaceutical companies that have a primary commitment to pharmaceutical research. Information on the effects of pharmaceutical price controls on research spending is one of the many topics covered at this site.

http://www.phrma.org

NumaWeb

This Numa Financial Systems site calls itself "the Internet's home page for financial derivatives." This site includes a reference index, a discussion forum, and links to many related sites.

http://www.numa.com/index.htm

Current Business Issues

*M*uch as we like profitable businesses, and the benefits and taxes that they bring us, there is always the possibility that the pursuit of profit will go "too far" and negatively affect other valuable parts of our lives— our environment, our future security, the morals of our children (and neighbors), and the reliability of our public utilities. Where is government regulation and limitation of business enterprise needed, appropriate, or inappropriate?

- Was the Financial Industry Responsible for the Economic Meltdown of 2008?
- Should the Government Be Responsible to Bailout Financial Institutions to Avert an Economic Disaster?
- Are the Risks of Derivatives Manageable?
- Should Price Gouging Be Regulated?

ISSUE 6

Was the Financial Industry Responsible for the Economic Meltdown of 2008?

YES: John C. Bogle, from "A Crisis of Ethic Proportions," *Wall Street Journal* (April 21, 2009)

NO: Lloyd C. Blankfein, from *Permanent Senate Subcommittee on Investigations* (June 2010)

ISSUE SUMMARY

YES: John Bogle laments the unchecked market forces, particularly in the fields of investment banking, banking, and finance that almost destroyed the global economy. He calls for the firms to make long-term investments, not short-term gains, and create an overall culture of ethics in all practices.

NO: Lloyd Blankfein, as the CEO of one of the largest global investment banks, does not believe that his financial firm was responsible for the market collapse of 2008. The blame could be placed on issues of risk management within the field instead.

T he market crash of 2008 is described as a breach of both ethics and traditional monetary practices and policies. In books and articles written on the topic, authors cite problems such as regulators and rating agencies failing to do their jobs; the unprecedented leverage placed on the financial system through complex derivatives, easy credit, and a lax attitude toward risk. Bogle cites additional problems in the financial community's inability to recognize the stark changes in the nature of capitalism. Much of the change that caused these breaches came after the 1999 revocation of the Glass–Steagall Act allowed giant financial institutions to have a different type of banking relationship/ownership. Rather than banks being a utility for customers, the banks became financial institutions working for "agents" of the owners. The owners of financial institutions weren't at risk for loss, but rather distant "others" were placed in risky financial settings in most cases without their knowledge. Our money managers now hold 75% of all shares of public companies, according to Bogle. He and others believe these money managers fostered the global crisis by engaging in dangerous speculation in a variety of ways. Some institutions created trenches of bonds around a subprime mortgage industry that was destined to fail. But superficial ratings and controls from financial firms allowed the investments to skyrocket and then plummet. Did Adam Smith understand that one day the "invisible hand" through which our self-interest advances the interests of society would be used to harm all but a few in the market? Smith contends that owner interest is always preferred to agent interest, because managers watch over their own funds with more vigilance than they watch over funds they don't own. Bogle asks that financial managers gain a much stronger sense of their ethical responsibilities to society. He predicts this will be no easy task.

Blankfein, who is chair and chief executive officer of one of the largest financial institutions in the world, thanks the American Congress for generously loaning his firm, Goldman Sachs, funds during the financial crisis of 2008. The government made unprecedented loans to most major financial firms, including Goldman Sachs—one loan under President George W. Bush for over $700,000 billion and a similar-in-size "bail out" loan under President Barack Obama. Blankfein states that he understands how Americans may be skeptical of the investment banking industry and their part in global market collapse. He explains that rating agencies and regulators failed to "sound the alarm that there was too much lending and too much leverage in the system—that credit had become too cheap." He blames much of the problem on complex derivatives that lacked transparency. Government regulations are a solution to the problem he states, and he says that Goldman Sachs will support regulations. However, most financial institutions eventually opposed many regulations that were proposed in the Dodd–Frank Wall Street Reform and Consumer Protection Act of 2010 and, and the Fraud Enforcement and Recovery Act of 2009. Blankfein explains that his firm's risk management processes "did not and could not provide absolute clarity." However, he states that maintaining his firm's reputation is paramount at all times. His final statement to the Senate panel investigating the financial crisis was, "We didn't have a massive short against the housing market and we certainly did not bet against our clients." This statement may be proven false. On July 3, 2011, Goldman Sachs was subpoenaed by the Manhattan District Attorney's office over their activities leading up to the financial crisis. The subpoena follows the April 2011 release of a 639-page Senate report that showed Goldman had steered investors toward mortgage securities it knew would likely fail. The report, which was the result of a Senate panel investigation of the financial crisis, found that Goldman marketed four sets of complex mortgage securities to banks and other investors. The report said the firm failed to tell the banks and investors that the securities were very risky, secretly bet against the investors' positions, and deceived them about its own positions. The panel's report found this was part of Goldman's effort to shift risk from its balance sheet to those of investors. Neither the report nor the subpoena is a conviction of fraud against the giant investment bank.

YES

John C. Bogle

A Crisis of Ethic Proportions

I recently received a letter from a Vanguard shareholder who described the global financial crisis as "a crisis of ethic proportions." Substituting "ethic" for "epic" is a fine turn of phrase, and it accurately places a heavy responsibility for the meltdown on a broad deterioration in traditional ethical standards.

Commerce, business and finance have hardly been exempt from this trend. Relying on Adam Smith's "invisible hand," through which our self-interest advances the interests of society, we have depended on the market-place and competition to create prosperity and well-being.

But self-interest got out of hand. It created a bottom-line society in which success is measured in monetary terms. Dollars became the coin of the new realm. Unchecked market forces overwhelmed traditional standards of professional conduct, developed over centuries.

The result is a shift from moral absolutism to moral relativism. We've moved from a society in which "there are some things that one simply does not do" to one in which "if everyone else is doing it, I can too." Business ethics and professional standards were lost in the shuffle.

The driving force of any profession includes not only the special knowledge, skills and standards that it demands, but the duty to serve responsibly, selflessly and wisely, and to establish an inherently ethical relationship between professionals and society. The old notion of trusting and being trusted—which once was not only the accepted standard of business conduct but the key to success—came to be seen as a quaint relic of an era long gone.

The proximate causes of the crisis are usually said to be easy credit, bankers' cavalier attitudes toward risk, "securitization" (which severed the traditional link between borrower and lender), the extraordinary leverage built into the financial system by complex derivatives, and the failure of our regulators to do their job.

But the larger cause was our failure to recognize the sea change in the nature of capitalism that was occurring right before our eyes. That change was the growth of giant business corporations and giant financial institutions controlled not by their owners in the "ownership society" of yore, but by agents of the owners, which created an "agency society."

The managers of our public corporations came to place their interests ahead of the interests of their company's owners. Our money manager agents—who in the U.S. now hold 75% of all shares of public companies—blithely accepted the change. They fostered the crisis with superficial security analysis and research and by ignoring corporate governance issues. They also traded stocks at an unprecedented rate, engaging in a dangerous spree of speculation.

Adam Smith presciently described the characteristics of today's corporate and institutional managers (many of whom are themselves controlled by giant financial conglomerates) with these words: "[M]anagers of other people's money [rarely] watch over it with the same anxious vigilance with which . . . [they] watch over their own . . . they . . . very easily give themselves a dispensation. Negligence and profusion must always prevail."

The malfeasance and misjudgments by our corporate, financial and government leaders, declining ethical standards, and the failure of our new agency society reflect a failure of capitalism. Free-market champion and former Federal Reserve chairman Alan Greenspan shares my view. That failure, he said in testimony to Congress last October, "was a flaw in the model that I perceived as the critical functioning structure that defines how the world works." As one journalist observed, "that's a hell of a big thing to find a flaw in."

What's to be done? We must work to establish a "fiduciary society," where manager/agents entrusted with managing other people's money are required—by federal statute—to place front and center the interests of the owners they are duty-bound to serve. The focus needs to be on long-term investment (rather than short-term speculation), appropriate due diligence in security selection, and ensuring that corporations are run in the interest of their owners. Manager/agents need to act in a way that reflects their ethical responsibilities to society. Making that happen will be no easy task.

Lloyd C. Blankfein

 **NO**

Causes and Consequences of the Financial Crisis

"We didn't have a massive short against the housing market . . . rather, we believe we managed our risk"

Prepared remarks by LLOYD C. BLANKFEIN, Chairman and CEO, Goldman Sachs *Delivered to a Senate panel investigating Goldman Sachs' mortgage-trading activities before the financial crisis, Washington, D.C., April 27, 2010*

Chairman Levin, Ranking Member Coburn and Members of the Subcommittee:

Thank you for the invitation to appear before you today as you examine some of the causes and consequences of the financial crisis.

Today, the financial system is still fragile but it is largely stable. This stability is a result of decisive and necessary government action during the fall of 2008. Like other financial institutions, Goldman Sachs received an investment from the government as a part of its various efforts to fortify our markets and the economy during a very difficult time.

I want to express my gratitude and the gratitude of our entire firm. We held the government's investment for approximately eight months and repaid it in full along with a 23% annualized return for taxpayers.

Until recently, most Americans had never heard of Goldman Sachs or weren't sure what it did. We don't have banking branches. We provide very few mortgages and don't issue credit cards or loans to consumers. Instead, we generally work with companies, governments, pension funds, mutual funds and other investing institutions. These clients usually come to Goldman Sachs for one or more of the following reasons: (1) they want financial advice; (2) they need financing; (3) they want to buy or sell a stock, bond or other financial instrument; or (a) they want help in managing and growing their financial assets. The 35,000 people who work at Goldman Sachs, the majority of whom work in the United States, are hardworking, diligent and thoughtful. Through them, we help governments raise capital to fund schools and roads. We advise companies and provide them funds to invest in their growth. We work with pension funds, labor unions and university endowments to help

Permanent Senate Subcommittee on Investigations, 2010.

build and secure their assets for generations to come. And, we connect buyers and sellers in the securities markets, contributing to the liquidity and vitality of our financial system. These functions are important to economic growth and job creation.

I recognize, however, that many Americans are skeptical about the contribution of investment banking to our economy and understandably angry about how Wall Street contributed to the financial crisis. As a firm, we are trying to deal with the implications of the crisis for ourselves and for the system. What we and other banks, rating agencies and regulators failed to do was sound the alarm that there was too much lending and too much leverage in the system—that credit had become too cheap. One consequence of the growth of the housing market was that instruments that pooled mortgages and their risk became overly complex. That complexity and the fact that some instruments couldn't be easily bought or sold compounded the effects of the crisis.

While derivatives are an important tool to help companies and financial institutions manage their risk, we need more transparency for the public and regulators as well as safeguards in the system for their use. That is why Goldman Sachs, in supporting financial regulatory reform, has made it clear that it supports clearinghouses for eligible derivatives and higher capital requirements for non-standard instruments.

As you know, ten days ago, the SEC announced a civil action against Goldman Sachs in connection with a specific transaction. It was one of the worst days in my professional life, as I know it was for every person at our firm. We believe deeply in a culture that prizes teamwork, depends on honesty and rewards saying no as much as saying yes. We have been a clientcentered firm for 140 years and if our clients believe that we don't deserve their trust, we cannot survive.

While we strongly disagree with the SEC's complaint, I also recognize how such a complicated transaction may look to many people. To them, it is confirmation of how out of control they believe Wall Street has become, no matter how sophisticated the parties or what disclosures were made. We have to do a better job of striking the balance between what an informed client believes is important to his or her investing goals and what the public believes is overly complex and risky.

Finally, Mr. Chairman, the Subcommittee is focused on the more specific issues revolving around the mortgage securitization market. I think it is important to consider these issues in the context of risk management. We believe that strong, conservative risk management is fundamental and helps define Goldman Sachs. Our risk management processes did not, and could not, provide absolute clarity; they highlighted uncertainty about evolving conditions in the housing market. That uncertainty dictated our decision to attempt to reduce the firm's overall risk.

Much has been said about the supposedly massive short Goldman Sachs had on the U.S. housing market. The fact is we were not consistently or significantly net "short the market" in residential mortgage-related products in 2007 and 2008. Our performance in our residential mortgagerelated business confirms this.

During the two years of the financial crisis, while profitable overall, Goldman Sachs lost approximately \$1.2 billion from our activities in the residential housing market.

We didn't have a massive short against the housing market and we certainly did not bet against our clients. Rather, we believe that we managed our risk as our shareholders and our regulators would expect. Mr. Chairman, thank you for the opportunity to address these issues. I look forward to your questions.

POSTSCRIPT

Was the Financial Industry Responsible for the Economic Meltdown of 2008?

Blankfein states that overall he was grateful for the government bailout of 2008, but his firm Goldman Sachs always displays integrity in their actions, which includes the period before the bailout as well as the present. Bogle finds that a lack of ethics throughout Wall Street was responsible for the bailout and doesn't excuse any one firm from responsibility. Is regulation the answer? To many analysts, regulations that were passed due to the financial crisis of 2008 seem weak in their ability to limit risk-taking for the institutions and instruments that threatened the overall stability of the global economic system. To date no one has been arrested or tried for his or her part in the overall scheme that caused trillion dollar losses and threatened global economic stability. To date leveraged derivatives continue to be a major financial vehicle despite the highly speculative nature that can be employed to enhance profits. Some government analysts call for additional reforms of investment banks and other financial institutions. They also ask that regulators have clear accountability to enforce constraints on risk. However, the American banking system has the largest lobby contingent in Washington, and as such many ethicists are skeptical of long-term changes.

Suggested Readings

Andrew A. Samwick, "Moral Hazard in the Policy Response to the 2008 Financial Market Meltdown," *CATO Journal* (vol. 19, no. 1, 2009), pp. 131–139.

Charles Ferguson. *Inside Job*. Perf. Matt Damon. 2010. Sony Picture Classics, DVD (2011).

John D. McKinnion and Maya Jackson Randall, "Panel Blames All for Meltdown," *Wall Street Journal—Eastern Edition* (January 26, 2011), p. A7.

Thomas E. Woods, *Meltdown: A Free-Market Look at Why the Stock Market Collapsed, the Economy Tanked, and Government Bailouts Will Make Things Worse* (Washington, D.C.: Regnery Publishing, 2009).

Walden Belle, "A meltdown primer," *New Internationalist* (vol. 417, 2008), pp. 34–35.

ISSUE 7

Should the Government Be Responsible to Bailout Financial Institutions to Avert an Economic Disaster?

YES: **Roger Lowenstein**, from *The End of Wall Street* (Penguin Press, 2010), pp. 273–284

NO: **Robert J. Samuelson**, from "The Perils of Prosperity," *Newsweek* (February 10, 2010), cited in *The Great Inflation and Its Aftermath: The Past and Future of American Affluence* (Random House, 2010)

ISSUE SUMMARY

YES: Roger Lowenstein details the collapse of the market of 2008 in a bleak excerpt from his book. The only ethical perspective for the American people to avoid a complete economic calamity was a government bailout.

NO: Robert Samuelson explains in an excerpt from his book that economies go boom and bust. He posits that in the future it is a better economic policy to allow an economy to naturally bust than to have government intervention.

One of the most difficult challenges for economic policymakers in the past 80 years has been the financial crisis of 2008. It may have hit its nadir but is still showing signs of harming global fiscal markets. The initial policy response from the Federal Reserve was to prop up major financial institutions through TARP (troubled asset relief program) capital. However, the market may have needed the bailout earlier, as downward spiral recession forced companies to layoff and fire large numbers of employees. Globally, hundreds of thousands of individuals lost their jobs because of the unstable market their employers were experiencing. Despite measures taken by the Federal Reserve to provide liquidity to a range of financial institutions to stem what could have blossomed into a full-scale global panic, government economists have found their reputations severely damaged. The damage is because few, if any, economists advising the government and others were able to predict the nature, timing, or severity of the crash. There were a few isolated early warnings, but none came close to the overall greed that had consumed the investment banking, mortgage, securities, and banks in general.

Three years after the first "shock" there is some stabilization in the market; however, hundreds of thousands of home owners owe more on their homes than they are worth, and unemployment numbers continue to climb. Robert Samuelson claims that as a result of these developments, there may be a need for an overhaul of economics as a discipline, arguing that much of the research in economics has been of little value or even counterproductive. He reminds us that the perils of prosperity caused much of the disaster many are facing today; government economists could share much of the blame for this problem. His claim is that when a market booms, it must also go bust, and the economists were aware of this, or should have been. He also believes that rather than the government bailing out institutions, that following the natural consequences of the prosperity boom is important. Rather than implementing "misguided" policies, perhaps in the future financial institutions should be allowed to fail. Most societies want to enjoy as much prosperity for as long as possible. Politicians would like to give them this prosperity, but Samuelson insists there are nasty and unintended side effects, such as eventually a housing market bubble will burst. For Samuelson, more frequent and milder recessions and financial setbacks should be accepted, rather than striving for the fantasy of a sustained prosperity.

For Lowenstein, the recent financial crisis was a failure of the economic practices of bankers, mortgage brokers, and regulators. These practices included inadequate risk-measurement and risk management systems at many financial firms. He also finds fault with the firms' business models, including an overreliance on unstable short-term funding and inordinate leverage. Firms took advantage of blind spots in the financial regulatory structures in the United States and globally. When TARP funds became necessary, more than $700 billion in aid was handed out in an effort to stabilize financial institutions and some large business. Months later, stimulus funds of $787 billion were handed out to give aid to states, reduce taxes, and encourage investments in industry. Lowenstein paints the picture of the destruction started by a few in banking and finance that spread destruction across the country and globe. There was no choice for government economists—too much damage would have occurred to innocents had the bailouts not been implemented.

YES

Roger Lowenstein

Great Recession

We must acknowledge that many in the financial community, including those at the Federal Reserve, failed to either detect or act upon the telltale signs of financial system excess.

Richard Fisher, President, Federal Reserve Bank of Dallas, February 2009

The injection of TARP capital proved to be the nadir of the financial crisis. In the significant sense of halting the plunge in credit markets, the program had an immediate and salutary effect: for banks and many corporations, borrowing costs would never again return to the skyscraper levels of mid-October. For the economy at large, however, the Treasury's intervention arrived too late. By the end of October 2008, the slowdown had mushroomed into what by many measures was the worst recession in seven decades.

Within days of Paulson's forced investment in banks, household-name businesses were firing hordes of workers. Citigroup let go 34,000; Bank of America, Goldman, Merrill, and Morgan Stanley thousands more. Nor was the slump confined to financial firms. The litany of Main Street corporations pruning payrolls soon included Merck, Chrysler, Pratt & Whitney, Yahoo, Xerox, Whirlpool, Alcoa, and Coca-Cola.

The recession was not only wide, it was deep. The mild downturn of 1990, like that of 2001, had seemed to verify Ben Bernanke's contention that economic cycles were moderating, but the present slump recalled the painful recessions of the smokestack America of the 1950s. Auto sales plunged 40 percent, a throwback to an era predating the abundance of credit, when only by scrimping and saving could Americans upgrade their automobiles. Home building plummeted to its lowest level in fifty years. Newer and greener industries, hallmarks of the modern, service economy, were devastated. Nortel, the telecom powerhouse, filed for Chapter 11. Pfizer sent 19,500 chemists and others packing. International trade collapsed; law firms, universities, and state agencies shrank their payrolls. In the dark winter of 2008–09, jobs were everywhere a scarce commodity. In Cambridge, Massachusetts, Harvard law grads had to struggle to find work. In Miami, when the city posted openings for thirty-five firefighters, it drew one thousand able-bodied applicants.

The Great Recession, as journalists dubbed it, rolled back the clock to an earlier, more vulnerable time. Pink slips from formerly recession-proof employers inflicted a psychological blow. Americans hooked on spending on credit reverted to the musty habit of their grandparents—saving. As they cut back on shopping, retail suffered a shock. Circuit City, the purveyor of electronics, filed for Chapter 11; so did General Growth Properties, the mall operator. As spending slumped, advertising crashed, and newspapers across the country shriveled, their reporters—media-savvy, educated, and urbane—laid off in droves. The prosperous upper middle of the country was unhinged from its breezy confidence, its expensive indulgences, and high-end tastes. Whole Foods, the organic retailer, hit the skids, its stock collapsing 80 percent. Starbucks saw its profits crash to less than a penny per drink and shuttered nine hundred stores.

Wall Street itself went into a terrible funk. Investment banks, already battered by the crash, fell idle. IPOs, derivatives, and private equity all stopped dead. Corporate America ceased doing deals. The stock market fell and kept falling (in this sense, October was far from the bottom). As confidence in business evaporated, investors shoveled their money at—and only at—the government until, in December, so much liquidity was offered to the Treasury that the yield on its T-bills touched zero. For a brief moment, American capitalism ventured into an illogical and absurd mathematical space; the yield on bills turned *negative*.

As the market crashed, the wealthy suffered with everyone else. The Yellowstone Club, a Montana ski resort offering lavish homes for the ultrarich (Bill Gates was a member) filed for bankruptcy. In New York, Christie's failed to auction works by Manet, Renoir, Cézanne, and de Kooning. The embarrassed auctioneer explained that the desired prices, determined during the summer, "were from an earlier time," as if from another century.

Not having lived through such a slump before, people did not know if, or how long, it would endure. Confidence in private markets evaporated; government was again a protector. An era of widespread regulation was foreseen, a tide of legislative reform. Jeff Madrick, an economist, published a tome with the suddenly plausible title, *The Case for Big Government*. Its thesis proved truer than its author dreamed.

Once they decided to bail out Wall Street, Paulson and Bernanke agreed there was no going back. And their interventions proved much broader than initially conceived. Paulson aggressively utilized the TARP; 650 banks received injections of public capital. The Fed became the dominant provider of mortgages, car loans, short-term commercial credit, and loans to banks. The central bank became the financier to the government itself, purchasing Treasury securities by the billions. Like a patient on ever-increasing doses of morphine, the country subsisted on public funds.

The Fed could offset the scarcity of lenders, but it could do little about the lack of *borrowers*, a more serious malady. Credit can always be manufactured—not so the willingness to borrow, which rests on faith in the future. In its absence, economies stagnate. Japan's had idled for a decade in the 1990s, and the fear of a similar lull fairly traumatized Bernanke. Neither people nor businesses wanted to borrow; they were overleveraged from the bubble years and they were uncertain that the future was worth borrowing for. The total of mortgage loans outstanding had risen in every quarter since the Federal Reserve began tracking such data, in 1946; now it fell for six straight quarters.

In December, three months after Lehman failed, Bernanke dared to emulate his mythical experiment of dropping cash from a helicopter in the sky. In a desperate effort to stimulate, the Fed lowered its target rate for overnight bank loans from a paltry 1 percent to a range of ¼ percent to *zero*—a record low and, indeed, abutting the theoretical extreme. The cut, however, was largely symbolic. Owing to a paucity of demand, the actual rate at which banks were borrowing had already fallen to a tenth of a percent. No one wanted the money.

The grim recession handed the Democrats a golden opportunity to retake the White House—and also, so the faithful hoped, roll back the credo of laissez-faire. On the campaign trail, Obama stirred hopes of a second FDR, or at least a second New Deal. He artfully blamed the financial crisis on eight years of extreme Republicanism. The truth was muddier. Given how boldly the administration had intervened to save the banks, Bush was no Herbert Hoover.[1] Nor were the Democrats free of blame for the crisis's origins. While Bush-style conservatives had loudly championed deregulation, Democrats such as Robert Rubin had deregulated in practice. The Democrats had done the most to insulate the mortgage twins, Fannie and Freddie, from demands that they reform and trim their balance sheets. On the other hand, blame for the ineffective or tardy response to the crisis rested with the Bush administration and with the GOP naysayers in the House. Obama hung his candidacy on the slogan of "Change," and by November 4, change was what the electorate wanted.

After the election, Obama's financial policy was more moderate than many expected; indeed, it was largely a continuation of the Paulson-Bernanke-Geithner regime. The president-elect ensured a smooth transition by elevating Geithner from the New York Fed to Treasury secretary. This was a clear signal that any "change" would be incremental. Paulson, comforted that his two principal partners would remain on the job, continued to intervene in the economy up to his last days in office.

The government's response to the financial crisis consisted of three main policies. The first was bailing out tottering banks and other companies. The second consisted of numerous Fed facilities to maintain a minimum level of liquidity in the banking system and in the economy. These two policies began, of course, well before the transition of power, and they continued seamlessly under Obama. The third was a massive government stimulus, which the Democratic Congress enacted during Obama's first thirty days.[2]

Taking these in order, the bailout reflex was especially hard to unlearn. A seminal moment occurred in November, weeks after the election, when Citigroup began to tremble. A stream of deposits left the bank as customers began to jump ship and, as in the previous death spirals, the stock cratered. In the third week of November, Citi's shares lost 60 percent, finishing on Friday, November 21, at under 4, its lowest level in sixteen years. Pandit, the CEO, lashed out in an employee conference call at "fearmongering." To avoid demoralizing the troops, the company stopped displaying its stock price at headquarters. Meanwhile, Robert Rubin, chairman of the executive committee, called Paulson, his former Goldman colleague, and pleaded for government help. Five U.S.

agencies were involved in the talks. Citi insisted that *it* wasn't the problem so much as the banking system—although Citi itself had written off $49 billion in charges over the previous four quarters, and its balance sheet was freighted with $2 trillion of assets that the market couldn't value or that (to judge from its plummeting stock) it refused to value.

The independent-minded Sheila Bair, head of the FDIC, dared to suggest that Citigroup be allowed to fail. Let the government protect the bank and its depositors, she argued, and allow the umbrella corporation, which had misused its capital by plowing it into CDOs, to suffer the market's justice. Paulson could not believe his ears. "I'm having an out-of-body experience here, Sheila," the secretary replied. "I can't believe we're having this discussion. You're talking about *Citigroup* going through receivership." Deliberations, in the usual pattern, continued through the weekend; Citi did not get a term sheet until nearly 10 P.M. on Sunday. The United States granted it roughly $250 billion in loss protection and invested $20 billion (in addition to the TARP money invested in October). In February, the Obama administration provided Citi with yet a third rescue. The government was compensated for its largesse with a one-third ownership in Citi, but the November bailout—struck after the financial panic had passed its worst—protected the bank's managers and directors from the full effects of years of horrendous decisions. What the government failed to do was to send a message that here was a bank too poorly managed *not* to fail.

A similar dynamic ensued when Paulson and Bernanke forced a deeply reluctant Ken Lewis to complete the acquisition of Merrill Lynch. (This was the same Bank of America chief who had ardently coveted Merrill as recently as September. In the waning days of 2008, as Merrill posted new and staggering losses, he tried to wriggle out.) As *his* stock tumbled, Lewis demanded government protection against potential losses. This time, it was Kevin Warsh of the Fed who questioned whether a bank shouldn't be left to take its lumps. Once again, the government ran to the rescue.

Nor did the bailouts end there. The government upped its investment in AIG—chipping in additional capital in November of '08 and still more in March of 2009—a point by which, the panic well past, AIG's Wall Street creditors might have been expected to share the pain. The United States provided tens of billions in capital and loans for Fannie and Freddie. It also widened the safety net to insure the credit subsidiary of John Deere, as well as GE Capital. It converted American Express and also GMAC, the auto finance company, to banks, and supplied both with capital from TARP.

And there was more. In the fall, auto executives had driven, in hybrid cars carefully selected for their political appeal,[3] to the nation's capital to plead for aid. On the advice of Secretary Paulson, General Motors and Chrysler were rescued by President Bush, one of his last presidential acts. Detroit did not present the same systemic risk as banking; the bailout was an old-fashioned subsidy (of the unions as well as the carmakers) disguised as financial necessity. The shrunken manufacturers closed two thousand dealerships, and Rick Wagoner, GM's chief executive, resigned at the government's behest. It was not enough. Months later, GM and Chrysler were forced to file for bankruptcy.

GM's filing was the fourth largest in American history (behind Lehman, Washington Mutual, and WorldCom).

The bailout policy—perhaps a necessary evil when the financial system was in extremis—was thus continued well beyond the banking emergency. It is hard to escape the conclusion that, having been widely criticized for allowing Lehman to fail,[4] regulators were afraid to let *any* large institution go under, even as the most acute phase of the crisis receded. Far from restoring confidence, the bailouts reaffirmed in the public's mind a dispiriting truth: private markets were helpless. Confidence would only return when private investors manifested courage. For that to occur, assets had to sink to a price at which private buyers would venture back.

While the bailouts were aimed at specific institutions, the Fed's actions to provide liquidity were aimed at salvaging the overall economy. Bernanke's Fed was easily the most energetic in history. The Fed single-handedly propped up the real estate market, pumping an average of $20 billion into mortgage securities every *week*. It lent to small businesses, car buyers, consumers. It partially offset the collapse in corporate liquidity by purchasing $350 billion of commercial paper. It stocked up on Treasury bonds in a deliberate attempt to hold down interest rates, lest the government's borrowing drive rates higher. The Fed's own assets ballooned two and a half times, as it scooped up mortgages and government bonds and financed investments in asset-backed securities such as student loans, credit card debts, mortgages—all of the unwanted detritus of the bubble years.

Still the economy kept shrinking. From October of '08 to the following March, GDP fell at an astounding annualized rate of 6 percent, the worst six-month stretch in fifty years. Fed governors, as well as private economists, were stunned by the sharpness of the downturn. Credit had been in ample supply for so long, it was forgotten that business couldn't function without it. A third of the country's manufacturing capacity was idled. General Electric, a mainstay of American industry, slashed its dividend for the first time since 1938. Companies that had operated profitably for decades saw their markets suddenly implode. Fastenal, a Winona, Michigan–based screw manufacturer with a stable business and a loyal customer base—the sort of bedrock company that had powered the economy through thick and thin—was an apt example. Fastenal had steadily increased sales for forty-two years. It did not take foolish risks or waste money on extravagances (executives traveling cross-country drove corporate cars and shared rooms in inexpensive hotels). Even in the spring of 2008, as the mortgage market was imploding; Fastenal was still reporting double-digit sales gains. Then, its business began to tail off. In the fall, it experienced a mild downturn. In the spring of 2009, Fastenal's sales plunged 25 percent. The stock fell by half and the workforce was pared by 11 percent. Such a brutal contraction defied every forecast.

The economic freeze sent the stock market into a tailspin that hit its worst in the two days after Obama's election, when the Dow plummeted one thousand points. By the end of 2008, the S&P 500 was down 38 percent, making it the worst year for stocks since 1937. The price of oil, a barometer of economic strength, plunged during the year from $96 a barrel to $46; junk bond portfolios were cut by a third. These were figures worthy of a Depression.

Stocks fell a further 11 percent between New Year's Day and Obama's inauguration, on January 20. From then to the second week of March, they fell 16 percent more. On the low of March 9, the Dow stood at 6,547, its lowest level since April 1997. Ford and Citi traded at $1 and Bank of America at 3, a plunge of 90 percent from when it had agreed to acquire Merrill, a mere six months earlier. Peak to trough, banking stocks dropped 88 percent and the broader market fell 57 percent—the worst slide since the Hoover market of 1929–32, when the market plunged 86 percent. Market pros who had lived through Black Monday and other information-age crashes that were over in days or hours found them themselves in new, more frightening terrain— a relentless slump, inexorable, seemingly endless. What everyone wanted to know, what no one could answer, was: Would the selling stop?

This was the atmosphere in which Obama took office—as frightening an economic landscape as had greeted any new president since FDR in 1933. In January, as Obama moved in to the White House, the economy shed 740,000 jobs, a record high. The following month, the value of the median home fell to $165,000, erasing a full six years' worth of gains.

The administration immediately proposed a stimulus. Congress exerted control over the specifics of the bill, resulting in a balkanized package ranging from funds for new technologies to highway repairs. Broadly, it allocated $787 billion for three purposes: aid to the states, which were in desperate shape because of falling tax receipts; cuts in federal taxes; and a potpourri of investments in industries such as high-speed rail and alternative energy.[5]

It took time for the money to be spent and, arguably, long-range investment was ill-suited to the short-term agenda of reigniting the economy. In the meantime, the economy kept sinking. Office buildings lost tenants and their rents plunged. Commercial loans were foreclosed on in droves, imperiling lenders. Throughout 2009, banks failed at a rate of nearly three per week. Incredibly, the performance of home mortgages deteriorated even from the abysmal standard of '08. By the spring of '09, 26.5 percent of subprime mortgage-holders were seriously delinquent and four in ten were either behind on their loans or in the process of foreclosure. About one in eight people with a mortgage of *any* kind—not just subprime—were in similar straits, and fully fifteen million families owed more than their homes were worth.

In the spring of 2009, the orgy of federal spending began to show effect. The economy kept shrinking, but at a slower rate. The stock market rebounded off its lows, and in the second quarter, housing prices, after falling for three straight years, eked out a gain. Finally, in the third quarter, the economy began to limp forward. By then, the GDP had contracted 3.8 percent, the greatest drop in national output since the demobilization after World War II. Save for that, the present slump was the worst recession since the 1930s. It was also the longest. The National Bureau of Economic Research determined that the Great Recession had begun in December 2007—nine months before the fall of Lehman. It lasted until approximately the middle of 2009. And then, the longest recession in living memory was over.

While a recovery commenced, the losses were far from expunged. Stocks remained a third off their highs and beneath their levels of a decade back.

Home prices, having fallen 32 percent, remained severely depressed. Although Obama, unlike Bush, made an effort to stem the tide of foreclosures, his policies were only marginally effective. Lenders were inundated with repossession proceedings; judges who wanted to work out accommodations between borrowers and banks found that the latter did not return their calls. Foreclosures rose throughout the first half of 2009, peaking only in July, when a record 360,000 families were stripped of their deeds. Thereafter foreclosures continued at abnormally high rates. (One foreclosed dwelling was the ranch house on East Jefferson Street in Dillon, South Carolina, that had been the childhood home of Ben Bernanke.) Commercial real estate remained in a severe downturn. Commercial paper outstanding did not hit bottom until late July. In August, the economy was still so weak that the Fed grimly extended its facility for purchasing asset-backed securities. Bank lending and consumer credit were declining well into the autumn of 2009.

Even after the crisis had ended, the federal government remained deeply involved in the ordinary business of American households and firms. As late as a year after the Lehman failure, government spending accounted for 26 percent of the U.S. economy—its biggest share since the Truman administration—and Washington continued to provide the financing for nine out of ten new home loans. As an indicator of its far-flung reach, the government was actively overseeing General Motors, AIG, Citigroup, Fannie Mae, and Freddie Mac—respectively the country's biggest car company, biggest insurer, former biggest bank, and the bulwarks of the mortgage industry.[6] And the Fed, as of September 30, remained swollen with $2.144 trillion in assets, including roughly $700 billion in the mortgage-backed securities that private investors no longer wanted.

The financial industry had not begun to recoup its losses. According to the IMF, U.S. banks wrote down a total of $610 billion in loans and securities through the second quarter of 2009, a goodly portion of which was suffered by Wall Street banks, the rest by their mortgage-banking comrades. The loss in market value of the biggest banks alone, even after stocks staged an impressive rally, was roughly a trillion dollars. Of course, three major investment banks failed or were acquired and more than one hundred depository institutions were seized.

The cost of the crash to ordinary citizens was astronomical. The total wealth of Americans plunged from $64 trillion to $51 trillion. Another cost—to be borne by future generations—was the huge growth in the federal deficit incurred to pay for the rescue.

The most punishing blow was the devastation in jobs, and for ordinary workers the pain continued long after the worst was over on Wall Street. In October 2009, unemployment hit double digits—10.2 percent. In California, cradle of the subprime loan, 12½ percent of the population was out of work; in Michigan, devastated by the collapse in auto sales, 15 percent. As a measure of how disproportionate was the Wall Street scourge. Wall Street itself, presumably one of the prime agents of the bust, shed 30,000 jobs; the entire United States lost a total of eight million. Never, since the end of World War II, had so many jobs disappeared so fast, and never had the power of finance to inflict damage on the society it serves been so painfully clear. By the recession's end, the economy had lost all the jobs that had been added during the boom years and more. Even with a population that was 20 million larger, the job market was smaller. In sum, the U.S. spent nearly a decade losing ground—a decade that, according to the country's highest sages, was to have ushered in an era of nearly uniformly advancing prosperity. The subprime binge that Bernanke had supposed was a contained problem turned out to be a symptom of a full credit mania. Ultimately, it destroyed the American workplace. Such was the bitter fruit of Wall Street's folly.

Notes

1. In truth, not even Hoover was a Hoover. Through programs such as the aforementioned Reconstruction Finance Corporation, which propped up thousands of banks, he was far more active in fighting the Depression than history recalls. His reputation for heartlessness stems mostly from his deep-freeze personality. Dour and remote, he failed to inspire and seemed not to empathize with the millions of his countrymen out of work. It was said by a contemporary that a rose would wilt at Hoover's touch—words never uttered about the outgoing and congenial Bush. But the two shared an ideological preference for aiding institutions (banks) rather than people. Thus, Hoover scorned welfare and Bush sidetracked foreclosure relief. However, the thirty-first president would have been horrified at Bush's blithe spending and reckless deficits. The son of a Quaker blacksmith, orphaned at ten, Hoover was a self-made striver famous for his efficiency campaigns and his rigid morals—the polar opposite of the happy-go-lucky White House heir.

2. Obama's policy also had a fourth element—financial reform. This is discussed in the concluding chapter.

3. Earlier, the executives had been widely criticized for flying to Washington on corporate jets.

4. A Treasury official remarked, "People felt burned by Lehman; we didn't want another."

5. The government effort to rescue the economy cost easily more, even in adjusted dollars, than the Louisiana Purchase, the *Apollo* moon shot, or the Korean War. The U.S.'s $170 billion investment in AIG alone cost more than the Marshall Plan to rebuild Europe—such is the penalty for speculative excess. In total, the United States committed more than $12 trillion to various forms of relief, but most of that (such as funds set aside for potential losses) will likely never be spent. Actual expenditures will likely fall in the range of $3.5 trillion to $4 trillion, fifteen times the cost of the S&L bailout of the late 1980s. Much of the money spent, such as for asset purchases or loans, will likely be recouped. The U.S. should earn a profit on the TARP investments in banks. However, the stimulus was a sheer expense, and recoveries from General Motors, in which the country invested $70 billion, as well as the approximately $225 billion handed to Fannie and Freddie, appear problematic.

6. The United States owned 34 percent of Citigroup, 80 percent of AIG and 60 percent of General Motors.

Robert J. Samuelson  **NO**

The Perils of Prosperity

We need to get the story straight. Already, a crude consensus has formed over what caused the financial crisis. We were victimized by dishonest mortgage brokers, greedy bankers, and inept regulators. Easy credit from the Federal Reserve probably made matters worse. True, debate continues over details. Fed chairman Ben Bernanke recently gave a speech denying that it had loosened credit too much, though he admitted to lax bank regulation. Just recently a congressionally created commission opened hearings on the causes of the crisis. Still, the basic consensus seems well established and highly reassuring. It suggests that if we toughen regulation, suppress outrageous avarice, and improve the Fed's policies, we can prevent anything like this from ever occurring again.

There's only one problem: the consensus is wrong—or at least vastly simplified.

Viewed historically, what we experienced was a classic boom and bust. Prolonged prosperity dulled people's sense of risk. With hindsight, we know that investors, mortgage brokers, and bankers engaged in reckless behavior that created economic havoc. We know that regulators turned a blind eye to practices that, in retrospect, were ruinous. We know that the Fed kept interest rates low for a long period (the overnight fed-funds rate fell to 1 percent in June 2003). But the crucial question is: why? Greed and shortsightedness didn't suddenly burst forth; they are constants of human nature.

One answer is this: speculation and complacency flourished because the prevailing view was that the economy and financial system had become safer. For a quarter century, from 1983 to 2007, the United States enjoyed what was arguably the greatest prosperity in its history. The boom was triggered by the conquest of high inflation, which had destabilized the economy since the late 1960s. From 1979 to 1984, inflation dropped from 13 percent to 4 percent. By 2001, it was 1.6 percent. As inflation fell, interest rates followed—though the relationship was loose—and as interest rates fell, the stock market and housing prices soared. From 1980 to 2000, the value of household stocks and mutual funds increased from about $1 trillion to nearly $11 trillion. The median price for existing homes rose from $62,200 in 1980 to $143,600 in 2000; by 2006, it was $221,900.

Feeling enriched by higher home values and stock portfolios, many Americans skimped on savings or borrowed more. The personal saving rate dropped from 10 percent of disposable income in 1980 to about 2 percent 20 years later. The parallel surge in consumer spending, housing construction, and renovation propelled the economy and created jobs, 36 million of them from 1983 to 2001. There were only two recessions in these years, both historically mild: those of 1990–91 and 2001. Monthly unemployment peaked at 7.8 percent in mid-1992.

The hard-won triumph over double-digit inflation in the early 1980s, engineered by then–Fed chairman Paul Volcker and backed by newly elected president Ronald Reagan, qualifies as one of the great achievements of economic policy since World War II. The temptation is to portray it as a pleasing morality tale. The economic theories that led to higher inflation were bad; the theories that subdued higher inflation were good. Superior ideas displaced inferior ones, and the reward was the increased prosperity and economic stability of the 1980s and later. But that, unfortunately, is only half the story.

Success also planted the seeds of disaster by creating self-defeating expectations and behaviors. The huge profits made in these decades by investors conditioned many to believe in the underlying benevolence of financial markets. Although they might periodically go to excess, they would ultimately self-correct without too much collateral damage. The greater stability of the real economy—by contrast, there had been four recessions from the late 1960s to the early 1980s—provided an anchor. The Fed was also a backstop: under Alan Greenspan, it was lionized for averting deep downturns after the stock-market crash of 1987 and the burst "tech bubble" in 2000. Money managers, regulators, economists, and the general public all succumbed to these seductive beliefs.

The explosion of the subprime-mortgage market early in the 2000s may now appear insane, but it had a logic. Housing prices would continue rising because they had consistently risen for two decades. Consumers could borrow and spend more because their wealth was constantly expanding and they were less threatened by recession. That justified relaxed lending standards. Homeowners with weak credit histories could refinance loans on more favorable terms in two or three years because the value of their houses would have risen. If borrowers defaulted, lenders could recover their money because the homes would be worth more.

The paradox is that, thinking the world less risky, people took actions that made it more risky. The pleasures of prosperity backfired. They bred carelessness and complacency. If regulation was lax, the main reason was that regulators—like the lenders, investors, and borrowers they supervised—shared the conventional wisdom. Markets seemed to be working. Why interfere? That was the lesson of experience, not an abstract devotion to the theory of "efficient markets," as is now increasingly argued.

Unless we get the story of the crisis right, we may be disappointed by the sequel. The boom-bust explanation does not exonerate greed, shortsightedness, or misguided government policies. But it does help explain them. It doesn't mean that we can't—or shouldn't—take steps to curb dangerous risk taking. Greater capital requirements would protect banks from losses; the ability to control the shutdown of large, failing financial institutions might avoid the chaos of the Lehman Brothers collapse; moving the trading of many derivatives (such as credit default swaps) to exchanges would create more transparency in financial markets. But it's neither possible—nor desirable—to regulate away all risk. Every bubble is not a potential depression. Popped bubbles and losses must occur to deter speculation and compel investors to evaluate risk. Finally, a single-minded focus on the blunders of Wall Street may also distract us from other possible sources of future crises, including excessive government debt.

The larger lesson of the recent crisis is sobering. Modern, advanced democracies strive to deliver as much prosperity as possible to as many people as possible for as long as possible. They are in the business of creating perpetual booms. The cruel contradiction is that this promise itself may become a source of instability because the more it is attained, the more people begin acting in ways that ultimately invite its destruction. Booms often have unintended and nasty side effects; even anticipated side effects that are ultimately unsustainable—stock-market bubbles, excessively tight labor markets—can be hard to police because they're initially popular and pleasurable.

The quest for ever-more and ever-better prosperity subverts itself. It might be better to tolerate more frequent, milder recessions and financial setbacks than to strive for a sustained prosperity that, though superficially more appealing, is unattainable and ends in a devastating bust. That's a central implication of the crisis, but it poses hard political and economic questions that haven't yet been asked, let alone answered.

POSTSCRIPT

Should the Government Be Responsible to Bailout Financial Institutions to Avert an Economic Disaster?

Should the government have bailed out the financial institutions that caused the crisis of 2008? For Lowenstein the answer is yes, and the end doesn't seem to be in sight. For Samuelson, the market will have booms and busts. Financial managers have to be much more diligent in keeping free enterprise afloat. Both Samuelson and Lowenstein would agree that the causes of the crisis are linked to various factors, including poorly structured incentives at many banks. Compensation practices at financial institutions often tied bonuses to short-term results and then didn't make adjustments for loss and risk. They would also find that top managers and lower-level employees, such as traders and loan officers, took excessive risks. There were massive problems with the application of the so-called originate-to-distribute model to subprime mortgages. In this disastrous practice, mortgage lenders and those who packaged the loans for sale to investors were compensated primarily on the quantity of "product" they were able to sell in the financial system. Little attention was paid to credit quality and untold numbers of loans were made without sufficient documentation or care in underwriting. Samuelson reminds us that markets will have booms and busts. When booms get too large, the bust will be too large as well. Lowenstein posits that, when financial disasters are as dire as the one in 2008, government intervention is needed to help with some stability.

Suggested Readings

Edmund L. Andrews, "Greenspan Concedes Flaws in Deregulatory Approach," *The New York Times,* late edn. (October 24, 2008), p. B1.

Michael W. Hudson, *The Monster: How a Gang of Predatory Lenders and Wall Street Bankers Fleeced America—and Spawned a Global Crisis* (New York: Times Books, 2010).

Gretchen Morgenson and Joshua Rosner, *Reckless Endangerment: How Outsized Ambition, Greed, and Corruption Led to Economic Armageddon* (New York: Times Books, 2011).

Jeremy J. Siegle, "Economy Blame Game," *Kiplinger's Personal Finance* (April 2008), p. 47.

David Singleton (Dir.), *The Flaw.* Film, New Video Group (2011).

ISSUE 8

Are the Risks of Derivatives Manageable?

YES: **Justin Welby**, from "The Ethics of Derivatives and Risk Management," *Ethical Perspectives* (vol. 4, no. 2, 1997)

NO: **Thomas A. Bass**, from "Derivatives: The Crystal Meth of Finance," *The Huffington Post* (May 5, 2009)

ISSUE SUMMARY

YES: In 2008, most of the world watched in horror as the U.S. stock market nearly collapsed, bringing down other monetary world markets with it. Justin Welby contends that derivatives are an important and ethical investment practice, but one that involves risks. He claims that the risks should be understood well before participating in these investment practices.

NO: Thomas Bass claims that the market failures were due in large part to mismanagement of these investments he compares to crystal meth. In this 2009 article, he recommends widespread regulation of these instruments or no use of them at all.

This business ethics book is filled with a variety of arenas of business ethics. Understanding these issues is vital for individuals to be well educated in both ethics and business concerns. The issue of derivatives is more specific than many of these issues, but in 2009, it is estimated to be one of the largest potential disasters lurking behind the scenes of many business transactions. In examining derivatives, we learn about many of the dangers behind these complex financial investments. Author Thomas A. Bass makes an analogy between derivatives and the "world's biggest betting parlor." Astute businessman Warren Buffett is quoted as calling them "financial weapons of mass destruction." It is estimated that in 2009, Buffett may have lost as much as $67 billion in derivative transactions. It is no surprise that Bass can't find any justification for continuing the practice of unregulated derivatives, but he doesn't hold much hope for this conclusion.

Valuing derivatives is generally determined by what someone else is willing to pay for a contract. Imagine the scenario that "A" will be worth "B" if

"C" happens. In some respects, it appears to be financial fantasy. As Justin Welby explains, derivatives are "financial instruments based on other products, whether physical or financial. The other products may themselves be derivative."

Welby is a business scholar and rector, and he finds that with care, derivative contracts can be appropriate with the proper balance of "courage and prudence." Welby calls derivatives powerful and reminds us that "power needs monitoring and controlling." It appears that in today's derivative market, there has been little monitoring, control, or ethical considerations of derivatives.

Derivative contracts are discussed in notional amounts because no one can determine the true values with certainty. Bass and others watching the markets estimate that the outstanding notional value of derivatives is more than $1.144 quadrillion. Quadrillion is probably a number not yet used in any of our readings. Bass explains that currently the U.S. real estate market is valued at $23 trillion, and the stock market is valued at less than $15 trillion. The U.S. gross domestic product is at $14.2 trillion.

YES

Justin Welby[1]

The Ethics of Derivatives and Risk Management

1 Derivatives

Derivatives are financial instruments based on other products, whether physical or financial. The other products may themselves be derivative. Three main forms of derivative exist: futures, options and swaps.

1.1 What Are They?

Futures—Futures originated in the agricultural markets, with the establishment of contracts for future delivery of produce. A farmer might sell next year's potatoes now, thus locking in his return. Derivatives based on physical products remain crucial and enormous markets, covering everything from orange juice to oil. A derivative contract was at this point a contract to take or deliver a given quantity of a specified quality of the product at a particular place and time in the future, and at a price agreed today.

In the 1970s there was a substantial growth in financial derivatives, starting in Chicago, and based on instruments such as US treasury bills and bonds (short or long term promissory notes of the US government). In the 1980s these derivatives spread geographically, with markets opening in London (LIFFE) and France (MATIF), as well as the Far East, in Tokyo, Osaka, Singapore and Hong Kong. All major financial centres now have a derivatives market. They have also spread in form, with new contracts being invented. These have covered all the principal physical products that were freely traded and most financial instruments.

Options—The most important development has been the invention of the option contract. This is fundamentally different from a futures contract in that on the buyer's side a right but not an obligation is obtained (other than the obligation to pay for the option), and on the seller's (technically 'writer's') an obligation but no rights.

Options are based on a complicated mathematical analysis of the volatility of the underlying product. A buyer of an option is making two assumptions at least, (1) that the product will move in value by more than the cost of the option, and (2) that volatility of price movement will at least not decrease. A writer makes one or both of the opposite assumptions. A trader of options

From *Ethical Perspectives*, July 1997, pp. 84–92. Copyright © 1997 by Ethical Perspectives. Reprinted by permission.

should be neutral as to the price but be taking a position on volatility. The earliest option contracts were in the Foreign Exchange (FX) market, on the 'cable' (to be traded internationally using the Atlantic telegraph cable) traded on the Philadelphia stock exchange. The market has developed rapidly so that most large cash contracts and futures contracts now have associated option contracts.

Swaps—The swap market was the last of the major developments in derivatives. It started in the late 1970s. Developing rapidly in size, it is now capable of supporting huge volumes of transactions and underpins a great deal of the activity in the international debt capital markets.

In a swap, two borrowers exchange interest rate obligations. Typically a party with floating rate interest obligation in a currency (e.g. £) undertakes to pay a fixed rate of interest on the same amount of principal to a second party with a fixed rate obligation who pays a rate of interest to the first party based on an agreed floating rate of interest. Each has then effectively exchanged cash flows. Variations on the theme are possible, for example, across two or more currencies. The advantages to each side are considerable. They can manage their exposure to interest rates without needing to raise new loans, and may take advantage of good access to a particular market (e.g., long term fixed interest rate pounds for a large UK company) without being forced to remain exposed to that market if they want a different obligation (for example floating interest rate US$).

1.2 Where Do They Happen?

Derivatives markets usually started as exchange based, linked to a geographical market such as the Chicago Board of Trade (CBOT). However, the financial derivatives (and some others, especially gold and oil) rapidly developed 'over-the-counter' markets (OTC), with no physical location. Major banks act as market-makers and trade the instruments for their own account. This was especially true in the swaps and options markets. It led to a deepening of liquidity and flexibility in the relevant markets and a proliferation of derivatives of derivatives. Examples are 'swaptions', options on swaps, and combinations of different derivatives intended to cause particular cash flow effects. This is where it is easy to lose money!

1.3 Who Uses Them, And Why?

There are three main categories of derivative user:

Producers—Almost all internationally traded commodities have a futures contract somewhere. Whether the producers are nations or companies, they tend to use the derivative markets to hedge price risk, that is, establish a certainty of future prices. This may be to protect a producers' price cartel, or simply as a means of avoiding sudden and unexpected adverse movements. Typically, producers are the most powerful single group in a commodity, but not a controlling group.

Consumers—Consumers are the mirror image of the producers in commodities, or almost any company of medium to large size in the financial derivatives markets. They may be issuers or investors in securities. Again the aim is to prevent surprises, or lock in what is seen as a favourable rate or price of a financial product or security.

Intermediaries—These may be banks, brokers or simply speculative traders. They are likely to provide up to 90% of the volume in any market, but their influence on price is less clear and is the subject of much argument. Their activity provides essential liquidity but also increases volatility. They will often have no underlying interest whatever in the commodity. However, without their participation the markets themselves could not exist. A technical mishap in the North Sea in the 1980s led to one US bank trading in oil futures becoming the proud owner of a physical tanker full of crude oil in a falling market, to the great satisfaction of many oil companies.

2.1 Should We Try to Manage Risk?

The ethical question with regard to financial risk has at its core the ethics of risk management, and the desire for predictability in the future. Risk management involves looking at the justice of the distribution of risk rather than only the relative benefits in a consequentialist manner.[2] In general terms this is obvious in the normal running of life. I should take normal precautions against harm provided that they do not lead to harm to someone less able to protect themselves. It is ethical to test the strength of ice before walking on it, but not to do so by putting my children on it first, on the grounds that their earning power is less than mine and they are therefore more expendable.

In retail finance this is seen in 1980s and 1990s legislation on Investor Protection. The burden of risk in ensuring that a product is suitable for the purchaser has shifted dramatically from a caveat emptor approach to fall squarely on the seller. Thus in any sale of life products the majority of the paperwork is less about the product than whether the purchaser has had all the legal and prudential warnings. It is recognized that a life company is in a far better position to assess risk than an individual, and must make sure that the investor has had the risk management carried out on their behalf. Legislation directs that more weight is given to an ethical than market driven distribution of risk.

2.2 The Risks of Risk Management

All action to resolve risk creates risk. Yet in financial markets inaction is in itself the adoption of a risk profile. As a portfolio manager, to invest or leave reserves in cash are both risk choices. In FX, to engage in the use of option strategies creates many risks, not to do so creates others. Even Boards of Directors have begun to recognize this as the risks of risk management have loomed larger in professional thinking.

In response to the Leeson affair, Proctor & Gamble, Metallgesellschaft, Orange County and lesser known events, the burden of managing risk management has grown, to the point where its consumption of resources in non-financial firms must begin to pose ethical questions even in consequentialist terms.[3]

3 Ethical Perspectives on Risk Management

The question must be asked whether it is ethically justified to use resources in this way. Risk is inherent in life; new financial instruments are often loosely thought of as hedges when they are risk management tools. There is a responsibility for managers who use them to recognize the true nature of what they are doing. Given that most instruments are copious users of energy and other intangible resources of the business, as well as having a risk profile deriving from their use at all, they must be justifiable in terms of consequence, rule or virtue.

3.1 Justifiable in Terms of Consequence

No market is morally neutral.[4] "It both expresses and needs a moral framework which is wider than the market itself. This framework can quite properly justify the basic operations of the system. But because it is a wider moral framework it will also correct and supplement those operations in the light of values to which the market itself appeals."[5]

This is true, but most ethical discourse in finance is essentially a form of debased utilitarianism or consequentialism. The question we ask too often is "does it have good results?", rather than "is it good?" There is a sense in which that is right: any ethical conclusion must have a reason, though the reason may become "God says so." But in business ethics the result has become more and more narrowly defined. One result of this is seen in the common and fallacious argument that ethical behaviour is good because it contributes to the bottom line. The moral framework becomes a subsidiary of the market. Looking at the subject of derivatives has brought this home to me with fresh power. My first thought was "what harm can they do?" I used derivatives for many years, without qualms, as a means of protecting the interests of the company for which I worked. They provide a focused, transparent and efficient method of adjusting price to supply and demand. In the oil industry they were certainly less damaging in their results than the cartel of the 1970s, OPEC, with its indifference to the poorer countries, its corruption and overwhelming greed. At least the derivatives market in oil seems impersonal. The counterparty is invisible.

This is a classically utilitarian argument of the greatest benefit to the greatest number. Similar arguments are ready to hand in other markets. Financial derivatives may lower the cost of capital by allocating it more efficiently to those best able to access it who then pass on some of the benefit through the swaps market. Currency derivatives may ease the risk of cross-currency investment. Some benefit in terms of risk management will at least be intended for all users of derivatives where the use is driven by commercial considerations other than those of trading in derivatives. Within the derivatives markets themselves this issue is extreme. It is a truism to say that a market price cannot be wrong, it is simply a price. In a futures trading pit no ethics exist except performing what you have promised.[6] Inevitably therefore, our comments are from outside the structure of concepts that many practitioners would consider valid.

The consequences of trading in complicated and risky instruments may be more subtle than accounting can reveal. Risk is not always measurable but at times may be inherent in the ethos of an organizational system, part of the culture, like safety. Whatever the controls, a company with a high risk ethos is likely to run high risks. In the early 1980s, at the time of the panic caused by the run on the US bank, Continental Illinois, the Financial Times commented, "Banks should be boring." The use in financial organizations of many of the new financial instruments requires the recruitment of teams whose rewards are usually linked to performance on a profit centre basis. This in itself creates a high risk ethos which is a ratchet that progresses inevitably, and whose culture is often more powerful than all the controls that can be invented.

Although many new financial instruments may benefit many companies and people (look at the example of the new availability of flexible fixed rate mortgages in the UK, all derivative based), like nuclear power, the accidents can have massive fall-out. It is far from clear that the greatest good of the greatest number is the result of the unfettered development of new financial instruments. Even the largest banks seem unable to prevent losses through rash or unauthorized dealing: "banks may have abandoned the safe role of the banker in roulette or the bookmaker at the races in favour of gambling themselves."[7]

3.2 Justifiable in Terms of Rule

The argument so far is that derivatives have their uses but also have a great potential for harm. They concentrate power without accountability. They distance markets from the reality of the people producing. They tend to self-deception about the nature of the world. But they cannot be banned. Nor should they be. Properly used they add flexibility and risk management to investment decisions, and can facilitate wealth creation. Three controls are suggested: capital adequacy, trading restriction and open declaration.

There should be strict limits on the amount of capital (and hence open positions) that any institution can commit to derivatives. This could include step ups in capital allocation once a certain size of position had been reached. There would have to be some concept of concert-party. The explicit aim should be to make it prohibitively expensive, and obviously unacceptable, for a small group of traders to run positions that can control a market. Trading should be restricted so as to prevent excessive volatility. This has worked in New York since 1987. After a certain move, trading must close for a period.

The companies or people who may trade need close regulation. Any use of derivatives over a de minimis level should require regulatory approval. In particular the use of exotics should require evidence of adequate systems to monitor and reveal risk, and a level of independent audit.

Finally, companies using derivatives that are not traders should have to publish a policy, for example after the statement of accounting basis, on the use, limits and intention of derivative involvement.

3.3 Justifiable in Terms of Virtue

3.3.1 Transparency

Both in the secular philosophical and the religious traditions of European thought, transparency is thought of as a virtue. Iago may be clever, but is nevertheless a villain because of his dissembling. In the Wagnerian cycle one may feel that Siegfried is a muscle bound idiot, but still a hero because of his transparency. Candide is naïve, but his transparency is seen by Voltaire as virtuous. John's first epistle has the famous exhortation to "walk in the light" with one another and with God. King David's uniqueness is not his moral uprightness but his honesty and openness in his walk of faith, expressed most clearly in Psalm 51. Straightforward dealing is a City virtue ("dictum meum pactum," the motto of the London Stock Exchange, etc.) and is enshrined in legislation and regulation.[8]

The virtue of transparency is not only ethical but a management aim in order to understand risk. Its benefits lie behind reforms in accounting, the break-up of conglomerates, the fashion for mission statements that control priorities, and concern over derivatives. We cannot manage what we cannot see. A recent Accounting Standard Board discussion paper on financial instruments aims for this. "The issue is that, whatever basis [of accounting] is used, it should be unambiguous, universal and simple."[9]

Transparency is not only for self-preservation, in that false information leads to false markets, but applies even when there is no obvious consequential harm, as is often seen in insider trading. Transparency is a virtue even of consenting adults in private, as well as in the open market, and its importance is being reinforced.

3.3.2 Self-awareness

Another virtue is self-awareness, considered as such from Aristotle onwards. New financial instruments compel a proper and well balanced view of the nature of the company and its outlook. They increase corporate self-awareness, and encourage a willingness to resist the fatalistic approach to the future that diminishes the significance of human free-will.[10] Like health and safety rules, they encourage the management of risk, and thus focus an organization on its proper objectives. They encourage a proper balance between prudence and risk, leading management to take the risks it should, and transfer others to those better able to carry them. An oil exploration and production company may hedge interest rate and foreign exchange risk, buying certainty in contrast to the vagaries of the drill-bit.

3.3.3 Between Recklessness and Immobility

An ethics of virtue raises questions when risk management becomes obsessive, and behaviour such as cowardice is first held in contempt and then treated as pathological in extreme cases. It is recognized that an obsession with risk paralyses action, and that there is a proper balance between recklessness and terrified immobility. An honest living with the fact of risk and its consequences is seen as a good. This is a view deeply rooted in all human ethical traditions, and in the European seen at its most sophisticated in the Stoics.

The same balance is reflected in the Judaeo-Christian tradition. Within the Bible there is a tension between faith in the ultimate goodness of God in all circumstances[11] and an avoidance of recklessness that tests providence and faithfulness.[12] This same tension is reflected in common law in the Anglo-Saxon tradition with the tests of reasonable care and contributory negligence. The search for a risk free life is seen in such absurdities as the famous McDonald's coffee lawsuit in the US, where a jury initially awarded damages of $2,000,000 (reduced on appeal) to a woman who was scalded while simultaneously driving and trying to drink a hot cup of coffee. In legal ethics such cases are seen as increasingly indefensible. The opposite extreme is found at the Pont du Gard, near Nîmes, an unrailed and crumbling Roman aqueduct with a vertical drop of over 100 feet. Anyone can walk across, if they dare, the only caution being a rusty sign saying "Les vents puissent s'enlever," perhaps translatable as "gone with the wind!."

If one takes the three main approaches to ethics, the consequentialist, deontological and virtue based, it is clear that the last two place risk management as one sensible preoccupation among others, without giving it primacy.

Conclusion

The widespread and elaborate use of new financial instruments among corporate entities and financial institutions requires justification. It faces the charge of increasing both the level and complexity of risk in the financial system under the pretext of reducing it. It is a prodigious user of management resources and IT. It obscures the integrity of the nature of the non-financial user.

It is not mere academic argument to question the ethics of certain instruments. Both in the US and the UK certain forms of financial instrument are deemed too risky to be used by all and sundry.[13] Other forms of instrument may be banned outright, even though many financial professionals will be perfectly capable of measuring the risk involved.[14] The force of this attack is recognized in the financial industry. One defence frequently put forward is similar to that of the National Rifle Association in the US about guns. It is the users, not the product, that are the problem. "One misconception is that derivatives are risky instruments that are used for speculation. It is more accurate to say that derivatives are instruments that can be used to alter risk profiles."[15] The mere fact of an instrument existing is no reason to use it. The biggest advocates of exotic options are bankers. Practising Treasurers spend much time seeking to distinguish between the fascinating idea which the bank's rocket scientist wants to try, and the derivative that will genuinely benefit the company. The fact that many of these instruments are harmful or spurious does not mean they should be banned, but neither does the absence of a ban make them ethical.

The ethical question to ask for the non-financial corporation has to do with the proper balance of courage and prudence. Will this instrument enable the company to carry out its proper task with more focus and self-awareness, or is it an attempt to neutralize the proper risks that we are paid to take? For financial corporations the inevitable presence of derivatives poses two issues. First, are they intrinsically valuable or simply so complicated that no client could use them and monitor the new exposures involved? Secondly, will the active management of our positions created by this activity result in a change in the nature of our business, and if so, has this been clearly communicated to the world around?

On reading this again I am once more struck by a remark made to me by a clergyman long before I was ordained. "What is an ethical Treasurer?" One of the major challenges in the field of financial ethics is the development of an adequate, and clearly communicated, measure of the intrinsic ethics of finance.

This paper is not arguing that derivatives are wrong, but that they are powerful, and power needs monitoring and controlling. The events of October 1987 are often referred to as the meltdown of the markets. My clear memory is of the whole executive board of directors standing in my office gazing in awe at a Topic Screen (showing FTSE prices) as waves of red chased across the screen. The use of nuclear metaphors was apt. A system that seemed safe had assumed a life of its own. There is little doubt that derivatives fuelled the reaction.

Notes

1. Justin Welby has been Rector of St. James's Anglican Church, Southam in Warwickshire, England, a small market town, since 1995. Before that he was assistant minister (curate) in a depressed urban industrial parish in the Midlands of England from 1992. Before being ordained he worked in the oil industry, first for Elf Aquitaine in Paris, and then as Group Treasurer of Enterprise Oil in the UK. During that time he had experience of projects throughout the world, especially in Nigeria and the North Sea. He is a member of the British Association of Corporate Treasurers, and is still involved in aspects of finance work. He holds degrees from Cambridge and Durham universities.

2. 'Risk' in *New Dictionary of Christian Ethics*. SCM, p. 557, see also *The Common Good*, Catholic Bishop's Conference 1996, § 77, p. 19.

3. Stewart Hodges, Director, Financial Operations Research Centre at the University of Warwick, pointed out, in a complicated article dealing with the effects of delta hedging using the Black-Scholes model, that "the risk exposure is constantly adjusted in response to market movements" and that this leads to very high turnover (thus costs and transaction risks); "in fact the expected level of turnover is proportional to the square root of the number of revisions [of the hedge following market movements], becoming unbounded in the limit." Cf. 'Current Research on Derivative Products' in *Treasurer*, November 1991, p. 6 and 9.

4. Dr Robert Song, at Cranmer Hall, Durham University, has been very helpful in discussing this.

5. Richard Harries, *Is There a Gospel for the Rich?* Mowbray, 1992, p. 95.

6. The film 'Trading Places,' with Eddie Murphy, is an enjoyable and generally accurate way of understanding this.

7. 'Editorial' in *Treasurer*, April 1995.

8. Stock exchange listing regulations, especially obligations on disclosure of material facts, insider trading legislation and Takeover Panel rules about concert parties, would be three examples.

9. David Creed (Group Treasurer Tate & Lyle PLC), 'A personal view of the ASB's Financial Instruments Discussion Paper' in *Treasurer*, October 1996, p. 16.

10. The basic argument in an article by Gay Evans (Chairman International Swaps and Futures Association), 'The Great Contradiction' in *Treasurer*, October 1996, p. 30.

11. e.g. Daniel 3:17–18 and Romans 8:28.

12. e.g. Deuteronomy 6:16 and Matthew 4:7.

13. Investing in private placements in the US, and the 'sophisticated investor' test under the FSA.

14. Pyramid selling schemes.

15. Gay Evans, *op. cit.*

 **NO**

Derivatives: The Crystal Meth of Finance

In May 2008, Warren Buffett, the great "value" investor from Omaha and America's second-richest man, announced on the eve of his annual shareholders' meeting that he had lost $1.6 billion in bad bets on derivatives. Most of this loss came from shorting put derivatives on Standard and Poor's Index of 500 leading stocks and on three other foreign stock indexes in Europe and Japan. In laymen's terms, Mr. Buffett had placed a bet—a very large bet, which wiped out 64% of Berkshire Hathaway's profits—that global stock markets would rise instead of fall.

Preparing for this year's shareholders' meeting, Mr. Buffett announced in February 2009 that his gambling on derivatives had resulted in an "accounting loss" of $14.6 billion, with $10 billion of this loss coming from his wrong-way bet that global stock prices would rise. On the eve of the meeting itself, on May 2nd, the *New York Times* reported that Buffett's "worst-case exposure" had risen to $67 billion. After the company's fourth quarter net income fell 96%, Berkshire was stripped of its triple-A debt rating by both Fitch and Moody's, and this was in spite of the fact that Buffett owns twenty percent of Moody's parent company.

How could the Oracle of Omaha be getting burned by derivatives? Was this the same Warren Buffett who in 2002 warned that "Derivatives are financial weapons of mass destruction, carrying dangers that, while now latent, are potentially lethal"? Buffett had promised his shareholders that he would avoid these "time bombs . . . for . . . the economic system," but here he was, seven years later, announcing that the crystal speed of derivatives had got a fearsome hold on him.

Derivatives have got a fearsome hold on all of us, but my fellow journalists, who missed the story in the first place, are still avoiding the subject. They file an avalanche of twitters describing every move made by someone like Bernie Madoff, because this is a story anyone can understand. "I trusted the guy. I gave him my money. He stole it." Camera cues to tears glistening on cheeks. It's a wrap.

But derivatives? Financial weapons of mass destruction? Shorting puts on the S&P 500? *Whoa, man, how am I going to get my mind around* this *story?* How am I going to explain the exquisite pleasure that comes from using this crystal meth of finance? Why do derivatives exist in the first place, and why have they become the world's biggest betting parlor, in spite of the fact that no one understands the size or nature of these bets?

As the Oracle of Omaha confessed in his recent "letter to shareholders,"

"Improved 'transparency'—a favorite remedy of politicians, commentators and financial regulators for averting future train wrecks—won't cure the problems that derivatives pose. I know of no reporting mechanism that would come close to describing and measuring the risks in a huge and complex portfolio of derivatives."

Buffett goes on to say,

"Auditors can't audit these contracts, and regulators can't regulate them. When I read the pages of 'disclosure' in 10-Ks of companies that are entangled with these instruments, all I end up knowing is that I don't know what is going on in their portfolios (and then I reach for some aspirin)."

By now the entire world is joining Mr. Buffett in reaching for some aspirin. Why, for example, did AIG, the biggest financial meth freak on the street, refuse for six months to report on what it had done with the $200 billion that the United States Treasury has dumped into its coffers, and why is there still no public disclosure of the company's assets and liabilities? The answer to the first question is that both AIG and the U.S. government were too embarrassed to announce, in this age of global markets, that much of the bailout money has gone overseas, with sixteen of the top twenty-two recipients being foreign banks. And how much more money will be required to keep AIG in the game? No one knows the answer to this question, or, to quote the great physicist Neils Bohr, "Prediction is difficult, especially of the future."

So why have derivatives got such a fearsome hold on our financial system? What is this speedy form of finance, and why, assuming that we will not be setting the clock back to Year Zero, will derivatives be around—transformed and traded differently, perhaps, but around—for the foreseeable future?

A derivative is something that takes its value from something else. It is a bet on a bet, a second order gamble that General Motors stock will rise or fall or that the S&P Index of 500 stocks (which includes General Motors) will rise or fall. As the Oracle of Omaha wrote in his 2002 letter to Berkshire Hathaway shareholders:

"derivatives . . . call for money to change hands at some future date, with the amount to be determined by one or more reference items, such as interest rates, stock prices, or currency values. If, for example, you are either long or short [on] an S&P 500 futures contract, you are a party to a very simple derivative transaction—with your gain or loss derived from movements in the index."

These deals get more complicated when you start betting on household mortgages or car or student loans. The underlying transactions are sliced and diced into financial securities that are tied to interest rate fluctuations or some other aspect of currency or financial futures.

The key word here is "future." If I sell you a share of General Motors stock, you pay me, and the deal is done. If I sell you a derivative contract with General Motors sliced into it, I am selling you a contingent future payment for which I could be liable twenty years down the road.

This is why my friends in finance *like* derivatives. They see them as a kind of voting system, where today's prices reveal people's expectations about the future. But this is also why Warren Buffett calls derivatives "financial weapons of mass destruction." Given the boom and bust nature of capitalism, betting that the markets will not explode twenty years down the road is a matter of faith, not finance.

Exploded derivatives contracts are called toxic waste, and the institutions holding these bad bets are called zombies, because they would be bankrupt and buried save for the public handouts that keep them among the "living dead." We have borrowed these terms from epidemiology and Afro-Caribbean voodoo because the situation is really quite terrifying.

Let's start with a simple question. How big is the market in derivatives? No one knows, because no one has been recording or regulating these contracts, many of which are traded over-the-counter via telephone calls or electronic signals from one banker or hedge fund trader to another. Derivatives are a kind of "shadow banking system" because the black box trading systems that deal in them can easily shade into black market operations good at money laundering, tax evasion, or outright theft.

Tom Foremski, a former reporter for the *Financial Times*, and British analyst D. K. Matai, using data compiled in 2007 by the Bank for International Settlements in Basel, Switzerland, estimate that the outstanding notional value of derivatives is $1.144 quadrillion. To help you get your mind around this number, we are talking about more than a thousand trillion dollars. This sum is made up of $548 trillion in listed credit derivatives and $596 trillion in over-the-counter derivatives, which includes trading on interest rates ($393 trillion), credit default swaps ($58 trillion), foreign exchange ($56 trillion), and commodities ($9 trillion).

These numbers indicate the face value of contracts currently traded, but if any of these contracts were to default, which has been happening recently with some frequency—either because the financial markets have frozen up or the financial institutions trading these contracts have gone belly up—then the numbers would be discounted. So instead of saying that the world is currently on the hook for a quadrillion dollars in derivatives, let's cut the number in half and say that the world's derivative bubble is only $500 trillion.

How big is $500 trillion?

The gross domestic product of the United States is $15 trillion. The money supply of the United States—all the greenbacks currently in circulation—is also about $15 trillion. The gross domestic product of the entire world is $50 trillion. The total value of the world's real estate is $75 trillion. The value of the world's stock and bond markets is about $100 trillion.

As you can see, the world's derivative markets—even with a "half-price" sticker of $500 trillion—are huge, and if somebody as smart as Warren Buffett can get burned by trading derivatives then imagine how the rest of us suckers are faring. Lest you think that you, oh, virtuous reader, would never dabble in derivatives, stand warned that TIAA-CREF, Fidelity, and other guardians of your financial futures are big players in the world's derivative markets. As the

Oracle of Omaha wrote in 2002: "The range of derivative contracts is limited only by the imagination of man (or sometimes, it seems, madmen)."

Again, I hate to disabuse any of you readers who are Marxists, Maoists, anarcho-syndicalists, or goldbugs, but, unless we crank the clock back to Year Zero and bring Pol Pot out of the jungle to reorganize our financial system, derivatives are here to stay. A few flavors might disappear off the menu. One example is the formerly-trendy product known as "portfolio insurance," which blew up during the crash of 1987, when the markets began gapping downward so fast that the "insurance" written against this risk proved worthless.

The market in mortgage-backed securities—frozen last fall but thawed this spring with TARP money—will return. The market in asset-backed securities (covering things such as student loans), which was dead in its tracks last fall, until being resurrected with TALF money, will return. The market in credit default swaps (CDSs), which was suffering from an absence of liquidity that resulted in hair-raising volatility, will return. Foreign exchange rate derivatives, commodity derivatives, equity-linked derivatives, all will be with us next year.

And why is this? Derivatives are fun. Trading shares in G.M. is grandad's game. Trading puts on the FTSE with a LIBOR chaser is the hepped up work of testosterone-driven bonus boys. Derivatives are useful. They speed up the velocity with which money changes hands, and increased velocity means more volume. Playing the overnight float in the Asian markets and then zipping your money back for a day's work at the Merc effectively doubles your bank, even before you get the mojo going that allows you to leverage your investment ten-fold.

Derivatives fill out the mathematical space of financial markets (an argument made best by quants and computers). They lay off risk—or so say my financial friends, when they are not being blown up by bad bets. Derivatives do the work of Adam Smith's invisible hand. They transmogrify individual greed into the collective good. They exist not because they are complicated, but because people find them useful—and I am not talking merely about the dealers who profit from them.

The world economy sits on top of the world financial markets, and there is no hope of engineering an economic recovery without a functioning financial system. This is why the government is printing money and pumping it as fast as possible into TARPs, TALFS, and other bailouts designed the get the markets back in business—not the markets that deal in stocks and commodities, but those that operate in the high-speed world of derivatives. This is the big financial story of the day, and any journalist interested in doing more than compiling an updated version of Gustave Flaubert's *Dictionary of Received Ideas* should be covering this story.

POSTSCRIPT

Are the Risks of Derivatives Manageable?

In the fall of 2008, the housing market in the United States and worldwide took a nosedive. But government bailouts haven't done much to bring the prices of these homes back. Mortgages were sold off to secondary buyers, and then a variety of derivative securities were devised based on those mortgages. Next the securities were traded on something else—maybe A, B, or C. However, the original value of the real estate may have no relevance to the determination of the current value of A, B, or C. (Justin Welby explains in a detailed footnote the derivative real estate problem in Europe.)[1]

To be well educated in today's business and ethics climate, a student, investor, politician, or ordinary citizen needs to know about derivatives and weigh in on solutions for the future.

Perhaps it is time for a slightly contrarian view and an attempt to suggest ways in which ethical finance is more than an oxymoron. First, arguably ethical aims do not of themselves make actions ethical. It is possible to do the right thing in such a wrong way that it becomes the wrong thing. Especially in the sub-prime market it is arguable that in many ways the aims were good. Home ownership brings a level of security and commitment to an area, tends to reduce crime and vandalism, and promotes good citizenship. Enabling low income families to own homes is good. The fact that banks sought to make money out of doing so is also perfectly reasonable. Even the packaging of loans and selling them on can be portrayed as reasonable and prudent balance sheet management. But in all the activity any potential virtue was lost in poor execution.

Loan making pushed the boundaries of what was wise and prudent by allowing (in the UK) self certification of income, developing products that had hidden and unsustainable costs, and losing sight of the interests of the client borrower. Profit was maximized through excessive slicing of risks and the use of instruments of such complexity that they could not be tracked or valued. At the heart of the whole complexity was the steady and then rapid distancing of the original product and the final investor. Disintermediation began with investors and clients separated through exchanges or trading of an asset. Once the risk began to be sliced, in the end all that is left is a financial flow, or even an off balance sheet exposure.

---

[1] J. Welby, "Ethics Finance and the Human Factor," *The European Weekly: New Europe* (Issue: 810, December 1, 2008).

ISSUE 9

Should Price Gouging Be Regulated?

YES: Jeremy Snyder, from "What's the Matter with Price Gouging?" *Business Ethics Quarterly* (vol. 19, no. 2, April 2009)

NO: Matt Zwolinski, from "Price Gouging, Non-Worseness, and Distributive Justice," *Business Ethics Quarterly* (vol. 19, no. 2, April 2009)

ISSUE SUMMARY

YES: Jeremy Snyder contends that price gouging conflicts with the goal of equitable access to goods essential to a minimally flourishing human life. Efficient provision of essential goods is not sufficient to prevent serious inequities. Regulations are needed for equitable access.

NO: Matt Zwolinski argues that price gouging can be morally permissible, even though this does not mean that price gougers are morally virtuous. Considerations of the availability of institutional alternatives and distributive justice may render price gouging morally acceptable. In any case, regulations cannot be expected to resolve the moral issues more satisfactorily than the market itself.

Price gouging is often associated with notions like the powerful harming the needy. Often a natural disaster of some type occurs and people are in extreme need of goods. Suddenly, supply is short and demand is intense. In this condition, prices go up. The law of supply and demand is one of the staples of the business world. This law would allow for price gouging, but eventually, as supply and demand adjust to one another, the price will go down. Price gouging is probably as old as the business market itself.

Some business ethicists believe that during times of extreme need, prices should be regulated by the government to bring about stability to the disaster area more rapidly. For example, gas companies should be held to a standard price in the aftermath of a hurricane. Grocers or merchants should keep prices fair and stable in an effort to alleviate some of the pain during a disaster.

Thomas Aquinas, in *Summa Theologica*,[1] brings up the notion of the "just price." In essence, the notion of the just price says that the seller must not sell

---

[1] Saint Thomas Aquinas, In: T. McDermott (Trans.), *Summa Theologiae: A Concise Translation* (Allen, Texas: Christian Classics, 1991).

something for a higher price simply because the buyer is in a needy condition. But how does a merchant in a position of holding the goods that others need utilize self-control and keep prices at a normal rate? "Savvy" might be the term some would use in characterizing an individual who raises prices on needed goods during a disaster, thereby making a large profit. "Unethical" might also be a term for this type of behavior. Adam Smith is known as a defender of the free market. In his *Wealth of Nations*,[2] he explains how famines intensify when the government enforces a "just price" during a period of "scarcity or dearth." Smith explains that it is unacceptable for the government to impose prices on merchants during a time of "dearth." He believes that the artificial regulation increases the length of the famine because of the withholding of produce by merchants or farmers. For Smith, the price-gouging traders are working to control mass starvation. These merchants might be derided for their "gouging," but Smith explains that they merely offer the supply to meet the demand. They save the hungry from starving.

Many economists have commented on price gouging since the time of Smith, including our two authors.[3] What really is price *gouging*? Is it fair? Is it an acceptable practice?

---

[2] Adam Smith, *The Wealth of Nations* (New York: Classic House Books, 2009).

[3] William Sundstrom introduced us to the price gouging writings by Aquinas and Smith. Sundstrom, an economist, contributes to the Web site for the Markkula Center for Applied Ethics at Santa Clara University.

YES

Jeremy Snyder

What's the Matter with Price Gouging?

Prices for essential goods are likely to increase when a disaster strikes, should that event decrease available supplies of these goods, increase demand, or both.[1] Sometimes these price increases are condemned as 'price gouging' or 'profiteering.' Such labels are not intended as simply descriptions of price increases; rather, they carry a strong negative moral valence. In many cases, the moral wrong of these price increases is identified as wrongfully gaining from another's misfortune. Consider the common view that "[t]hings like selling generators for four and five times their cost is not free enterprise, that's taking advantage of other people's misery" (Rushing 2004, A-l). In other cases, price gouging is condemned as unfairly taking advantage of others' needs, language that is often associated with exploitation.[2]

But it isn't clear from these kinds of sentiments when a price increase amounts to price gouging or why, if at all, certain price increases following disasters are morally worrisome. Moreover, there are many reasons to think that price increases can create a net benefit for a community following a disaster. As one critic of anti-price gouging legislation puts it:

> Price to the left of the intersection of the supply-and-demand curve and you are guaranteed to vaporize whatever you are attempting to keep inexpensive. . . . The reason that gasoline is disappearing from service stations across the nation is because station owners aren't gouging with sufficient gusto. Whether out of a misguided sense of kindness, concern about what politicians might think, fear of bad press, or the desire to keep customers happy, they are pricing below what the market would otherwise bear and, as a result, their inventory has disappeared. Now, how are the poor being helped by service stations closing down for lack of fuel? Gas at $6 a gallon, after all, is better than gas unavailable at any price. (Taylor 2005)

Price increases lead to rationing by consumers and encourage increased production of scarce goods. If the aim of anti-gouging legislation is to prevent vendors from profiting too much from a supply disruption, then achieving this aim may come at the cost of a swift return to normal market conditions.

From *Business Ethics Quarterly*, April 2009, pp. 275–293. Copyright © 2009 by *Business Ethics Quarterly*. Reprinted by permission of The Philosophy Documentation Center, publisher of *Business Ethics Quarterly*.

In this paper, I discuss what moral wrongs, if any, are most reasonably ascribed to accusations of price gouging. This discussion keeps in mind both practical and moral defenses of price gouging following disasters.[3] In the first section of this paper, I examine existing anti-gouging legislation for commonalities in their definitions of gouging. I then present arguments in favor of the permissibility of gouging, focusing on the economic benefits of price increases following disasters. In the third section I present a critique of gouging based on specific forms of a failure of respect for others. This critique is followed by a discussion of means for avoiding gouging in practice and responses to objections to my view. As I will argue, even when morally defensible anti-gouging legislation is not in place, individual vendors will have a duty not to gouge their customers.

Price Gouging in the Law

At present, thirty-two states and the District of Columbia have passed some form of anti-gouging legislation. Although there is no federal anti-gouging law in the US, a bill targeting fuel price increases passed the House of Representatives in 2007. In order to develop a better sense of what actions raise worries about price gouging, I will briefly examine this body of legislation.

Anti-gouging legislation is typically triggered by the declaration of a state of emergency or disaster. This declaration may be made by the state governor, local officials, or even the President. In substantially fewer cases, anti-gouging legislation requires a declaration by public officials in addition to a declaration of emergency. The duration of the activation of anti-gouging controls can vary from the length of the declaration of a disaster to a fixed length of time or some mix of the two.[4]

Laws against price gouging limit price increases for goods during their period of activation. For the most part, price increases are allowed when they reflect increases in the cost of doing business following the disaster and, to some extent, changes in the market. For example, the Federal Trade Commission defined price gouging as occurring when "a firm's average monthly sales price for gasoline in a particular area is higher than for a previous month, *and* where such higher prices are not substantially attributable to *either* (1) increased costs, or (2) national or international market trends" (Federal Trade Commission 2006, 137). In many cases, these caps seek to factor in changes in the market and costs by allowing the price of goods to increase a certain percentage above the pre-disaster price. Otherwise, vague language prohibiting "unconscionable" or "gross" increases in prices is used.[5] At their most extreme, anti-gouging legislation may forbid *any* increase in the prices of goods beyond those justified by higher business costs. These more extreme restrictions are unusual and at present limited to Georgia, Louisiana, Mississippi, and Connecticut.[6]

Anti-gouging laws can be tied to all goods and services following activation of anti-gouging statutes[7] or limited to specific, essential goods. What counts as an essential good is often left undefined but can explicitly include dwelling units, gasoline, food, water, supplies for home repair, and pharmaceuticals.[8]

Despite many broad commonalities in state anti-gouging legislation, this overview reveals four key areas of disagreement and vagueness in determining what constitutes price gouging. First, there is disagreement as to how much of a price increase, particularly beyond what can be justified by increases in business costs, is allowable. Second, state legislatures disagree as to whether prohibitions of price increases should be extended to all goods and services or limited only to certain exchanges, although most favor the latter. Third, when legislation is limited to certain exchanges, there is disagreement as to what goods and services should be covered. Fourth, and most importantly from the perspective of this paper, when anti-gouging legislation uses moral language to justify itself, this language tends to be vague.[9]

In Defense of Price Increases

Anti-gouging legislation and charges of price gouging are common. While the precise nature of the moral wrong associated with gouging is unclear, there is widespread agreement that *something* is wrong about these price increases. Yet, there are many reasons to think that price increases condemned as gouging are morally innocent at worst and, more often, create a positive and morally praiseworthy benefit for all concerned.

In a gouging situation following a disaster, both vendor and customer understand the exchange to be to their advantage. Since the good being exchanged is likely to be something essential to the well-being of the customer (e.g., food, water, shelter), the exchange is actually likely to provide proportionally greater utility to the customer than the vendor even at the higher than usual price. While the vendor may stand to clear a larger than normal profit as a result of the disaster, the essential nature of the goods mean that they will be of enormous, possibly even life saving, benefit to the consumer. Despite the harms to the consumer and possibly vendor as a result of the disaster, the high price exchange does no harm in itself when compared to the welfare of each person following the disaster. Rather, the exchange will provide the customer with essential goods that increase her welfare.

While disasters create a temporary increase in the pricing power of vendors, this shift can easily be explained and justified by the rules of the market. A disaster is likely to cause a reduction in essential supplies. For example, fuel may no longer be able pass through ruptured pipes or closed roads. These disasters—or even the threat of one—may also create an increase in demand for essential goods, such as plywood for protecting homes. The resulting shift in the equilibrium point between supply and demand predictably creates an increase in prices for goods, especially for essential goods that have inelastic demand, without any untoward manipulation of the market. From the standpoint of the dynamic functioning of the market, these higher prices should be allowed and the market can be trusted to maintain itself (Jacoby 2004).

Not only are price increases explainable as a result of the natural functioning of the market, it is argued, they serve a beneficial purpose. High prices for essential goods have the effect of helping the market to return to pre-disaster prices. These prices achieve a signaling effect for both vendors and consumers (Hayek 1945). The high prices charged by vendors will lure other suppliers into the market, quickly increasing supplies of essential goods. An increase in supplies will meet increased demand and help move prices toward pre-disaster levels. Without these price increases, vendors may lack both the information and motivation necessary to enter the post-disaster market and increase supplies.

Defenders of price gouging argue that higher prices also aid in the conservation of scarce goods by making it more likely that they will be purchased by those who place the greatest value on them. These high prices also tend to ensure that scarce essential goods will be used sparingly. While ice might be valuable to those seeking to keep their beer cold following a hurricane, higher prices will tend to ensure that those purchasing ice put it to more highly valued uses such as preserving medicine and scarce food. This efficiency of allocation is coupled with a rationing effect created by higher prices. When fuel prices spike, generators that might have been used to power the air conditioning in an entire house will instead be limited to cooling a single room. As a result, fuel supplies that would have been exhausted quickly at pre-disaster prices are now prolonged (*Wall Street Journal* 2005).

The promise of price increases following a disaster can also help increase supplies of essential goods prior to the event. If the disaster is foreseeable (as in the case of a hurricane), suppliers can pre-position goods in the area likely to be affected. The prospect of higher prices encourages such preemptive actions and acts in the long run to keep prices relatively low, meeting the needs of far more people than otherwise would have been the case.

Some extra profit following a disaster can also serve as a fair reward for the efforts and risks undertaken by vendors. Vendors of scarce goods may go to extraordinary lengths to get goods to the market following a disaster. A vendor might pre-position goods in a likely disaster area at considerable cost to himself and at considerable risk if the disaster destroys these stocks or strikes too far away for the supplies to be of use. Vendors in the affected area might act to protect existing stocks of supplies from damage at great expense to themselves and perhaps at some sacrifice to their own safety. If some of these supplies are lost, the local vendor, too, will be a victim of the disaster. Those who bring needed goods into the affected area after the event may also forgo opportunities for profit at home, face high costs in transporting the goods to the affected area, and may be subjected to bodily danger if the disaster is still ongoing or law and order have broken down.

Given these positive economic effects, price increases following a disaster need not be morally troubling. In fact, it could be argued, given that the needs of the affected population are especially strong, the so-called gouger might even deserve special praise for her efforts. At the very least, her self-interested motives in the post-disaster market are not obviously different from those typically judged to be morally innocent in a normal market.

Price Gouging and Respect for Others

If there is something morally wrong with price gouging, it is not that gouging causes direct harms or economic inefficiency. In fact, a critique of price gouging will need to confront the positive moral value of the efficiencies and rationing effect created by price increases.

As I have noted, many anti-gouging laws are limited to price increases on certain goods that are tied to basic human needs. I believe that this characteristic of anti-gouging legislation offers an important insight regarding what is morally objectionable about price gouging. As not all types of price increases trigger the worry about gouging, it is not price increases themselves that motivate this concern. Rather, I would like to argue, it is price increases that undermine equitable access to certain, essential goods that motivate the worry about price gouging.

Put another way, worries about price gouging are engaged when price increases cut off poor consumers from necessary goods, not when price increases are unfair. We might think that price increases following a disaster are unfair in the sense that they allow for a large shift in the social surplus of the interaction in the favor of the vendor. If the normally functioning market serves as a benchmark for a fair transaction and fair distribution of the social surplus generated by that transaction, then the disaster shifts the equilibrium point between supply and demand in such a way that the vendor can now charge unfair prices for her products (Wertheimer 1996).

To see that it is not fairness, *per se,* that motivates concerns over price gouging, consider an example. An avalanche outside of an exclusive ski resort blocks the only road to the resort on New Year's eve. Because this road is blocked, a group of wealthy revelers at the resort no longer have access to a resupply of champagne that was to be used to celebrate the new year. While there is food, drink, and shelter to meet everyone's essential needs until the road is cleared, there is far too little champagne on hand to ensure that everyone will be able to make a toast at midnight. Because of the high value placed on participating in the midnight toast by the resort's wealthy patrons, the owners of the limited remaining supply of champagne are able to clear unusually high profits by selling their supplies.

The actions of these vendors could certainly be considered unfair by the lights of the normally functioning market. But to label these actions as a case of price gouging strains the normal use of the term.[10] Consider that the language surrounding gouging typically focuses on the vulnerability created by the disaster and the desperation of consumers to meet their basic needs. As the Attorney General of Texas put it, following gouging accusations in the wake of hurricane Ike, "They took advantage of the fear and the needs of people who were evacuating the Gulf Coast region, and they jacked up prices" (Elliott 2008). Price hikes for gasoline following that same hurricane again focus on the absolute needs of consumers: "It's sad to think that merchants would take advantage of people who are already struggling to fill their gas tanks just to get from home to work or from home to church and back" (*Jackson Sun* 2008). While the would-be champagne drinkers may be desperate to participate in the New Year's toast and willing to pay unusually high prices to do so, their desperation is of an entirely different kind than that which normally motivates the charge of gouging. It is the desperation of individuals for essential goods, rather than simply the unfairness of the transaction, that motivates accusations of price gouging following a disaster.

Having located the wrongness of price gouging in access to essential goods, we can now say more about the duty that price gouging violates. To be specific, I would like to argue that price increases following a disaster can undermine equitable access to the goods essential to minimal human functioning. When price increases do so, they violate the norm of equal respect for persons. Respect for persons is often understood in terms of a duty to treat others as ends in themselves. More specifically, this respect is expressed both through recognizing that human animals are capable of forming and acting on a conception of the good life but need material support in order to do so (Hill 1991).[11]

Proponents of various ethical theories can agree that basic respect for human persons will entail two components: Negatively, we should not interfere with others as they live out their conception of the good life given reciprocal respect and non-interference. Positively, we should aid others in forming and living out their conception of the good life, particularly by ensuring that they have the minimal means of developing such a conception. An attitude of respect for others will be expressed through our actions, including non-interference, positive support, and other expressions of the equal value of all human persons (Anderson 1993).

At first glance, it would seem that placing limits on the functioning of the market through anti-gouging legislation would run counter to the goal of respecting others' freedom to pursue their conception of the good life. In the first place, I have discussed how price increases efficiently bring new supplies of essential goods into the market and help ration existing supplies. In this way, free markets serve as a means of supplying the goods essential to forming and acting on a conception of the good life.

Secondly, in their ideal form, markets carry their own value as institutions that protect and enlarge human freedom.[12] By offering a space in which consumers can freely negotiate, consummate, and exit exchanges, markets ensure that consumers are not beholden to any particular vendor in their pursuit of the good life.[13] Adam Smith specifically defends markets in terms of their historical role in undermining the oppressive feudal system of production (Satz 2007). Under a feudal system, serfs are tied to single masters and denied the freedoms of movement and exit created by a well-functioning market. Without the freedom to exit from the feudal relationship, the serf is condemned to take whatever terms of exchange are offered by her master. In a market, on the other hand, the "tradesman or artificer derives his subsistence from the employment, not of one, but of a hundred or thousand different customers. Though in some measure obliged to them all, therefore, he is not absolutely dependent on any one of them" (Smith 1976, 420). Markets guarantee legal protections for persons so that the equal right to make exchanges is enshrined as an entitlement, creating political equality between richer and poorer (Anderson 2004). The moral concern that justifies the idealized institution of the market, then, is an interest in providing the material means to and institutional protection of individual freedom.

Conditions following a disaster can be highly non-ideal for a market, however, at least from the perspective of a stable balance between supply and demand. A disaster potentially results in a reduction of supply and spike in demand for some or all essential goods. While price increases reflect a new, post-disaster balance between supply and demand, over the short-term this new equilibrium point can be particularly disruptive to the lives of the poorest members of a community. Until the pricing signals created by the new equilibrium increase supplies of essential goods, prices will remain high and supplies may be insufficient to meet demand. This gap between supply and demand is morally troubling because the goods in question are essential to minimal human functioning and may be out of reach for the poorest members of the affected community. While price increases in a free market represent one means of restoring supplies and rationing existing stocks of essential goods, anti-gouging legislation offers an alternative approach to this problem.

There are many good reasons to think that, following a disaster, an unfettered free market does not best serve the freedom-enhancing purpose by which it is morally justified. While unfettered price increases work toward *efficiently* promoting increases in the supply of essential goods following a disaster, the concern that motivates price gouging laws is that an unfettered market in these goods runs counter to the goal of *equity*, a key component of respect for persons. This failure of equity takes place in terms of the distribution of scarce essential goods within the affected community.[14]

While price increases can decrease consumption rates of essential goods, they do so at the cost of giving the wealthiest members of a community the greatest access to limited supplies. This access is created in two ways. First, and most obviously, wealthy persons will have greater financial means with which to bid on scarce resources when they have been located (Ramasastry 2005).[15] Second, these persons will likely have greater access to the information and transport needed to locate and reach scarce resources. In an idealized market, free competition lowers prices in order to put essential goods into the hands of all but the poorest members of a community. Following a disaster, free competition gives greater access to these goods to those who have the greatest resources within a community.

Avoiding Price Gouging in Practice

A vendor concerned about the effects of unconstrained price increases on equitable access to essential goods might respond by retaining pre-disaster prices for his poorest customers while allowing price increases for the remainder. That is, instead of allowing price increases according to the market, a vendor might adjust prices according to each consumer's ability to pay. This response would have the benefit of protecting the vendor against committing the moral wrongs I have described while preserving some of the price signaling and rationing effects of price increases.

In practice, vendors will face a range of difficulties should they attempt to price goods according to consumers' ability to pay. A great deal of information will often not be available to the merchant, particularly the means available to customers for purchasing essential goods. While some vendors in smaller communities will be intimately familiar with the needs and vulnerabilities of their customers, typically this will not be the case, particularly if the vendor enters the market from outside of the community in response to a disaster.

Given this problem, legislators and vendors can take two steps in order to avoid the moral wrong that I have argued is associated with price gouging. First, legislators can adopt a typical strategy found in existing state price gouging legislation and limit price increases to the going market rate prior to the disaster, plus increases for additional costs and risks to the vendor. When legislation of this kind has not been enacted within a community, individual vendors should still take it upon themselves to moderate their price increases. The aim of this moderation is to prevent vendors from receiving windfall profits in the face of the desperate need of their individual customers. By raising prices only to reflect changes in costs and risks in the post-disaster market, vendors maintain their own access to essential goods without unduly worsening others' access.

This strategy presumes that the going fair market price enabled members of the community generally to meet their essential needs prior to the disaster. Of course, this is an imperfect strategy since some persons will be priced out of competitive markets for essential goods even under normal conditions. If the local market prior to the disaster does not provide access to essential goods for a large portion of the community prior to the disaster, then this benchmark for setting prices should be discarded. This problem demonstrates that pre-disaster prices can serve as a useful shortcut under conditions of uncertainty only; these prices do not carry normative weight of their own. Nonetheless, a competitive market, in conjunction with a social safety net to make up for those priced out of the market, will serve as a useful mechanism for distributing goods essential to basic functioning.

Because the exchanges under discussion are mutually advantageous, there is good reason to allow for prices to exceed slightly the pre-disaster rate. As I have noted, price increases following a disaster have the positive effect of increasing supplies, encouraging rationing, and discouraging waste. Insofar as the prices charged by merchants aim at these goals, they can also serve the goal of equitable access to essential goods. Therefore, limited price increases even beyond those justified by increased costs and risks can be justified. Otherwise, price increases merely promote the vendor's self-interest at the cost of the basic needs of those around her.

While even limited price increases achieve a rationing effect, they will typically need to be supplemented with non-price rationing mechanisms, such as caps on purchases. As a second step, legislators should impose caps on the purchase of essential goods in order to ration these goods without distributing them according to ability to pay. When these caps are not mandated by law, individual vendors should impose caps on the sale of their own stocks of essential goods. The limits placed by these caps should depend on supplies and demand for essential goods following a disaster and the needs of the local population. For example, rationing of generators will not be necessary in a post-disaster setting where ample electricity remains available. Therefore, attention to the context in which the disaster takes place will be essential to the proper execution of this step.

Caps on purchases retain some of the rationing effect of unlimited price increases without rationing according to ability to pay. Instead of distributing scarce goods to those with the greatest financial resources in a community, caps on purchases mimic a lottery for essential goods, treating all persons as equally deserving of the goods essential to basic human functioning. In practice, those individuals with the greatest resources within a community will retain some advantage in obtaining scarce goods under a system of purchasing caps. Well-off members of a community may be better able to obtain information about the location of scarce goods, to travel to the location of these goods, and to have the time to wait in line to obtain these goods compared to less well-off persons.

A coordinated, community-wide cap on purchases of essential goods would seemingly reduce this problem. A central authority could distribute equal numbers of vouchers for essential goods to each member of the community, and vendors would be required to sell essential goods only to those customers holding a voucher. Moreover, these vouchers could be accepted in lieu of payment, with the local government repaying vendors at a later time for their goods. This policy would limit all members of the community to the same numbers of essential goods with the added benefit of ensuring that even very poor persons would have an equal opportunity to access essential goods.

However, the level of coordination between vendors required for a community-wide cap is likely to be impractical given the disruption created by the disaster, at least over the short-term.[16] A system of caps on purchases enforced by individual vendors represents a compromise between achieving a rationing effect that is to the benefit of all persons within a community and ensuring that this benefit is spread evenly throughout the community. Insofar as the state and federal government are able to distribute supplies, those supplies should be distributed on a lottery basis.

Both of the steps I have recommended are restricted to essential goods. Since the moral concerns facing price increases are triggered by the capacity of customers to engage in minimal human functioning, those goods not necessary to this purpose may be given whatever price the post-disaster market will bear. Following a disaster, for example, an individual might desperately wish to replace a damaged wide screen, high definition television. If many other persons in the local community share this desire and supplies of the product have been disrupted by the disaster, we can expect that the market price of high-end televisions will rise substantially. But, because this product is non-essential, television vendors can ethically charge whatever price the market will bear for their products.[17] While would-be customers might resent this situation, by the standards of price gouging the merchant does not act unethically.

Recall that state price gouging legislation is divided on what price increases were acceptable following a disaster and on what goods should be covered by the legislation. My account suggests that, for the vendor operating under conditions of uncertainty, equal respect for all members of a community will require: 1) Limited price increases beyond those justified by increases in costs and risk; and 2) Caps on purchases of essential goods in order to ration supplies of these goods. Neither of these restrictions should apply to persons selling non-essential goods. These guidelines will be most relevant when the pre-disaster market is reasonably successful at meeting the basic needs of all members of the community. Therefore, contextual factors make these guidelines defeasible.

Objections

Matt Zwolinski (2008) argues against both the effectiveness of price gouging legislation and the immorality of price increases that are typically condemned as gouging. His positive argument hinges largely on the benefits created by price increases, which I have largely granted in this paper.[18] In order to strengthen my argument as to the immorality of these price increases, I will respond to two of Zwolinski's central arguments. First, I will address the 'non-worseness claim' (NWC) that it cannot be morally worse to engage in a voluntary and mutually beneficial exchange than no exchange at all. Second, I will consider Zwolinski's argument that price increases do not exhibit a failure of respect for consumers.

Zwolinski asks how we can criticize vendors who engage in voluntary and mutually beneficial exchanges while we ignore those who do nothing to help the needy in disaster areas:

> On the one hand, to the extent that we hold that price gougers are guilty of mutually beneficial exploitation, we hold that they are acting wrongly even though their actions bring *some* benefit to disaster victims. On the other hand, many of *us* do *nothing* to relieve the suffering of most disaster victims, and we generally do not view ourselves as acting wrongly in failing to provide this benefit—or, at least, we do not view ourselves as acting *as* wrongly as price gougers. (Zwolinski 2008, 356–57)

This "non-worseness claim" asks why we should condemn those who help bring needed supplies into disaster areas as "gougers" when we do not condemn those who stay home, helping no one.[19] That is, how can it be morally worse to engage in a voluntary and mutually beneficial interaction than to do nothing at all?[20]

In response, I believe that we must take the long view when assessing the moral principles underlying our actions. Individual actions, such as charging high prices for essential goods or sitting on one's couch in response to a disaster, may not tell the full story as to one's responsiveness toward the basic needs of others. One is not required to respond to every disaster nor every needy person in order to live a morally praiseworthy life. However, a *pattern* of failure to respond to the needs of others can exhibit a greater level of indifference toward the basic needs of others than is exhibited through a single instance of price gouging.

Zwolinski is right to note that some of those who charge market clearing prices following a disaster might be motivated both by self-interest and the benefits created for some consumers (Zwolinski 2008, 337–68). These motives may be morally superior to those of the person motivated to enter the disaster zone purely by self-interest. My point is that the person who chooses not to enter the disaster zone may be motivated purely by self-interest or have other, morally laudable responses toward the basic needs of her fellow humans. As the non-gouger's duty of beneficence has not been specified in the way that, as I have argued, the gouger's duty has been specified, she retains leeway as to how she will discharge this duty.

In order to assess a non-gouger's underlying moral motivation, we must consider her responsiveness to others who lack access to essential goods. For example, does the non-gouger rise from her couch to help some other persons in situations of desperate need? Or is she solely moved to maximize her own welfare? In the latter case, the non-gouger can be accurately assessed as being guided by more morally problematic principles than those that guide a gouger who is motivated both by self-interest and the needs of others. The NWC, then, is false when motivations are assessed through sets of actions rather than single, morally ambiguous actions.

A second concern raised by Zwolinski also hinges on the positive consequences created by price gouging. Given that the exchanges I have been discussing are mutually beneficial and voluntary, Zwolinski questions whether placing limits on these exchanges is in keeping with respect for others:

> Exploitation might plausibly be argued to manifest a lack of respect for the personhood of the exploitee. But laws against price gouging both manifest and encourage similar or greater lack of respect. They manifest a lack of respect for both merchants and customers by preventing them from making the autonomous choice to enter into economic exchanges at the market-clearing price. They send the signal, in effect, that *your* decision that this exchange is in your best interest is unimportant, and that the law will decide for you what sorts of transactions you are allowed to enter into. (Zwolinski 2008, 352–53).

That is, if consumers are not forced into these exchanges—and in fact they desperately seek them out—how can it be consistent with respect for others' choices to rule them out of bounds?

I have argued that proper respect for the needs of others demands that vendors moderate their price increases and engage in non-price rationing. This argument does not hold that agreements between vendors and consumers at market clearing prices are coercive. Rather, vendors ought to limit their price increases and legislators ought to pass laws requiring vendors to do so. These restrictions aim to aid the entire post-disaster community while distributing essential goods more equitably. My claim is not that individual freedom is unimportant, but that the market may not support freedom equitably following a disaster.

Zwolinski defends his position by noting, "Price gougers treat their fellow human beings as traders, rather than as brothers and sisters in the Kingdom of Ends. But to treat someone as a trader is still a far cry more respectful than treating him as an object" (Zwolinski 2008, 359). Perhaps so, but I have argued that a disaster disrupts the market in a way that makes it *inappropriate* to treat one's fellow human beings as traders. When the market is functioning under normal conditions, it can be appropriate to treat one's fellow humans as traders in market transactions, especially in the presence of an adequate social safety net. This is so because the institution of the market creates a space in which self-interest and hard bargaining enhances the freedom of all persons. Following a disaster, however, the market fails to behave in this way over the short-term, pricing the poorest members of the community out of the market for essential goods.

Conclusions

If my account of the wrongness of price gouging is correct, it supports three major conclusions. First, the moral wrongs associated with price gouging should be understood generally as failures of respect for others. Vendors who ration scarce essential goods according to ability to pay undercut the goal of equitable access to essential goods within their community. This failure of respect takes place in a setting where the vendor owes a specified duty of benef-icence to her customers and alternative means of achieving price signaling (through modest price increases) and rationing (through purchasing caps) are available.

Second, price gouging is only possible in transactions involving some good essential to living a distinctly human life. Price increases for diamonds, for example, are not instances of price gouging under my account. Moral wrongs, such as unfairness, may accompany price increases for non-essential goods. These wrongs, however, are distinct from the wrongs I have ascribed to price gouging.

Finally, the potential for price gouging will depend on the extent and strength of non-market social institutions for distributing essential goods. If these institutions are in place prior to a disaster and survive that event, price gouging is unlikely to occur even if vendors freely raise their prices in the post-disaster market. Individuals are more highly susceptible to price gouging in communities where entitlements to essential goods are weak or non-existent. Therefore, the moral wrong of price gouging cannot be reduced merely to price increases for essential goods following a disaster, even if these prices cannot be justified by increased costs.

The general shape of anti-gouging legislation gives a good rule of thumb for avoiding gouging. Price gouging legislation should allow for price increases justified by changes in the costs and risks of doing business. Otherwise, price increases should be limited and vendors should be required to ration their goods by placing caps on the number of purchases of essential goods. These limits on the market should be triggered by declarations of a state of emer-gency and limited to essential goods. Price controls should be restricted to the area affected by the disaster rather than entire states (Rapp 2005/2006). If price gouging legislation along these lines should prove to be deeply impractical or has not been enacted in a community, vendors should still constrain their market transactions along these lines.

Many cases of what are sometimes popularly called gouging are not morally problematic under my account nor considered cases of gouging. We should expect price increases on many goods following a disaster and many, if not most, of these increases will be justified by increases in cost, supply disruptions, and increased risk. However, in the most egregious cases, price increases cannot be justified in these ways, giving justification to the charge of price gouging as representing a kind of moral wrong.

These observations depend on an account of price gouging as a kind of failure of respect for others, but I hope to have shown that this account tracks well with widespread intuitions as to when and why certain price increases are morally problematic while revealing where those intuitions are unjustified. In practice, determining whether gouging has taken place will require great attention to local context, as shaped by the goal of equitable access to goods that meet the essential needs of consumers.

Notes

1. I am grateful to Robert Leider, Maggie Little, Daniel Levine, Leigh Anne Palmer, David Skarbek, Justin Weinberg, and Matt Zwolinski for their extensive comments on earlier versions of this paper. I am also thankful to the participants in a presentation of an earlier version of this paper at the 2008 APA Pacific Division Annual Meeting.

2. For example, a proposed federal anti-gouging law bans "taking unfair advantage of the circumstances related to an energy emergency to increase prices unreasonably." See . . . (accessed May 28, 2008). New York's anti-gouging law (NY GEN BUS S 396-r) is justified by the need to prevent vendors "from taking unfair advantage of consumers during abnormal disruptions of the market." In broader terms, USA Today condemns gougers as 'Vultures' (McCarthy 2004). Similarly, Florida Governor Charlie Crist complained that "It is astounding to me, the level of greed that someone must have in their soul to be willing to take advantage of someone suffering in the wake of a hurricane" (Jacoby 2004, F11).

3. I will use the term "disasters" to include any event that creates physical damage to a discrete area, disrupting the normal functioning of the market. These events include both natural disasters such as hurricanes and man-made disasters such as terrorist attacks.

4. For a helpful summary of US anti-gouging laws, see Skarbek & Skarbek 2008.

5. See, for example, Michigan (Mich. Stat. Ann. §445.903(z)), Missouri (15 CSR §60-8.030), and Texas (Tex. Bus & Com. Code §17.46(b)(27)).

6. See Geoffrey Rapp (2005/2006).

7. For example, California, Connecticut, the District of Columbia, Hawaii, and Mississippi make general prohibitions against price increases. California prohibits price increases generally for consumer goods and services (Cal. Pen. Code §396), Connecticut includes any item (Conn. Gen. Stat. §42-230), DC any merchandise or service (D.C. Code §28.4101 to 4102), Hawaii any commodity (Haw. Rev. Stat. §209-9), and Mississippi all goods and services (Miss. Code Ann. §75-24-25).

8. See generally the American Bar Association's summary of state legislation at: . . . (accessed May 28, 2008).

9. When explicit justification for anti-gouging legislation is given, references to 'unfair' prices is most common. The language of unconscionable and gross price increases, drawn from the common law tradition, are frequent as well (Rapp 2005/2006).

10. If one feels that 'price gouging' can appropriately apply to the champagne example, we can discriminate between two senses of price gouging. 'Fairness gouging' can apply to price increases on all goods following a disaster or other market disruption while 'needs gouging' will be limited to price increases on essential goods. As I argue, 'needs gouging' is at the heart of the moral wrong that is typically associated with gouging.

11. The goods essential to minimal human functioning are supported through various non-essential goods. For this reason, I will also discuss non-essential goods like electrical generators, gasoline, and ice that are, in many communities, instrumental to the durability of essential goods such as food, water, and adequate shelter. Insofar as the essential goods are relevant to the wrongness of gouging, these non-essential goods will be relevant as well.

12. Of course, disagreement will take place as to what corresponding regulatory environment best supports this freedom-enhancing function.

13. This point has been made by authors as diverse as Milton Friedman (1962) and Amartya Sen (1999).

14. There is a long history within Judeo-Christian and Islamic thought condemning excessive price increases against vulnerable populations. These restrictions are motivated by concerns about oppression of the weak. Consider, for example, Leviticus 25:14: "And if thou sell ought unto thy neighbor, or buyest ought of thy neighbor's hand, ye shall not oppress one another." More generally, see Brewer 2007, 1104–06.

15. In some cases, even wealthy persons following a disaster may not have the immediately available resources to afford price increases on essential goods. When referencing 'the wealthy' I intend those with the resources available to afford price increases rather than those with the greatest savings and assets within a community. My thanks to an anonymous reviewer for pointing out this ambiguity.

16. Moreover, such a system, even if it could be established, would likely create or exacerbate a black market in essential goods (Rockoff 2002). See also Abhi Raghunathan (2005).

17. By the standards of fairness, the price *might* be morally problematic. At the least, however, the vendor does not gouge his customer by the standard I am proposing.

18. There is some disagreement on this point, however. Geoffrey Rapp (2005/2006, 553–59) argues that anti-gouging laws are economically justified in two ways. First, they help preserve hard currency reserves when a disaster or terrorist attack disrupts electronic payment systems such as ATMs. Second, they counteract the effects of pricing irrationality that prevent efficient pricing during market disruptions.

19. Zwolinski discusses price increases among vendors who bring goods into the post-disaster market whereas I have focused my discussion on vendors with goods already in the market. The risks and opportunity costs faced

by outsiders may be different from those of locals, meaning that outsiders and locals may be justified in offering different prices for their goods based on different levels of risk and cost. I discuss the relevance of vendors' risks and costs to post-disaster prices in the previous section. The source of these goods, however, is not relevant to the basic moral wrong of price gouging.

20. Alan Wertheimer (1996, 289–93) describes the non-worseness claim as holding that an interaction Y between A and B cannot be morally worse than no interaction at all if Y makes both A and B better off when compared to a baseline of no interaction. In other words, the NWC denies the possibility that a mutually beneficial exploitative interaction can be morally worse than no interaction at all.

Bibliography

Anderson, Elizabeth. 1993. *Value in ethics and economics.* Cambridge, MA: Harvard University Press.

_____. 2004. Ethical assumptions in economic theory: Some lessons from the history of credit and bankruptcy. *Ethical Theory and Moral Practice,* 7: 347–60.

Brewer, Michael. 2007. Planning disaster: Price gouging statutes and the shortages they create. *Brooklyn Law Review,* 72: 1101–37.

Elliott, Janet. 2008. Two hotels face lawsuits for raising rates. *The Houston Chronicle* (October 3).

Federal Trade Commission. 2006. *Investigation of gasoline price manipulation and post-Katrina gasoline price increases.* . . .

Friedman, Milton. 1962. *Capitalism and freedom.* Chicago: University of Chicago Press.

Hayek, Friedrich. 1945. The use of knowledge in society. *American Economic Review,* 35(4): 519–30.

Hill, Thomas. 1991. *Autonomy and self-respect.* New York: Cambridge University Press.

Jackson Sun. 2008. Go after those who may be price gouging. *The Jackson Sun* (September 17).

Jacoby, Jeff. 2004. Bring on the 'price gougers.' *The Boston Globe* (August 22): F11.

Kittay, Eva. 1999. *Love's labor: Essays on women, equality, and dependency.* New York: Routledge.

McCarthy, Michael. 2004. After the storm come the vultures. *USA Today* (August 20): 6B.

Nussbaum, Martha. 2000. *Women and human development.* New York: Cambridge University Press.

Page, Edward, & Cho, Min. 2006. Price gouging 101: A call to Florida lawmakers to perfect Florida's price gouging law, *Florida Bar Journal,* 80: 49–52.

Raghunathan, Abhi. 2005. South Florida shortages fuel black market. *St. Petersburg Times* (October 29): 1B.

Ramasastry, Anita. 2005. Assessing anti-price-gouging statutes in the wake of hurricane Katrina: Why they're necessary in emergencies, but need to be rewritten. *Findlaw* (September 15). Available at. . .

Rapp, Geoffrey. 2005/2006. Gouging: Terrorist attacks, hurricanes, and the legal and economic aspects of post-disaster price regulation. *Kentucky Law Journal,* 94: 535–60.

Reader, Soran. 2003. Distance, relationship and moral obligation. *The Monist,* 86: 367–81.

Rockoff, Hugh. 2002. Price controls. In David R. Henderson (Ed.), *The Concise Encyclopedia of Economics.* Indianapolis: Liberty Fund, Inc. Available at...

Rushing, J. Taylor. 2004. Storms stir up price gouging. *Florida Times-Union* (September 18):A-1.

Satz, Debra. 2007. Liberalism, economic freedom, and the limits of markets. *Social Philosophy and Policy,* 24: 120–40.

Sen, Amartya. 1992. *Inequality reexamined.* Cambridge, MA: Harvard University Press.

———. 1999. *Development as freedom.* New York: Knopf.

Skarbek, Brian R., & Skarbek, David B. 2008. The price is right: Regulation, reputation, and recovery. *Dartmouth Law Journal,* 6(2): 235–76.

Smith, Adam. 1976 (1776). *An inquiry into the nature and causes of the wealth of nations.* Ed. R. H. Campbell, Andrew Skinner, and W. B. Todd. Oxford: Oxford University Press.

Snyder, Jeremy. 2008. Needs exploitation. *Ethical Theory and Moral Practice,* 11: 389–405.

Taylor, Jerry. 2005. Gouge on. *National Review Online* (September 2). ...

Treaster, Joseph. 2004. With storm gone, Floridians are hit with price gouging. *New York Times* (August 18): A1.

Waldron, Jeremy. 2003. Who is my neighbor?: Humanity and proximity. *The Monist,* 86: 333–54.

Wall Street Journal. 2005. In praise of 'gouging.' *Wall Street Journal* (September 7): A16.

Wertheimer, Alan. 1996. *Exploitation.* Princeton, NJ: Princeton University Press.

Zwolinski, Matt. 2008. The ethics of price gouging. *Business Ethics Quarterly,* 18: 347–78.

Matt Zwolinski  **NO**

Price Gouging, Non-Worseness, and Distributive Justice

Price gouging tends to evoke from humane and decent people an immediate and overwhelming sense of repugnance.[1] Most people have a strong sense that price gouging involves a kind of predatory behavior—a ruthless satisfaction of individual greed at the expense of the vulnerable—and that it must therefore constitute a serious moral wrong. Indeed, recent research in moral psychology suggests that this kind of "gut" reaction against price gouging might be very deeply rooted in us indeed. Instinctive and powerful reactions against the exploitation of the vulnerable may have served our early ancestors well by promoting the cohesion and survival of the small groups in which they lived.[2] But while reliance on automatic emotional reactions might have worked well for our primitive ancestors, such reactions are of little help in coming to a sophisticated and subtle understanding of the many and varied questions bearing on the morality of price gouging.[3] For such an understanding requires us to do more than simply decide whether "price gouging" is "good" or "bad." It requires us to discriminate among the many forms price gouging can take—between, for instance, an established merchant's raising prices to cover increased costs of supplies and risk, and a low-level entrepreneur who is drawn by the lure of high profits to begin selling items for the first time in the wake of a disaster. And it requires us to discriminate between the many different kinds of moral evaluations we can make of price gouging—whether it ought to be morally permissible or impermissible; whether it is morally praiseworthy, morally blameworthy, or merely morally tolerable; whether we have good moral reasons to prohibit it by law or by social pressure; and so forth. Each of these questions in turn raises a host of differing and difficult subsidiary questions that require both careful empirical research and thoughtful philosophical analysis to fully address.

Fortunately, Jeremy Snyder's paper on the subject contains no shortage of precisely this sort of thoughtful analysis.[4] Although his conclusions differ in some ways from my own,[5] he nevertheless provides a carefully argued case for the immorality of price gouging, while at the same time demonstrating an admirable sensitivity to the many morally attractive features of a free-market price system. Still, in spite of its many strengths, there are some points at which Snyder's position is less clear or less well-defended than it might be. Rather than continuing to sing the praises of what is generally a very fine piece of work, then, I shall focus my comments on what I take to be two problematic areas of his paper—first, Snyder's rejection of the non-worseness claim appears to be based on a misunderstanding of the kind of moral objects to which that principle is meant to apply; and second, Snyder's appeal to considerations of distributive justice and equal respect for persons is flawed insofar as it rests on two false assumptions—that price gouging undermines equitable access to vital goods, and that a regime in which price gouging is banned promotes equitable access. I will conclude with some brief comments on how Snyder's evaluation of price gouging compares with my own.

1. The Non-Worseness Claim

One of Snyder's major objections to my argument stems from my use of the "nonworseness claim" (NWC) to defend price gouging against the charge that it is wrongfully exploitative. NWC, as I described it, holds that "in cases where A has a right not to transact with B, and where transacting with B is not worse for B than not transacting with B at all, then it cannot be seriously wrong for A to engage in this transaction, even if its terms are judged to be unfair by some external standard" (Zwolinski 2008: 357). If the NWC is true, then it is hard to see how standard cases of price gouging can be serious moral wrongs. After all, most of us would think that an individual who could sell generators to victims of a disaster but chose not to do so would be acting within his rights (even if we also believe that she would be acting less than fully virtuously), and it also seems clear (Snyder himself concedes this [Snyder 2009: 277–78]) that those who buy from price gougers at inflated prices are nevertheless better off as a result than they would have been had the transaction not taken place at all. So, since gouging someone is better for them than neglecting them, and we have a moral right to neglect them, must we not therefore have a moral right to gouge them as well? How could gouging possibly be worse than neglect?

Snyder takes issue with this argument by holding that it fails when "motivations are assessed through sets of actions rather than single, morally ambiguous actions" (Snyder 2009: 288). Price gougers might indeed be acting in ways that help their customers, Snyder concedes, but they might be doing so only out of the vicious motive to extract as much profit as possible out of people in desperate need. Of course, they *might* be doing it out of a sense of morally virtuous beneficence as well. We can't tell just by looking at one action in isolation. To determine whether a person is properly motivated by a responsiveness to the needs of others, we need to look at their pattern of action as a whole, and not just one isolated instance.

This reasoning seems correct, as far as it goes. But it is not clear what lesson Snyder thinks he can draw from it. At times, Snyder writes as though he is making a point about the *moral character* of the price gouger and what it takes to lead a "morally praiseworthy life" (Snyder 2009: 287). With this point I am in full agreement—indeed it is one which I tried to make myself in part five of my paper (Zwolinski 2008: 366–68). One's moral character is a matter of one's general disposition to see the needs of others as reason-giving and to respond appropriately to those reasons. And the act of price gouging is too morally ambiguous for us to read this disposition (or its absence) off of it. But NWC is not a thesis about moral character, it is a thesis about the wrongness of moral *acts*. And this is importantly different. Vicious people can perform morally permissible actions. Think, for instance, of Kant's shopkeeper who returns the correct change to a naïve customer *only* out of a selfish concern for his own reputation and long-term profit. If he could be sure he could steal a penny from a child's change and get away with it, he would, but prudence dictates restraint. Such a person has a bad moral character. But the act he is performing—giving the child back her correct change—is perfectly innocent. The distinction between these two moral assessments becomes clear, and especially important to recognize, when we think about their respective implications for third parties. If we see a person—vicious or innocent—performing a morally *impermissible* action then, all else being equal, we should try to stop him, either as individuals or perhaps through the collective institutions of the state. But there is no comparable reason for us to try to stop someone from doing that which it is morally permissible for her to do, even if the person doing it is morally vicious. Her moral viciousness might give us *other* kinds of reason for action. We might have reason to censure her and get her to see the intrinsic value of all persons. And, in the case of Kant's shopkeeper, we might be very hesitant to patronize her store for fear that circumstances in the future will *not* always tip the scales of self-interest toward the side of honesty. But we do not have reason to interfere with her performance of a morally permissible act, or even to morally condemn the act, though we might have reason to morally condemn the agent.

Thus, Snyder's concerns about NWC do not give us reason to prohibit price gouging, or even condemn it. For all his arguments show (correctly, I think) is that price gouging can sometimes be done by morally vicious people. They do not show that the act of price gouging itself is morally impermissible. And that is all that my use of NWC was ever meant to deny.

2. Distributive Justice

One of the most common criticisms of price gouging, and one which is central to Snyder's argument as I understand it, is that it leads to vital resources being distributed in a morally objectionable way. Because price gouging involves charging a higher than normal price for goods, it disadvantages those who are poor relative to those who are well off. According to Snyder, price gouging thus undermines equitable access to essential goods, and thereby manifests a lack of equal respect for persons (Snyder 2009: 280).

However, the claim that price gouging undermines equitable access to goods is problematic for two reasons. First, it is the *emergency* that undermines equitable access, not whatever price gouging may occur in response to that disaster. Prior to the emergency, there is generally a well-functioning market in food, water, and other vital goods that generally ensures that all who need these goods will be able to purchase them. Emergencies lead to either a sharp increase in the demand for, or a sharp decrease in the supply of, these goods, and it is *this fact* that undermines equitable access. When supply and demand are radically altered so that there are not enough goods to go around, *no* method of distribution will produce equitable access—at least not at levels sufficient to meet people's needs.[6] Some people will get the goods, and others will not.

This is true of all methods of distribution, including Snyder's proposed method involving legislatively imposed caps on both the price of essential goods and on the amount of those goods that any consumer can purchase. Such a method of distribution, Snyder says, "mimic[s] a lottery for essential goods, treating all persons as equally deserving of the goods essential to basic human functioning" (Snyder 2009: 285). But the lottery metaphor, while apt in its characterization of a system of this sort, is puzzling as a way of highlighting the alleged distributive justice of such a system. For a lottery has seemed to many—most memorably to John Rawls—the paradigm case of moral arbitrariness (Rawls 1971: 74). In a lottery, some will obtain goods, some will not, and the difference between the two is nothing more than brute luck. In Snyder's lottery-like system, people will likewise be divided into "Haves" and "Have-Nots," and the difference between them will be based on who manages to get in line before supplies run out. This may not be *entirely* a matter of luck—perhaps it gives an edge to the perceptive, or those with a lot of time on their hands to stand in line. But it can hardly be said to be a system that distributes in accordance with any characteristic of great moral significance.

Furthermore, the sense in which it can be said to be a system that treats people as "equals" is at best a highly attenuated one. Because the context in which such a system operates is one where demand greatly exceeds supply, it is highly unlikely that the result of such a system will be equal units of vital goods being distributed to each person. For non-divisible goods like generators and radios, there will simply be no alternative to some people getting the good while others go away empty-handed. Other goods like ice could theoretically be divided into equally sized units for each person. But such a proposal is rife with practical difficulties. What if the portions of the good, once equally divided, are too small to be of any practical use? A bag of 300 ice cubes equally divided among 300 people is almost infinitely less useful than the same bag of ice in one person's hands. How is the relevant 'community' among which equal distribution is to take place to be defined? How are shopkeepers to determine what an equal unit of the good should be? And, most significantly, what sort of restrictions are to be put on the use to which people's shares of the good may be put? Will people be allowed to sell their goods to others—even though this would be certain to undermine equitable access?[7] Or will such secondary markets be prohibited?

The only kind of equality that Snyder's system can hope to achieve, then, is equality of *opportunity* to access vital goods. But this too, on closer examination, turns out to be less satisfying from a moral perspective than we might have hoped for. For in reality, opportunity under Snyder's proposed system will *not* be equal. Even if the system runs perfectly, those who show up first to a vendor will have a better opportunity than those who show up later. And in reality, rationing systems like the one proposed are often subject to corruption that favors 'insiders'—those with a personal, religious, ethnic, or other connection to those with resources or the power to affect their distribution.[8] It is true that nothing in Snyder's proposed system directly makes access to vital goods contingent on wealth, so with respect to *that* variable opportunity may be said to be equal. But in reality, and with respect to other equally if not more arbitrary variables, opportunity will not be equal.

Finally, it is worth noting that while Snyder's proposed distributive mechanism seeks to mimic while improving upon the *allocative* function of prices, it makes *no* effort to mimic their equally if not more important *signaling* function.[9] Prices that increase and decline in response to changes in supply and demand are important not only to allocate scarce resources among competing uses, but to signal when too much or too little social resources are being invested in a particular activity. In particular, the high prices that vital goods like water, sandbags, and hotel rooms command in the wake of a disaster signal to entrepreneurs to provide *more* of these goods, and indicate that larger-than-normal profits can be made by doing so. Post-disaster high prices thus convey both the *information* that increased supply is needed, and the *incentive* to provide that additional supply. But in so doing, high prices provide their own best corrective—as profit-seeking entrepreneurs rush to reap the windfall profits that the radically altered balance of supply and demand makes possible, they increase supply and in doing so drive the price down to something approximating its pre-disaster equilibrium. This means that the window of opportunity during which price gouging can occur is narrow, *but only if individuals are free to set prices as they see fit.*

This point is crucial. No one, not even those of us who argue that price gouging is morally permissible, thinks that price gouging is unqualifiedly *good* in the sense of being something that would occur in an ideal world. Cases of price gouging occur in circumstances of desperate need and terrible suffering. And in the short run, price gouging is just one more allocative mechanism among others, with the result that some people's needs—often the needs of the poorest and most vulnerable—will go unmet. But policies and moral injunctions that prevent prices from rising freely in the wake of a disaster do not diminish the desperation of the short run; they simply make it harder to move past that short run into a period of recovery. This might not be the case if we could rely on all people to act on the principles of beneficence that Snyder enjoins. And indeed, one of the most heartening aspects of some of the recent natural disasters in the United States has been the extent to which beneficence *has* been effective in delivering vital goods and services to those who so desperately need them. But it is probably a permanent feature of the human condition that there will always be less beneficence to go around than is needed. And in such a condition we would do well to take as much advantage as we can of the market's ability to channel individual self-interest toward socially desirable ends. In some cases, as is demonstrated in the response of Wal-Mart and Home Depot to Hurricane Katrina, even narrow self-interest will not lead to price gouging, and this is a happy result.[10] But where it does, we should recognize that gouging ought to be tolerated not as an end in itself, but merely as a method of making a very bad short-run situation less bad (by conserving scarce resources and allocating them effectively) and also of making that short run as short as possible (by providing incentives to increase supply).

3. Conclusion

Despite the concerns raised above, Snyder's ultimate position on the morality of price gouging does not seem to be too distant from my own. We both believe that price increases in the wake of a disaster can, in some circumstances, be not only morally permissible but positively morally desirable insofar as they serve to promote the interests of those suffering in the wake of a disaster. And we both believe that under other circumstances, price gouging can be wrongfully exploitative. The main differences between our views seem to be two: we differ regarding the precise conditions under which price gouging becomes wrongfully exploitative, and we differ regarding the desirability of the legal regulation of price gouging.

On the first of these differences, Snyder's position is somewhat unclear. He states that some "price increases condemned as gouging are morally innocent at worst and, more often, create a positive and morally praiseworthy benefit for all concerned" (Snyder 2009: 277). They do this, he notes, in many of the ways I discussed in my own paper: they aid "in the conservation of scarce goods by making it more likely that they will be purchased by those who place the greatest value on them" (Snyder 2009: 278), they send signals which lead "other suppliers into the market, quickly increasing supplies of essential goods" (Snyder 2009: 278), they provide an incentive to merchants to "increase supplies of essential goods prior to the [disaster]" (Snyder 2009: 278), and they serve as a "fair reward for the efforts and risks undertaken by vendors" (Snyder 2009: 278). And Snyder seems to indicate that insofar as price increases are necessary to serve these morally praiseworthy goals, they are morally permissible, as when he writes that "price increases even beyond those justified by increased costs and risks can be justified" insofar as they increase supplies, encourage rationing, and discourage waste (Snyder 2009: 285).

The question this raises, then, is under what conditions price gouging *will not* be morally acceptable on Snyder's account. The only clue Snyder provides to an answer is that price increases will be unacceptable when they "undermine equitable access to certain, essential goods" (Snyder 2009: 279). But this is puzzling, since price increases can presumably serve the morally praiseworthy goals described above (e.g. increasing rationing, discouraging waste) while *at the same time* undermining the equitable access of individuals to those goods. Indeed, it seems likely that the only way that price increases *can* promote goals like allocative efficiency and signaling new supply is by undermining equitable access, since these price increases will operate in a context in which individuals will face dramatically different budget constraints. This suggests that we cannot hope for both equitable access and the morally attractive benefits of price increases, and it is not clear which of these Snyder's account counsels us to choose in the (possibly ubiquitous) cases of conflict.

The second difference between Snyder's account and my own is that I favor the repeal of all laws prohibiting or regulating price gouging, whereas Snyder thinks some regulation is appropriate. Here, again, it is easy to overstate the differences between our accounts. We both think, as far as I can tell, that current laws are a bad idea insofar as they prohibit many mutually beneficial exchanges that would not be objectionably exploitative. But Snyder does seem to suggest that there is some role for the legal regulation of price gouging, and that it will involve limiting permissible price increases to those necessary to promote allocative efficiency, signal new supply, and compensate for increased risk and costs to merchants (Snyder 2009: 285). Now, I actually think that Snyder provides a fairly exhaustive list of the morally praiseworthy aspects of price increases, such that somebody who knowingly increased her price beyond this level could properly be described as satisfying her individual greed with no morally redeeming side-effects. So as an account of the conditions under which price increases are *morally praiseworthy*, I don't have much to disagree with in Snyder's proposal. But as a proposal for the *legal regulation* of price gouging (or even the social regulation of price gouging in the forms of boycotts/social pressure), I have a serious problem with it. The problem is that by Snyder's standard, it is virtually impossible to know whether any given price increase is moral or immoral.[11] What percentage price increase is necessary to encourage the optimal level of rationing among one's consumers? In trying to answer this question, the merchant at least has the advantage of observing the behavior of her customers and seeing who responds in what way to a certain rate of price increase. But how will the merchant know who *should* be buying less, and who *should* be buying more? How would legislators know this? And what hope does a merchant or a legislator have—even if she is lucky enough to have a PhD in econometrics—of predicting the level of price increase necessary to attract sufficient supply to where it is needed?[12]

Thus, even if Snyder's list of morally relevant criteria is complete, it is useless as a standard of regulation because we cannot ever know if we are satisfying it. My contention is that the best hope we have of finding a price that approximates the satisfaction of these criteria is to let that price emerge through the free choices of numerous individuals in the market. This, too, is an imperfect mechanism, since actual prices do not always and necessarily reflect a proper balance of supply and demand, nor do they even purport to approximate "fair rewards" for risk and effort. Market prices, in other words, are not a perfect measure of moral significance. My claim, though, is that given the constraints in knowledge faced by those who would be charged with regulating prices, reliance on market prices in post-disaster contexts does a better job at promoting our moral values than any feasible alternative mechanism.

Notes

1. For a discussion of the role of repugnance as a reaction to price gouging and other forms of market exchange, see Roth 2007: 43–44.
2. For an overview of the possible evolutionary origins of "deontic" moral intuitions, such as those which tend to be invoked against the permissibility of mutually beneficial exploitation, see Greene 2007; Haidt 2001; Prinz 2008.

3. They may also be less helpful in a world in which distant, impersonal relationships have replaced close-knit societies as the locus of interpersonal interaction, and in which the distant indirect and non-obvious effects of our actions have an increasingly great relative causal significance on human well-being as the direct and visible ones. On this point, see Hayek's discussion of the extended order in Hayek and Bartley 1988: chap. 1, but also the concluding sections of Greene 2007.

4. Snyder 2009.

5. See Zwolinski 2008. See also Zwolinski forthcoming.

6. Of course, one could guarantee equity of a sort with a policy that bans distribution of the good altogether. Such a policy, if effectively enforced, could result in each person getting an equitable share of nothing.

7. Here we face a problem similar to that illustrated by Robert Nozick's famous Wilt Chamberlain example (Nozick 1974: 160–64). The maintenance of an initially equal distribution will require either a prohibition on trades or continual redistribution. And since Snyder's proposal is not to initially distribute *all* resources equally, but only to provide equal access to certain vital resources, the difficulty of maintaining equality will be even greater.

8. See, for a discussion, Alchian and Allen 1968: 95–99.

9. On this distinction, see Zwolinski 2008: 360–64.

10. Steven Horowitz has documented the response of the private sector to Hurricane Katrina, noting that in the two weeks following the disaster Wal-Mart shipped over 2500 truckloads of needed goods to Louisiana, a substantial portion of which was given away free. This quick response time was made possible by Wal-Mart's elaborate mechanisms for tracking storms before they hit in order to ensure that its stores are well stocked prior to the time that demand increases. Neither Home Depot nor Wal-Mart engaged in price gouging in the aftermath of Katrina. And while it is possible that this restraint was at least partly motivated by altruistic concerns, no doubt a large part of it was motivated by the recognition that their behavior during this highly public and emotionally charged disaster situation would affect consumers' future willingness to give them their business. For established retailers, post-disaster deals are but one move in a long series of iterated prisoners' dilemmas with customers, and in such contexts mutual cooperation is often the strategy best in accord with individual self-interest (Axelrod 1984). Or, as one Home Depot executive put it, "I can't think of a quicker way to lose customers than price gouging." See Horowitz 2008; Horowitz forthcoming.

11. The problem is that no individual or group of individuals has sufficient information to know what price would be necessary to satisfy the criteria Snyder sets out. This problem is essentially just a specific instance of the more general knowledge problem discussed by Friedrich Hayek in Hayek 1937, 1945; and elsewhere.

12. There is strong evidence that even well-trained economists are severely limited in their ability to predict how actual markets will respond to events like a change in the general price level, much less a change in the price charged by one particular merchant. See, for a discussion, Gaus forthcoming; Gaus 2007.

Bibliography

Alchian, A., and W. Allen. 1968. *University Economics,* 2nd ed. New York: Wadsworth.

Axelrod, R. 1984. *The Evolution of Cooperation.* New York: Basic Books.

Gaus, G. F. 2007. "Social Complexity and Evolved Moral Principles," in *Liberalism, Conservatism, and Hayek's Idea of Spontaneous Order,* ed. P. McNamara. London: Palgrave Macmillan.

———. Forthcoming. "Is the Public Incompetent? Compared to Whom? About What?" *Critical Review.*

Greene, J. 2007. "The Secret Joke in Kant's Soul," in *Moral Psychology, Vol. 3: The Neuroscience of Morality: Emotion, Disease, and Development,* ed. W. Sinnott-Armstrong. Cambridge, Mass.: MIT Press.

Haidt, J. 2001. "The Emotional Dog and Its Rational Tail: A Social Intuitionist Approach to Moral Judgment," *Psychological Review* 108: 814–34.

Hayek, F. A. 1937. "Economics and Knowledge," *Economica* 4: 33–54.

———. 1945. "The Use of Knowledge in Society," *American Economic Review* 35(4): 519–30.

Hayek, F. A., and W. W. Bartley III. 1988. *The Fatal Conceit: The Errors of Socialism.* Chicago: University of Chicago Press.

Horowitz, S. 2008. *Making Hurricane Response More Effective: Lessons from the Private Sector and the Coast Guard During Katrina.* Washington, D.C.: Mercatus Center.

———. Forthcoming. "Wal-Mart to the Rescue: Private Enterprise's Response to Hurricane Katrina," *The Independent Review* 13(4).

Nozick, R. 1974. *Anarchy, State, and Utopia.* New York: Basic Books.

Prinz, J. 2008. *The Emotional Construction of Morals.* Oxford: Oxford University Press.

Rawls, J. 1971. *A Theory of Justice,* 1st ed. Cambridge: Belknap Press.

Roth, A. 2007. "Repugnance as a Constraint on Markets," *Journal of Economic Perspectives* 21(3): 37–58.

Snyder, J. 2009. "What's the Matter with Price Gouging?" *Business Ethics Quarterly.* 19(2) (April): 275–93.

Zwolinski, M. 2008. "The Ethics of Price Gouging," *Business Ethics Quarterly* 18(3): 347–78.

———. Forthcoming. "Price Gouging and Market Failure," in *New Essays on Philosophy, Politics & Economics: Integration and Common Research Projects,* ed. G. Gaus, J. Lamont, and C. Favor. Stanford, Calif.: Stanford University Press.

POSTSCRIPT

Should Price Gouging Be Regulated?

Consumers are thinking about the people who make the products they purchase and the conditions in which they work. American retailers and name brands have produced clothing, shoes, toys, and more. Store shelves are filled with merchandise made in sweatshops where often the workers conduct their labor in unsafe conditions with little pay. Many of these retailers say there are strict codes of conduct and on-site monitoring. However business ethicists believe that some factories have found ways to conceal abuses and to keep double sets of books to fool auditors. At some factories individuals are tutored with a script to recite to auditors. The script is different than the real conditions at the sweatshop. What can Americans ethically believe about what they wear and use? Is a Kantian ideal being followed in the production of these goods?

Will the poorest in society still be able to purchase the goods and services they need in times of disaster? Probably not, and they could very well perish. The invisible hand of the market (the law of supply and demand) may seem harsh in times such as these.

Society could strive to reduce situations in which buyers or sellers are desperate. Warding off natural disasters is impossible, but perhaps better preparation for any disaster might keep members of a society more in line with the free market in times when price gouging seems savvy.

A reply by Matt Zwolinski is also found in Business Ethics Quarterly *19:2 (April 2009), pp. 303–308, in which he answers some of Snyder's concerns, and clarifies his points that it is not morally justified to have laws prohibiting price gouging; that it is morally permissible behavior to engage in price gouging; and that price gouging doesn't reflect badly on the moral character of those who participate in it.*

Suggested Readings

Henry Altman, "Who's Gored by Gouging?" *Nation's Business* (June 1987).

Mark Kahler, "Fight Price Gouging," (September 1, 2009) Budgettravel.about .com/od/cheapgroundtransportation/a/price_gouging_2.htm

Miranda Okker, "Bad-business Ethics/Price Gouging," *Ad Traps* (April 25, 2005) http://www.marketingprofs.com/

Harris R. Sherline, "Price Gouging and Excess Profits," (May 24, 2008) http:// www.articlesbase.com/ethics-articles/price-gouging-and-excess-profits-425486 .html

Internet References . . .

Workplace Fairness

Workplace Fairness is a nonprofit organization that was founded to assist individuals, both employed and unemployed, in understanding, enforcing, and expanding their rights in the workplace.

http://www.nerinet.org

WorkNet@ILR

The School of Industrial and Labor Relations at Cornell University offers this site consisting of an index of Internet sites relevant to the field of industrial and labor relations; a list of centers, institutes, and affiliated groups; and an electronic archive that contains full-text documents on the glass ceiling, child labor, and more.

http://www.ilr.cornell.edu/

WorkNet: Alcohol and Other Drugs in the Workplace

This site of the Canadian Centre on Substance Abuse provides news, databases, bibliographies, resources, and research on alcohol and other drugs in the workplace.

http://www.ccsa.ca/ccsa/

Employee Incentives and Career Development

This site is dedicated to the proposition that effective employee compensation and career development is a valuable tool in obtaining, maintaining, and retaining a productive workforce. It contains links to pay-for-knowledge, incentive systems, career development, wage and salary compensation, and more.

http://www.snc.edu/socsci/chair/336/group1.htm

Executive PayWatch

Executive PayWatch, sponsored by the American Federation of Labor—Congress of Industrial Organizations (AFL-CIO), is a working families' guide to monitoring and curtailing the excessive salaries, bonuses, and perks in CEO compensation packages.

http://www.aflcio.org/corporateamerica/paywatch/

Human Resources: The Corporation and Employees

*W*hat is a just wage—for a worker near the poverty line, or for a multimillionaire corporate executive? What is a just employment policy? What rights does the employer have to limit employee privacy for company interests? And what right does an employee have to denounce an employer publicly for wrongdoing? The limits of employer and employee rights are never fixed, but require repeated examination and balancing.

- Does Blowing the Whistle Violate Company Loyalty?
- Is Employer Monitoring of Employee Social Media Justified?
- Is "Employment-at-Will" Good Social Policy?
- Is CEO Compensation Justified by Performance?

ISSUE 10

Does Blowing the Whistle Violate Company Loyalty?

YES: Sissela Bok, from "Whistleblowing and Professional Responsibility," *New York University Education Quarterly* (Summer 1980)

NO: Robert A. Larmer, from "Whistleblowing and Employee Loyalty," *Journal of Business Ethics* (vol. 11, 1992)

ISSUE SUMMARY

YES: Philosopher Sissela Bok asserts that although blowing the whistle is often justified, it does involve dissent, accusation, and a breach of loyalty to the employer.

NO: Robert A. Larmer argues, on the contrary, that putting a stop to illegal or unethical company activities may be the highest type of loyalty an employee can display.

T he whistle-blower is a nearly mythical character—the brave, lonely person who exposes evil in the corporate or governmental bureaucracy. Since the readings are very general, some specific cases might be useful. In a fascinating treatment of the phenomenon, N. R. Kleinfeld portrays five of the early whistle-blowers, some of whom have become famous as case studies in business schools across the country. Each one has an interesting story to tell; each claims that if he had it to do over again he would, for he likes living with a clear conscience. But each has paid a price: great stress, sometimes ill health, career loss, financial ruin, and/or loss of friends and family. Worst of all is the universal suspicion of anyone who can be characterized as a "snitch" or a "tattletale."

Whistle-blowing has been cast in a new light with the recent passage of the Dodd–Frank Wall Street Reform and Consumer Protection Act of 2010. The incentives for bringing factual allegations of fraud forward have increased. However, ethical dilemmas associated with whistle-blowing remain. Ethical issues surrounding whistle-blowing within business and finance often center on notions of fair warning and loyalty. Internal whistle-blowing involves someone within a firm alleging wrongdoing within that firm. In ideal ethical cases, the individual should only report on cases where facts can be established; where there is a possibility for significant harm; where the employee can follow a chain of command in reporting the wrongdoing; and where it should be understood that reporting of the wrongdoing will make important changes for the firm.

Curtis C. Verschoor ("Increased Motivation for Whistleblowing," *Strategic Finance*, November 2010, pp. 60–62) explores the promise of internal whistle-blowing in light of the recent legal changes of 2010. Verschoor contends that whistle-blowing may be an attractive option in today's marketplace because of the market collapse of 2008. He notes that distrust increases when employees are asked to file fraudulent statements or reports. The new legislation of 2010 now allows these employees to report the fraudulence before it is uncovered. Under specific conditions, these employees can also be awarded a percentage of the funds that were deemed fraudulent. For example, awards can range from 10 percent to 30 percent of the amount of monetary sanctions in cases over $1 million. The Dodd–Frank Act gives other incentives for whistle-blowing as well. Releasing information to outside regulators or other entities is known as external whistle-blowing. In these cases the employer doesn't have the oppor-tunity to address the wrongdoing. In other external cases, someone outside the firm would bring forward the information to the regulatory agency without first notifying the firm. Presently, the government regulators are encouraging these forms of whistle-blowing, and it would be discouraged by corporations.

The monitory reward of whistle-blowing may be a strong incentive for some individuals. However, often both the whistle-blower and the individual involved in the wrongdoing are treated as suspect. Whether or not the alle-gations are eventually proven, both the whistle-blower and those accused of wrongdoing pay a price. Implicit and explicit retaliation often accompanies the charges. A whistle-blower may innocently come forward with allegations against another, only to face severe scrutiny and charges of disloyalty. Some analysts cite that more than 60 percent of whistle-blowers suffered at least one negative consequence, such as being pressured to withdraw their charges, being ostracized by coworkers, and even being threatened with a lawsuit. Whistle-blowers can be fired and "blackballed" in the industry. Because of the negative consequences, analysts find that few whistle-blowers would again press allegations against a fellow employee.

In an effort to avoid whistle-blowing, some businesses have created an internal ethics office responsible for developing and sustaining policies that value open communication with employees. Policies should privilege those who use the open door policy to report concerns and problems that have a fac-tual basis. The policies would posit that the employee should want the firm to be protected from allegations of wrongdoing, and would understand the firm's position of investigating the charges. The employee would never be asked to follow up on an investigation.

Do these recent legal and internal corporate policy changes mitigate the concern about whistle-blowing being a form of company disloyalty? Done from a concern for public interest and in accordance with a company's own apparent commitment to ethics, is whistle-blowing necessarily an act of disloyalty?

YES

Sissela Bok

Whistleblowing and Professional Responsibility

Whistleblowing is a new label generated by our increased awareness of the ethical conflicts encountered at work. Whistleblowers sound an alarm from within the very organization in which they work, aiming to spotlight neglect or abuses that threaten the public interest.

The stakes in whistleblowing are high. Take the nurse who alleges that physicians enrich themselves in her hospital through unnecessary surgery; the engineer who discloses safety defects in the braking systems of a fleet of new rapid-transit vehicles; the Defense Department official who alerts Congress to military graft and overspending: all know that they pose a threat to those whom they denounce and that their own careers may be at risk.

Moral Conflicts

Moral conflicts on several levels confront anyone who is wondering whether to speak out about abuses or risks or serious neglect. In the first place, he must try to decide whether, other things being equal, speaking out is in fact in the public interest. This choice is often made more complicated by factual uncertainties: Who is responsible for the abuse or neglect? How great is the threat? And how likely is it that speaking out will precipitate changes for the better?

In the second place, a would-be whistleblower must weigh his responsibility to serve the public interest against the responsibility he owes to his colleagues and the institution in which he works. While the professional ethic requires collegial loyalty, the codes of ethics often stress responsibility to the public over and above duties to colleagues and clients. Thus the United States Code of Ethics for Government Servants asks them to "expose corruption wherever uncovered" and to "put loyalty to the highest moral principles and to country above loyalty to persons, party, or government."[1] Similarly, the largest professional engineering association requires members to speak out against abuses threatening the safety, health, and welfare of the public.[2]

A third conflict for would-be whistleblowers is personal in nature and cuts across the first two: even in cases where they have concluded that the

From *New York University Education Quarterly*, vol. 11, Summer 1980, pp. 2–7. Copyright © 1980 by Sissela Bok. Reprinted by permission of the author.

facts warrant speaking out, and that their duty to do so overrides loyalties to colleagues and institutions, they often have reason to fear the results of carrying out such a duty. However strong this duty may seem in theory, they know that, in practice, retaliation is likely. As a result, their careers and their ability to support themselves and their families may be unjustly impaired.[3] A government handbook issued during the Nixon era recommends reassigning "undesirables" to places so remote that they would prefer to resign. Whistleblowers may also be downgraded or given work without responsibility or work for which they are not qualified; or else they may be given many more tasks than they can possibly perform. Another risk is that an outspoken civil servant may be ordered to undergo a psychiatric fitness-for-duty examination,[4] declared unfit for service, and "separated" as well as discredited from the point of view of any allegations he may be making. Outright firing, finally, is the most direct institutional response to whistleblowers.

Add to the conflicts confronting individual whistleblowers the claim to self-policing that many professions make, and professional responsibility is at issue in still another way. For an appeal to the public goes against everything that "self-policing" stands for. The question for the different professions, then, is how to resolve, insofar as it is possible, the conflict between professional loyalty and professional responsibility toward the outside world. The same conflicts arise to some extent in all groups, but professional groups often have special cohesion and claim special dignity and privileges.

The plight of whistleblowers has come to be documented by the press and described in a number of books. Evidence of the hardships imposed on those who chose to act in the public interest has combined with a heightened awareness of professional malfeasance and corruption to produce a shift toward greater public support of whistleblowers. Public service law firms and consumer groups have taken up their cause; institutional reforms and legislation have been proposed to combat illegitimate reprisals.[5]

Given the indispensable services performed by so many whistleblowers, strong public support is often merited. But the new climate of acceptance makes it easy to overlook the dangers of whistleblowing: of uses in error or in malice; of work and reputations unjustly lost for those falsely accused; of privacy invaded and trust undermined. There comes a level of internal prying and mutual suspicion at which no institution can function. And it is a fact that the disappointed, the incompetent, the malicious, and the paranoid all too often leap to accusations in public. Worst of all, ideological persecution throughout the world traditionally relies on insiders willing to inform on their colleagues or even on their family members, often through staged public denunciations or press campaigns.

No society can count itself immune from such dangers. But neither can it risk silencing those with a legitimate reason to blow the whistle. How then can we distinguish between different instances of whistleblowing? A society that fails to protect the right to speak out even on the part of those whose warnings turn out to be spurious obviously opens the door to political repression. But from the moral point of view there are important differences between the aims, messages, and methods of dissenters from within.

Nature of Whistleblowing

Three elements, each jarring, and triply jarring when conjoined, lend acts of whistleblowing special urgency and bitterness: dissent, breach of loyalty, and accusation.

Like all dissent, whistleblowing makes public a disagreement with an authority or a majority view. But whereas dissent can concern all forms of disagreement with, for instance, religious dogma or government policy or court decisions, whistleblowing has the narrower aim of shedding light on negligence or abuse, or alerting to a risk, and of assigning responsibility for this risk.

Would-be whistleblowers confront the conflict inherent in all dissent: between conforming and sticking their necks out. The more repressive the authority they challenge, the greater the personal risk they take in speaking out. At exceptional times, as in times of war, even ordinarily tolerant authorities may come to regard dissent as unacceptable and even disloyal.[6]

Furthermore, the whistleblower hopes to stop the game; but since he is neither referee nor coach, and since he blows the whistle on his own team, his act is seen as a violation of loyalty. In holding his position, he has assumed certain obligations to his colleagues and clients. He may even have subscribed to a loyalty oath or a promise of confidentiality. Loyalty to colleagues and to clients comes to be pitted against loyalty to the public interest, to those who may be injured unless the revelation is made.

Not only is loyalty violated in whistleblowing, hierarchy as well is often opposed, since the whistleblower is not only a colleague but a subordinate. Though aware of the risks inherent in such disobedience, he often hopes to keep his job.[7] At times, however, he plans his alarm to coincide with leaving the institution. If he is highly placed, or joined by others, resigning in protest may effectively direct public attention to the wrongdoing at issue.[8] Still another alternative, often chosen by those who wish to be safe from retaliation, is to leave the institution quietly, to secure another post, and then to blow the whistle. In this way, it is possible to speak with the authority and knowledge of an insider without having the vulnerability of that position.

It is the element of accusation, of calling a "foul," that arouses the strongest reactions on the part of the hierarchy. The accusation may be of neglect, of willfully concealed dangers, or of outright abuse on the part of colleagues or superiors. It singles out specific persons or groups as responsible for threats to the public interest. If no one could be held responsible—as in the case of an impending avalanche—the warning would not constitute whistleblowing.

The accusation of the whistleblower, moreover, concerns a present or an imminent threat. Past errors or misdeeds occasion such an alarm only if they still affect current practices. And risks far in the future lack the immediacy needed to make the alarm a compelling one, as well as the close connection to particular individuals that would justify actual accusations. Thus an alarm can be sounded about safety defects in a rapid-transit system that threaten or will shortly threaten passengers, but the revelation of safety defects in a system no longer in use, while of historical interest, would not constitute whistleblowing. Nor would the revelation of potential problems in a system not yet fully designed and far from implemented.[9]

Not only immediacy, but also specificity, is needed for there to be an alarm capable of pinpointing responsibility. A concrete risk must be at issue rather than a vague foreboding or a somber prediction. The act of whistleblowing differs in this respect from the lamentation or the dire prophecy. An immediate and specific threat would normally be acted upon by those at risk. The whistleblower assumes that his message will alert listeners to something they do not know, or whose significance they have not grasped because it has been kept secret.

The desire for openness inheres in the temptation to reveal any secret, sometimes joined to an urge for self-aggrandizement and publicity and the hope for revenge for past slights or injustices. There can be pleasure, too— righteous or malicious—in laying bare the secrets of co-workers and in setting the record straight at last. Colleagues of the whistleblower often suspect his motives: they may regard him as a crank, as publicity-hungry, wrong about the facts, eager for scandal and discord, and driven to indiscretion by his personal biases and shortcomings.

For whistleblowing to be effective, it must arouse its audience. Inarticulate whistleblowers are likely to fail from the outset. When they are greeted by apathy, their message dissipates. When they are greeted by disbelief, they elicit no response at all. And when the audience is not free to receive or to act on the information—when censorship or fear of retribution stifles response—then the message rebounds to injure the whistleblower. Whistleblowing also requires the possibility of concerted public response: the idea of whistleblowing in an anarchy is therefore merely quixotic.

Such characteristics of whistleblowing and strategic considerations for achieving an impact are common to the noblest warnings, the most vicious personal attacks, and the delusions of the paranoid. How can one distinguish the many acts of sounding an alarm that are genuinely in the public interest from all the petty, biased, or lurid revelations that pervade our querulous and gossip-ridden society? Can we draw distinctions between different whistleblowers, different messages, different methods?

We clearly can, in a number of cases. Whistleblowing may be starkly inappropriate when in malice or error, or when it lays bare legitimately private matters having to do, for instance, with political belief or sexual life. It can, just as clearly, be the only way to shed light on an ongoing unjust practice such as drugging political prisoners or subjecting them to electroshock treatment. It can be the last resort for alerting the public to an impending disaster. Taking such clear-cut cases as benchmarks, and reflecting on what it is about them that weighs so heavily for or against speaking out, we can work our way toward the admittedly more complex cases in which whistleblowing is not so clearly the right or wrong choice, or where different points of view exist regarding its legitimacy—cases where there are moral reasons both for concealment and for disclosure and where judgments conflict. . . .

Individual Moral Choice

What questions might those who consider sounding an alarm in public ask themselves? How might they articulate the problem they see and weigh its injustice before deciding whether or not to reveal it? How can they best try to make sure their choice is the right one? In thinking about these questions it helps to keep in mind the three elements mentioned earlier: dissent, breach of loyalty, and accusation. They impose certain requirements—of accuracy and judgment in dissent; of exploring alternative ways to cope with improprieties that minimize the breach of loyalty; and of fairness in accusation. For each, careful articulation and testing of arguments are needed to limit error and bias.

Dissent by whistleblowers, first of all, is expressly claimed to be intended to benefit the public. It carries with it, as a result, an obligation to consider the nature of this benefit and to consider also the possible harm that may come from speaking out: harm to persons or institutions and, ultimately, to the public interest itself. Whistleblowers must, therefore, begin by making every effort to consider the effects of speaking out versus those of remaining silent. They must assure themselves of the accuracy of their reports, checking and rechecking the facts before speaking out; specify the degree to which there is genuine impropriety; consider how imminent is the threat they see, how serious, and how closely linked to those accused of neglect and abuse.

If the facts warrant whistleblowing, how can the second element— breach of loyalty—be minimized? The most important question here is whether the existing avenues for change within the organization have been explored. It is a waste of time for the public as well as harmful to the institution to sound the loudest alarm first. Whistleblowing has to remain a last alternative because of its destructive side effects: it must be chosen only when other alternatives have been considered and rejected. They may be rejected if they simply do not apply to the problem at hand, or when there is not time to go through routine channels or when the institution is so corrupt or coercive that steps will be taken to silence the whistleblower should he try the regular channels first.

What weight should an oath or a promise of silence have in the conflict of loyalties? One sworn to silence is doubtless under a stronger obligation because of the oath he has taken. He has bound himself, assumed specific obligations beyond those assumed in merely taking a new position. But even such promises can be overridden when the public interest at issue is strong enough. They can be overridden if they were obtained under duress or through deceit. They can be overridden, too, if they promise something that is in itself wrong or unlawful. The fact that one has promised silence is no excuse for complicity in covering up a crime or a violation of the public's trust.

The third element in whistleblowing—accusation—raises equally serious ethical concerns. They are concerns of fairness to the persons accused of impropriety. Is the message one to which the public is entitled in the first place? Or does it infringe on personal and private matters that one has no right to invade? Here, the very notion of what is in the public's best "interest" is at issue: "accusations" regarding an official's unusual sexual or religious experiences may well appeal to the public's interest without being information relevant to "the public interest."

Great conflicts arise here. We have witnessed excessive claims to executive privilege and to secrecy by government officials during the Watergate scandal in order to cover up for abuses the public had every right to discover. Conversely, those hoping to profit from prying into private matters have become adept at invoking "the public's right to know." Some even regard such private matters as threats to the public: they voice their own religious and political prejudices in the language of accusation. Such a danger is never stronger than when the accusation is delivered surreptitiously. The anonymous accusations made during the McCarthy period regarding political beliefs and associations often injured persons who did not even know their accusers or the exact nature of the accusations.

From the public's point of view, accusations that are openly made by identifiable individuals are more likely to be taken seriously. And in fairness to those criticized, openly accepted responsibility for blowing the whistle should be preferred to the denunciation or the leaked rumor. What is openly stated can more easily be checked, its source's motives challenged, and the underlying information examined. Those under attack may otherwise be hard put to defend themselves against nameless adversaries. Often they do not even know that they are threatened until it is too late to respond. The anonymous denunciation, moreover, common to so many regimes, places the burden of investigation on government agencies that may thereby gain the power of a secret police.

From the point of view of the whistleblower, on the other hand, the anonymous message is safer in situations where retaliation is likely. But it is also often less likely to be taken seriously. Unless the message is accompanied by indications of how the evidence can be checked, its anonymity, however safe for the source, speaks against it.

During the process of weighing the legitimacy of speaking out, the method used, and the degree of fairness needed, whistleblowers must try to compensate for the strong possibility of bias on their part. They should be scrupulously aware of any motive that might skew their message: a desire for self-defense in a difficult bureaucratic situation, perhaps, or the urge to seek revenge, or inflated expectations regarding the effect their message will have on the situation. (Needless to say, bias affects the silent as well as the outspoken. The motive for holding back important information about abuses and injustice ought to give similar cause for soul-searching.)

Likewise, the possibility of personal gain from sounding the alarm ought to give pause. Once again there is then greater risk of a biased message. Even if the whistleblower regards himself as incorruptible, his profiting from revelations of neglect or abuse will lead others to question his motives and to put less credence in his charges. If, for example, a government employee stands to make large profits from a book exposing the inequities in his agency, there is danger that he will, perhaps even unconsciously, slant his report in order to cause more of a sensation.

A special problem arises when there is a high risk that the civil servant who speaks out will have to go through costly litigation. Might he not justifiably try to make enough money on his public revelations—say, through books or public speaking—to offset his losses? In so doing he will not strictly speaking have *profited* from his revelations: he merely avoids being financially crushed by their sequels. He will nevertheless still be suspected at the time of revelation, and his message will therefore seem more questionable.

Reducing bias and error in moral choice often requires consultation, even open debate[10]: methods that force articulation of the moral arguments at stake and challenge privately held assumptions. But acts of whistleblowing present special problems when it comes to open consultation. On the one hand, once the whistleblower sounds his alarm publicly, his arguments will be subjected to open scrutiny; he will have to articulate his reasons for speaking out and substantiate his charges. On the other hand, it will then be too late to retract the alarm or to combat its harmful effects, should his choice to speak out have been ill-advised.

For this reason, the whistleblower owes it to all involved to make sure of two things: that he has sought as much and as objective advice regarding his choice as he can *before* going public; and that he is aware of the arguments for and against the practice of whistleblowing in general, so that he can see his own choice against as richly detailed and coherently structured a background as possible. Satisfying these two requirements once again has special problems because of the very nature of whistleblowing: the more corrupt the circumstances, the more dangerous it may be to seek consultation before speaking out. And yet, since the whistleblower himself may have a biased view of the state of affairs, he may choose not to consult others when in fact it would be not only safe but advantageous to do so; he may see corruption and conspiracy where none exists.

Notes

1. Code of Ethics for Government Service passed by the U.S. House of Representatives in the 85th Congress (1958) and applying to all government employees and office holders.

2. Code of Ethics of the Institute of Electrical and Electronics Engineers, Article IV.

3. For case histories and descriptions of what befalls whistleblowers, see Rosemary Chalk and Frank von Hippel, "Due Process for Dissenting Whistle-Blowers," *Technology Review* 81 (June–July 1979); 48–55; Alan S. Westin and Stephen Salisbury, eds., *Individual Rights in the Corporation* (New York: Pantheon, 1980); Helen Dudar, "The Price of Blowing the Whistle," *New York Times Magazine,* 30 October 1979, pp. 41–54; John Edsall, *Scientific Freedom and Responsibility* (Washington, D.C.: American Association for the Advancement of Science, 1975), p. 5; David Ewing, *Freedom Inside the Organization* (New York: Dutton, 1977); Ralph Nader, Peter Petkas, and Kate Blackwell, *Whistle Blowing* (New York: Grossman, 1972); Charles Peter and Taylor Branch, *Blowing the Whistle* (New York: Praeger, 1972).

4. Congressional hearings uncovered a growing resort to mandatory psychiatric examinations.

5. For an account of strategies and proposals to support government whistle-blowers, see Government Accountability Project, *A Whistleblower's Guide to the Federal Bureaucracy* (Washington, D.C.: Institute for Policy Studies, 1977).

6. See, e.g., Samuel Eliot Morison, Frederick Merk, and Frank Friedel, *Dissent in Three American Wars* (Cambridge: Harvard University Press, 1970).

7. In the scheme worked out by Albert Hirschman in *Exit, Voice and Loyalty* (Cambridge: Harvard University Press, 1970), whistleblowing represents "voice" accompanied by a preference not to "exit," though forced "exit" is clearly a possibility and "voice" after or during "exit" may be chosen for strategic reasons.

8. Edward Weisband and Thomas N. Franck, *Resignation in Protest* (New York: Grossman, 1975).

9. Future developments can, however, be the cause for whistleblowing if they are seen as resulting from steps being taken or about to be taken that render them inevitable.

10. I discuss these questions of consultation and publicity with respect to moral choice in chapter 7 of Sissela Bok, *Lying* (New York: Pantheon, 1978); and in *Secrets* (New York: Pantheon Books, 1982), Ch. IX and XV.

Robert A. Larmer  **NO**

Whistleblowing and Employee Loyalty

Whistleblowing by an employee is the act of complaining, either within the corporation or publicly, about a corporation's unethical practices. Such an act raises important questions concerning the loyalties and duties of employees. Traditionally, the employee has been viewed as an agent who acts on behalf of a principal, i.e., the employer, and as possessing duties of loyalty and confidentiality. Whistleblowing, at least at first blush, seems a violation of these duties and it is scarcely surprising that in many instances employers and fellow employees argue that it is an act of disloyalty and hence morally wrong.[1]

It is this issue of the relation between whistleblowing and employee loyalty that I want to address. What I will call the standard view is that employees possess *prima facie* duties of loyalty and confidentiality to their employers and that whistleblowing cannot be justified except on the basis of a higher duty to the public good. Against this standard view, Ronald Duska has recently argued that employees do not have even a *prima facie* duty of loyalty to their employers and that whistleblowing needs, therefore, no moral justification.[2] I am going to criticize both views. My suggestion is that both misunderstand the relation between loyalty and whistleblowing. In their place I will propose a third more adequate view.

Duska's view is more radical in that it suggests that there can be no issue of whistleblowing and employee loyalty, since the employee has no duty to be loyal to his employer. His reason for suggesting that the employee owes the employer, at least the corporate employer, no loyalty is that companies are not the kinds of things which are proper objects of loyalty. His argument in support of this rests upon two key claims. The first is that loyalty, properly understood, implies a reciprocal relationship and is only appropriate in the context of a mutual surrendering of self-interest. He writes,

> It is important to recognize that in any relationship which demands loyalty the relationship works both ways and involves mutual enrichment. Loyalty is incompatible with self-interest, because it is something that necessarily requires we go beyond self-interest. My loyalty to my friend, for example, requires I put aside my interests some of the time. . . . Loyalty depends on ties that demand self-sacrifice with no expectation of reward, e.g., the ties of loyalty that bind a family together.[3]

From *Journal of Business Ethics*, vol. 11, 1992, pp. 125–128. Copyright © 1992 by Springer Science and Business Media. Reprinted by permission via Rightslink.

The second is that the relation between a company and an employee does not involve any surrender of self-interest on the part of the company, since its primary goal is to maximize profit. Indeed, although it is convenient, it is misleading to talk of a company having interests. As Duska comments,

> A company is not a person. A company is an instrument, and an instrument with a specific purpose, the making of profit. To treat an instrument as an end in itself, like a person, may not be as bad as treating an end as an instrument, but it does give the instrument a moral status it does not deserve . . .[4]

Since, then, the relation between a company and an employee does not fulfill the minimal requirement of being a relation between two individuals, much less two reciprocally self-sacrificing individuals, Duska feels it is a mistake to suggest the employee has any duties of loyalty to the company.

This view does not seem adequate, however. First, it is not true that loyalty must be quite so reciprocal as Duska demands. Ideally, of course, one expects that if one is loyal to another person that person will reciprocate in kind. There are, however, many cases where loyalty is not entirely reciprocated, but where we do not feel that it is misplaced. A parent, for example, may remain loyal to an erring teenager, even though the teenager demonstrates no loyalty to the parent. Indeed, part of being a proper parent is to demonstrate loyalty to your children whether or not that loyalty is reciprocated. This is not to suggest any kind of analogy between parents and employees, but rather that it is not nonsense to suppose that loyalty may be appropriate even though it is not reciprocated. Inasmuch as he ignores this possibility, Duska's account of loyalty is flawed.

Second, even if Duska is correct in holding that loyalty is only appropriate between moral agents and that a company is not genuinely a moral agent, the question may still be raised whether an employee owes loyalty to fellow employees or the shareholders of the company. Granted that reference to a company as an individual involves reification and should not be taken too literally, it may nevertheless constitute a legitimate shorthand way of describing relations between genuine moral agents.

Third, it seems wrong to suggest that simply because the primary motive of the employer is economic, considerations of loyalty are irrelevant. An employee's primary motive in working for an employer is generally economic, but no one on that account would argue that it is impossible for her to demonstrate loyalty to the employer, even if it turns out to be misplaced. All that is required is that her primary economic motive be in some degree qualified by considerations of the employer's welfare. Similarly, the fact that an employer's primary motive is economic does not imply that it is not qualified by considerations of the employee's welfare. Given the possibility of mutual qualification of admittedly primary economic motives, it is fallacious to argue that employee loyalty is never appropriate.

In contrast to Duska, the standard view is that loyalty to one's employer is appropriate. According to it, one has an obligation to be loyal to one's employer and, consequently, a *prima facie* duty to protect the employer's interests. Whistleblowing constitutes, therefore, a violation of duty to one's employer and needs strong justification if it is to be appropriate. Sissela Bok summarizes this view very well when she writes

> the whistleblower hopes to stop the game; but since he is neither referee nor coach, and since he blows the whistle on his own team, his act is seen as a violation of loyalty. In holding his position, he has assumed certain obligations to his colleagues and clients. He may even have subscribed to a loyalty oath or a promise of confidentiality. Loyalty to colleagues and to clients comes to be pitted against loyalty to the public interest, to those who may be injured unless the revelation is made.[5]

The strength of this view is that it recognizes that loyalty is due one's employer. Its weakness is that it tends to conceive of whistleblowing as involving a tragic moral choice, since blowing the whistle is seen not so much as a positive action, but rather the lesser of two evils. Bok again puts the essence of this view very clearly when she writes that "a would-be whistleblower must weigh his responsibility to serve the public interest *against* the responsibility he owes to his colleagues and the institution in which he works" and "that [when] their duty [to whistleblow] . . . *so overrides loyalties to colleagues and institutions,* they [whistleblowers] often have reason to fear the results of carrying out such a duty."[6] The employee, according to this understanding of whistleblowing, must choose between two acts of betrayal, either her employer or the public interest, each in itself reprehensible.

Behind this view lies the assumption that to be loyal to someone is to act in a way that accords with what that person believes to be in her best interests. To be loyal to an employer, therefore, is to act in a way which the employer deems to be in his or her best interests. Since employers very rarely approve of whistleblowing and generally feel that it is not in their best interests, it follows that whistleblowing is an act of betrayal on the part of the employee, albeit a betrayal made in the interests of the public good.

Plausible though it initially seems, I think this view of whistleblowing is mistaken and that it embodies a mistaken conception of what constitutes employee loyalty. It ignores the fact that

> the great majority of corporate whistleblowers . . . [consider] themselves to be very loyal employees who . . . [try] to use 'direct voice' (internal whistleblowing), . . . [are] rebuffed and punished for this, and then . . . [use] 'indirect voice' (external whistleblowing). They . . . [believe] initially that they . . . [are] behaving in a loyal manner, helping their employers by calling top management's attention to practices that could eventually get the firm in trouble.[7]

By ignoring the possibility that blowing the whistle may demonstrate greater loyalty than not blowing the whistle, it fails to do justice to the many instances where loyalty to someone constrains us to act in defiance of what that person believes to be in her best interests. I am not, for example, being disloyal to a friend if I refuse to loan her money for an investment I am sure will bring her financial ruin; even if she bitterly reproaches me for denying her what is so obviously a golden opportunity to make a fortune.

A more adequate definition of being loyal to someone is that loyalty involves acting in accordance with what one has good reason to believe to be in that person's best interests. A key question, of course, is what constitutes a good reason to think that something is in a person's best interests. Very often, but by no means invariably, we accept that a person thinking that something is in her best interests is a sufficiently good reason to think that it actually is. Other times, especially when we feel that she is being rash, foolish, or misinformed we are prepared, precisely by virtue of being loyal, to act contrary to the person's wishes. It is beyond the scope of this paper to investigate such cases in detail, but three general points can be made.

First, to the degree that an action is genuinely immoral, it is impossible that it is in the agent's best interests. We would not, for example, say that someone who sells child pornography was acting in his own best interests, even if he vigorously protested that there was nothing wrong with such activity. Loyalty does not imply that we have a duty to refrain from reporting the immoral actions of those to whom we are loyal. An employer who is acting immorally is not acting in her own best interests and an employee is not acting disloyally in blowing the whistle.[8] Indeed, the argument can be made that the employee who blows the whistle may be demonstrating greater loyalty than the employee who simply ignores the immoral conduct, inasmuch as she is attempting to prevent her employer from engaging in self-destructive behaviour.

Second, loyalty requires that, whenever possible, in trying to resolve a problem we deal directly with the person to whom we are loyal. If, for example, I am loyal to a friend I do not immediately involve a third party when I try to dissuade my friend from involvement in immoral actions. Rather, I approach my friend directly, listen to his perspective on the events in question, and provide an opportunity for him to address the problem in a morally satisfactory way. This implies that, whenever possible, a loyal employee blows the whistle internally. This provides the employer with the opportunity to either demonstrate to the employee that, contrary to first appearances, no genuine wrongdoing had occurred, or, if there is a genuine moral problem, the opportunity to resolve it.

This principle of dealing directly with the person to whom loyalty is due needs to be qualified, however. Loyalty to a person requires that one acts in that person's best interests. Generally, this cannot be done without directly involving the person to whom one is loyal in the decision-making process, but there may arise cases where acting in a person's best interests requires that one act independently and perhaps even against the wishes of the person to whom one is loyal. Such cases will be especially apt to arise when the person to whom one is loyal is either immoral or ignoring the moral consequences of his actions. Thus, for example, loyalty to a friend who deals in hard narcotics would not imply that I speak first to my friend about my decision to inform the police of his activities, if the only effect of my doing so would be to make him more careful in his criminal dealings. Similarly, a loyal employee is under no obligation to speak first to an employer about the employer's immoral actions, if the only response of the employer will be to take care to cover up wrongdoing.

Neither is a loyal employee under obligation to speak first to an employer if it is clear that by doing so she places herself in jeopardy from an employer who will retaliate if given the opportunity. Loyalty amounts to acting in another's best interests and that may mean qualifying what seems to be in one's own interests, but it cannot imply that one take no steps to protect oneself from the immorality of those to whom one is loyal. The reason it cannot is that, as has already been argued, acting immorally can never really be in a person's best interests. It follows, therefore, that one is not acting in a person's best interests if one allows oneself to be treated immorally by that person. Thus, for example, a father might be loyal to a child even though the child is guilty of stealing from him, but this would not mean that the father should let the child continue to steal. Similarly, an employee may be loyal to an employer even though she takes steps to protect herself against unfair retaliation by the employer, e.g., by blowing the whistle externally.

Third, loyalty requires that one is concerned with more than considerations of justice. I have been arguing that loyalty cannot require one to ignore immoral or unjust behaviour on the part of those to whom one is loyal, since loyalty amounts to acting in a person's best interests and it can never be in a person's best interests to be allowed to act immorally. Loyalty, however, goes beyond considerations of justice in that, while it is possible to be disinterested and just, it is not possible to be disinterested and loyal. Loyalty implies a desire that the person to whom one is loyal take no moral stumbles, but that if moral stumbles have occurred that the person be restored and not simply punished. A loyal friend is not only someone who sticks by you in times of trouble, but someone who tries to help you avoid trouble. This suggests that a loyal employee will have a desire to point out problems and potential problems long before the drastic measures associated with whistleblowing become necessary, but that if whistleblowing does become necessary there remains a desire to help the employer.

In conclusion, although much more could be said on the subject of loyalty, our brief discussion has enabled us to clarify considerably the relation between whistleblowing and employee loyalty. It permits us to steer a course between the Scylla of Duska's view that, since the primary link between employer and employee is economic, the ideal of employee loyalty is an oxymoron, and the Charybdis of the standard view that, since it forces an employee to weigh conflicting duties, whistleblowing inevitably involves some degree of moral tragedy. The solution lies in realizing that to whistleblow for reasons of morality is to act in one's employer's best interests and involves, therefore, no disloyalty.

Notes

1. The definition I have proposed applies most directly to the relation between privately owned companies aiming to realize a profit and their employees. Obviously, issues of whistleblowing arise in other contexts, e.g., governmental organizations or charitable agencies, and deserve

careful thought. I do not propose, in this paper, to discuss whistleblowing in these other contexts, but I think my development of the concept of whistleblowing as positive demonstration of loyalty can easily be applied and will prove useful.

2. Duska, R.: 1985, 'Whistleblowing and Employee Loyalty,' in J. R. Desjardins and J. J. McCall, eds., *Contemporary Issues in Business Ethics* (Wadsworth, Belmont, California), pp. 295–300.

3. Duska, p. 297.

4. Duska, p. 298.

5. Bok, S.: 1983, 'Whistleblowing and Professional Responsibility,' in T. L. Beauchamp and N. E. Bowie, eds., *Ethical Theory and Business,* 2nd ed. (Prentice-Hall Inc., Englewood Cliffs, New Jersey), pp. 261–269, p. 263.

6. Bok, pp. 261–2, emphasis added.

7. Near, J. P. and P. Miceli: 1985, 'Organizational Dissidence: The Case of Whistle-Blowing', *Journal of Business Ethics* **4**, pp. 1–16, p. 10.

8. As Near and Miceli note 'The whistle-blower may provide valuable information helpful in improving organizational effectiveness . . . the prevalence of illegal activity in organizations is associated with declining organizational performance' (p. 1).

The general point is that the structure of the world is such that it is not in a company's long-term interests to act immorally. Sooner or later a company which flouts morality and legality will suffer.

POSTSCRIPT

Does Blowing the Whistle Violate Company Loyalty?

Whistleblowers are hard role models. What would you do in their shoes? The corporation, incidentally, is not the only setting for whistles. Would you tell about a friend's drug abuse, cheating on exams (or on his wife), stealing just a little bit of money? How do you weigh the possibility of damage done to the community against the security of your own career (some damage done to many people versus much damage done to a few people)? If you can see nothing but painful consequences all around if you blow the whistle, does that settle the problem—or does simple justice and fidelity to law have a claim of its own, as Ernest Fitzgerald argued? At what point do you decide that you cannot survive as a moral person unless you take action to end an evil that is being concealed—that the value of your own integrity outweighs the certain penalties of honesty?

Should we, as a society, protect the whistleblower with legislation designed to discourage corporate retaliation? Richard De George and Alan Westin, the earliest business ethics writers to take whistleblowing seriously, agree that the best policy is one that precludes the need for such heroics. "The need for moral heroes," De George concludes, "shows a defective society and defective corporations. It is more important to change the legal and corporate structures that make whistle blowing necessary than to convince people to be moral heroes" (*Business Ethics*, 2nd edition, 1986, p. 236). "The single most important element in creating a meaningful internal system to deal with whistle blowing is to have top leadership accept this as a management priority," says Westin, "This means that the chief operating officer and his senior colleagues have to believe that a policy which encourages discussion and dissent, and deals fairly with whistle-blowing claims, is a good and important thing for their company to adopt. . . . They have to see it, in their own terms, as a moral duty of good private enterprise" (*Whistle-Blowing!* 1981, p. 141). He cites Alexander Trowbridge, former secretary of commerce, on the importance of creating the proper organizational climate within the corporation: "It must be one that fosters the development of discipline in response to strong leadership and yet creates an atmosphere in which the individual, when confronted with something clearly illegal, unethical or unjust, can feel free to speak up—and to bring the problem to the attention of those high enough up in the corporation to solve it" (Ibid., p. 142). We need clear policies that permit and encourage the employees to communicate their doubts, and we need to train our managers to be responsive instead of punitive when the doubts are communicated.

But these are not enough. "Even the best drafted policy statements and management training programs will not resolve all the questions of illegal, dangerous, or improper conduct that might arise," Westin concludes. "There has to be a clear process of receiving complaints, conducting impartial investigations, defining standards of judgment, providing a fair-hearing procedure, and reaching the most objective and responsible decision possible. Such a procedure has to be fair both to the complaining employee and to company officials if morale is to be preserved and general confidence in management's integrity is to be the general expectation of the work force" (Ibid., p. 143). The company can "establish channels whereby those employees who have moral concerns can get a fair hearing without danger to their position or standing in the company," suggests De George, "Expressing such concerns, moreover, should be considered a demonstration of company loyalty and should be rewarded appropriately" (De George, p. 237). Possibilities for appropriate mechanisms include company ombudsmen, employee advocates, and committees of the board of directors.

Yes, but suppose that *these* are not enough. We run a moral company, we think; we have mechanisms in place to receive and process complaints, we think; but it will still happen that under the pressure of competition, company policies may bend, and the ombudsmen and advocates may become co-opted into the company agenda. At this point, do we as a society have any remaining interest in protecting the whistleblower? Laws are already in place protecting those who expose their companies' illegal activities; but we have always had protections for those who help the authorities bring lawbreakers to justice, so those laws are nothing novel. The question is really, does society as a whole have any collective interest in the monitoring of private organizations in the economic sphere? And if it does, and it seems that it does, is the legal protection of the whistle-blower the appropriate way to express that interest?

Suggested Reading

A. Bather and M. Kelly, "Whistleblowing: The Advantages of Self-Regulation." Department of Accounting Working Paper Series, Number 82 (Hamilton, New Zealand: University of Waikato, 2005).

Colin Grant, "Whistle Blowers: Saints of Secular Culture," *Journal of Business Ethics* (vol. 39, no. 2, September 2002).

Roberta Ann Johnson, *Whistle Blowing: When It Works and Why* (New York: L. Reinner Publishers, 2002).

Wim Vandekerchkhove and M. S. Ronald Commers, "Whistle Blowing and Rational Loyalty," *Journal of Business Ethics* (vol. 53, no. 1–2, August 2004).

ISSUE 11

Is Employer Monitoring of Employee Social Media Justified?

YES: Brian Elzweig and Donna K. Peeples, from "Using Social Networking Web Sites in Hiring and Retention Decisions," *SAM Advanced Management Journal* (Autumn 2009), pp. 27–35

NO: Eric Krell, from "Privacy Matters: Safeguarding Employees' Privacy Requires an Effective Policy, Sound Practices and Ongoing Communication" *HR Magazine* (February 2010), pp. 43–46

ISSUE SUMMARY

YES: Brian Elzweig and Donna K. Peeples write that although an employer does need to be respectful of their employees' privacy, they also have the responsibility to avoid negligent hiring and negligent retention. They find that the monitoring of an employee's, or a potential employee's, social media is a viable way to avoid these potentially serious problems. This is not to say that an employer's monitoring of social media should be without limits. Special care should be taken in respect to state privacy laws regarding expected privacy and laws regarding the protection of employees outside of company time.

NO: Eric Krell recognizes the importance of employee privacy and believes that it must be safeguarded. To appropriately do so, he believes that a concrete, written plan needs to be drafted, and often reevaluated, in coordination with each company's human resource department and a VP of employee security. This will ensure not only a uniform policy throughout the company, but will disclose to the employees if and in what ways their social media will be monitored.

2010 was a big year for the popular social networking Web site Facebook. Not only was its creator, Mark Zuckerberg, and the site's tumultuous beginnings, the subject of an award-winning movie, *The Social Network,* but the site itself reached the 500-million-user milestone and shows no signs of slowing its growth. Sites like Facebook, such as Twitter, MySpace, and personal blogs, allow their users to stay in touch with friends and family as well as make new connections by posting photos, messages of varying length, and comments to other users' sites. As these forms of social media grow in size and number, so do the questions of their appropriate use by the creators and receivers of the information. Although the previous generation's employee privacy ethics focused on issues such as e-mail privacy, the advent and growth of this new use of the Internet has made employer monitoring of employees' social networking the twenty-first century's central employee privacy issue.

Although social networking has proven to be a useful tool for many companies, creating another inexpensive way to advertise products and events is not without drawbacks. Time wasted by employees updating their personal sites on company time has led many businesses to block access to such sites on work premises to maintain a productive environment. Although this step seems reasonable to most, it is not the only way a company's interests can be affected by an employee's decisions regarding social media. Disgruntled and careless employees have been known to take to their personal sites to air their grievances and share possibly damaging company or client information. This leads many to ask, should an employee's use of social media outside of the office affect their job?

With a plethora of personal information not normally found on a resume or application now readily available with the click of a mouse, more and more employers are using social media in hiring and employee retention decisions. As a result, as social media use increases, so has the number of people fired or passed over for jobs because of information found on their personal sites not directly related to their job. Items such as questionable photos and personal, defamatory remarks about their bosses and co-workers have been causes of dismissal.

Although social media has been used to help businesses identify which employees could prove to be a liability to the company, employer perusal of these sites can itself prove to be a liability. As mentioned previously, these sites often contain information not asked for on job applications, often times for legal reasons. A person's social profile, whether blatantly or by association with certain groups, can often contain information about one's religion, sexuality, gender, disabilities, or other indicators of minority status.

These sites have a myriad of ways to personalize security and block unauthorized persons from viewing profiles, or even just pieces of information. In their privacy policy, Facebook reminds us that one should "Always consider your privacy settings before sharing information on Facebook." With these layers of protection, can privacy be expected on the Internet, or considering the wise words of Benjamin Franklin, can three people keep a secret only if two of them are dead? Is the use of these settings a legitimate claim to privacy, or simply a false comfort?

While reading the following articles, consider whether information on the Internet can truly be considered as private. Does an employer have a right to access employee information on social media sites if precautions have not been taken to otherwise prevent their access? And should employers disclose their intention to use information found on social media sites?

YES

**Brian Elzweig and
Donna K. Peeples**

Using Social Networking Web Sites in Hiring and Retention Decisions

Social networking Web sites are a relatively new format that allows people to post personal information to be viewed by "private" friends and the public as well. Managers may wish to access these sites, with or without permission, and use that information in hiring and retention decisions. Managers may, in fact, be required to monitor employees' social networking sites to defend against the possibility of negligent hiring and retention lawsuits being filed against their companies. However, use of this information must be weighed against the expectation of privacy by the person posting the information. A better understanding of the law can provide guidelines of when and how managers may access this information, thus avoiding liability for invading the privacy of current or potential employees.

An Interesting Example of What Not To Do

Many people have heard stories about how some employees have lost their jobs because of what they posted on a social networking Web site. For example, Stacy Snyder (*Snyder v. Millersville University*, 2008), student at Millersville University, was dismissed from her job as a student teacher at a high school and denied her teaching credential when officials from the university were made aware of a photograph and a post on her MySpace.com (hereinafter MySpace) site.

The post also included what the *New York Times* described as a "surprisingly innocuous" picture containing a head shot of Ms. Snyder wearing a pirate hat while drinking from a plastic cup. In a self-titled caption she called the photograph "drunken pirate" (Stross, 2007). Nicole Reinking, who was Snyder's coordinating teacher at Conestoga Valley High School (CV), had been critical of Snyder's classroom performance and professionalism (*Snyder v. Millersville University*, 2008).

Millersville University claimed that Ms. Snyder's dismissal was due to her competency as a teacher; however, the court held that her dismissal was based at least in part on the MySpace posting. Millersville University stated that the photograph was "unprofessional" and may "promote underage drinking." The college also claimed that Ms. Snyder was in violation of a section of the teacher's handbook requiring teachers to be "well groomed and appropriately dressed" (Stross, 2007). Snyder sued Millersville University alleging that

From *SAM Advanced Management Journal*, Autumn 2009, pp. 27–35. Copyright © 2009 by Society for Advancement of Management. Reprinted by permission.

her "First Amendment right to free expression protected the text and photograph in her . . . MySpace posting" (*Snyder v. Millersville University*, 2008). The United States District Court for the Eastern District of Pennsylvania ruled that Snyder was acting as an employee of CV, not as a student at Millersville University, when she was a student teacher. In doing so, the court denied her First Amendment claim stating that Snyder "was a public employee . . . when she created her MySpace posting, [therefore] she would be obligated to show that the posting related to matters of public concern to receive First Amendment protection" (*Snyder v. Millersville University*, 2008).

Snyder's case illustrates a dilemma facing many managers today and gives rise to important questions. First, may information available on a personal Web site be legally used in decisions relating to hiring or other employee decisions such as retention? Second, if such information may be used legally, should a manager seek this information and act on it? These fairly new questions are exacerbated by the prevalence of social networking sites and the potential wealth of information contained on them. Some interesting findings are:

- According to Ipsos Insight's (2007) latest "Face of the Web" study, social networking is becoming the dominant online behavior. The study found that 24% of American adults have visited a social networking Web site, with two thirds visiting within the 30 days previous to the polling. This usage is even higher in other countries such as South Korea, where 49% of adults had visited a social networking site at least once (Ipsos Insight, 2007).
- The two most popular social networking sites are MySpace and Facebook.com (Facebook) (Hitwise, 2008).
- In May of 2008, Facebook had 123.9 million unique visitors and MySpace had 114.6 million (McCarthy, 2008).
- The fastest growing demographic on Facebook is those who are 25 years old and older (ComScore, 2007).
- More than half of its users are over age 35 (Comscore, 2006).

With this many users, most of whom have their own Web page, it would seem that for a manager who is trying to hire the best employees, these sites (along with hundreds of smaller ones) are a veritable treasure trove of information (Boyd and Ellison, 2007). Ostensibly, information that is not available on a resume may be available on a job candidate's Web site. The problem for managers, however, is that while they may want to mine the sites for information about a candidate, the site's creator may have a legal right to privacy, and there may also be problems with accuracy of data obtained.

Can Managers Use Social Networking Web Sites in Hiring Decisions?

According to a recent survey by Careerbuilders.com,

- 22% of hiring managers used social networking Web sites to screen job candidates, double the amount from two years ago.

- Of those using the sites for screening, 34% reported that the information obtained caused them not to hire a particular candidate.
- 24% found content favorable to the candidate in their hiring decision.
- The number of hiring managers using social networking Web sites is likely to increase in the future as 9% who reported not using them planned to do so in the future (Grasz, 2008).

Since this has become a source of information, would a manager be remiss in *not* using these sites? Before deciding, managers should address some liability issues that generally revolve around the expectation of privacy.

Right to Privacy—Or Not?

In this age of information, especially information posted on the Internet by private individuals, should there be an expectation of privacy? Does utilizing the Web sites' privacy settings create an expectation of privacy? These are not simple questions with answers fully tested in the courts.

Whether or not there is an expectation of privacy may depend on how the user's account is set up and the information provided by the site regarding the conditions of privacy. Both Facebook and MySpace allow a user to set up a private site so that only those given permission by the user should be allowed access. It has been suggested that Snyder's biggest mistake was "not knowing or choosing to turn on any sort of privacy controls on her social network profile page . . . which would have prevented anyone except those who were accepted as Snyder's friends, [anyone who had been granted access, and those exempted by the terms of service/use], to have access to the items she posted. Facebook also offers extensive privacy controls that should be configured" (Perez, 2008).

This answer appears overly simplistic. While there is probably no expectation of privacy for a user who does not use privacy settings, a general expectation cannot be relied upon just by using the privacy settings.

Terms of Service—The Great Unread Section

When joining either MySpace or Facebook, the user must agree to the terms of service and to the Web sites privacy policies. These policies weaken a user's argument that just setting the site's privacy control functions guarantees privacy. The Facebook Principles notes that: "Facebook helps you share information with your friends and people around you . . . And you control the users with whom you share that information through the privacy settings on the Privacy page" (Facebook Principles). This is contrasted later in the policy:

> You post User Content . . . on the Site at your own risk. Although we allow you to set privacy options that limit access to your pages, please be aware that no security measures are perfect or impenetrable. We cannot control the actions of other Users with whom you may choose to share your pages and information. Therefore, we cannot and do not guarantee that User content you post on the Site will not be viewed by unauthorized persons. We are not responsible for circumvention of

any privacy settings or security measures contained on the Site. You understand and acknowledge that, even after removal, copies of User Content may remain viewable in cached and archived pages or if other Users have copied or stored your User Content. (Facebook Principles).

MySpace goes further in its safety settings noting that: "Every profile has the option of being 'private.' This means that only you and those you have added and approved as friends can see the details of your profile, including your blog, photos, interests, etc." (MySpace safety tips and settings: Safety settings).

That is contrasted with specific warnings in another part of the same document:

> *Don't forget that your profile and MySpace forums are public spaces. . . . Don't post anything that would embarrass you later.* It's easy to think that only our friends are looking at our MySpace page, but the truth is that everyone can see it. Think twice before posting a photo or information you wouldn't want your parents, potential employers, colleges or boss to see!" (MySpace safety tips and settings: General tips). [Emphasis added].

Is "Privacy" a Misnomer on Social Networking Sites?

Web sites themselves recognize that setting privacy options to limit access to a social networking site does not prevent all unwanted users from seeing the site's content. It has been suggested that hiring companies can access applicants' sites in a variety of ways. Facebook allows college students to give blanket access to anyone in their college. Recent graduates who remain active in their college's social network may become useful to their new employer because of their access to the Web sites of students still attending the school from which they graduated. Some companies may also hire current students who can access their peers' social networking profiles (Brandenburg, 2008). While searching for a specific person on both Facebook and MySpace, even before becoming a "friend" and being able to access a person's private site, certain information is still shared with the default settings. A user's "profile picture" (the picture that identifies their page) is available, as well as place of residence. MySpace also identifies the person's age, and Facebook shows other networks they are affiliated with (which can relate to work, hobbies, interests, politics, and a myriad of other things). In addition, Facebook allows someone doing a search to access the "target's" list of friends. Thus, a hiring company could ask a third party to access a potential hire's Web site for them.

Is There Tort Liability for Invasion of Privacy?

No case law directly addresses the point of whether there is an expectation of privacy on a social network Web site. Analogies must be made from case law as to expectations of privacy in other areas. The right to bring a private action for invasion of privacy was first discussed in legal literature in an 1890 *Harvard Law Review* article by Samuel Warren and Louis Brandies. This article led to courts creating tort claims for invasion of privacy (Warren and Brandeis, 1890). The seminal case in this area is *Katz v. United States*, in which the Supreme Court first recognized that "the Fourth Amendment protects people, not places." The issue in the Katz case was whether a wiretap of a telephone booth could be used as evidence against [Katz] the defendant, who was on trial for illegally transmitting bets or wagers by wire. The defendant argued that he had an expectation of privacy in the telephone booth; therefore, a warrant would be needed. In a concurring opinion that found for the defendant, Justice Harlan laid out the test for when a search and seizure requires a warrant: "There is a twofold requirement, first, that a person have exhibited an actual (subjective) expectation of privacy and, second, that the expectation be one that society is prepared to recognize as reasonable" (*Katz v. United States*, 1967).

The basic principle in Katz has been tested in the context of cyberspace, but not specifically in the context of social networking Web sites. In *United States v. Maxwell*, the Court of Appeals for the Armed Forces examined the expectation of privacy as it pertained to e-mail communications. The court contrasted e-mail, if considered to be the equivalent of first-class mail and telephone conversations—both with high expectations of privacy—with e-mail if considered to be "postcards," which have lower expectations of privacy. In addition, the court also noted that if the e-mail communication was sent to a chat room then the public at large would have access—much like placing a letter on a public bulletin board. Once the communication is given public access, then the expectation of privacy would be eliminated (*U.S. v. Maxwell* as discussed by Hodge, 2006). However, other courts have not found a blanket expectation of privacy in e-mails after they are sent, noting that the recipient should be figured into whether there is still an expectation of privacy (*U.S. v. Charbonneau* as discussed by Hodge, 2006).

Cases such as these would surely be used by a court determining if there is a reasonable expectation of privacy for a person's social networking site. The court should take into account that with a social network site, the user permits many people to have access. If access is allowed to some people, it is hard to know how a court would rule on a claim of privacy if the people who were allowed access gave other people access. However, it should also be noted that a person who took steps to ensure privacy, such as enacting privacy settings within their Web site, would have a higher expectation of privacy than those who did not (Brandenburg, 2008).

It has been suggested by Brandenburg (2008) that the following elements would be relevant in deciding whether or not a person using a social networking site would have a reasonable expectation of privacy:

1. Whether privacy settings are available;
2. Whether the social networker attempted to or did enable the privacy settings;

3. The level of privacy the networker attempted to or was able to set with an eye to the spectrum of privacy settings and measures available to the social networker;
4. The kinds of people and groups to whom that networker chose to disclose the information he or she later claims to be sensitive and private; and
5. Whether the unwanted or unauthorized person who accessed the networker's information was able to happen upon the information or had to hack through security measures to find the information (Brandenburg, 2008).

The question that has not been answered yet by the courts is how these factors would withstand scrutiny under the Katz test. Katz requires that the person claiming privacy must have a subjective expectation of privacy. It is hard to tell where the courts would draw the line to say that expectation was met. The more effort a user of a social networking site expends in attempting to maintain privacy the more likely the court will find that the first part of the Katz test was met. However, a court would most likely consider these elements in light of the user agreement and would have to decide if any privacy claims would be waived by that agreement. In addition, these elements do not address the second part of the Katz test. A court may see the pervasiveness of social networking Web sites as society accepting their use. Some courts may see this as society accepting the use of these sites to disseminate private information, and so the expectation of privacy would be reasonable. However, other courts may see examples like Snyder's as a warning. The more public stories there are about people having adverse employment decisions, the more likely it is that a court would rule that expecting privacy is not reasonable.

Stored Communications Act

In addition to the potential tort liability for invasion of privacy, another area of concern for managers is the Stored Communications Act (SCA) (18 U.S.C. §§ 2701–2711 (2000). The SCA makes it illegal to "intentionally access without authorization a facility through which an electronic communication service is provided" (18 U.S.C. §§ 2701(a)(1)). However, the SCA has a specific exception for "conduct authorized . . . by a user of that service with respect to a communication of or intended for that user . . ." 18 U.S.C. §§ 2701(c)(2). Questions arise as to what would qualify as conduct "authorized by a user" under the SCA. Certainly a user of a social networking Web site who allows access by designating others as "friends" would be authorizing their use. However, more questionable would be whether someone who was not granted access, such as an employer, was given information that was accessed by a "friend." Since the original person was authorized, the exception would probably apply. However, if an employer were to hack into a site without permission of the networker, then that employer would probably have liability under the SCA (Brandenburg, 2008).

Does the Right to Privacy Extend to Off-duty Current Employees

Davis (2007) has suggested that there should be an expectation of privacy for off-duty conduct of current employees, and that this expectation of privacy should extend to employees' social networking habits. The analysis is based on the issuance of lifestyle protection laws and some specific federal laws suggesting that once a person leaves work, they "expect to be let alone" (Davis, 2007). These laws soften the traditional employment-at-will doctrine available in most states. Two states, Colorado and North Dakota, have enacted broad protection for current employees. Colorado code states that it is a

> discriminatory or unfair employment practice for an employer to terminate the employment of any employee due to that employee's engaging in any lawful activity off the premises of the employer during nonworking hours unless such a restriction . . . [r]elates to a bona fide occupational requirement or is reasonably and rationally refted to the employment activities and responsibilities of a particular employee or a particular group of employees, rather than to all employees of the employer (Colo. Rev. Stat. Ann. § 24-34-402.5 (2008)).

Similarly, in North Dakota,

> [i]t is a discriminatory practice for an employer to fail or refuse to hire a person; to discharge an employee; or to accord adverse or unequal treatment to a person or employee with respect to application, hiring, training, apprenticeship, tenure, promotion, upgrading, compensation, layoff, or a term, privilege, or condition of employment, because of race, color, religion, sex, national origin, age, physical or mental disability, status with respect to marriage or public assistance, **or** *participation in lawful activity off the employer's premises during nonworking hours which is not in direct conflict with the essential business-related interests of the employer . . ."* (N.D. Cent. Code § 14-02.4-03 (2008). [Emphasis added].

Davis (2007) notes that other states have also enacted less broad protections for off-duty conduct, such as New York, which protects off-duty conduct including legal recreational activities, consumption of legal products, political activity, and union membership. In addition "[o]ther states have enacted much more limited statutes protecting specific categories of lawful off-duty conduct and lifestyle, including consumption of tobacco products, sexual orientation, and marital status" (Davis, 2007).

Using these examples and the rationale that people have an expectation of privacy outside of the workplace, Davis concludes that "[i]n a world where people simply have begun to conduct much of their social lives over the Internet, the same expectations apply: an employer should not be snooping into an employee's personal life when it has nothing to do with business" (Davis, 2007). This may be correct, but courts have interpreted what is considered to be "related to," "in direct conflict with the essential business-related interests of the employer," or other similar language. In *Marsh v. Delta Airlines,* Marsh, a Delta Air Lines baggage handler wrote a letter to the editor the *Denver Post* that criticized Delta. He was subsequently fired due to the publication of the letter (Marsh, 2007). Marsh then sued, claiming he was wrongfully terminated under the Colorado lifestyle statute. The court held in favor of Delta stating that there "is an implied duty of loyalty, with regard to public communications, that employees owe to their employers" (Marsh, 1997). In finding that Marsh violated the implied duty of loyalty, his firing was justified as this duty was a *bona fide* occupational requirement as contemplated in the exception to the broad-reaching Colorado statute. The court interpreted the statute to protect off-duty privacy as a shield for employees who are engaged in activities that are legal but are distasteful to their employers, such as homosexuality or political affiliation.

In the only case interpreting the North Dakota statute, a chaplain was fired from his job after it was revealed that he was caught masturbating in an enclosed public restroom of a department store. The chaplain claimed that he had broken no law since the enclosure prohibited him from being found guilty. The court held that it is a factual dispute whether this behavior was unlawful. If it is not, the court implied that the statute may protect him since it "may fit the protected status of lawful activity off the employer's premises" (Hougham, 1998).

The off-duty lifestyle statutes seem to protect activities that are completely divorced from the employer in that to protect an employee they must take place off-site, during nonworking hours, and have no relationship to the employer's interests (Sprague, 2007). Even if there is an expectation of privacy, the legitimate needs of the employer may override. The cases in which employers have been found to invade privacy are ones in which the "employer has pried into the employee's life far beyond a legitimate business need" (Sprague, 2007).

While there is a suggestion that there should be an expectation of privacy for off-duty social networking, outside of the exceptions noted, no laws make it illegal to search an employee's *publicly available social networking Web site*. Still, since the argument relating to the public or nonpublic nature of information on a social networking site is not clearly settled, employers using such information may be doing so at their own peril. On the other hand, an employer *not using* such information may create liability by the "negligent hiring" or "negligent retention of an individual." A negligent hiring claim suggests that at the time an employee was hired, it was negligent for an employer to engage the employee's services based on what the employer knew or should have known about the employee. (*McGuire v. Dean J. Curry*, 2009). Negligent retention liability is typically predicated on an "employer . . . placing a person with known propensities, or propensities which should have been discovered by reasonable investigation, in an employment position in which, because of the circumstances of the employment, it should have been foreseeable that the hired individual posed a threat of injury to others" (*Mandy v. 3M*, 1996). The negligent retention occurs "when, during the course of employment, the employer becomes aware or should have become aware of problems with an employee that indicated his unfitness, and the employer fails to take further action such as investigating, discharge, or reassignment" (*Mandy v. 3M*, 1996).

It is important to note that the tort[s] of negligent hiring and retention [are] based on the principle that a person conducting an activity through employees is subject to liability for harm resulting from negligent conduct "in the employment of improper persons or instrumentalities in work involving risk of harm to others." (quoting [in part] Restatement (Second) of Agency [s]ection 213(b) (1958)). . . . The duty to hire employees who are competent and not dangerous is, by its very nature, a duty of a master or employer, and this duty is nondelegable. . . . Thus, the liability of an employer for the negligent supervision or hiring of an unfit employee is an entirely separate and distinct basis from the liability of an employer under the doctrine of *respondeat superior. (Magnum Foods, Inc. v. Continental Cas. Co.*, 1994 (*original citations deleted*).

Negligent hiring and negligent retention only require constructive notice of the employee's propensity to cause injury and can be imputed to an employer who fails to take reasonable care in determining an employee's fitness for a position. The more contact an employee has with the public, the higher this duty to investigate becomes (*McGuire v. Dean J. Curry*, 2009). This would make it dangerous for an employer *not* to check any information to which the organization could have access. The evidence for negligent hiring and negligent retention claims can come outside of the theory *respondeat superior.* Therefore, the evidence that may be used to show that someone was negligently hired or retained may come from actions that happened outside of the scope of employment. As such, they are attractive to plaintiff's lawyers, and the number of these claims has increased in recent years (Richmon, 2001).

While there is little case law on social networking Web sites themselves, courts are increasingly looking for evidence that may be obtained from the Internet. Courts are recognizing "Googling" and "Internet searches" on parties as part of a due diligence search for missing defendants and have overturned cases when this was not done. Practitioners have warned that to find potentially relevant evidence lawyers need to look past traditional avenues and should include social networking Web sites in their search for evidence (Levitt and Rosch, 2007). Language on the sites tends to be frank and graphic and often includes pictures that show very well to juries. To effectively represent a party, an attorney needs to know what has been posted on the Internet and should assume that if it were posted publicly, the other party already has it. Once something has been posted on the Internet, it is difficult to remove all traces of it (Menzies, 2008). However, since the Katz analysis allows for a subjective expectation of privacy as one part of the test, a user believing that the information was erased may persuade a court that the privacy expectation exists.

It appears that courts, when determining whether an employer had constructive notice of information that could lead to a negligent hiring or negligent retention claim, need to examine the ease of availability of the information. Similarly, a job applicant's expectation of privacy would probably depend on similar factors that were discussed previously. Managers, it would seem, may have an affirmative duty to at least check for information available to the general public on social networking Web sites, but the practice may be considered an invasion of privacy if they were to hack into a private site without permission. However, managers should be cautioned to check their state's privacy and lifestyle laws before making any decisions that affect employment, since violation of these may create liability for the employer. Even if the employer is in a state with broad privacy and lifestyle rights (Colorado and North Dakota), managers should search for public information on their employees. Those states, as well as states with limited protections, allow exceptions to the lifestyle provisions for *bona fide* conflicts with the employer's business. It would seem that if Snyder had been in one of those states, as a teacher, her actions may still have been directly contrary to the employer's business. For example, if she were to have hurt a student while intoxicated, her MySpace posting would have been strong evidence against the school board in a negligent retention lawsuit.

Penalties for Invasion of Privacy

If a court were to hold that the social networker had an expectation of privacy for his or her Web site, and an employer used this in making a negative employment decision, the potential employer could be liable for the invasion of privacy. The employer may also subject itself to an action for wrongful termination of a current employee. Kirkland suggests this would be a proper remedy for employees who are fired for blogging (a similar activity using a social networking Web site) on their own time (Kirkland, 2006). In addition, it should be noted that the two states that have blanket privacy and lifestyle rights both enacted them as part of the state's anti-discrimination statutes. Courts looking for guidance may use this persuasive authority to help determine a penalty. As such, the penalty for invading the privacy of an employee, and using the information gained to make a negative hiring decision, could subject the employer to penalties similar to those found in discrimination cases, which are indeed substantial.

Other Potential Problems

The Potential for Liability for Discrimination

As discussed, information may be made available about a specific job candidate by searching their MySpace and Facebook accounts. On many social networking sites, information available without being a "friend" include a user's profile picture (usually the user's picture), age, networks in which they are members (which could include religious, political, sexual orientation, and other interests of the user), as well as other information. This information would not appear on a traditional job résumé and could lead to discriminatory acts. Many questions that are not typically asked in interviews, since they may lead to discriminatory hiring practices, may be answered by the job candidate's social networking site. The profile picture may tell the employer the candidate's sex or race, and other information may give clues about the candidate's religion or national origin. Using information gained from the social networking Web site in hiring decisions could run afoul of Title VII of the Civil Rights Act of 1964, the Age Discrimination in Employment Act, the Americans with Disabilities Act, or state discrimination laws. The social networking Web site may reveal information that would show a candidate to be in a protected class or category. Since this information is now provided prior to seeing a candidate face to face, the candidate could be passed up for an interview based on one of those factors. Human resource managers must have procedures in place to ensure that this does not occur (Davis, 2007). Evidence of an employer routinely checking potential job candidates' social networking profiles could easily be used to make a case for discrimination if they do not have enough workers who are members of protected classes.

The Possibility for Inaccurate Information in an Employment Decision

Another problem for potential employers is that the information contained in a social networking site may be false or inaccurate. One commentator imagines a scenario where a candidate is competing for a highly coveted job, knowing that the employer may do an online search of the candidates. The candidate then makes a Web site containing false or misleading information about one of the competitors for the job. The competitor may be eliminated from consideration without knowing why and may never know of the false information (Davis, 2007). Even without malicious intent, a manager's biases may come into play. If there is a picture of a job candidate drinking, will the manager think that person is an alcoholic? If a person is pictured holding a hunting rifle, is that person homicidal or a member of a militia? The manager's biases, triggered by one picture or bit of information, could wrongly frame his or her entire view of the candidate (Davis, 2007). Even the 24% of employers (Grasz, 2008) who made positive employment decisions based on a social networking Web site could be doing this on misinformation. A site that shows great communication skills or looks very professional may not have been designed by the person who owns it. Many people hire others to make their Web sites.

Additionally, information may be posted about a candidate by someone else, and the candidate themselves may not know about it. Both MySpace and Facebook allow "friends" to post things on other "friends" sites. The owner of the site can remove the posts, but the manager may see it before the candidate does. Any of the above scenarios, and many others, could allow a hiring manger to make adverse employment decisions using inaccurate information.

What Now?

Reviewing the current information on social networking sites and applying it to good business practices, it would appear that an employer would be remiss if the Internet was *not* routinely searched for information regarding *potential* employees. Searching for information on *current* employees may be constrained by the time and effort required. Certainly if there is a reason to update information, such as a transfer, promotion or a behavior issue, a search would be to protect the organization. The following are suggestions for employers before accessing and using information obtained from the Internet.

- Check social networking sites before making employment decisions in order to gain important information—good or bad.
- Verify accuracy of the information gathered.
- Recognize the purpose of the sites. Do not have unrealistic expectations of propriety.
- Consider the age of the employee or potential employee.
- Develop clear policies and procedures regarding use of social networking sites. Clearly disseminate this information to employees.
- Post information regarding your potential use of social networking sites on your job postings and application forms.
- Have employees and persons seeking employment sign consent forms prior to accessing information.
- Check state statute for privacy and lifestyle laws. Many states have some protections even if there is not a blanket protection for off-duty conduct.
- Train all employees on the important issues discussed in this paper.

Conclusion

With social networking Web sites becoming more prevalent, especially among individuals in the workforce, use of them is becoming more common in employment hiring and retention decisions. Since social networking sites are relatively new to users as well as employers, there are many issues to consider before using them for employment decisions. Employers should take steps to avoid invading privacy or committing discriminatory acts in using the sites, but should not fear using them if they have a legitimate interest at stake. These Web sites contain a treasure trove of publicly available information. Employers may be at risk if they *do not*, in fact, check for publicly available information on their current and potential employees. Employers should also take steps to ensure the accuracy of the information gathered. In addition, employees and job seekers should be put on notice that employers are using these sites to gather information and should assume that nothing posted on them is actually kept private.

References

Boyd, D. M., and Ellison, N. B. (2007). Social network sites: Definition, history, and scholarship. *Journal of Computer-Mediated Communication, 13*(1), article 11.

Brandenburg, C. (2008). The newest way to screen job applicants: A social networker's nightmare. *Federal Communications Law Journal, 60*(3), 597.

Colo. Rev. Stat. Ann. B 24-34-402.5 (2008).

ComScore press release: Facebook sees flood of new traffic from teenagers and adults (2007, July 5). Retrieved December 19, 2008 from http://www.comscore.com/press/release.asp?press=1519

ComScore press release: More than half of MySpace visitors are now age 35 or older, as the site's demographic composition continues to shift. (2006, October 5). Retrieved February 4, 2009 from http://www.comscore.com/press/release.asp?press=1019

Davis, D. (2007). My Space isn't your space: Expanding the fair credit reporting act to ensure accountability and fairness in employer searches of online social networking services. *Kansas Journal of Law and Public Policy, 16,* 237.

Facebook Principles (n.d.). Retrieved on January 21, 2009 from http://www .facebook.com/policy.php

Grasz, J. (2008, September 10). One-in-five employers use social networking sites to research job candidates, CareerBuilder.com survey finds. Retrieved December 18, 2008 from http://careerbuilder.com/share/aboutus/press releasesdetail.aspx?id= pr459&sd=9%2f10%2f2008&ed=12%2f31%2f2008&siteid=cbpr&sc_cmp1=cb_pr459_

Hitwise US-Top 20 websites-October, 2008. Retrieved December 18, 2008 from http:]]www.hitwise.com/datacenter/rankings.php

Hodge, M. (2006). The fourth amendment and privacy issues on the "new" internet: Facebook.com and MySpace.com. *Southern Illinois University Law Journal, 31,* 95.

Hougam v. Valley Memorial Homes, 1998 ND 24 (Supreme Court of North Dakota 1998).

Ipsos Insight Marketing Research Consultancy: Online video and social networking websites set to drive the evolution of tomorrow's digital lifestyle (2007, July 5). Retrieved December 18, 2008 from http://www.ipsosinsight.com/ pressrelease.aspx?id=3556

Katz v. United States, 389 U.S. 347 (1967).

Kirkland, A. (2007). You got fired? On your day off?! Challenging termination of employees for personal blogging practices. *University of Missouri Kansas City Law Review, 75,* 545.

Levitt, C., and Rosch, M. (2007, February). Making internet searches part of due diligence. *Los Angeles Lawyer, 29,* 46.

Magnum Foods, Inc. v. Continental Cas. Co., 36 F.3d 1491 (United States Court of Appeals for the Tenth Circuit 1994).

Mandy v. 3M, 940 F. Supp 1463 (United States District Court for the District of Minnesota 1996).

Marsh v. Delta Air Lines, 952 F. Supp. 1458 (United States District Court for the District of Colorado 1997).

McCarthy, C. (2008, June 20). ComScore: Facebook is beating MySpace worldwide.

CNet News. Retrieved from http://news.cnet.com/830113577_3-9973826-36.html

McGuire v. Dean J. Curry, 766 N.W.2d 501 (Supreme Court of South Dakota 2009).

Menzies, K.B. (2008, July). Perils and possibilities of online social networks. *Trial, 44,* 58.

MySpace safety tips and settings: General tips. (n.d.). Retrieved on January 21, 2009 from http://www.myspace.com/index.cfm?fuseaction=cms.viewpage&placement= safety_pagetips

MySpace safety tips and settings: Safety settings. (n.d.). Retrieved on January 21, 2009 from http://www.myspace.com/index.cfm?fuseaction=cms.viewpage& placement=safety_pagetips & sspage=4

N.D. Cent. Code B14-02.4-03 (2008).

Perez, S. (2008, December 5). Social network profile costs woman college degree. *Read Write Web*. Retrieved from http://www.readwriteweb.com/archives/social_network_profile_costs_woman_college_degree.php

Richmon, A. (2001). Note: restoring the balance: Employer liability and employer privacy. *Iowa Law Review, 86*(4), 1337.

Snyder v. Millersville University, Civil Action No. 07-1660, 2008 WL 5093140 (E.D. Pa December 3, 2008).

Sprague, R. (2007). From Taylorism to the Omnipticon: Expanding employee surveillance beyond the workplace. *John Marshall Journal of Computer & Information Law, 25*(1), 1.

Stored Communications Act, 18 U.S.C. BB 2701-2711 (2000).

Stross, R. (2007, December 30). How to lose your job on your own time. *The New York Times*. Retrieved from http://www.nytimes.com/2007/12/30/business/30digi.html

United States v. Charbonneau, 979 F. Supp. 1177 (United States District Court for the Southern District of Ohio 1997).

United States v. Maxwell, 45 M.J. 406 (United States Court of Appeals for the Armed Forces 1996).

Warren, S.V. and Brandeis L.D. (1890). The right to privacy. *Harvard Law Review, 4*(5), 193.

Eric Krell

Privacy Matters: Safeguarding Employees' Privacy Requires an Effective Policy, Sound Practices and Ongoing Communication

Beverly Widger, SPHR, senior vice president for human resources at Claremont Savings Bank in Claremont, N.H., introduces new hires to the realm of corporate privacy during orientation. "We are constantly aware of our customers' privacy as well as our own employees' privacy," says Widger, a member of the Society for Human Resource Management's (SHRM) Employee Relations Special Expertise Panel.

Widger and other HR managers at companies with mature privacy programs emphasize that creating privacy policies represents only one of several components necessary for effective privacy management. They say managing the policies requires board-level action, an ongoing collaborative management effort, employee education and, just as important, making the policies meaningful to all employees.

That explains why HR professionals play a crucial role in managing privacy policies and why Widger presents real-world scenarios related to privacy during orientation and in workforce communication.

Says Bernard Ruesgen, SPHR, logistics HR group manager for Sports Authority in Englewood, Colo.: "Whether you're talking about Internet security, e-mail security, personnel files, health care or other privacy issues that touch almost every element of the business, you have to make it meaningful." In short, HR professionals need to place these policies in a context that employees can relate to.

This communication effort never ends, privacy experts say, because of the expanding use of technology and communication in personal and business lives. The risks of mismanaging employees' privacy can be severe: lost revenue, lost productivity, legal or regulatory actions, declines in brand value and shareholder value, and recruiting and retention problems.

HR professionals need to understand privacy issues to manage and mitigate the risks associated with the data they work with, says J. Trevor Hughes, executive director of the International Association of Privacy Professionals (IAPP) in York, Maine.

An Emerging Patchwork

Corporate privacy generally covers customer and employee privacy, with sub-categories including the privacy of job applicants and how vendors such as benefits providers protect the privacy of client companies' employees. The emergence of the chief privacy officer position reflects the growing importance of corporate privacy management. (See "New Face in the C-Suite" in the January 2010 issue of *HR Magazine*.)

Hughes says HR professionals should sharpen their skills in spotting privacy issues, an area of expertise covered in the Certified Information Privacy Professional designation that the IAPP offers members. Yet, spotting such issues can be tricky, given the fluctuations in privacy regulations globally.

The European Union requires companies doing business in its member countries to adhere to employee privacy principles. The U.S. government has not passed a sweeping privacy law since the Electronic Communications Privacy Act of 1986, which regulates how employers monitor employee telephone calls.

Since then, a patchwork of requirements has slowly developed, notes Philip Gordon, a shareholder in Littler Mendelson's Denver office and chair of the employment and labor law firm's data privacy and protection practice.

The Americans with Disabilities Act of 1990 contains confidentiality requirements, and the Health Insurance Portability and Accountability Act of 1996 includes rules protecting the security and privacy of employee health data. Most recently, the Genetic Information Nondiscrimination Act of 2008—which prevents employers from using genetic information, including family medical histories, in staffing decisions—and several state laws governing personal data have been enacted. In addition, the threat of identity theft casts privacy protection in a new light; many state laws require notice when there has been a privacy breach.

As such privacy protection increases, corporate policies concerning privacy require improvement, insists Lewis Maltby, president and founder of the National Workrights Institute in Princeton, N.J., and author of *Can They Do That? Retaking Our Fundamental Rights in the Workplace* (Portfolio, 2010).

At many companies, the privacy policy "is what employees see on their screens when they turn their computers on," Maltby explains. "That so-called notice is really a reservation of rights. It doesn't really indicate anything about the company's actual privacy practice."

As a result, employees' expectations and employers' actions concerning privacy frequently are misaligned, creating problems. Maltby notes that 25 percent of employers have fired employees because of "inappropriate" e-mails, yet many organizations fail to define what "inappropriate" means.

"Some privacy advocates suggest that employers are Big Brother and want to spy on employees," Maltby says. "That's not the case. This is a sin of omission. . . . Employees have virtually no privacy in e-mail communications, text messages or web sites that they visit at work. And when they find out, it damages morale and productivity in ways that don't usually get noticed. On occasion, it affects recruitment and retention."

Creating a Policy

The first step in aligning privacy expectations involves creating a corporate privacy policy.

Many companies create two types of policies, says Gordon. An employee-facing policy provides relatively high-level principles governing the organization's collection, use, disclosure, safeguarding and disposal of employee data. An operational policy or manual is directed internally for people who access and use employee data to perform legitimate job functions.

The principles typically describe what employee data the company collects and how the data are collected; used; shared, if applicable; accessed; stored; and, when necessary, disposed of. The operational policy usually consists of numerous policies tailored to the privacy issues of different departments and groups. Companies such as Claremont Savings Bank, Sports Authority and Eastman Kodak Co. in Rochester, N.Y., follow the approach Gordon describes.

For example, when job candidates visit Kodak's job-posting site, they see a privacy notice geared toward them; this notice differs from both the policy employees see and the policies directed at customers.

Widger and Ruesgen emphasize that developing a corporate privacy policy is a board-level effort requiring regular and deep collaboration among HR, legal, information technology (IT) and privacy professionals. "Create a cross-functional team," Gordon says. "No single person has all of the knowledge or skills necessary."

Each year, Claremont Savings Bank's compliance officer and at least one other senior officer review the bank's privacy policy. After that, the policy goes to the board for approval. Then, Widger and her team communicate the policy—focusing on updates and areas requiring attention—to managers and employees, who are required to sign off annually. Training, online or in person, accompanies the effort.

A compliance officer develops the policies and makes updates, and an internal auditor ensures that the policies are being adhered to, says Widger, who recently worked with her compliance officer, the bank's top IT executive and other senior-level officers to expand the policy to address social media issues.

HR's Role

HR professionals help craft and communicate the policies while operating as perhaps the organization's most important protectors of employee privacy.

"HR professionals may be touching more-sensitive, and potentially more-damaging, personal data than anyone else," says Hughes. "As our concept of sexual harassment evolved, HR professionals became educated and more sophisticated in their management of those issues. As our concept of privacy in the marketplace evolves, HR professionals are going to have to step up once again and get themselves educated on, and aware of, these issues."

This awareness extends beyond having employees sign receipts for handbooks that contain the privacy policy and even beyond the company's walls.

"Incorporate the elements of the policy into your daily discussions," Ruesgen says. "If you have a managers' meeting that covers leave-of-absence policies, a natural segue into privacy exists, and you have to leverage that conversation." In the situation Ruesgen describes, for example, explain to managers that if an employee takes leave for a personal medical or financial reason, that information must remain confidential.

One reason Brian O'Connor, Kodak's chief security and privacy officer, works closely with HR colleagues: "HR can help by making sure that what you are drafting can be understood by the average employee," he says.

And don't just look at your own organization, Widger notes. "Look at your payroll provider, your benefits provider, your 401(k) provider—any vendor that you use—to understand what they have in place to protect your employees' information."

Claremont Savings Bank requires relevant vendors to complete Statement of Auditing Standards (SAS) 70 audits and to sign a privacy policy agreement stating that they will keep employee information confidential and protected.

SAS 70 audits were developed by the American Institute of Certified Public Accountants in the late 1980s and finished in the early 1990s. Their use has increased since enactment of the Sarbanes-Oxley Act of 2002. The audits come in two types, depending on their rigor, and are designed to help vendors show client companies that internal privacy controls are up to snuff.

All of this can sound overwhelming to HR professionals in organizations without formal privacy functions or pre-Inter-net-era policies in hard-copy employee handbooks. Fortunately, there are several steps that can kick-start improvement efforts. (See the sidebar "Get Started.") The most important step for HR professionals involves understanding and accepting their key roles in shaping and disseminating privacy policies.

"The more personal stories that you can give to help drive home the importance of the policy, the better," Widger advises.

POSTSCRIPT

Is Employer Monitoring of Employee Social Media Justified?

Our personal privacy is important to us. However, privacy seems to be a larger employment issue now than at any time in the past. Actions today that are shown on someone's social media site could harm one's potential future employment. Current employment could also be damaged by imprudent postings on social media. Solutions to loss of privacy could include policies and procedures that clearly inform employees when social media will be monitored. This may not be enough. Some employers may find the firm's reputation more important than employee privacy and keep vigilant watch on employees' social media sites. The future will probably present many more ethical implications on this issue.

Suggested Readings

Victoria Brown and E. Vaughn, "The Writing on the (Facebook) Wall: The Use of Social Network Sites in Hiring Decisions," *Journal of Business & Psychology* (vol. 26, no. 2, 2011), pp. 219–225.

John Browning, "Employers Face Pros, Cons with Monitoring Social Networking," *Houston Business Journal* (February 26, 2009).

Steven Greenhouse, "Labor Board Says Rights Apply on Net," *New York Times* (November 9, 2010), p. 1.

Karen E. Klein, "Establish a Commonsense Social Media Policy," *BusinessWeek.com* (2011), p. 9.

ISSUE 12

Is "Employment-at-Will" Good Social Policy?

YES: Richard A. Epstein, from "In Defense of the Contract at Will," *University of Chicago Law Review* (Fall 1984)

NO: John J. McCall, from "A Defense of Just Cause Dismissal Rules," *Business Ethics Quarterly* (April 2003)

ISSUE SUMMARY

YES: Richard Epstein defends the at-will contract as an appropriate expression of autonomy of contract on the part of both employee and employer and as a means to the most efficient operations of the market.

NO: John McCall argues that the defense of the employment-at-will doctrine does not take account of its economic and social consequences and is in derogation of the very moral principles that underlie private property and freedom of contract.

How can there possibly be any objection to freedom? If I want to make a deal with my neighbor that I will help him move some boxes on Saturday, and he will pay me $20, what could be wrong with that? Suppose I do a really good job moving his boxes. It turns out that he runs an appliance store, and he wants to hire me to move boxes every day. I have the time, the pay's all right, but I have one problem—suppose something better comes along, and I want to up and leave, no offense? Maybe he has a problem, too: There's machinery out there that might make my job unnecessary, and he might want to invest in it next year. So we make a further stipulation: I can leave on thirty days' notice, he can terminate my job on thirty days' notice. We've both bought ourselves more freedom in the future. What's wrong with that?

Note that we don't have to do it that way. I could have said no, I have better things to do Saturday, and no, I don't want to move boxes every day, at least not at that pay. Or, on the other hand, either one of us might be coming off a really bad experience with unreliable bosses or employees, and we might decide to write restrictive terms into the contract—we might make it a five-year contract, with strong penalties on both sides for premature termination, or, as a college professor, I might insist on lifetime tenure in the job before I'll take it. (He might change his mind about hiring me at that point.) If one of those alternatives looks better to us, we can go that way—the law allows us a wide range of freedom in forging our own contracts. But if we choose the first way, what's wrong with it?

Epstein is in the stronger position here, for he only has to say, over and over again, that freedom is good, that autonomy is morally preferable to servitude, and that intelligent people should therefore be free to decide the terms of their own contracts on the basis of their own perceived interests. But the story above is not the situation that raises the question of just-cause dismissal. The story that raises that question is of the employee who took the job in the shop right out of high school, or in the office right out of college, and has now been a faithful employee for twenty-two years. A new boss comes in and decides that the productivity of the shop is not high enough, or the office doesn't look smart enough, so she fires most of the older employees to hire new young people who will look better and work harder. Should she be able to do that?

The point is, as McCall points out, that after twenty-odd years of work, it doesn't seem fair to be tossed out on your ear with only thirty days' notice, too late in your life to make a new career or, often, even to get another job, after all those years of making it to work through rain and snow, loyal to the company, assuming that you'd be at the company working hard for the rest of your life. Contract or no contract, it is not in accordance with justice to reciprocate an effective lifetime of labor with a thirty-day termination. When your employer hired you year after year, wasn't he entering into some kind of super-contract with you, that you would always be there for him and he would always be there for you? If your boyfriend hangs out with you for twenty years, you can call yourself married in the common law, and you can get a financial award from the man if he walks out on you. Shouldn't employment be bound by the same presumptions?

Ask yourself, as you read these selections, what you will expect of an employer. If you're doing your job, shouldn't you be allowed to keep it? If times change and the employer wants something else, shouldn't you have the opportunity to upgrade yourself before your employer upgrades for you?

YES

Richard A. Epstein

In Defense of the Contract at Will

. . . The persistent tension between private ordering and government regulation exists in virtually every area known to the law, and in none has that tension been more pronounced than in the law of employer and employee relations. During the last fifty years, the balance of power has shifted heavily in favor of direct public regulation, which has been thought strictly necessary to redress the perceived imbalance between the individual and the firm. In particular the employment relationship has been the subject of at least two major statutory revolutions. The first, which culminated in the passage of the National Labor Relations Act in 1935,[1] set the basic structure for collective bargaining that persists to the current time. The second, which is embodied in Title VII of the Civil Rights Act of 1964,[2] offers extensive protection to all individuals against discrimination on the basis of race, sex, religion, or national origin. The effect of these two statutes is so pervasive that it is easy to forget that, even after their passage, large portions of the employment relation remain subject to the traditional common law rules, which when all was said and done set their face in support of freedom of contract and the system of voluntary exchange. One manifestation of that position was the prominent place that the common law, especially as it developed in the nineteenth century, gave to the contract at will. The basic position was well set out in an oft-quoted passage from *Payne v. Western & Atlantic Railroad:*

> [M]en must be left, without interference to buy and sell where they please, and to discharge or retain employees at will for good cause or for no cause, or even for bad cause without thereby being guilty of an unlawful act *per se*. It is a right which an employee may exercise in the same way, to the same extent, for the same cause or want of cause as the employer.[3]

The survival of the contract at will, and the frequency of its use in private markets, might well be taken as a sign of its suitability for employment relations. But the contract at will has been in retreat even at common law, as the movement for public control of labor markets has now spilled over into the judicial arena. The judicial erosion of the older position has been spurred on by academic commentators, who have been almost unanimous in their condemnation of the at-will relationship, often treating it as an archaic relic that should be jettisoned along with other vestiges of nineteenth-century laissez-faire.[4] . . .

. . . The contract at will is not ideal for every employment relation. No court or legislature should ever command its use. Nonetheless, there are two ways in which the contract at will should be respected: one deals with entitlements against regulation and the other with presumptions in the event of contractual silence.

First, the parties should be permitted as of right to adopt this form of contract if they so desire. The principle behind this conclusion is that freedom of contract tends both to advance individual autonomy and to promote the efficient operation of labor markets.

Second, the contract at will should be respected as a rule of construction in response to the perennial question of gaps in contract language: what term should be implied in the absence of explicit agreement on the question of duration or grounds for termination? The applicable standard asks two familiar questions: what rule tends to lend predictability to litigation and to advance the joint interests of the parties?[5] On both these points I hope to show that the contract at will represents in most contexts the efficient solution to the employment relation. . . .

I. The Fairness of the Contract At Will

The first way to argue for the contract at will is to insist upon the importance of freedom of contract as an end in itself. Freedom of contract is an aspect of individual liberty, every bit as much as freedom of speech, or freedom in the selection of marriage partners or in the adoption of religious beliefs or affiliations. Just as it is regarded as prima facie unjust to abridge these liberties, so too is it presumptively unjust to abridge the economic liberties of individuals. The desire to make one's own choices about employment may be as strong as it is with respect to marriage or participation in religious activities, and it is doubtless more pervasive than the desire to participate in political activity. Indeed for most people, their own health and comfort, and that of their families, depend critically upon their ability to earn a living by entering the employment market. If government regulation is inappropriate for personal, religious, or political activities, then what makes it intrinsically desirable for employment relations?

It is one thing to set aside the occasional transaction that reflects only the momentary aberrations of particular parties who are overwhelmed by major personal and social dislocations. It is quite another to announce that a rule to which vast numbers of individuals adhere is so fundamentally corrupt that it does not deserve the minimum respect of the law. With employment contracts we are not dealing with the widow who has sold her inheritance for a song to a man with a thin mustache. Instead we are dealing with the routine stuff of ordinary life; people who are competent enough to marry, vote, and pray are not unable to protect themselves in their day-to-day business transactions.

Courts and legislatures have intervened so often in private contractual relations that it may seem almost quixotic to insist that they bear a heavy burden of justification every time they wish to substitute their own judgment for that of the immediate parties to the transactions. Yet it is hardly likely that remote public bodies have better information about individual preferences than the parties who hold them. This basic principle of autonomy, moreover, is not limited to some areas of individual conduct and wholly inapplicable to others. It covers all these activities as a piece and admits no ad hoc exceptions, but only principled limitations. . . .

II. The Utility of the Contract At Will

The strong fairness argument in favor of freedom of contract makes short work of the various for-cause and good-faith restrictions upon private contracts. Yet the argument is incomplete in several respects. In particular, it does not explain why the presumption in the case of silence should be in favor of the contract at will. Nor does it give a descriptive account of *why* the contract at will is so commonly found in all trades and professions. Nor does the argument meet on their own terms the concerns voiced most frequently by the critics of the contract at will. Thus, the commonplace belief today (at least outside the actual world of business) is that the contract at will is so unfair and one-sided that it cannot be the outcome of a rational set of bargaining processes any more than, to take the extreme case, a contract for total slavery. While we may not, the criticism continues, be able to observe them, defects in capacity at contract formation nonetheless must be present: the ban upon the contract at will is an effective way to reach abuses that are pervasive but difficult to detect, so that modest government interference only strengthens the operation of market forces.[6] . . .

In order to show the interaction of all relevant factors, it is useful to analyze a case in which the problem of bilateral control exists, but where the overtones of inequality of bargaining power are absent. The treatment of partnership relations is therefore very instructive because partners are generally social and economic equals between whom considerations of inequality of bargaining power, so evident in the debate over the contract at will, have no relevance. To be sure, the structural differences between partnership and employment contracts must be identified, but these will in the end explain why the at-will contract may make even greater sense in the employment context. . . .

The case for the contract at will is further strengthened by another feature common to contracts of this sort. The employer is often required either to give notice or to pay damages in lieu of notice; damages are traditionally equal to the wages that the employee would have earned during the notice period. These provisions for "severance pay" provide the worker with some protection against casual or hasty discharges, but they do not interfere with the powerful efficiency characteristics of the contract at will. First, lump-sum transfers do not require the introduction of any "for cause" requirement, which could be the source of expensive litigation. Second, because the sums are definite, they can be easily computed, so that administrative costs are minimized. Third, because the payments are unconditional, they do not create perverse incentives for the employee or heavy monitoring costs for the employer: the terminated employee will not be tempted to avoid gainful employment in order to run up his damages for wrongful discharge; the employer, for his part, will not have to monitor the post-termination behavior of the employee in order to guard against that very risk. Thus, provisions for severance pay can be used to give employees added protection against arbitrary discharge without sacrificing the advantages of a clean break between the parties. . . .

The contract at will is also a sensible private adaptation to the problem of imperfect information over time. In sharp contrast to the purchase of standard goods, an inspection of the job before acceptance is far less likely to guarantee its quality thereafter. The future is not clearly known. More important, employees, like employers, *know what they do not know.* They are not faced with a bolt from the blue, with an "unknown unknown." Rather they face a known unknown for which they can plan. The at-will contract is an essential part of that planning because it allows both sides to take a wait-and-see attitude to their relationship so that new and more accurate choices can be made on the strength of improved information. ("You can start Tuesday and we'll see how the job works out" is a highly intelligent response to uncertainty.) To be sure, employment relationships are more personal and hence often stormier than those that exist in financial markets, but that is no warrant for replacing the contract at will with a for-cause contract provision. The proper question is: will the shift in methods of control work a change for the benefit of both parties, or will it only make a difficult situation worse? . . .

1. *Administrative Costs.* There is one last way in which the contract at will has an enormous advantage over its rivals. It is very cheap to administer. Any effort to use a for-cause rule will in principle allow all, or at least a substantial fraction of, dismissals to generate litigation. Because motive will be a critical element in these cases, the chances of either side obtaining summary judgment will be negligible. Similarly, the broad modern rules of discovery will allow exploration into every aspect of the employment relation. Indeed, a little imagination will allow the plaintiff's lawyer to delve into the general employment policies of the firm, the treatment of similar cases, and a review of the individual file. The employer for his part will be able to examine every aspect of the employee's performance and personal life in order to bolster the case for dismissal. . . .

Conclusion

The recent trend toward expanding the legal remedies for wrongful discharge has been greeted with wide approval in judicial, academic, and popular circles. In this paper, I have argued that the modern trend rests in large measure upon a misunderstanding of the contractual processes and the ends served by the contract at will. No system of regulation can hope to match the benefits that the contract at will affords in employment relations. The flexibility afforded by the contract at will permits the ceaseless marginal adjustments that are necessary in any ongoing productive activity conducted, as all activities are, in conditions of technological and business change. The strength of the contract at will should not be judged by the occasional cases in which it is said to produce unfortunate results, but rather by the vast run of cases where it provides a sensible private response to the many and varied problems in labor contracting. All too often the case for a wrongful discharge doctrine rests upon the identification of possible employer abuses, as if they were all that mattered. But the proper goal is to find the set of comprehensive arrangements that will minimize the frequency and severity of abuses by employers and employees alike. Any effort to drive employer abuses to zero can only increase the difficulties inherent in the employment relation. Here, a full analysis of the relevant costs and benefits shows why the constant minor imperfections of the market, far from being a reason to oust private agreements, offer the most powerful reason for respecting them. The doctrine of wrongful discharge is the problem and not the solution. This is one of the many situations in which courts and legislatures should leave well enough alone.

Notes

1. Act of July 5, 1935, ch. 372, 49 Stat. 449 (codified as amended at 29 U.S.C. §§ 151–169 (1982)).

2. Pub. L. No. 88–352, 78 Stat. 253 (codified as amended at 42 U.S.C. §§ 2000e to 2000e–17 (1982)).

3. Payne v. Western & Atl. R.R., 81 Tenn. 507, 518–19 (1884), *overruled on other grounds,* Hutton v. Waters, 132 Tenn. 527, 544, 179 S.W. 134, 138 (1915). The passage continues as follows:

   He may refuse to work for a man or company, that trades with any obnoxious person, or does other things which he dislikes. He may persuade his fellows and the employer may lose all his hands and be compelled to close his doors; or he may yield to the demand and withdraw his custom or cease his dealings, and the obnoxious person be thus injured or wrecked in business.

   81 Tenn. at 519. It should be noted that *Payne* did not itself involve the discharge of an employee for a bad reason or no reason at all. As the last two quoted sentences indicate, the question of the status of the contract arose obliquely, in a defamation suit by a merchant against a railroad. The railroad's yard master had posted a sign that read: "Any employee of this company on Chattanooga pay-roll who trades with L. Payne from this date will be discharged. Notify all in your department." *Payne,* 81 Tenn. at 510.

   The plaintiff Payne claimed that his business, which had been heavily dependent upon the trade of railroad workers, had thereby been ruined. The court held for the defendant on the grounds that (a) there was no defamation implicit in the announcement and (b) the employer's notice to its employees was within its rights because all the contracts with its workers were terminable at will. *Hutton* overruled *Payne,* not on the ground that contracts at will were against public policy, but on an abuse-of-rights theory according to which an employer cannot use his right to discharge employees for the sole purpose of harming third-party interests. The propriety of the *Hutton* theory is a difficult question, but my views tend toward those of the *Payne* court. *See* Epstein, *A Common Law for Labor Relations: A Critique of the New Deal Labor Legislation,* 92 YALE L.J. 1357, 1367–69, 1381 (1983).

4. *E.g.*, Blackburn, *Restricted Employer Discharge Rights: A Changing Concept of Employment at Will,* 17 AM. BUS. L.J. 467, 491–92 (1980); Blades, *Employment at Will v. Individual Freedom: On Limiting the Abusive Exercise of Employer Power,* 67 COLUM. L. REV. 1404, 1405–06, 1413–14, 1435 (1967); Blumrosen, *Employer Discipline: United States Report,* 18 RUTGERS L. REV. 428, 428–34 (1964); Feinman, *The Development of the Employment at Will Rule,* 2 AM. J. LEGAL HIST. 118, 131–35 (1976); Murg & Scharman, *Employment at Will: Do the Exceptions Overwhelm the Rule?,* 23 B.C.L. REV. 329, 338–40, 383–84 (1982); Peck, *Unjust Discharges from Employment: A Necessary Change in the Law,* 40 OHIO ST. L.J. 1, 1–10 (1979); Summers, *Individual Protection Against Unjust Dismissal: Time for a Statute,* 62 VA. L. REV. 481, 484 (1976); Weynard, *Present Status of Individual Employee Rights,* PROC. N.Y.U. 22D ANN. CONF. ON LAB. 171, 214–16 (1970); Note, *Guidelines for a Public Policy Exception to the Employment at Will Rule,* 13 CONN. L. REV. 617, 641–42 (1980); Note, *Protecting Employees at Will Against Wrongful Discharge: The Public Policy Exception,* 96 HARV. L. REV. 1931, 1931–35 (1983); Note, *Protecting At Will Employees Against Wrongful Discharge: The Duty to Terminate Only in Good Faith,* 93 HARV. L. REV. 1816, 1824–28 (1980) [hereinafter cited as Note, *Wrongful Discharge*]; Note, *A Common Law Action for the Abusively Discharged Employee,* 26 HASTINGS L.J. 1435, 1443–46 (1975); Note, *Implied Contract Rights to Job Security,* 26 STAN. L. REV. 335, 337–40 (1974); Note, *California's Controls on Employer Abuse of Employee Political Rights,* 22 STAN. L. REV. 1015, 1015–20 (1970).

5. The traditional rule has been codified under current California law: "An employment, having no specified term, may be terminated at the will of either party on notice to the other." CAL. LAB. CODE § 2922 (West 1971). Indeed, this should mean, as it now does, that where a contract speaks of "permanent" employment, the presumption should again be that the contract is terminable at will, for all that "permanent" connotes is the absence of any definite termination date. It does not imply one in which there is a lifetime engagement by either employer or employee, especially where none of the subsidiary terms for such a long-term relationship is identified by the parties. The proper rule of construction should be that the contract is terminable at will by either side.

6. Kronman, *Paternalism and the Law of Contracts,* 92 YALE L.J. 763, 777 (1983). The point is especially important in connection with the law of undue influence, where there is a long historical dispute over the relationship between the adequacy of consideration received and the procedural soundness of the underlying transaction. *See* Simpson, *The Horwitz Thesis and the History of Contracts,* 46 U. CHI. L. REV. 533, 561–80 (1979). Nonetheless, paternalistic explanations, whatever their force elsewhere, have little power in connection with employment relations. Indeed, if one thought it appropriate to restrict the powers of workers to make their own decisions during negotiations over the terms of employment, it might follow that restrictions on their right to participate in unions could be justified as well, for in both instances workers have proven that they often need to be protected against their own folly.

John J. McCall  **NO**

A Defense of Just Cause Dismissal Rules

I. Introduction

. . . Discussion of business practices often proceeds as if market principles are the only criteria needed in order to assess whether a practice is wise and reasonable. However, purely market-based analyses fail to acknowledge an indisputable fact: all markets operate in a social space that is defined by the moral values of the culture in which they are embedded. An example that illustrates this fact is the difference between U.S. and European practices governing the dismissal of individual employees. If we understand the legal differences between the U.S. and Europe, as well as management's response to those differences, we can see how differences in particular accepted moral norms give a different shape to the marketplace.

In dismissal policy, U.S. law follows a modified Employment at Will (EAW) approach. Corporations have wide discretion in both the procedures and reasons governing an individual employee's termination. For example, except for a handful of reasons identified as illegitimate by statute or past judicial precedent, employers may terminate for any or even for no reason. (Legally prohibited reasons include firings based on race or those in violation of clear public policy.) Employees who successfully press a wrongful discharge case through the courts may stand to recover very sizable awards (in the millions of dollars). However, winning a suit requires that the employee bear the initial burden of establishing that the discharge was for one of the identified illegitimate reasons.

Most European corporations operate in a much different legal environment. There, the legal systems usually mandate a Just Cause approach to dismissal. Under this approach, corporations must notify non-probationary employees of intent to dismiss. They are also significantly limited in the reasons the law will accept as adequate grounds for dismissal. Corporations must supply the employee with the reason for intended dismissal and the employee has the right to challenge the reason, usually in a pre-termination hearing and always before an external, easily accessible, and independent arbiter. Further, the initial burden of proof is on the employer. If, say, an employer wishes to dismiss an employee for poor productivity, the employer must have both clear, previously announced performance standards and evidence that the particular

From *Business Ethics Quarterly*, vol. 13, issue 2, April 2003, pp. 151–153, 161–175. Copyright © 2003 by Business Ethics Quarterly. Reprinted by permission of The Philosophy Documentation Center, publisher of Business Ethics Quarterly. References omitted.

employee has failed to meet those standards. If successful, aggrieved employees can receive remedies such as some small multiple of wages or re-instatement (though the latter happens in a very small minority of cases). This Just Cause approach places substantially greater limits on the power of European employers to dismiss a worker.

Legal differences, though, are only part of the difference between the U.S. and European dismissal policies. Interviews I have conducted with executives from across the European Community revealed a strong and almost universal moral endorsement of Just Cause requirements. Senior managers in a wide variety of firms (from small local manufacturers to mega-firms whose products are recognizable in the international marketplace, from large national retailers to EC-wide food distributors) expressed the same sentiment when responding to questions about their attitude towards legally mandated Just Cause: The employee deserves not only an in-house hearing but also an external "court of appeal" where he/she can challenge the reasons for dismissal. Management sometimes mentioned the difficulties encountered under such a system but also often described those difficulties as a cost of doing business, a cost that was required by the moral values to which they were committed.

This commitment seems to extend beyond the few managers that I interviewed. No concerted efforts by business specifically to repeal Just Cause dismissal rules has been part of recent European legal reform. There has been a significant change, however, in that the percentage of temporary and part-time work has grown substantially in Europe over the past decade as regulations governing fixed-term employment contracts have been relaxed. Some attribute this change to corporate desires for a more flexible labor law. There is some truth to this. However, we need to be careful in identifying just what flexibility employers desire. Is it, for example, in rules governing individual dismissal or in rules governing severance in cases of collective dismissals? My interviews found the latter to be more a source of complaint.

In the U.S., on the other hand, corporate lobbying efforts historically have resisted legally mandated Just Cause dismissal rules. Just Cause proposals have been introduced in the legislatures of any number of states over the last decades, but only in the case of Montana has the proposal been enacted into law. While quite a number of large U.S. corporations have adopted internal appeals mechanisms and have promised workers that they will be dismissed only for cause, those systems are voluntary and without the easily accessible external appeals mechanisms available to Europeans. (Non-unionized U.S. workers usually must make their case in the court system, a potentially expensive and daunting proposition.) And recently, many U.S. corporations, in a move to prevent costly wrongful firing suits, are requiring workers to sign waiver statements that indicate acceptance of Employment at Will. Even some corporations that have extensive, voluntarily adopted grievance systems have done this. In the U.S., notwithstanding the common cultural heritage with Western Europe, the traditional emphases on economic liberty, competition, and individualism have given a different shape to the labor market. It would appear, at least at first blush, that the U.S. and Europe have sharply different values that are reflected in how employees are treated.

What are the possible responses for ethicists confronted by circumstances where markets are shaped by such conflicting value assumptions? One response, of course, is to retreat into an easy moral and cultural relativism that views cultural differences as simply brute, irresolvable disagreement. That would be too easy, however. For while some disagreements between cultures may be incapable of rational resolution, others might be settled by careful argument. For instance, it may be that analysis could show that one of the conflicting opinions is inadequate even on the basis of its own foundational assumptions. It is always possible that a given particular normative commitment is not justified by the fundamental principles of its own value system. To assume, without analysis, that any particular extant cultural norm is coherent with the basic values espoused by the culture is to assume too much.

Another response is available, then, for ethicists who wish to analyze cultural difference. It is to assess the degree to which the specific conflicting judgments of the cultures are (or are not) reasonable given their respective supporting arguments and underlying principles. In the pages that follow, I suggest that such an analysis will find fault with the arguments advanced in the U.S. against Just Cause. I want to argue that, given the underlying principles revealed by those arguments, the U.S. should drop its opposition and, instead, institute Just Cause protections for workers.

Typically, the arguments against Just Cause divide into two broad categories: those based on predicted dire social consequences and those based on individual right claims. For instance, the more *laissez faire* U.S approach is often defended as both a) more productive, and b) required by the rights to property and freedom of contract. I want to argue, however, that: 1) the empirical prediction of productivity losses with Just Cause is not supported by the evidence; 2) the economic arguments based on ideal market analyses are fraught with difficulties; and 3) the appeals to property or contract rights are insufficient to trump the claimed right of employees to freedom from arbitrary dismissal. Accordingly, I will propose that a Just Cause legal regime is preferable to the current U.S. model.

II. Consequences

Consequentialist objections to Just Cause themselves fall into two broad categories. One is associated with practical management and organizational behavior worries; the other comes from the ideal market analyses of law and economics theorists. Both types of argument are substantially speculative and I believe both have serious shortcomings. . . .

A. Market Arguments

The claims that job security provisions are costly to workers themselves can also be challenged. In order to determine whether workers are better off with job security, we need to identify, in the words of a classic jazz tune, "Compared to What?" Even if, for the sake of argument, we accept that there is a wage premium for workers without job security under EAW rules (contrary to some suggestions above), we need to ask whether workers with job security under a legal EAW regime are economically worse off, not only than workers without job security in that EAW system, but also than workers under a Just Cause regime that grants job security as the initial entitlement (Hager, 1991). Under the latter approach, of course, it is management that must buy the right to terminate at will from employees. Once again, the judgment will likely be influenced by the starting assumptions one makes about the distribution of entitlements.

The previously cited experimental evidence in Millon (1998) about the outcomes of parallel bargaining circumstances where entitlements were reversed is relevant here as well. The evidence cited concerning waivable employment default rules (rules that establish initial legal rules that the parties are free to negotiate around) showed that those persons favored by a default rule do better in negotiations than if the default rule were the opposite. Millon argues that this evidence indicates that workers both with and without job security under a job security default rule will be better off than workers employed at will under an EAW default rule.

Finally, Epstein's argument about the probability of error and the attendant possible harms has fatal flaws. His claim that employer abuse is improbable is discredited by problems noted above. The claim that unfairly dismissed but competent employees are unlikely to suffer serious harm may be an inaccurate description of potential employers' criteria of evaluation. There are reasons for suspecting that an employee who was dismissed, even unfairly, is permanently seen as suspect goods. Additionally, the ease with which even competent employees can find replacement work is overstated. Finally, his appeal to the potential damage to the corporation of large jury verdicts is a red herring, at least as an argument against Just Cause. For, recall that Just Cause policies typically give increased job security for employees in exchange for decreased corporate exposure to the "litigation lottery." For example, in the U.K. there was a limit of £11,000 on unfair dismissal awards (Donkin, 1994). Under Montana's Unfair Dismissal From Employment Act, the maximal award is four times earnings less what one could reasonably have been expected to earn since the termination (Bierman et al., 1993). The potential for large jury awards is irrelevant when assessing the costs of Just Cause.

The preceding theoretical market-based arguments against Just Cause thus fare no better than do those driven by practical management concern for worker productivity. In neither case is there a preponderance of argument to establish that Just Cause damages productivity. And so, these speculative concerns about the potential harmful consequences cannot lead to a rejection of Just Cause.

This final paragraph on the consequential arguments against Just Cause may be an appropriate place to note a tension between the two broad categories of consequential argument we have identified. The motivation argument claimed that workers needed to be motivated by fear of job loss. Such motivation can only be effective if job loss is perceived as both a real possibility and a serious harm. However, some market-based arguments claim that job security provisions are unnecessary and that unfairly dismissed employees are not seriously damaged. But these claims cannot both be true. For if the market already deters abuse, provides for job security, and minimizes the harm of unfair discharge, then the motivational argument loses all force since job loss is unlikely and not harmful. Alternatively, if, as I suspect is more likely, the motivational argument is correct in holding that workers see job loss as a serious harm, then that would disclose the absolute unreality of some of the law and economics objections to Just Cause.

We need now to move to a consideration of the rights based objections to Just Cause policies.

III. Rights
A. Rights Objections

Typically, rights arguments against Just Cause appeal to two members of the generally recognized pantheon of rights—property and freedom of contract (Werhane, 1985; Werhane and Radin, 1999).

Property rights are traditionally understood to involve an owner's entitlement to control goods in specific ways. Owners are entitled, among other things, to possess, to use, to benefit from, to dispose of, and to limit others' use of, benefit from, and access to the thing owned. If we take one's house or car as paradigmatic examples, ownership entitles one to deny access or use rights to others and to revoke previously granted access and use rights. Concretely, I have a right to control who enters my house and a right to ask any guest to leave. Opponents of Just Cause treat corporate property analogously. They argue that owners (or more usually, the agents of owners—managers) retain the right to deny employees further access to the work site, that is, to terminate employment. Legally mandated job security policies are thus unjust interferences with owners' property rights.

The second rights argument against Just Cause sees it as a violation of the right of free individuals to engage in voluntary exchanges with others. By prohibiting contracts with terms that specify employment at will, Just Cause policies interfere with persons' abilities to negotiate for themselves whatever contract provisions they find most desirable. For instance, under some Just Cause regimes, workers may be prohibited from choosing at will employment in exchange for greater income. As such, this second argument claims that Just Cause policies are unjust limits on market agents' freedoms of contract and association (Maitland, 1984; Narveson, 1992; Nozick, 1974). (This claim may not be true, of course. It is possible that Just Cause merely functions as the default interpretation when contracts are silent about dismissal terms, or it could make the job security entitlement one that is waivable by the right holder but only in exchange for at least a statutorily guaranteed minimum consideration.)

B. Method

These arguments are not easily dismissed. The rights they appeal to have powerful rhetorical force, especially in the U.S. But before we accept them as cogent objections, we need to clarify the circumstances of the debate. The debate over Just Cause is a case of conflicting right claims. Management and owners claim rights to property and freedom of contract. Workers claim conflicting rights to freedom from arbitrary and unfair discharge. It is true that the first two rights have existing recognition while, in the U.S. at least, the third is at best what Joel Feinberg calls a manifesto right, one claimed to be supported by good reasons but not yet socially sanctioned. However, its manifesto status is not a reason for allowing property and freedom of contract rights immediately to "trump" job security. For it may be that, on analysis, we decide that our current understanding of rights fails in not recognizing a right to job security.

A more reasonable method for resolving conflicts between rights claims must directly assess the merits of the competing claims. Moreover, a reasonable method will do more than consider the relative importance of the conflicting rights in some general and abstract way. Rather, resolving conflicts between rights requires us to focus on the particular cases where the conflict arises since the conflict between rights typically occurs in defined marginal areas. Recognizing job security rights, for example, will not interfere with conceptions of non-corporate property rights, nor will it impact other aspects of corporate property rights, such as the right freely to sell one's shares in the market.

We can satisfy these requirements for a reasonable assessment of rights conflicts if we ask two questions of each of the competing claims: 1) What are the justifying or foundational reasons for this right (why is it a right)? 2) What harm would be done to those underlying values if we recognized a conflicting right claim and thus marginally constrained the scope of a particular right? Here, for instance, we need to ask what are the foundations of property, freedom of contract, and job security rights, and what harm would be done to those respective values if we denied a right to job security and gave owners the right to terminate at will or, alternatively, if we denied owners that right and instituted a Just Cause policy.

C. Response to Property Objections

What are the foundations of property rights? There is a very clear historical tradition of argument justifying rights to private ownership of property (that is rights privately to control goods, to benefit from them, to exclude others from using them, etc). In the modern period, individual rights to possess property privately have three significant foundations: autonomy, fairness, and utility. First, private control over property has been presented as instrumentally advancing an owner's autonomy by providing her a secure base of material possessions that frees her from over-reliance on the decisions of others. Second, it has been upheld as the only approach that fairly rewards the effort expended or the risk assumed in a productive activity. Finally, it has been urged as providing incentive for people to work and invest, thus raising the total amount of economic production and, in turn, the net standard of living.

Interestingly, the claimed right of employees to job security can be argued to rest on the same grounds: Dismissals can be arbitrary (fairness). They can damage the worker's ability to gain a wage, and thus make life both less happy (utility) and less within his/her control (autonomy). Workers who are no longer able to rely on secure income will have many significant life choices foreclosed (autonomy). Just Cause, then, can be defended on the same grounds of autonomy, fairness, and utility that are the traditional supports for private property rights.

What harm to these three underlying values would be done if corporations were required by Just Cause rules to extend job security to their workers? Would constraining the scope of an owner's right to deny access to corporate property hamper fairness or autonomy for owners? Would overall social utility be decreased if workers had a right to be free from arbitrary and unfair dismissal?

1. Fairness

First, consider the question about relative impacts on fairness. As was previously noted, property rights, and the associated rights to benefit from and to control goods, are historically justified, in part, on fairness grounds. But fairness, as the parent of any young child will attest, is often simultaneously both an overused and underdefined moral concept. Nonetheless, appeals to fairness can be more reasonably grounded than the simple assertion of "That's not fair!" if clear criteria are available. Criteria for assessing the fairness of a distribution, for example, typically will refer to three considerations: contribution, risk, and/or arbitrariness. Fair treatment requires that allocations of goods (and entitlements over them) be proportional to a person's contribution or risk assumed in creating the goods. It also requires that goods and benefits not be allocated to (or removed from) a person for arbitrary reasons. Since investors bear risk and make a contribution, risk and contribution are intuitively good, not arbitrary, moral reasons for allocating to them rights to privately control corporate property.

However, Just Cause rules do not erase owners' control over corporate property; they merely alter the right to control at the margins. Owners, even under Just Cause, still retain substantial control over assets—they can sell their shares freely; they can collectively dictate to management (with some limits) corporate policy, they retain rights to residual income, etc. This marginal decrease in an owner's control over property under Just Cause seems, whether on grounds of contribution or risk, insufficient to override an employee claim to job security because employees can also point to past contribution and risk as well. In addition, they can assert that they ought not be removed from employment without good cause, that is, for arbitrary reasons. Thus, recognizing an employee claim of dismissal only for good cause simply reduces the owner's marginal control. Moreover, evidence above also suggests that the Just Cause may have small impact on the owner's return/benefit.

Some, of course, will object to this analysis by arguing that the wages paid by the market assure fair treatment of workers (presumably because the wage rate is consensual). In this argument, so long as employees are paid for their past work, they have been fully compensated for their effort, risk, and contributions. They thus have no claim on future employment.

A number of points can be made in response to this argument that wages are full and fair compensation. The assumption (that past wages are adequate compensation for past contribution) may be challenged. Consider, for example, evidence from some analyses of internal labor markets (the labor market as it operates within a firm). These analyses claim that employees are paid less than their marginal contribution to the firm in the earlier years of their career and more than their marginal contribution later in their career (because wages and benefits tend to rise over time in a way that is not based purely on increased productivity). This deferred compensation of the early years is recouped only gradually. Employers can also use the deferral as a mechanism to reduce monitoring costs and to bind a worker to the firm, thus also reducing turnover costs (since a voluntary quit means foregoing deferred wages). Employers reap benefits from this aspect of the internal labor market. However, when an employee is fired without good cause, employers can also opportunistically and unfairly seize the promised future wages. (Blair, 1995; Lazear, 1992; Osterman, 1992; and Weiler, 1990) Thus, it is not necessarily the case that past wages can be assumed to be full and fair compensation for previous contribution. Terminating without good cause may instead be a paradigmatically unfair seizure.

However, even if we assume that the wage already paid is fair compensation for one's past risk and contribution, the issue here is whether terminating a relationship without good cause is acceptable on fairness grounds. It may not be if certain conditions are present. For example, even where pay for past contributions is morally adequate, it is possible that management actions created an expectation of future employment, expectations upon which employees relied. (See, for instance, Kim, 1999 and Singer, 1988, for discussions of ways in which reliance is elicited by particular firms and by economic institutions more broadly. It is worth noting that such reliance has historically been to the firm's advantage, allowing it to secure long term labor and to reduce monitoring costs.) What is fair can be a function not only of wages agreed to but also of promises made (explicitly and implicitly) and of consequent patterns of reliance.

Moreover, the fact that representations upon which employees relied were made by the firm's agents is not the only relevant consideration here. Such representations may be sufficient to raise questions of fairness but they are not necessary. Fairness norms can be implicated as well when, even without clear representations that created reliance, one party has come to depend in basic ways on a relationship or practice. When others crucially depend on and expect continued participation in a cooperative enterprise, it appears patently unfair to abruptly end the relationship without notice and without good reason, an idea we reflect in our common moral assessments of contexts as varied as marriage, housing, and access to traditional routes of public passage through private property. (See Singer, 1989 and Beerman and Singer, 1988 for extended discussions of how these moral assessments are reflected in much of our settled law in areas other than employment.) Thus, giving either party in an employment relationship the power to terminate the relationship without due process and good cause violates commonly held norms of fairness where there is long-standing dependence and expectation. It is especially unfair when one party has the preponderance of power.

The preceding point is merely an instance of a more general point: fair treatment in employment relationships often involves more than consensual monetary exchange. Employees clearly can be paid adequately but nonetheless treated unfairly if subjected to harassment or merely to ridicule. Thus there is clear need to consider when termination, even when past wages were adequate, is compatible with reasonable criteria of fairness. It is presumptively not when corporate actions create expectations of future employment. Dismissal without good reason from one's source of income, from one's social network, and from all the other goods associated with employment would seem to run afoul of this reliance criterion of fairness as well. So, even if past wages were adequate, it is still possible that a dismissal is unfair if it is based on arbitrary reasons.

We have, then, strong reasons for suggesting that firing without good cause, and thus removing a person from a source of income upon which he/she crucially depends, is inherently arbitrary and unfair. We need however to become more precise about what constitutes good cause and whether the set of reasons described as "good cause" is equivalent to the set of reasons accepted under Just Cause policies. It may, of course, be the case that Just Cause rules are more substantively restrictive than merely requiring that dismissal be for morally acceptable, good cause. We can evaluate whether this is the case by identifying the cases where Just Cause rules differ from EAW in the substantive grounds for permissible discharge. Recall that both Just Cause and EAW allow dismissal on grounds of inadequate performance, theft, absenteeism, etc. There are, though, at least three main scenarios where Just Cause is more restrictive than EAW. These are its prohibitions on dismissal for no reason, for personal reasons that are unrelated to productivity, and for the reason that there is a more productive replacement available for a currently adequate employee.

The first and second of these reasons seem to be paradigmatic examples of unfair treatment. Terminating a person's employment for no reason or for purely personal reasons is the epitome of arbitrary treatment. The third reason seems more defensible, however. Maintaining a current employee who merely performs adequately when there are others available who project to be superior performers certainly appears to damage the interests of the firm, as well as the interests of owners and, indeed, of other workers. Dismissing such an employee and replacing him with the predicted superior performer could, from that perspective, be argued as neither arbitrary nor unfair. Under this analysis, cause for termination exists whenever the firm possesses any competitive economic reason for dismissal.

We should reiterate here the previous point about the systemic effects of a firm's labor practices. Allowing the contemplated replacement policy is not a simple exchange of two workers, one for the other. Instead, it alters the entire system of employee relations. As noted above, it is not obvious that the potential gain of the more productive worker is greater than the opportunity costs inherent in adopting this replacement policy. Here, however, the question is not the productivity impact of the replacement but its fairness. At least two serious questions may be raised about the fairness of a policy that allows the replacement of an adequate performer whenever another is available who projects to be superior.

First, we need to ask which persons might be placed at greater risk by allowing such replacement. Arguably, allowing an adequate performer to be replaced would differentially impact more mature workers who might have both higher wages and declining productivity. The removal of longer-term employees whose loyalty has been a benefit to the firm in the past would seem to run counter to notions of fair treatment (for reasons of both contribution and expectation), and would seem to impose unreasonable demands for productivity over the course of a working career. A replacement policy of the sort under discussion here conjures the image of persons (human resources) being used up and disposed of.

Of course, the current American structure is not strict EAW but rather an EAW modified by numerous pieces of employment legislation, legislation that includes a prohibition on age discrimination. Thus, the fact that strict EAW might have this differential impact on mature workers is not to say that current U.S. legal standards would have this impact. This is true enough. But nonetheless, Just Cause would differ from even the modified U.S. version of EAW in that it places the burden of proof in termination on the employer rather than on the employee (as the U.S. law does). This fact is not insignificant given the substantial hurdles faced by plaintiffs under U.S. law and given the attitudinal sea change that would be indicated by adoption of Just Cause policy.

Second, and more importantly, allowing the replacement of an adequate performer has unacceptable implications for ideas about what corporations are entitled to. If we assume that a corporation has set reasonable standards of adequate performance, an open-ended policy permitting replacement of adequate performers essentially entails that employers can threaten dismissal unless ever-increasing productivity demands are satisfied. This demand for optimal, "110%" productivity goes beyond what any partner to an economic relationship is morally entitled. Employers are entitled to reasonable productivity and may morally threaten dismissal if a worker fails to meet that standard. Of course, a necessary condition for a reasonable demand is that a worker could meet it but being able to meet a demand is not sufficient to establish its reasonableness. For a demand to be reasonable, it must be one that can be met, not at any cost, but at a reasonable cost. That is, what is a reasonable demand must be seen in light of what we believe a decent human life to include. Demands that jeopardize goods that are constitutive of such a life are demands that are unreasonable. (Consider, from a wholly different context, Judith Thomson's (1971) analysis of what demands can reasonably be placed on a woman in order for her to avoid having to accept responsibility for pregnancy.) Workplace productivity demands that have seriously damaging impacts on family and social existence are, on any account of a decent human life, demands that are unreasonable. More generally, workplace demands that so exhaust a person's energy or time that other central aspects of life must be neglected are demands that go beyond what a corporation is reasonably entitled to. Given the unavoidable and central role that employment plays in contemporary life, a policy that allows employers to demand ever-increasing productivity under threat of dismissal is an unreasonable policy.

We have, then, grounds for believing that the set of morally good reasons for dismissal map on to that set of reasons for dismissal allowed under Just Cause rules. We can also see that some of the reasons for dismissal allowed under even the limited EAW of the U.S. are reasons that fall outside the set of morally good reasons. And, as argued above, firing without good reasons is arbitrary and, hence, unfair. Thus, the very considerations of fairness that are used in the American tradition to justify private property suggest that corporate property rights be limited by the adoption of Just Cause constraints on dismissal.

2. Autonomy

A private property right justified by appeal to autonomy seems a similarly unlikely candidate for overriding a right to be free from arbitrary dismissal. In Locke's original formulation of the argument, private property gave landowners some autonomy because it conferred on them an economic independence, especially from the powers of the crown. In the contemporary environment, most workers have whatever measure of economic independence they possess, not from landed estates, but from the security of the income gained by selling their labor on the market. To the degree that income is at risk from job loss, then to that degree workers have lost independence. Arbitrary dismissal, therefore, can substantially damage the ability of a worker to control important aspects of his/her life. On the other hand, precluding arbitrary dismissal through a Just Cause policy does not seriously decrease the degree to which the share-holders' investment in stock provides for economic independence and, hence, does not impact the ability of investors to have control over their lives. (For a more complete version of this analysis of the relation between autonomy, property, and employee rights, see McCall, 2001.)

Of course, someone might argue that Just Cause policies decrease the owner's autonomy and independence because they would decrease value of the investment. That presupposes that productivity and/or profits will decline as a result of job security. As was noted above, that assumption has not been shown to be warranted. But even if stock value or investment income did marginally decline, proponents of job security could respond by arguing that owners are entitled not to maximal return but merely to returns compatible with a requirement to treat others fairly. An invocation of the preceding fairness argument, then, has the potential to blunt even the speculative concern that job security would decrease share value or return.

It should be noted that the preceding analyses have been assuming as a context a moderately large, publicly traded corporation. Analyzing the impact of Just Cause on fairness and autonomy might be different for smaller ventures or ones that are owned by individuals or small numbers of partners. Citibank and the mom and pop corner grocery are at different extremes and may require different policies in practice. Requiring the corner grocer, or for that matter a regular employer of a household worker, to follow the same dismissal procedures as Citibank may more seriously damage the employer's control over his/her life. There may then be an argument for limiting the scope of Just Cause policies to businesses over a certain threshold size. We need to be aware, however, that even in small firms, arbitrary dismissal can still have a devastating impact on the employee and his/her family. Perhaps some mandatory severance but without the procedural requirements would be in order even for the smaller employer. If that were a known requirement, it could be planned for and calculated into the total cost of a person's employment, just as employer Social Security payments already are.

3. Utility

The analysis of the impact of mandated job security on net utility is perhaps less clear, partly because projections about future social consequences are so speculative. But some have claimed, as we have seen, that job security requirements will lower return to investors (thus depressing investment and production), reduce productivity, lower wages for employees, and depress overall employment. A number of points have been made in rebuttal of these charges above. These will not be repeated here. As for the impact on total employment, Just Cause would seem to have little net effect. It does not commit employers to keep workers who are unproductive, nor does it require them to keep workers when there is a downturn in demand. Just Cause may have an impact on the care and speed with which firms select permanent employees but it should not affect total employment levels. (See a similar analysis even for the more costly requirements of severance and restrictions on layoffs in Abraham and Houseman, 1993 and 1994, as well as Houseman, 1990.)

An item to watch, however, is whether Just Cause will increase the incentive of companies to hire temporary workers in order to avoid the process requirements for discharging employees who have completed the probationary period. This would be a significant effect given the income, benefits, and security differences between permanent and temporary work. Recent revisions in European law might provide a test case for this; the evidence is still out. I suspect, moreover, that the evidence of increased use of temporary workers is not clearly due to Just Cause rather than to other, more expensive requirements attaching to treatment of fulltime employees (e.g., other benefits or layoff provisions).

Whether the wages of other workers would decline and thus have an impact on overall utility will depend on whether there really is a wage premium for workers employed at will. This may not be the case since Just Cause appears to have little impact on net corporate income and, therefore, little effect on the employers' wage bargaining stance. Moreover, the evidence cited by Millon (1998) and discussed above makes the assumption of a wage premium problematic. However, if there nonetheless *is* a wage premium and workers under Just Cause are precluded from gaining that premium (which of course would only occur under non-waivable Just Cause rules), a utilitarian justification of Just Cause will depend in part on the benefits and costs of job security to workers, and on the relative size of the employee populations interested respectively in security or the potentially greater income gained without security. Pursuit of these questions will be left for the next section's discussion of freedom of contract.

D. Response to the Freedom of Contract Argument

In order to assess the conflict between freedom of contract rights and rights to job security, we need to ask about the foundations of freedom of contract just as we have asked about the foundations of property and job security rights. Freedom of contract has been defended on grounds of utility in that each person, as best judge of his/her own interests, is also in the best position to optimize the satisfaction of those interests. Allowing each person in the competitive marketplace to determine which goods he/she desires and how much he/she is willing to pay for them will, it is claimed, maximize the net satisfaction of interests.

A second defense of freedom of contract is on grounds of individual autonomy in that freedom of contract will obviously allow persons more direct control over their lives than if the ability to negotiate one's own terms were restricted. For instance, some will argue that employees should have the freedom to choose the job rules they prefer rather than be forced by legal mandates to accept "benefits" they do not wish to have. (Compare Narveson's (1992) argument on mandated worker participation.)

Of course, our commitment to autonomy does not result in absolute freedom of contract, as those in favor of Just Cause will be quick to note. In employment law in particular, we already accept a myriad of limits on the power of parties to set the terms of contracts. Laws governing discrimination, workplace safety, minimum wage, and sexual harassment are just a few instances where we constrain both employers and employees in negotiating contract terms. Since freedom of contract is not equivalent to absolute freedom of contract, the argument against Just Cause is incomplete unless it can show that Just Cause limits are inappropriate while other limits are acceptable. (I do not mean to suggest that all current legal limits on contracts, or even all those just mentioned, must be accepted. Rather, the point is that if one accepts any limits on contracts then one needs to distinguish those from the limits one does not accept. I also take it that a position which rejects all limits is *prima facie* an unreasonable one.)

Some might respond that acceptable limits are ones that are needed to correct for clear market failures. But, the argument continues, there are no clear failures with respect to job security. We have already discussed in Section II the reasons for suspecting that market failures of knowledge, power, and mobility might explain the relative absence of job security provisions in U.S. contracts. To the degree that those points are telling, then this attempt fails to distinguish job security from other market correcting limits on contracts.

However, even if there are no market failures with respect to job security, the response is problematic for other reasons. Not every justifiable limit on freedom of contract exists merely to remedy market failure. It would be odd indeed to claim that Civil Rights protections against discrimination and sexual harassment are responses to classic market failures. Rather, it is more natural to see such laws as expressing the belief that jeopardizing a person's employment for these morally arbitrary reasons is degrading and simply wrong.

So, some limits on contract freedoms can be defended on grounds other than correction of market failures. This is true of job security protections as well. If we accept the preceding fairness arguments, we might use Just Cause limits on employment contracts to underscore social opposition to the serious, avoidable, and arbitrary harms caused by at-will dismissals. Or, if we modeled an autonomy argument on traditional utility analysis, we might construct a "net autonomy" case for Just Cause as follows. Workers dismissed without cause suffer at least temporary loss of income, the stress that comes with that and, in all probability, loss of seniority and firm specific investment. These harms are proportionally greater the more that the dismissal would impact one's future employment applications. All of these economic losses will have serious impacts on the real life choices available to the dismissed worker. There is significant impact, then, on autonomy. The limits caused by job security requirements on the autonomy of other workers who might wish to trade security for increased income are not nearly so great. They merely lose the (speculative) marginal wage increase that might be available under at-will contracts. Moreover, this loss is not a necessary consequence of Just Cause rules. It occurs only when those rules are mandated as un-waivable; they need not be. Constraining freedom of contract, then, might produce more net autonomy for workers than would a discharge at will rule.

So, job security protections may be a rational choice for society either because workers who want them are unable to negotiate for them successfully (the market failure explanation) or because we simply want, as part of a commitment to fairness, institutionally to express an opposition to dismissals without just cause, or because we believe such protections maximize net autonomy.

Finally, we should note the following with respect to utility claims. Some provision prohibiting firing without cause is one of the first demands of union contracts. It would be surprising if unorganized workers somehow desired job security less. More reasonable is the assumption that they desire it but have been unable to secure individually for themselves what organized workers have secured. If this is true and workers generally want security, then perhaps net satisfaction would be also increased by legally proscribed protections against unfair dismissal.

IV. Conclusion

A review of the objections to Just Cause, both on grounds of consequences and rights, reveals them to be seriously deficient. Most seriously, the very foundational values of the rights commonly used in the U.S. to oppose Just Cause suggest, instead, that job security should be pursued. Concerns for fairness and autonomy arguably ought to drive the U.S. toward Just Cause requirements rather than away from them. The American resistance to Just Cause seems unwarranted on its own grounds once one recognizes that the American system of private property and freedom of contract depend on fairness and autonomy.

There is, however, a reason for resisting the introduction of Just Cause requirements that we have not yet addressed. It may be, despite the rhetoric, that Just Cause policies are simply ineffective at protecting workers from unfair dismissals. That is, while a Just Cause mechanism may be necessary for protecting workers, it may be that it alone is not sufficient. After all, most extant Just Cause policies place significant limits on the compensation available to employees when arbitrators judge them to have been unfairly dismissed. So, some might argue that current Just Cause policies cannot achieve their stated goals because they provide disincentives that are insufficient to deter arbitrary dismissals.

In fact, a survey of the Montana Bar Association completed in 1993 suggests that the Montana Wrongful Discharge from Employment Act may not adequately protect workers. More than half of the attorney respondents claimed that they personally declined to represent a plaintiff in a wrongful discharge suit. Most who said this cited as their reason the inadequate compensation available under the act given the complexity and hours involved in such suits. Perhaps more strikingly, a number of respondents reported that they believed that the act's reduction in liability for corporations had made some corporations more likely to discharge unfairly since they were no longer concerned about large damage awards (Bierman et al., 1993).

It might be that, since punishments under some extant Just Cause regimes, particularly in Montana and the U.K., are relatively small, employers who are not already committed to principles of fair dismissal will have little reason not to discharge without cause. If that is the case, what could the advantage of Just Cause be over the current American approach that at least poses the threat of the litigation lottery? There may still be two reasons for preferring Just Cause. First, a smaller, but highly probable, award for cases of unjust dismissal seems preferable to a litigation lottery where only some unfairly dismissed workers are even eligible for compensation (e.g., if they have been subject to the few unacceptable grounds enumerated under the U.S. approach). Unfairly dismissed workers are treated more equitably as a class and in relation to each other under Just Cause. And, the greater probability of an award might still serve as a disincentive for unjust termination, especially were the maximum awards more generous than those in the U.K. and Montana.

Second, the adoption of a Just Cause approach serves as a statement of public opposition to dismissal without cause. Law, in addition to its deterrence function, can also be a vehicle for educating and for creating or re-enforcing publicly important values. Law can serve the purpose of public notice of society's basic value commitments. The Civil Rights laws of the 1960s may be an historical example of how law can play a role in reshaping extant social norms that are incompatible with the espoused foundational values of the culture. So, while some currently extant Just Cause approaches may not alone guarantee protection for workers against unfair dismissal, properly constructed and publicized Just Cause laws can assist in readjusting a value system so that employers are more likely to be socialized to accept the principles of Just Cause. This would be a benefit in that it would make American employment practice more adequately reflect the espoused foundational values of its own culture.

Precisely how any U.S. Just Cause protections ought to be codified requires more debate than is possible here. Three distinct possibilities suggest themselves. (See Sunstein, 2001 and 2002, Eastlund 2002, Millon 1998.) One is that Just Cause merely be made the default rule when employment contracts fail to specify dismissal rules. This approach would allow employers and employees to contract around the default rules by adopting specific alternate provisions in the employment contract. Another approach is to make Just Cause the default but also mandate that any opting out of the default rule will provide both for some specified minimum level of compensation and some specific remaining employment protection. A third option would be to follow the lead of most of the industrialized world and to mandate non-waivable Just Cause protections for workers in all firms exceeding a small minimum size. Which of these approaches fits best with the moral values underlying the modern American commitment to private property is a matter for further argument. That argument will have to wait for another article. However, even without that analysis, we can conclude that some Just Cause protections for employees have very strong presumptive support.

Note

I would like to thank George Brenkert for some helpful comments that made this paper more cogent and more clear. I would also like to hold him responsible for any serious argumentative gaffes—but I doubt I can get away with that.

Bibliography

Abraham, Katherine, and Susan Houseman. 1993. *Job Security in America*. Washington, D.C.: The Brookings Institute.

_____. 1994. "Does Employment Protection Inhibit Labor Market Flexibility?" In *Social Protection versus Economic Flexibility*. Rebecca Blank, ed. Chicago: University of Chicago Press.

Beerman, Jack, and William Singer. 1989. "Baseline Questions in Legal Reasoning: The Case of Property in Jobs." *Georgia Law Review* 23: 911.

Bierman, Leonard, et at. 1993. "Montana's Wrongful Discharge from Employment Act: The Views of the Montana Bar." *Montana Law Review* 54: 367.

Blair, Margaret M. 1995. *Ownership and Control: Rethinking Corporate Governance for the Twenty-First Century*. Washington, D.C.: The Brookings Institute.

Donkin, Richard. 1994. "Making Fairness Work." *The Financial Times*, Management Section. September 7, 1994, p. 12.

Dworkin, Ronald. 1977. *Taking Rights Seriously*. Cambridge, Mass.: Harvard University Press.

Eastlund, Cynthia. 2002. "How Wrong Are Employees about Their Rights, and Why Does it Matter?" *New York University Law Review* 77: 6.

Epstein, Richard. 1984. "In Defense of Contract at Will." *University of Chicago Law Review* 51: 947.

Hager, Mark. 1991. "The Emperor's Clothes Are Not Efficient." *American University Law Review* 41: 7.

Houseman, Susan. 1990. "The Equity and Efficiency of Job Security." In *New Developments in the Labor Market*. K. Abraham and R. McKersie, eds. Cambridge, Mass: MIT Press.

Kim, Pauline T. 1997. "Bargaining with Imperfect Information: A Study of Worker Perceptions of Legal Protection in an At-Will World." *Cornell Law Review* 83: 105.

_____. 1999. "Norms, Learning and Law: Exploring the Influences on Workers' Legal Knowledge." *University of Illinois Law Review* 1999: 447.

Lazear, Edward P. 1992. "Compensation, Productivity and the New Economics of Personnel." In *Research Frontiers in Industrial Relations and Human Resources*. D. Lewin et al., eds. Madison, Wis.: Industrial Relations Research Association.

Maitland, Ian. 1989. "Rights in the Workplace." *Journal of Business Ethics* 8: 951.

McCall, John J. 2001. "Employee Voice in Corporate Governance: A Defense of Strong Participation Rights." *Business Ethics Quarterly* 11: 1.

Millon, David. 1998. "Default Rules, Wealth Distribution and Corporate Law Reform." *University of Pennsylvania Law Review* 146: 975.

Narveson, Jan. 1992. "Democracy and Economic Rights." In *Economic Rights*. E. Paul et al., eds. Cambridge: Cambridge University Press.

Nozick, Robert. 1974. *Anarchy, State and Utopia*. New York, N.Y.: Basic Books.

Osterman, Paul. 1992. "Internal Labor Markets in a Changing Environment." In *Research Frontiers in Industrial Relations and Human Resources*. D. Lewin et al., eds. Madison, Wis.: Industrial Relations Research Association.

Singer, Joseph William. 1988. "The Reliance Interest in Property." *Stanford University Law Review* 40: 614.

Sunstein, Cass R. 2001. "Human Behavior and the Law of Work." *Virginia Law Review* 87: 205.

_____. 2002. "Switching the Default Rule." *New York University Law Review* 77: 106.

Thomson, Judith Jarvis. 1971. "In Defense of Abortion." *Philosophy and Public Affairs* 1: 1.

Weiler, Paul. 1990. *Governing the Workplace*. Cambridge, Mass.: Harvard University Press.

Werhane, Patricia. 1985. *Persons, Rights and Corporations*. Englewood Cliffs, N.J.: Prentice Hall.

Werhane, Patricia, and Tara Radin. 1999. "Employment at Will and Due Process." In *Ethical Issues in Business: A Philosophical Approach,* 6th ed. Thomas Donaldson and Patricia Werhane, eds. Upper Saddle River, N.J.: Prentice Hall.

POSTSCRIPT

Is "Employment-at-Will" Good Social Policy?

Ultimately, the rights of Americans are determined by law. In Europe, as McCall points out, the laws are much more protective of the employee than they are in the United States. Epstein and others claim that European-style laws lead to less "efficiency"; that it is more difficult in Europe for investors to make money quickly. McCall and others argue that we should not be trampling fundamental notions of justice in order to achieve trifles more of efficiency. What do you think?

Suggested Readings

If the subject interests you, you might find the following readings interesting:

Cynthia Eastlund, "How Wrong Are Employees about Their Rights, and Why Does It Matter?" *New York University Law Review* 77:6, 2002.

Richard Green et al., "On the Ethics of At-Will Employment in the Public Sector," *Public Integrity*, vol.8, no.4, Fall 2006.

Edward P. Lazear, "Compensation, Productivity and the New Economics of Personnel," in D. Lewin et al., eds., *Research Frontiers in Industrial Relations and Human Resources* (Madison, WI: Industrial Relations Research Association).

Thomas Donaldson and Thomas Dunfee, *Ties That Bind* (Boston: Harvard University Press, 1999).

ISSUE 13

Is CEO Compensation Justified by Performance?

YES: Ira T. Kay, from "Don't Mess with CEO Pay," *Across the Board* (January/February 2006)

NO: Edgar Woolard, Jr., from "CEOs Are Being Paid Too Much," *Across the Board* (January/February 2006)

ISSUE SUMMARY

YES: Ira Kay, a consultant on executive compensation for Watson Wyatt Worldwide, argues that in general the pay of the CEO tracks the company's performance, so in general CEOs are simply paid to do what they were hired to do—bring up the price of the stock to increase shareholder wealth.

NO: Edgar Woolard, a former CEO himself, holds that the methods by which CEO compensation is determined are fundamentally flawed, and suggests some significant changes.

"**C**EOs are paid a lot to face facts, however unpleasant," writes Geoffrey Colvin in *Fortune*, "so it's time they faced this one: The issue of their pay has finally landed on the national agenda and won't be leaving soon." He ticks off the sources of national discontent with the enormous sums (and stocks, etc.) paid to the corporate chiefs: that layoffs continue, that the lowest-paid workers advance only slowly, that Japanese CEOs are paid much less for much more productivity—but mostly, just that paying one person more money than he can ever spend on anything worthwhile for himself or his family, while the world's millions struggle, suffer, and starve, just seems to be wrong.

For the fifth edition of this text (1998), the "No" side of the debate was carried by John Cassidy's 1997 *New Yorker* article "Gimme." Even then we could not use Colvin's 1992 article. For since Colvin wrote, Cassidy pointed out, chief executive compensation had gone much higher—by a factor of four for the average compensation, up to factors of fifteen and twenty for fortunate individuals. Colvin had clucked at annual compensation from $1.5 million to as high as $3 million a year; Cassidy observed compensation already at the $18 million and $20 million level. For the sixth edition of this text (2000), Cassidy no longer sufficed. Compensation had gone up to $60, $70, $90 million. The reason for the increase is clear enough—stock prices have gone up, shareholder wealth has increased enormously, and for reasons detailed in both of the selections that follow, shareholders wish to compensate management of their companies according to the increase in the price of the stock. Two questions arise immediately: First, if that's the system, what are we to do with compensation "insurance" policies that guarantee the same compensation no matter where the stock goes? Don't those arrangements kind of miss the point? And the second question is, Is this right? The shareholders' interests legitimately dictate some aspects of corporate policy, and the salaries have been agreed upon by the legally appropriate parties, but if the result is substantially unjust, should not the people as a whole step in and rectify the situation?

Urgency was added to the issue in the recession that followed the election of George W. Bush in 2000. As the computers rolled in early April 2001, stocks had undergone a sudden "correction," read, gone very far south, and shareholder wealth decreased substantially. Do we find CEO compensation humbly bowing to the facts of the ROI? Not in the least. "While typical investors lost 12 percent of their portfolios last year [2000], based on the Wilshire 5000 total market index, and profits for the Standard & Poor's 500 companies rose at less than half their pace in the 1990s, chief executives received an average 22 percent raise in salary and bonus." So we found out from a Special Report on Executive Pay from the *New York Times* on April 1, 2001 (First Business Page), and that was no April Fool. Not much had changed in 2005, according to *Forbes,* when Peter Cartwright of Calpine, which runs gas-fired power plants, took home (over the last six years) average annual compensation of $13 million while the ROI of the company over the same period was 7 percent. Average compensation over the last five years for Terry Semel of Yahoo came to $258.3 million; for Barry Diller of IAC/Inter-ActiveCorp, $239.9 million; for William McGuire of UnitedHealth Group, $342.3 million. That last is cause for pause: Your health care dollars and mine fueled that income. We knew the doctors weren't getting rich; now we know who is. You see how these 2005 figures dwarfed those that so bothered Geoffrey Colvin.

Should the American people step in and claim the right to set limits in the name of justice to the outsized amounts lavished on the fortunate sons of capitalism? That possibility is precisely what troubles Colvin. If CEOs will not regulate their own compensation, Congress and the SEC could surely step in and do a bit of regulating on their own. The prospect is not enticing to the business community. On the other hand, is this not exactly why we have government—so that when private motives get out of hand, the people as a whole can step in and defend their long-term interests?

Bear in mind, as you read the following selections, that the corporation was set up as a private enterprise, literally: a voluntary contract among investors to increase their wealth by legal means. But it is chartered and protected by the state, in the service of the state's long-term interest in a thriving economy. Adam Smith would be pleased; he argued that leaving investors to make money as best they could for their own selfish interests would best increase the welfare of the whole body of the people. The question that confronts us is, At what point do we conclude that the legal means set up for private parties to serve our interests by serving their own have failed in their purported effect and should be modified or revised? Or do we have any right to do that at this point? What do you think?

Ira T. Kay

Don't Mess with CEO Pay

For years, headlines have seized on dramatic accounts of outrageous amounts earned by executives—often of failing companies—and the financial tragedy that can befall both shareholders and employees when CEOs line their own pockets at the organization's expense. Images of lavish executive lifestyles are now engraved in the popular consciousness. The result: public support for political responses that include new regulatory measures and a long list of demands for greater shareholder or government control over executive compensation.

These images now overshadow the reality of thousands of successful companies with appropriately paid executives and conscientious boards. Instead, fresh accusations of CEOs collecting huge amounts of undeserved pay appear daily, fueling a full-blown mythology of a corporate America ruled by executive greed, fraud, and corruption.

This mythology consists of two related components: the myth of the failed pay-for-performance model and the myth of managerial power. The first myth hinges on the idea that the link between executive pay and corporate performance—if it ever existed—is irretrievably broken. The second myth accepts the idea of a failed pay-for-performance model and puts in its service the image of unchecked CEOs dominating subservient boards as the explanation for decisions resulting in excessive executive pay. The powerful combination of these two myths has captured newspaper headlines and shareholder agendas, regulatory attention and the public imagination.

This mythology has spilled over into the pages of *Across the Board*, where the September/October cover story links high levels of CEO pay to the country's growing income inequality and wonders why U.S. workers have not taken to the streets to protest "the blatant abuse of privilege" exercised by CEOs. In "The Revolution That Never Was," James Krohe Jr. manages to reference Marie Antoinette, Robespierre, Adam Smith, Alexis de Tocqueville, Andrew Jackson, Kim Jong II, Jack Welch, guerrilla warfare, "economic apartheid," and police brutality in Selma, Ala., in an article that feeds virtually every conceivable element of the myth of executive pay and wonders why we have not yet witnessed calls for a revolution to quash the "financial frolics of today's corporate aristocrats."

In a very different *Across the Board* feature story published a few months earlier, the myth of managerial power finds support in an interview with one of the myth's creators, Harvard professor Lucian Bebchuk, who believes that the pay-for-performance model is broken and that executive control over boards is to blame. Bebchuk is a distinguished scholar who has significant insights into the executive-pay process, but he greatly overestimates the influence of managerial power in the boardroom and ignores empirical evidence that most companies still operate under an intact and explicit pay-for-performance model. And although he acknowledges in his interview with *ATB* editor A.J. Vogl that "American companies have been successful and executives deserve a great deal of credit," his arguments about managerial power run counter to the realities of this success.

Fueling the Fiction

These two articles, in different ways, contribute to what is now a dominant image of executives collecting unearned compensation and growing rich at the expense of shareholders, employees and the broader community. In recent years, dozens of reporters from business magazines and the major newspapers have called me and specifically asked for examples of companies in which CEOs received exorbitant compensation, approved by the board, while the company performed poorly. Not once have I been asked to comment on the vast majority of companies—those in which executives are appropriately rewarded for performance or in which boards have reduced compensation or even fired the CEO for poor performance.

I have spent hundreds of hours answering reporters' questions, providing extensive data and explaining the pay-for-performance model of executive compensation, but my efforts have had little impact: The resulting stories feature the same anecdotal reporting on those corporations for which the process has gone awry. The press accounts ignore solid research that shows that annual pay for most executives moves up and down significantly with the company's performance, both financial and stock-related. Corporate wrongdoings and outlandish executive pay packages make for lively headlines, but the reliance on purely anecdotal reporting and the highly prejudicial language adopted are a huge disservice to the companies, their executives and employees, investors, and the public. The likelihood of real economic damage to the U.S. economy grows daily.

For example, the mythology drives institutional investors and trade unions with the power to exert enormous pressure on regulators and executive and board practices. The California Public Employees' Retirement System—the nation's largest public pension fund—offers a typical example in its Nov. 15, 2004, announcement of a new campaign to rein in "abusive compensation practices in corporate America and hold directors and compensation committees more accountable for their actions."

The AFL-CIO's website offers another example of the claim that managerial power has destroyed the efficacy of the pay-for-performance model: "Each year, shocking new examples of CEO pay greed are made public. Investors are concerned not just about the growing size of executive compensation packages, but the fact that CEO pay levels show little apparent relationship to corporate profits, stock prices or executive performance. How do CEOs do it? For years, executives have relied on their shareholders to be passive absentee owners. CEOs have rigged their own compensation packages by packing their boards with conflicted or negligent directors."

The ROI of the CEO

As with all modern myths, there's a grain of truth in all the assumptions and newspaper stories. The myths of managerial power and of the failed pay-for-performance model find touchstones in real examples of companies where CEOs have collected huge sums in cash compensation and stock options while shareholder returns declined. (You know the names—there's no need to mention them again here.) Cases of overstated profits or even outright fraud have fueled the idea that executives regularly manipulate the measures of performance to justify higher pay while boards default on their oversight responsibilities. The ability of executives to time the exercise of their stock options and collect additional pay through covert means has worsened perceptions of the situation both within and outside of the world of business.

These exceptions in executive pay practices, however, are now commonly mistaken for the rule. And as Krohe's article demonstrates, highly paid CEOs have become the new whipping boys for social critics concerned about the general rise in income inequality and other broad socioeconomic problems. Never mind that these same CEOs stand at the center of a corporate model that has generated millions of jobs and trillions of dollars in shareholder earnings. Worse, using CEOs as scapegoats distracts from the real causes of and possible solutions for inequality.

The primary determinant of CEO pay is the same force that sets pay for all Americans: relatively free—if somewhat imperfect—labor markets, in which companies offer the levels of compensation necessary to attract and retain the employees who generate value for shareholders. Part of that pay for most executives consists of stock-based incentives. A 2003 study by Brian J. Hall and Kevin J. Murphy shows that the ratio of total CEO compensation to production workers' average earnings closely follows the Dow Jones Industrial Average. When the Dow soars, the gap between executive and non-executive compensation widens. The problem, it seems, is not that CEOs receive too much performance-driven, stock-based compensation, but that non-executives receive too little.

The key question is not the actual dollar amount paid to a CEO in total compensation or whether that amount represents a high multiple of pay of the average worker's salary but, rather, whether that CEO creates an adequate return on the company's investment in executive compensation. In virtually every area of business, directors routinely evaluate and adjust the amounts that companies invest in all inputs, and shareholders directly or indirectly endorse or challenge those decisions. Executive pay is no different.

Hard Realities

The corporate scandals of recent years laid bare the inner workings of a handful of public companies where, inarguably, the process for setting executive pay violated not only the principle of pay-for-performance but the extensive set of laws and regulations governing executive pay practices and the role of the board. But while I condemn illegal actions and criticize boards that reward executives who fail to produce positive financial results, I know that the vast majority of U.S. corporations do much better by their shareholders and the public. I have worked directly with more than a thousand publicly traded companies in the United States and attended thousands of compensation-committee meetings, and I have *never* witnessed board members straining to find a way to pay an executive more than he is worth.

In addition, at Watson Wyatt I work with a team of experts that has conducted extensive research at fifteen hundred of America's largest corporations and tracked the relationship between these pay practices and corporate performance over almost twenty years. In evaluating thousands of companies annually, yielding nearly twenty thousand "company years" of data, and pooling cross-sectional company data over multiple years, we have discovered that for both most companies and the "typical" company, there is substantial pay-for-performance sensitivity. That is, high performance generates high pay for executives and low performance generates low pay. Numerous empirical academic studies support our conclusions.

Our empirical evidence and evidence from other studies have produced the following key findings:

1. Executive pay is unquestionably high relative to low-level corporate positions, and it has risen dramatically over the past ten to fifteen years, faster than inflation and faster than average employee pay. But executive compensation generally tracks total returns to shareholders—even including the recent rise in pay.
2. Executive stock ownership has risen dramatically over the past ten to fifteen years. High levels of CEO stock ownership are correlated with and most likely the cause of companies' high financial and stock-market performance.
3. Executives are paid commensurate with the skills and talents that they bring to the organization. Underperforming executives routinely receive pay reductions or are terminated—far more often than press accounts imply.
4. CEOs who are recruited from outside a company and have little influence over its board receive compensation that is competitive with and often higher than the pay levels of CEOs who are promoted from within the company.
5. At the vast majority of companies, even extraordinarily high levels of CEO compensation represent a tiny fraction of the total value created by the corporation under that CEO's leadership. (Watson Wyatt has found that U.S. executives receive approximately 1 percent of the net income generated by the corporations they manage.) Well-run companies, it bears pointing out, produce significant shareholder returns and job security for millions of workers.

Extensive research demonstrates a high and positive correlation between executive pay and corporate performance. For example, high levels of executive stock ownership in 2000, created primarily through stock-option awards, correlated with higher stock-market valuation and long-term earnings per share over the subsequent five-year period. In general, high-performing companies are led by highly paid executives—with pay-for-performance in full effect. Executives at low-performing companies receive lower amounts of pay. Reams of data from other studies confirm these correlations.

Why CEOs Are Worth the Money

The huge gap between the realities of executive pay and the now-dominant mythology surrounding it has become even more evident in recent years. Empirical studies show that executive compensation has closely tracked corporate performance: Pay rose during the boom years of the 1990s, when U.S. corporations generated huge returns, declined during the 2001–03 profit slowdown, and increased in 2004 as profits improved. The myth of excessive executive pay continued to gain power, however, even as concrete, well-documented financial realities defied it.

The blind outrage over executive pay climbed even during the slowdown, as compensation dropped drastically. During this same period, in the aftermath of the corporate scandals, Congress and the U.S. regulatory agencies instituted far-reaching reforms in corporate governance and board composition, and companies spent millions to improve their governance and transparency. But the critics of executive pay and managerial power were only encouraged to raise their voices.

It might surprise those critics to learn that CEOs are not interchangeable and not chosen by lot; they are an extremely important asset to their companies and generally represent an excellent investment. The relative scarcity of CEO talent is manifested in many ways, including the frenetic behavior of boards charged with filling the top position when a CEO retires or departs. CEOs have significant, legitimate, market-driven bargaining power, and in pay negotiations, they use that power to obtain pay commensurate with their skills. Boards, as they should, use their own bargaining power to retain talent and maximize returns to company shareholders.

Boards understand the imperative of finding an excellent CEO and are willing to risk millions of dollars to secure the right talent. Their behavior is not only understandable but necessary to secure the company's future success. Any influence that CEOs might have over their directors is modest in comparison to the financial risk that CEOs assume when they leave other prospects and take on the extraordinarily difficult task of managing a major corporation, with a substantial portion of their short- and long-term compensation contingent on the organization's financial success.

Lucian Bebchuk and other critics underestimate the financial risk entailed in executive positions when they cite executives' large severance packages, derided as "golden parachutes." Top executive talent expects and can command financial protections commensurate with the level of risk they assume. Like any other element of compensation, boards should and generally do evaluate severance agreements as part of the package they create to attract and retain talent. In recent years, boards have become more aware of the damage done when executive benefits and perquisites are excessive and not aligned with non-executive programs, and are now reining in these elements.

Properly designed pay opportunities drive superior corporate performance and secure it for the future. And most importantly, many economists argue, the U.S. model of executive compensation is a significant source of competitive advantage for the nation's economy, driving higher productivity, profits, and stock prices.

Resetting the Debate

Companies design executive pay programs to accomplish the classic goals of any human-capital program. First, they must attract, retain, and motivate their human capital to perform at the highest levels. The motivational factor is the most important, because it addresses the question of how a company achieves the greatest return on its human-capital investment and rewards executives for making the right decisions to drive shareholder value. Incentive-pay and pay-at-risk programs are particularly effective, especially at the top of the house, in achieving this motivation goal.

Clearly, there are exceptions to the motivational element—base salaries, pensions, and other benefits, for example—that are more closely tied to retention goals and are an essential part of creating a balanced portfolio for the employee. The portfolio as a whole must address the need for income and security and the opportunity for creating significant asset appreciation.

A long list of pressures, including institutional-investor pushback, accounting changes, SEC investigations, and scrutiny from labor unions and the media, are forcing companies to rethink their executive-compensation programs, especially their stock-based incentives. The key now is to address the real problems in executive compensation without sacrificing the performance-based model and the huge returns that it has generated. Boards are struggling to achieve greater transparency and more rigorous execution of their pay practices—a positive move for all parties involved.

The real threat to U.S. economic growth, job creation, and higher living standards now comes from regulatory overreach as proponents of the mythology reject market forces and continue to push for government and institutional control over executive pay. To the extent that the mythology now surrounding executive pay leads to a rejection of the pay-for-performance model and restrictions on the risk-and-reward structure for setting executive compensation, American corporate performance will suffer.

There will be more pressure on boards to effectively reduce executive pay. This may meet the social desires of some constituents, but it will almost surely cause economic decline, for companies and the U.S. economy. We will see higher executive turnover and less talent in the executive suite as the most qualified job candidates move into other professions, as we saw in the 1970s, when top candidates moved into investment banking, venture-capital firms, and consulting, and corporate performance suffered as a result.

Our research demonstrates that aligning pay plans, incentive opportunities, and performance measures throughout an organization is key to financial success. Alignment means that executives and non-executives alike have the opportunity to increase their pay through performance-based incentives. As new regulations make it more difficult to execute the stock-based elements of the pay-for-performance model, for example, by reducing broad-based stock options, we will see even less alignment between executives' compensation and the pay packages of the rank-and-file. We are already witnessing the unintended consequences of the new requirement for stock-option expensing as companies cut the broad-based stock-option plans that have benefited millions of workers and given them a direct stake in the financial success of the companies for which they work.

Instead of changing executive pay plans to make them more like pay plans for employees, we should be reshaping employee pay to infuse it with the same incentives that drive performance in the company's upper ranks. A top-down regulatory approach to alignment will only damage the entire market-based, performance-management process that has worked so well for most companies and the economy as a whole. Instead of placing artificial limits on executive pay, we should focus squarely on increasing performance incentives and stock ownership for both executive and non-executive employees and rewarding high performers throughout the organization, from top to bottom. Within the context of a free-market economy, equal opportunity—not income equality by fiat—is the goal.

The short answer to James Krohe's question of why high levels of executive pay have not sparked a worker revolution is that the fundamental model works too well. Workers vote to support that model every day when they show up for work, perform well, and rely on corporate leadership to pursue a viable plan for meeting payroll and funding employee benefits. Shareholders vote to support the model every time they purchase shares or defeat one of the dozens of proposals submitted in recent years to curb executive compensation. Rejecting the pay-for-performance model for executive compensation means returning to the world of the CEO as caretaker. And caretakers—as shown by both evidence and common sense—do not create high value for shareholders or jobs for employees.

In some ways, the decidedly negative attention focused on executive pay has increased the pressure that executives, board members, HR staffs, and compensation consultants all feel when they enter into discussions about the most effective methods for tying pay to performance and ensuring the company's success. The managerial-power argument has contributed to meaningful discussions about corporate governance and raised the level of dialogue in boardrooms. These are positive developments.

When the argument is blown into mythological proportions, however, it skews thinking about the realities of corporate behavior and leads to fundamental misunderstandings about executives, their pay levels, and their role in building successful companies and a flourishing economy. Consequently, the mythology now surrounding executive compensation leads many to reject a pay model that works well and is critical to ongoing growth at both the corporate and the national economic level. We need to address excesses in executive pay without abandoning the core model, and to return the debate to a rational, informed discussion. And we can safely leave Marie Antoinette out of it.

Edgar Woolard, Jr.

 **NO**

CEOs Are Being Paid Too Much

There's a major concern out there for all of us. I personally am extremely saddened by the loss of the respect that this country's corporate leaders have experienced. We've had a double blow in the last ten years or so. The first one we know way too much about—the fraud at Enron, Tyco, Adelphia, World-Com, and many others.

The CEOs say there were a few rotten apples in that barrel, and maybe that's the answer—but there are a hell of lot more rotten apples than I would have ever guessed. But that's just the base of one of the issues that has eroded the trust and confidence in American business leaders.

The second one is the perception of excess compensation received by CEOs getting worse year by year. And if directors agree, they can be the leaders in making a very important change. I'd like to deal with it by describing several myths about compensation and trying to undermine them.

Myth #1: CEO Pay by Competition

The first is the myth that CEO pay is driven by competition—and to that I say "bull." CEO pay is driven today primarily by outside consultant surveys, and by the fact that many board members have bought into the concept that your CEO has to be at least in the top half, and maybe in the top quartile. So we have the "ratchet, ratchet, ratchet" concept. We all understand it well enough to know that if everybody is trying to be in the top half, everybody is going to get a hefty increase every year. If Bill and Sally get an increase in their total compensation, I have to get an increase so that I will stay in the top half.

How can we change that?

In 1990, we addressed this issue at DuPont. I became CEO in 1989, and I was concerned about what was evident even then. A 1989 *Business Week* article talked about executive pay—who makes the most and are they worth it: Michael Eisner, $40 million in 1988; Ross Johnson, $20 million; and others. I don't know Eisner, but I know that even fifteen years later he's one of the most criticized CEOs in the country.

What we did at DuPont was go to a simple concept: internal pay equity. I went to the board and the compensation committee and said, "We're going to look at the people who run the businesses, who make decisions on prices and new products with guidance from the CEO—the executive vice presidents—and we're going to set the limit of what a CEO in this company can be paid at 1.5 times the pay rate for the executive vice president—50 percent."

From *Across the Board*, January/February 2006. Copyright © 2006 by Conference Board, Inc. Reprinted by permission.

That to me seemed equitable. It had been anywhere from 30 to 50 percent in the past. I said, "Let's set it at 50 percent, and we're not going to chase the surveys." And this is the way DuPont has done it ever since. I think we have tweaked it up a little bit since then, but using a multiple still is the right way to go.

Board members can do this by suggesting that the HR and compensation people look at what's happened to internal pay equity, and seriously consider going in that direction. That will solve this problem in a great way.

Myth #2: Compensation Committees Are Independent

I give a "double bull" to this one. It could be that committees are becoming more independent, but over the last fifteen years they certainly haven't been.

Let me describe how it works: The compensation committee talks to an outside consultant who has surveys that you could drive a truck through and that support paying anything you want to pay. The consultant talks to the HR vice president, who talks to the CEO. The CEO says what he'd like to receive— enough so he will be "respected by his peers." It gets to the HR person, who tells the consultant, and the CEO gets what he's implied he deserves. The members of the compensation committee are happy that they're independent, the HR person is happy, the CEO is happy, and the consultant gets invited back next year.

There are two ways to change that as well. Here's the first one. When John Reed came back to the New York Stock Exchange to try to clean up the mess after Dick Grasso, he made the decision—which I admire him for—that the board was going to have its own outside consultant, one who was not going to be allowed to talk to internal people—not to the HR vice president, not to the CEO.

I'm the head of the comp committee at the NYSE, and when I talk with our outside consultant, he gives us his ideas of what he thinks the pay package ought to be. Then, with the consultant there, I talk to the compensation committee, and we make a decision. I talk to the HR vice president to see if he has any other thoughts, but the committee is totally independent.

The other way to change things is to truly insist on pay-for-performance, which everyone likes to talk about but no one does. Boards pay everybody in the top quartile whether they have good performance or bad performance—or even if they're about to be fired.

Well, I was on a board fifteen years ago, and four CEOs were on the compensation committee, and for two consecutive years, we gave the CEO and the executives there no bonus, no salary increase, and modest stock options, because their performance was lousy those years. After that, they did extremely well, and we paid them extremely well. That's how pay-for-performance should work.

Myth #3: Look How Much Wealth I Created

This one is really a joke. It was born in the 1980s and '90s during the stock-market bubble, when all CEOs were beating their chest about how much wealth they were creating for shareholders. And I'd look to the king, Jack Welch. Jack's the best CEO of the last fifty years, and I've told him this. But he likes to say, "I created $400 billion worth of wealth." No, Jack—no, you didn't. He said that when GE's stock was at 60, but when the bubble burst it went to 30, and it's in the low 30s now. So he created $150 to $200 billion.

But besides the actual figure, there are two things wrong with his claim. Now, I don't care how much money Jack Welch made. God bless him; I think he's terrific. But what did it do? It set a new level for CEO pay based on the stock-market bubble; all the other CEOs were saying, "Look how much wealth I created."

So you've got this more recent high level of executive pay, and then you've got the ratcheting effect in the system. Those things have to change.

Myth #4: Severance for Failing

The last one is the worst of all. Any directors who agree to give these huge severance pay packages to CEOs who fail—Philip Purcell of Morgan Stanley got $114 million, Carly Fiorina of Hewlett-Packard got $20 million—why are you doing that? No one else gets paid excessively when they fail. They get fired; they get fair severance.

All of this is killing the image of CEOs and corporate executives. When it comes to our image, we're in the league with lawyers and politicians. I don't want to be there, and I don't think you do either. We need the respect of our employees and the general public. And there's a lot of skepticism about leaders in politics and in churches and in the military—but we can't have it in the business community, because we're the backbone of the market system that has made this country great and created so many opportunities for people. We can't be seen as either dishonest or greedy.

What can you do about it?

Some of you CEOs need to show leadership and say, "We're going to do internal pay equity." It's easy to get the data, and then you can decide what you think is fair and how much you think the CEO contributes versus the other business leaders who make their companies so strong.

Compensation committees need to seriously consider implementing internal pay equity. Pay only for outstanding performance. Quit giving people money just because Bill and Sally are getting it. Consider going to an independent consultant that deals only with the board while you deal with HR and the CEO.

Last, take a look at stock-option packages. Not just for one year but the mega-grants that built up in the 1980s and '90s. If you've given huge stock-option packages for the last five years, look at their value. There's nothing in the Bible that says that you have to give increased stock options every year. Give a smaller grant; give a different kind of grant; put some kind of limits on.

There are many ways to do it, but it's important to get the system back under control. It's important for our image, for our reputation, for integrity, for trust, and for our leadership in this country.

POSTSCRIPT

Is CEO Compensation Justified by Performance?

In 1992, when Geoffrey Colvin wrote the article bringing the problem of CEO compensation to public attention, he was worried about the country's perception of annual outlays of $1.7 million average total CEO compensation for almost 300 large companies, with pay going up to a whopping $3.2 million annually for the really big companies. By 1995, the CEO of a multibillion-dollar company received an average of $4.37 million in compensation, up 23 percent from 1994. And it got worse from there, with 1996 figures going through the roof: how on earth could Jack Welch, CEO of General Electric, spend the $21.4 million in salary and performance bonuses (and about $18 million in stock options) that he received in 1996, or Green Tree Financial Corporation's Lawrence Coss spend his $102.4 million in salary and bonus (plus stock options worth at least $38 million)? The Business Section of *The New York Times* at the end of 1997 glowed with projected bonuses of $11 billion for Wall Street that year—that was over and above salary, and before stock options. Two years later, Jack Welch was pulling in $68 million. As per the introduction to this issue, the amounts then tripled, quadrupled, into amounts per individual that dwarf the annual health budgets of most of the world. The situation is not correcting itself.

The political impact of these salaries is muted for the present, probably due to the failure of the American left, or liberal political orientation, to find a powerful spokesperson who might gain the confidence of the American people. The moral dimensions of the problem have not changed since the days of the prophet Amos of the Hebrew Scriptures: What right have the rich to enjoy their warm palaces and mansions, dining plentifully on the best food from all the world, while the poor suffer from hunger and cold? But the political dimensions are volatile, and dependent upon the rest of the system to provide context and opportunity. This issue will be with us for a while.

Suggested Readings

Lucian Bebchuk and Jesse Fried, *Pay Without Performance: The Unfulfilled Promise of Executive Compensation* (Cambridge: Harvard University Press, 2006).

Rocco Huang, "Because I'm Worth It? CEO Pay and Corporate Governance," *Business Review* (Federal Reserve Bank of Philadelphia) (2010), pp. 12–19.

Ira Kay and Steven Van Putten, *Myths and Realities of Executive Pay* (Cambridge: Cambridge University Press, 2007).

Jean MacGuire, et al., "CEO Incentives and Corporate Social Performance," *Journal of Business Ethics* (vol. 45, no. 4, July 2003).

Ben Steverman, "CEOs and the Pay-for-Performance Puzzle," *BusinessWeek Online* (p. 2, 2009).

Ronald A. Wirtz, "Goldilocks in the Corner Office," *The Region* (The Federal Reserve Bank of Minneapolis) (vol. 20, no. 4, 2006), pp. 22–35.

Internet References . . .

Advertising World

Advertising World, maintained by the Department of Advertising at the University of Texas at Austin, links to numerous sites on marketing and advertising. Among the many indexed topics are ethics and self-regulation, consumer interest, public relations, and market research.

http://advertising.utexas.edu/world/

Overlawyered.com

Overlawyered.com explores an American legal system that too often turns litigation into a weapon against guilty and innocent alike, erodes individual responsibility, rewards sharp practice, enriches its participants at the public's expense, and resists even modest efforts at reform and accountability. This page focuses on litigation over auto safety.

http://overlawyered.com/topics/auto.html

The Pew Initiative on Food and Biotechnology

The Pew Initiative on Food and Biotechnology was established as an independent and objective source of information that encourages research and debate on agricultural biotechnology. It is the purpose of this site to provide a resource that would enable consumers as well as policymakers to make their own informed decisions on the subject.

http://pewagbiotech.org

Consumer Issues

*W*hat does the customer have a right to expect from the maker of the products that he buys? The answer, essentially, is quality and honesty. It sounds simple, but somehow we cannot be sure that the manufacturers are giving us good products and the salesmen are telling the truth about them; the controversies have never ceased.

- Should Advertising Directed at Children be Restricted?
- Should Homeowners Employ Strategic Default Options with Mortgages?
- Should We Require Labeling for Genetically Modified Food?

ISSUE 14

Should Advertising Directed at Children be Restricted?

YES: **Stephanie Clifford**, from "A Fine Line When Ads and Children Mix," *The New York Times* (February 14, 2010)

NO: **Patrick Basham and John Luik**, "A Happy Meal Ban is Nothing to Smile About," *cato.org* (November 9, 2010)

ISSUE SUMMARY

YES: Stephanie Clifford cites studies that show that advertising for children is often barely distinguishable from regular programming. She cites harms that can come to children through advertising that seems more fact than promotion to the child.

NO: Patrick Basham and John Luik find no credence in studies linking harms to child-directed advertising. They cite research that shows that advertising has little effect on the market associated with children.

In our capitalist economy, markets are influenced by advertisements that drive consumers to a vast array of products. Advertisers employ specific tactics that are designed to attract consumers. As adults, we each use our own personal filters to decide which products will benefit us, to choose which products we want, to decipher which products are good for us and which are not.

Children do not have the fully developed cognitive skills necessary for making such an informed decision. They can be influenced and manipulated more easily by information that is presented to them. We cannot expect children to be able to make the decisions at the same level of understanding and rationality as an adult.

Because of this, advertisers have come under more and more scrutiny lately for the ways they market to children. Stephanie Clifford addresses the impact that this has had on the publications that depend on support from their advertisers. The stringent marketing guidelines have forced some children's publications to end. Others have flat out refused any advertising, and still others have required their advertisers to develop new, subtler ways of advertising.

Is this a good thing? Should marketing directed toward children be restricted in any way? Patrick Basham and John Luik approach the question by considering the impact marketing food to children has on children's consumption of food and their levels of obesity. They introduce the topic by giving the example of the ban of McDonald's Happy Meals, which they say is driven by four false assumptions regarding the alleged connections between children, obesity, health costs, and advertising. Basham and Luik discuss a study that indicates that there is no significant correlation between the size of a particular market and the level of advertisement for that product. Furthermore, they state that there is no direct correlation between obesity and advertising.

Yet this does not mean that there is no association between other products directed toward children and the level of marketing those products to children. Take the example of toys. As Basham and Luik state, McDonald's includes the toy in the Happy Meal to "tempt" children. Although the product the corporation is trying to sell may be food, the means of its marketing and what they are really selling is the toy. Young children cannot be expected to make this distinction. Also, if there is no effect on advertising and consumption, why would McDonald's bother placing the toy in the meal when they could bypass it, saving money while experiencing negligible effect on sales?

The issue cannot be approached from a teleological or consequentialist perspective. It does not matter if advertisements targeting children greatly stimulate the market and, therefore, the entire economy; the issue at stake is the impact specifically and solely on the children. The ethics of marketing to children must be considered from the deontological perspective. We need to ask ourselves, what do we owe children to protect their development as healthy and rational adults? What are we ethically obligated to protect children from, and how do we go about doing so?

YES

Stephanie Clifford

A Fine Line When Ads and Children Mix

When an arts and crafts company placed an ad in Discovery Girls magazine for Tulip Glam-It-Up iron-on crystals, it hardly seemed controversial. The ad, which ran last summer, showed a young girl wearing a T-shirt swirled with paint and crystals. "I glam rock it up," the girl was saying.

But when the reviewers assigned to monitoring children's advertising at the Council of Better Business Bureaus saw it, they saw problems. It was not clearly marked as an ad, for instance, and they worried that children might think they could mimic the design from crystals alone. The Children's Advertising Review Unit of the bureau contacted Duncan Enterprises, which ran the ad, and suggested several changes last month.

"We don't want to deceive anyone," said Alyson Dias, director for marketing communications at Duncan Enterprises. "They're just asking for more clarity and more disclosure than ever before, and if that's what's needed to advertise to the tween and under-13 crowd, then that's fine—we'll do it."

Still, she said, "it is difficult, advertising to children." Wary of getting into hot water with advocacy or standards groups, advertisers are increasingly cautious about taking out ads aimed at children. And that is hammering magazines like Sports Illustrated Kids, National Geographic Kids and Boys' Life.

At the same time, all the attention about advertising to children has an interesting side effect. Publishers and advertisers are becoming more creative about such ads, and are running games, contests and events where the advertiser has only a subtle presence—exactly the opposite of what some of the advocacy groups were aiming for.

"Obviously there have been all sorts of issues that have arisen as a consequence" of directly advertising to children, like "childhood obesity, diabetes and other social issues—and that's why it's a much more difficult environment to advertise directly in," said Stuart Hazlewood, the chief strategy officer of the advertising agency DDB New York. "They have to be a lot more subtle about it these days."

Marketers began paying closer attention to how they advertised to children in the 1970s, when consumer advocates complained about the ways commercialism permeated society. In 1974, the industry created the Children's Advertising Review Unit. Today, that unit has about seven reviewers who contact companies when they judge ads are misleading or inappropriate.

"Especially where advertising is concerned, children have certain vulnerabilities because of their age and how they perceive things, their cognitive abilities," said Wayne J. Keeley, director for the program.

More recently, regulators pressured the industry to limit food advertising in response to concerns about childhood obesity. In 2006, major food marketers began joining the Children's Food and Beverage Advertising Initiative, another program from the Council of Better Business Bureaus.

Four marketers—Coca-Cola, Mars, Hershey and Cadbury Adams USA—said they would not advertise at all to children. Others announced nutritional standards that their products had to meet if they were advertised to children. While these tended to ban products with the highest fat and sugar levels, each company could set its own standards, and the list of approved products includes processed foods like Kid Cuisine Constructor Cheeseburger, Apple Jacks and Cocoa Puffs.

The debate over what is appropriate for children continues, with the Federal Communications Commission seeking opinions about online marketing to children, and the Federal Trade Commission holding a hearing in December on food marketing to children.

All the scrutiny has put children's magazines under pressure.

While almost all magazines suffered in 2009, magazines for children posted some of the lowest overall ad-page numbers. Nickelodeon magazine ceased publication with its December 2009/January 2010 issue.

In response, some magazines are taking a more expansive view of how advertisers can reach children.

"We've really built our business around a strategy, when it comes to advertising partners, of allowing them to really make use of our ability to get this youth audience in all the ways that they're out there, so we get them in school, we get them in print, we get them when they're out of school and having fun through sports," said Bob Der, managing editor of Sports Illustrated Kids and who also oversees editorial content in Time for Kids.

That means programs like "Sports Dad of the Year," sponsored by Wendy's, and a design-your-own-game contest for Pepperidge Farm's Goldfish crackers that S.I. Kids helped create.

"The days of single-page advertising, it doesn't exist that way anymore," said Eileen Masio, executive director of integrated marketing for S.I. Kids and Time for Kids. "It's really making their messaging and what they stand for come to life." National Geographic Kids is taking a similar approach.

Patrick Basham and John Luik  **NO**

A Happy Meal Ban Is Nothing to Smile About

A Happy Meal is not a healthy meal, at least according to the San Francisco Board of Supervisors. The board last week approved a preliminary ban that would strip toys from fast-food meals in San Francisco. The ban's backers claim the legislation gives parents a chance to convince their children to go for the healthier choice, without being tempted by a Shrek toy. If the final vote is approved this week, the ban will begin in December 2011.

The San Francisco ban, and similar proposals on both sides of the Atlantic, are predicated upon four false assumptions: the fast food sold by McDonald's and its competitors makes kids fat; fast-food marketing causes childhood obesity; fat children grow into unhealthy adults; fat kids incur significantly higher health care costs than skinny ones.

First, there is no evidence to support the assumption that fast-food outlets and the food they sell make people overweight and obese. And, in fact, this assumption is contradicted by a considerable amount of research. For example, in 2004 a team of researchers, after conducting a study with 14,000 American children, found that eating junk food did not lead to obesity among children. A similar conclusion was reported in Canada the year after, when researchers concluded that eating in fast-food restaurants was not associated with an increased risk of obesity, even in children who ate in such restaurants more than three times a week.

The claim about the association between the number of fast-food outlets and levels of obesity is equally unfounded. A 2005 study of elementary school children in the US found no significant associations between either fast-food prices or outlet density. Two years later, Russ Lopez, of the Boston University School of Public Health, reported similar non-significant findings for fast-food density.

Second, the Happy Meal ban assumes that fast-food marketing is a cause of childhood overweightedness and obesity. Therefore, it is argued, restrictions on food marketing and advertising are necessary.

In order to establish an evidence-based case for this claim, one would have to demonstrate that such advertising has an independent effect on children's weight. This, in turn, would require a study design that controlled for the multiple other risk factors connected with childhood obesity (by some estimates, there are dozens such factors). However, none of the studies purporting to demonstrate that food advertising causes childhood obesity control for more than a handful of these other risk factors. These studies therefore cannot establish an evidence-based case for the connection between food advertising and children's weight.

Further, the causal thesis is undermined by the fact that, in the UK for example, advertising for food and drink has been falling in real terms since 1999 and is now roughly at 1982 levels, even while rates of overweightedness and obesity allegedly have been rising. Again, there is a substantial body of econometric literature that disproves the alleged connection between advertising, diets and weight.

In his research into food advertising in the UK, Peter Kyle, of the University of Lancaster, found no evidence to support the causal claim that advertising increased market size. Another researcher, Martyn Duffy, has looked at the impact of advertising on 11 food categories and found that advertising had no effect on demand. More specifically, professor Harry Henry has examined the effect of advertising on breakfast cereals and biscuits, both frequently cited as culprits in the childhood obesity epidemic. He concluded that advertising had no affect on market size.

Finally, Bob Eagle and Tim Ambler looked at the impact of advertising on chocolate consumption in five European countries in order to test the claim that a reduction in advertising would reduce consumption. They reported no significant association between the amount of advertising and the size of the chocolate market. Eagle and Ambler's work is corroborated by evidence from the Canadian province of Quebec and from Sweden, both of which have imposed advertising bans on foods to children, with Quebec's in operation since 1980. In both jurisdictions, however, there have not been significant reductions in childhood obesity or any marked differences in obesity rates compared with other adjacent areas.

Third, it is unclear that being a fat child carries significant health risks or increases one's risk of becoming a fat adult. For example, a long-running study in Aberdeen, Scotland, which looked at the health outcomes of children born in the 1950s, found that the body mass index (BMI) of children was not associated with increased risk for stroke and heart attack in later life.

In addition, the work of a group of British researchers into child health and epidemiology directly contradicts the assumption that overweight or obese children are at greater health risk and that reducing children's weight benefits adult health. Their 'Thousand Families Study' followed 1,000 families in the city of Newcastle in north-east England from 1954 in an effort to track the effects of childhood obesity on adult health. The study found that, contrary to the claim that fat children become fat adults burdened with health problems, there was little tracking from childhood overweightedness to adulthood obesity. Indeed, over 80 per cent of the obese adult participants in the study became obese as adults.

The assumption of a link between childhood and adult obesity is also contradicted by a recent US Preventive Services Task Force analysis of the efficacy of dyslipidemia screening and weight-reduction programmes for children. It found that the evidence for effectiveness is 'lacking, of poor quality, or conflicting.'

The evidence also shows that the goal of encouraging children to eat low-fat diets is not only unsupported by the evidence but also risks significant harm in terms of adverse effects on growth and nutrient intake. The best evidence indicates that a 'substantial proportion of children under age 12 or 13, even with BMIs above the ninety-fifth percentile, will not develop adult obesity.'

Revealingly, the American data has shown that fat children generally consume no more food nor are less physically active than those of 'normal' weight. And multiple studies have failed to find a link in children between physical activity levels, food intake and obesity. American, British, Australian, French, and Spanish studies have all found little evidence to support a relationship between energy intake in children and their weight.

Indeed, to blame either these children or their parents for being fat contradicts much of the accumulating evidence on just how small a contribution to obesity is made by the factors that anyone—parents, children or the state—can control. One recent American study found that for twins, for example, the shared environment effect for both BMI and waist circumference is only 10 per cent.

Fourth, what about the claims about how much all of these fat children are costing the health system? After all, we all know, don't we, that fat children incur significantly higher health care costs than their slender peers?

In fact, this is not true, either. A 2008 US study examined the healthcare costs of 8,404 children in Kansas City and found that there was no relationship between a child's BMI and his or her visits to a doctor or casualty rooms. The only extra costs associated with the obese children were down to the fact that they were 5.5 times more likely to have had extra lab screening tests ordered. It had nothing to do with the them being less healthy.

The evidence-less Happy Meal ban should remind us that the entire idea of fat children is largely a cultural construct, not a scientific one. A hundred years ago, today's penchant for thin children would have been considered a shocking instance of child neglect.

The idea that children weighing over a certain amount are fat or obese has no scientific foundation, as the dividing line between fat and normal is purely arbitrary, representing nothing more than a public health bureaucrat's notion of where normal ends and fat begins.

POSTSCRIPT

Should Advertising Directed at Children be Restricted?

Clifford holds that advertising directed at children needs to be restricted. In most cases, a child and an adult are not tried for the same crime in the same court, by the same approach; likewise, a child and adult should not be corralled into the same advertising realm, in the same manner. Children and adults have different cognitive abilities, and the difference needs to be addressed and respected. There is a categorical imperative to protect children from manipulation by advertising. The question is how to incorporate marketing strategies that do not manipulate the minds of children. Our society needs to determine how we are going to handle advertising. Basham and Luik state that the link between childhood and adult obesity is unscientific and inaccurate. They claim that most data has shown that fat children generally are not less physically active, nor do they consume more food than "normal" children. The finding is that "normal" is a bureaucratic notion from a public health department, and that there is no reason to restrict advertising to children.

Suggested Readings

Rebecca A. Clay, "Advertising to Children: Is it Ethical," *Monitor on Psychology* (vol. 31, no. 8, 2000), p. 52.

Matthew Grimm, "Is Marketing to Kids Ethical?" *Brandweek* (vol. 45, no. 14, 2004), pp. 44–48.

Michelle M. Mello, "Federal Trade Commission Regulation of Food Advertising to Children: Possibilities for a Reinvigorated Role," *Journal of Health Politics, Policy & Law* (vol. 35, no. 2, 2010), pp. 227–276.

Elizabeth S. Moore, "Children and the Changing World of Advertising," *Journal of Business Ethics* (vol. 52, no. 2, 2004), pp. 161–167.

Mark Ritson, "A Junk Food 'Tax' Would Benefit Children More Than Any Ad Ban," *Marketing* (September 18, 2003), p. 16.

Juliet B. Schor, *Born to Buy: The Commercialized Child and the New Consumer Culture* (New York: Scribner, 2005).

Louise Thornley, Louise Signal, and George Thomson, "Does Industry Regulation of Food Advertising Protect Child Rights?" *Critical Public Health* (vol. 20, no. 1, 2010), pp. 25–33.

ISSUE 15

Should Homeowners Employ Strategic Default Options with Mortgages?

YES: Roger Lowenstein, from "The Way We Live Now: Walk Away from Your Mortgage," *The New York Times Magazine* (January 10, 2010)

NO: Rick Moran, from "The Ethics of 'Walking Away' from Your Mortgage," *The Moderate Voice* (February 4, 2010)

ISSUE SUMMARY

YES: Roger Lowenstein explains that often businesses decide to walk away from enterprises that aren't sound investments. He uses this analogy to conclude that it is acceptable for homeowners to walk away from their home investment when the value of the home is much less than the overall loan on the home.

NO: Rick Moran explains that just because businesses walk away from poor investments doesn't mean that Americans should also lack ethics. He encourages home buyers to remain true to their ethical obligations with their housing investment even though the economic costs can be high.

A mortgage is a promise. The citizen—a competent adult of mature years and sound judgment—wants to buy a home for himself and his family, a secure shelter from physical and social storms, a nurturing refuge for growing children, repository for valued possessions and base for all family activity. He does not have enough cash to buy the home he wants outright, so he takes out a loan from a local bank—a "mortgage" on the house—which he promises will be paid back over the next 30 years in monthly payments. (Of course there's wiggle room—serious illness or other eventualities could lead to an arrangement to space out the payments, for example.) He and the bank have figured out that it's a good deal for both of them. The payments are not too much for his income; the bank will make an acceptable profit from the interest it charges him; the risk of default—of his not paying off the loan—is sufficiently small that it is balanced by the expected profit; and at the end of 30 years, he will own free and clear the home he treasures, and the bank will have its money back, able to lend again. Just beyond the edge of the transaction, we should note that the stability of the community, and the mortgage market at large, depends on his conscientious payment of the loan.

The source of the borrower's obligation lies not, however, in its importance to the community, let alone to the real estate market across the country. It lies in the homeowner's promise, freely made, in possession of all the information that a rational person would want to have, that he will pay back the loan; the source of the obligation is deontological, not teleological. It is also central to the enterprise of business: In the first attempt to define the nature of justice, in Plato's *Republic*, the businessman Cephalos summarizes it as "Tell the truth and pay your debts," no ifs, ands, or buts. Once the autonomous human being has freely committed himself, that commitment binds through all circumstances—or almost all. The question for us here rises in a situation of vastly changed circumstances: Does the obligation still hold with its original force?

Roger Lowenstein calls attention to the fact that the world of commerce has changed radically since the period when contract replaced inherited duties (attached to one's station in life) as the source of economic obligation. For a business, "loan repayment" has no moral weight at all; the terms of the loan, which spell out the penalty for default (in the case of the mortgage, the loss of the property), determine whether or not it is in the borrower's interest to repay the loan. If the penalty is of greater value than the amount left to be paid, then it is in his interest to repay; otherwise not. When the mortgage is "under water," the amount to be paid greater than the value of the property, it is clearly not in his interest to repay. No business, as Lowenstein points out, would hesitate a moment in such circumstances—drop the keys in an envelope addressed to the bank ("jingle mail"), accept the penalty, and walk away.

What has changed between the traditional view of the mortgage on the home and the new businesslike perspective? We've lost two essential quantities: first, the sentimental emotional value of the home, the place of love, the family's shelter from a heartless world, now replaced by a mere investment; second, the strict obligation to repay based on the promise freely made—Cephalos' imperative to pay your debts has changed from categorical (keep your promises) to hypothetical (only if it is in your interest to do so).

Can the global economy afford these losses? The case of the underwater mortgage raises far-reaching questions about the place of moral commitment in business dealings. After all, the fulfillment of a contract is rarely as much in the interest of the contracting parties as is the making of the contract (that's why we have contracts with penalties for nonfulfillment). If every fulfillment depends on a canny businessman's determination that he won't get away with default (which is what he'd like to do), the business community is going to be spending a lot more time in the courts of law.

What in general, and in the case of the underwater mortgage in particular, is the place of the firm moral commitment in the face of business disaster? Keep the question in mind as you read the following selections.

The Way We Live Now: Walk Away from Your Mortgage

John Courson, president and C.E.O. of the Mortgage Bankers Association, recently told The Wall Street Journal that homeowners who default on their mortgages should think about the "message" they will send to "their family and their kids and their friends." Courson was implying that homeowners—record numbers of whom continue to default—have a responsibility to make good. He wasn't referring to the people who have no choice, who can't afford their payments. He was speaking about the rising number of folks who are voluntarily choosing not to pay.

Such voluntary defaults are a new phenomenon. Time was, Americans would do anything to pay their mortgage—forgo a new car or a vacation, even put a younger family member to work. But the housing collapse left 10.7 million families owing more than their homes are worth. So some of them are making a calculated decision to hang onto their money and let their homes go. Is this irresponsible?

Businesses—in particular Wall Street banks—make such calculations routinely. Morgan Stanley recently decided to stop making payments on five San Francisco office buildings. A Morgan Stanley fund purchased the buildings at the height of the boom, and their value has plunged. Nobody has said Morgan Stanley is immoral—perhaps because no one assumed it was moral to begin with. But the average American, as if sprung from some Franklinesque mythology, is supposed to honor his debts, or so says the mortgage industry as well as government officials. Former Treasury Secretary Henry M. Paulson Jr. declared that "any homeowner who can afford his mortgage payment but chooses to walk away from an underwater property is simply a speculator—and one who is not honoring his obligation." (Paulson presumably was not so censorious of speculation during his 32-year career at Goldman Sachs.)

The moral suasion has continued under President Obama, who has urged that homeowners follow the "responsible" course. Indeed, HUD-approved housing counselors are supposed to counsel people against foreclosure. In many cases, this means counseling people to throw away money. Brent White, a University of Arizona law professor, notes that a family who bought a three-bedroom home in Salinas, Calif., at the market top in 2006, with no down payment (then a common-enough occurrence), could theoretically have to wait

60 years to recover their equity. On the other hand, if they walked, they could rent a similar house for a pittance of their monthly mortgage.

There are two reasons why so-called strategic defaults have been considered antisocial and perhaps amoral. One is that foreclosures depress the neighborhood and drive down prices. But in a market society, since when are people responsible for the economic effects of their actions? Every oil speculator helps to drive up gasoline prices. Every hedge fund that speculated against a bank by purchasing credit-default swaps on its bonds signaled skepticism about the bank's creditworthiness and helped to make it more costly for the bank to borrow, and thus to issue loans. We are all economic pinballs, insensibly colliding for better or worse.

The other reason is that default (supposedly) debases the character of the borrower. Once, perhaps, when bankers held onto mortgages for 30 years, they occupied a moral high ground. These days, lenders typically unload mortgages within days (or minutes). And not just in mortgage finance, but in virtually every realm of our transaction-obsessed society, the message is that enduring relationships count for less than the value put on assets for sale.

Think of private-equity firms that close a factory—essentially deciding that the company is worth more dead than alive. Or the New York Yankees and their World Series M.V.P. Hideki Matsui, who parted company as soon as the cheering stopped. Or money-losing hedge-fund managers: rather than try to earn back their investors' lost capital, they start new funds so they can rake in fresh incentives. Sam Zell, a billionaire, let the Tribune Company, which he had previously acquired, file for bankruptcy. Indeed, the owners of any company that defaults on bonds and chooses to let the company fail rather than invest more capital in it are practicing "strategic default." Banks signal their complicity with this ethos when they send new credit cards to people who failed to stay current on old ones.

Mortgage holders do sign a promissory note, which is a promise to pay. But the contract explicitly details the penalty for nonpayment—surrender of the property. The borrower isn't escaping the consequences; he is suffering them.

In some states, lenders also have recourse to the borrowers' unmortgaged assets, like their car and savings accounts. A study by the Federal Reserve Bank of Richmond found that defaults are lower in such states, apparently because lenders threaten the borrowers with judgments against their assets. But actual lawsuits are rare.

And given that nearly a quarter of mortgages are underwater, and that 10 percent of mortgages are delinquent, White, of the University of Arizona, is surprised that more people haven't walked. He thinks the desire to avoid shame is a factor, as are overblown fears of harm to credit ratings. Probably, homeowners also labor under a delusion that their homes will quickly return to value. White has argued that the government should stop perpetuating default "scare stories" and, indeed, should encourage borrowers to default when it's in their economic interest. This would correct a prevailing imbalance: homeowners operate under a "powerful moral constraint" while lenders are busily trying to maximize profits. More important, it might get the system unstuck. If lenders feared an avalanche of strategic defaults, they would have an incentive to renegotiate loan terms. In theory, this could produce a wave of loan modifications—the very goal the Treasury has been pursuing to end the crisis.

No one says defaulting on a contract is pretty or that, in a perfectly functioning society, defaults would be the rule. But to put the onus for restraint on ordinary homeowners seems rather strange. If the Mortgage Bankers Association is against defaults, its members, presumably the experts in such matters, might take better care not to lend people more than their homes are worth.

Rick Moran  **NO**

The Ethics of 'Walking Away" from Your Mortgage

It should be clear to all of us by now that the single driving factor in this economic downturn was the meltdown in home values. All the talk about how the big banks screwed us over is relevant only as it relates to the massive devaluation of our largest personal asset; our homes. If home values had stayed relatively stable, or come down at a reasonable rate, the bank crisis may have been manageable. It may have been seen as a bad couple of quarters rather than the catastrophe it became.

But that didn't happen so here we are. And where we are may very well precipitate another huge devaluation of homes which would then lead to another round of bailouts and takeovers. This is because according to most experts, there is still slack in home values that has yet to be taken in; that our homes are still overvalued despite dropping 30–35–40%.

This has created a situation that is evidently not unprecedented except in scale; people with "underwater" mortgages—where they owe more than their house is worth—simply mailing the keys to their domicile to the bank and walking away from their mortgage obligations. Many simply stop payments and dare the bank to foreclose and evict them. Others find cheaper quarters by either renting, or taking advantage of cheaper mortgages.

There were a few of these walkaways during the housing bust of the early 1990s. But today, nearly 5 million mortgages—about 10% of all residential mortgages in the country—are underwater (defined as a mortgage where the value of the house is 75% or less than the principle). And while no one is keeping track, one outfit has estimated that a half million people took the walkaway route last year.

Financial advisors are at the point of actually urging their clients to walkaway. Sure, their credit rating will take a hit. Better that than pouring money down a black hole where you will never realize any return on your investment.

There are a couple of ethical questions associated with walkaways that need to be addressed; one is personal, the other is an apparent double standard in the application of society's disapproval.

Case in point; a New York developer walked away from paying the loan on 11,000 apartments in Manhattan.

From *The Moderate Voice*, February 4, 2010, pp. 1–4. Copyright © 2010 by The Moderate Voice. Reprinted by permission.

The rules are different, though, for the walkaway of all walkaways.

That title is reserved for what happened to one of New York's trophy properties, the 56-building Stuyvesant Town and Peter Cooper Village complex. Spanning 80 acres on Manhattan's east side, it's the largest single-owned residential area in the city. Its red brick buildings, built by Metropolitan Life in the 1940s for World War II veterans, are still a haven for the city's middle class.

Commercial real-estate firm Tishman and its partner, investment firm BlackRock, paid $5.4 billion to buy the property from MetLife in late 2006—right at the market's peak. They hoped to make money by converting rent-regulated apartments into luxury condos and raising rents.

Then the housing crash hit. The value now: $1.8 billion.

And you thought you overpaid for your house.

"They made assumptions that things would grow to the moon, and things certainly did not," said Len Blum, a managing partner at investment bank Westwood Capital.

Tishman said last week that it was turning the property back over to creditors to avoid filing for bankruptcy protection. In recent weeks, Tishman failed to restructure $4.4 billion in debt, and couldn't find another buyer, according to a statement from the company.

Will Tishman come in for less disapprobation than a homeowner who walks away from a mortgage where he is paying 40% more than the house is worth? It's a certainty that banks are treating Tishman differently than the ordinary homeowner:

Walking away isn't risk-free. A foreclosure stays on a consumer's credit record for seven years and can send a credit score (based on a scale of 300 to 850) plunging by as much as 160 points, according to Fair Isaac Corp., which provides tools for analyzing credit records. A lower credit score means auto and other loans are likely to come with much higher interest rates, and credit card issuers may charge more interest or refuse to issue a card.

In addition, many states give lenders varying degrees of scope to seize bank deposits, cars or other assets of people who default on mortgages.

Even so, in neighborhoods with high concentrations of foreclosures, "it's going to be really difficult to prevent a cascade effect" as one strategic default emboldens others to take that drastic step, says Paola Sapienza, a professor of finance at Northwestern University. A study by researchers at Northwestern and the University of Chicago found that as many as one in four defaults may be strategic.

The double standard is easy to understand, less easy to justify. The fact is, a bank is less apt to severely penalize someone who owes them billions as opposed to someone who is into them for a few hundred thousand. The "sin" may be similar, but repentance is more complicated. It's as if a rich man and a poor man both stole a loaf of bread; the poor man was forced to knee walk up a rocky mountain and say the rosary while the rich man got away with saying one our father, one hail mary, and a glory be (old line catholics will recognize that penance immediately).

Ideally, the same sin should engender the same penance or punishment regardless of wealth or social station. But in this case, we hold people and corporations to different standards of behavior and hence, different attitudes toward walkaways.

But it is the personal ethics of abandoning a promise to repay monies loaned in good faith by a lending institution based on your past history of good credit and timely repayment that is of most relevance for us. What happens when so many walk away from their obligations not because they can't pay but because paying what they owe is a bad personal financial decision?

We can all sympathize with the walkaway and wonder if we'd do the same in their situation. But from an ethical standpoint, this is really rotten. By walking away, these homeowners are making it more difficult for the rest of us to get a homeloan or refinance our existing home. This is an inherently selfish act in that the walkaway fails to take into account the effect on the community and society.

And then there's the prospect if there are enough walkaways, a tipping point will be reached and all that bad paper that is still on the balance books of major banks will cause another meltdown necessitating still more bailouts and takeovers when home values go into another death spiral.

What happens if five million Americans decide to stop overpaying their mortgages and mail the keys back to the bank? There would be a sharp decline in housing values. There would be another downward leg to the financial crisis, with a big hit to the capital of banks and other institutions holding large mortgage portfolios.

I think the housing decline would be a healthy thing, as this market is still overvalued. I don't believe we would see a deflationary spiral, a widespread collapse of debt values, and a descent into a full-fledged Great Depression II. This was the great fear when the bubble first started popping in late 2006.

But since late 2008, the Bernanke Doctrine has showed that the modern Fed has the tools to keep this from happening. Administration officials can say whatever they want, but Too-Big-To-Fail is still reality.

What of the decline in individual purchasing power, the so-called adverse wealth effect, that would come with lower housing values? It would be muted because making mortgage payments on an overvalued house diminishes purchasing power just as badly.

But the net effect of the Great Walkaway would still be a strong downdraft in the overall economy.

I don't for a moment believe that 5 million people will strategically default on their mortgages. But who can guess where the tipping point might be? Who can be sure that 1 million or 2 million such defaults wouldn't crash the economy again?

All because people selfishly took stock of their personal financial situation and decided it was OK to saddle the rest of us with what is, after all, their problem. I say they have no ethical right to do it and that Congress should make it easier for banks to collect from these voluntary deadbeats.

Not surprisingly, Congress will treat these people as victims and no doubt either bail them out (one estimate is it would take about $750 billion to pay off the difference between what underwater borrowers owe and what their houses are worth), or make some accommodation with credit reporting services to give these strategic deadbeats a pass. Encouraging irresponsibility has been the hallmark of the Obama administration housing policies so why should we expect anything to be different here?

For the vast majority of us who have suffered a big hit on the value of our homes but continue to remain faithful to our obligations, this whole walkaway phenomenon is a slap in the face. We are being played for suckers. And it's depressing to think that rewards will accrue to those ethically challenged scofflaws who don't play by the rules but come out smelling like roses anyway.

POSTSCRIPT

Should Homeowners Employ Strategic Default Options with Mortgages?

We need to restructure the complex world of loans and mortgages. A current ethical and economic problem in the housing market often confronts a conscientious citizen who pays his debts. Now, with his home losing half its value, how does he escape from the obligation to take a large financial loss? The homeowner who needs to sell now is at a systematic disadvantage. How about the smart businessperson who operates entirely within the law, but without the added goal of moral concern? Is the home ownership dilemma easier to solve? It may be that the entire structure of business law grew in response to situations of this kind—to level the balance between the conscience-driven and the advantage-driven individual. These authors, in different ways, find that laws need to change to cover these new cases.

Suggested Readings

Thomas M. Anderson, "Walking Away from a Mortgage," *Kiplinger's Personal Finance* (vol. 64, no. 10, 2010), pp. 37–58.

James R. Hagerty and Nick Timiraos, "Debtor's Dilemma: Pay the Mortgage or Walk Away," *Wall Street Journal—Eastern Edition* (December 17, 2009), p. A22.

Kevin A. Hassett, "Mortgage Morality," *National Review* (vol. 62, no. 4, 2010), pp. 20–22.

Jody Shenn, "Mortgages: Strategic Defaults Are on the Rise," *Bloomberg BusinessWeek* (May 6, 2010), pp. 45–46.

Brent T. White, "Underwater Home: What Should You Do If You Owe More on Your Home Than It's Worth," *Createspace* (2010).

ISSUE 16

Should We Require Labeling for Genetically Modified Food?

YES: Philip L. Bereano, from "The Right to Know What We Eat," *Seattle Times* (October 11, 1998)

NO: Joseph A. Levitt, from Statement before the Health, Education, Labor, and Pensions Committee, United States Senate (September 26, 2000)

ISSUE SUMMARY

YES: The consumer's interest in knowing where his food comes from does not necessarily have to do with the chemical and nutritional properties of the food. Kosher pastrami, for instance, is identical to the nonkosher product, and dolphin-safe tuna is still tuna. But we have a real and important interest in knowing the processes by which our foods arrived on the table, Bereano argues, and the demand for a label for bioengineered foods is entirely legitimate.

NO: Levitt points out that as far as the law is concerned, only the nutritional traits and characteristics of foods are subject to safety assessment. Labeling has been required only where health risks exist, or where there is danger that a product's marketing claims may mislead the consumer as to the food's characteristics. Breeding techniques have never been subject to labeling, nor should genetic engineering techniques.

How much weight can a little label bear? We have seen a profound change in the function of the label over the course of the last century. At first, the label, if such there was, said only what the container contained and the brand name. "Carter's Little Liver Pills." "Argo Cornstarch." With advances in packaging, the labels became more attractive, brighter, eye-catching, and began to carry marketing claims. That was the label's purpose: to sell the product, by featuring a trusted brand name (logo, trademark) and an advertisement for the product, in a design aimed at capturing attention.

Poisons, of course, had to be labeled as such, to warn consumers to use them carefully—and to warn off the vulnerable. Remember the frightening skull and crossbones?

The consumer movement changed all that. Calling upon the police power of the state (the right and obligation of the state to protect the health, safety, and morals of the citizens), the Food and Drug Administration began requiring labels to fulfill serious informational functions. Now actual weights have to be listed on the package, a list of ingredients in order of weight must appear on any complex product, and the real nutritional content has to be listed in a plainly visible uniform panel on the back of the package (even for little candy bars). Even nonfood items have labeling requirements; garments and bedding must state the materials from which they are made, and bedding labels must warrant that those materials are new.

Those who would like genetically modified (GM) foods to be labeled as such do not conceal their interest in the same agenda. They would like to see all GM foods (corn, for instance) and all processed foods containing GM ingredients (vegetable oil, for instance) labeled as such, so that consumers will be worried by the labels, so that eventually GM foods will be taken off the market. In the light of the general profitability of GM foods, it seems politically more feasible to get a labeling requirement than a prohibition. Besides, in some polls, up to 70 percent of consumers have said that they would want to know if the product they bought was genetically modified. Who could object to full information about a product, the process by which it was produced as well as its content, being given to the consumer?

As it turns out, there are many objections. One is the sheer mass of effort required to sort out foods that contain GM products (practically ubiquitous at this point), especially processed foods like cereals and bake mixes. More important, whether or not a label designates a difference in a product, the consumer must assume it does and must assume, unless there is proof to the contrary, that it designates a dangerous difference. There was no doubt as to the intention or the effect of the requirement of labeling for tobacco products. There is every reason to think that a required label, "Contains Genetically Modified Products," would be read as a skull and crossbones.

Not every political agenda justifies labeling, after all. How would we react to a request to label as such all boxes of tampons or sanitary pads that were packed by African Americans? Suppose we could come up with a survey that showed that up to 70 percent of white women in a particular area would want to have that information. Would that influence our reaction? Ask yourself, as you read the following selections, just what political agenda or secondary purposes we want attached to the police power of the state. Is the demand for "labeling" justified or not?

YES

Philip L. Bereano

The Right to Know What We Eat

"I personally have no wish to eat anything produced by genetic modification, nor do I knowingly offer this sort of produce to my family or guests. There is increasing evidence that many people feel the same way."

—Prince Charles, *London Telegraph,* June 8, 1998.

Genetic engineering is a set of new techniques for altering the basic makeup of plants and animals. Genes from insects, animals, and humans have been added to crop plants; human genes have been added to pigs and cattle.

Although genetic-engineering techniques are biologically novel, the industry and government are so eager to achieve financial success that they say the products of the technologies are pretty much the same ("substantially equivalent") as normal crops. Despite the gene tinkering, the new products are not being tested extensively to find out how they differ and to be sure that any hazards are within acceptable limits.

These foods are now appearing in the supermarkets and on our dinner plates, but the industry and government have been vigorously resisting consumer attempts to label these "novel foods" in order to distinguish them from more traditional ones.

The failure of the U.S. government to require that genetically engineered foods (GEFs) be labeled presents consumers with quandaries: issues of free speech and consumers' right to know, religious rights for those with dietary restrictions, and cultural rights for people, such as vegetarians, who choose to avoid consuming foods of certain origins.

The use of antibiotic-resistant genes engineered into crop plants as "markers" can contribute to the spread of antibiotic-tolerant disease bacteria; this resistance is a major public-health problem, as documented by a recent study of the National Academy of Sciences. Some genetic recombinations can lead to allergic or auto-immune reactions. The products of some genes which are used as plant pesticides have been implicated in skin diseases in farm and market workers.

The struggle over labeling is occurring because industry knows that consumers do not want to eat GEFs; labeled products will likely fail in the marketplace. However, as the British publication *The Economist* noted, "if Monsanto cannot persuade us, it certainly has no right to foist its products on us." Labels would counter "foisting" and are legally justifiable.

The Government's Rationale

In 1992, the government abdicated any supervision over GEFs. Under Food and Drug Administration's rules, the agency does not even have access to industry information about a GEF unless the company decides voluntarily to submit it. Moreover, important information on risk-assessment questions is often withheld as being proprietary, "confidential business information." So "safety" cannot be judged in a precautionary way; we must await the inevitable hazardous event.

According to a former FDA official, the genetic processes used in the development of a new food are "NOT considered to be material information because there is no evidence that new biotech foods are different from other foods in ways related to safety."

James Maryanski, FDA biotechnology coordinator, claims that whether a food has been genetically engineered is not a "material fact" and FDA would not "require things to be on the label just because a consumer might want to know them."

Yet a standard law dictionary defines "material" as "important," "going to the merits," "relevant." Since labeling is a form of speech from growers and processors to purchasers, it is reasonable, therefore, to interpret "material" as comprising whatever issues a substantial portion of the consuming public defines as "important." And all the polls show that whether food is genetically engineered falls into such a category.

Last May, several religious leaders and citizen groups sued the FDA to change its position and to require that GEFs be labeled.

Process Labels

Some government officials have said that labeling should be only about the food product itself, not the process by which it is manufactured. Yet, the U.S. has many process food labels: kosher, dolphin-free, Made in America, union-made, free-range (chickens, for example), irradiated, and "green" terms such as "organic."

For many of these products, the scientific difference between an item which can carry the label and that which cannot is negligible or nonexistent. Kosher pastrami is chemically identical to non-kosher meat. Dolphin-free tuna and tuna caught by methods which result in killing of dolphins are the same, as are many products which are "made in America" when compared to those made abroad, or those made by unionized as opposed to nonunion workers.

These labeling rules recognize that consumers are interested in the processes by which their purchases are made and have a legal right to such knowledge. In none of these labeling situations has the argument been made that if the products are substantially equivalent, no label differentiation is permissible. It is constitutionally permissible for government rules to intrude slightly on the commercial speech of producers in order to expand the First Amendment rights of consumers to know what is of significant interest to them.

Substantial Equivalence

In order to provide an apparently rational basis for its refusal to exercise regulatory oversight in this regard, the U.S. government has adopted the industry's position that genetically engineered foods are "substantially equivalent" to their natural counterparts. The FDA ignores the contradictory practice of corporations in going to another government agency, the Patent Office, where they argue that a GEF is novel and different (in order to justify receiving monopoly protection).

"Substantial equivalence" is used as a basis for both eliminating regulatory assessment and failing to require labels on GEFs. However, the concept of substantial equivalence is subjective and imprecise.

Most genetic engineering is designed to meet corporate—not consumer—needs. Foods are engineered, for instance, to produce "counterfeit freshness." Consumers believe engineered characteristics such as color and texture indicate freshness, flavor and nutritional quality. Actually the produce is aging and growing stale, and nutritional value is being depleted. So much for "substantial equivalence."

The Precautionary Principle

Consumers International, a global alliance of more than 200 consumer groups, has suggested that "because the effects (of GEFs) are so difficult to predict, it is vital to have internationally agreed and enforceable rules for research protocols, field trials and post-marketing surveillance." This approach has become known as the "precautionary principle" and has entered into the regulatory processes of the European Union.

The principle reflects common-sense aphorisms such as "Better safe than sorry" and "An ounce of prevention is worth a pound of cure." It rests on the notion that parties who wish to change the social order (often while making money or gaining power and influence) should not be able to slough the costs and risks onto others. The new procedure's proponents should have to prove it is safe rather than forcing regulators or citizens to prove a lack of safety.

Look Before You Eat

For GEFs, labeling performs important functions in carrying out the precautionary principle. It places a burden on industry to show that genetic manipulations are socially beneficial and provides a financial incentive for them to do research to reduce uncertainty about the consequences of GEFs.

Democratic notions of free speech include the right to receive information as well as to disseminate it. It is fundamental to capitalist market theory that for transactions to be most efficient all parties must have "perfect information." The realities of modern food production create a tremendous imbalance of knowledge between producer and purchaser. Our society has relied on the government to redress this imbalance and make grocery shopping a fairer and more efficient—as well as safer—activity.

In an economic democracy, choice is the fundamental prerogative of the purchaser.

As some biologists have put it, "The risk associated with genetically engineered foods is derived from the fact that, although genetic engineers can cut and splice DNA molecules with precision in the test tube, when those altered DNA molecules are introduced into a living organism, the full range of effects on that organism cannot be predicted or known before commercialization. The introduced DNA may bring about unintended changes, some of which may be damaging to health."

Numerous opinion polls in the U.S. and abroad in the past decade have shown great skepticism about genetic alteration of foods; a large proportion of respondents, usually majorities, are reluctant to use such products. Regardless of whether they would consume GEFs, consumers feel even more strongly that they should be labeled.

In a *Toronto Star* poll reported on June 2, 98 percent favored labeling. Bioindustry giant Novartis surveyed U.S. consumers and found 93 percent of them wanted information about genetic engineering of food.

Alice Waters, originator of the legendary Berkeley restaurant Chez Panisse and recently selected to organize a new restaurant at the Louvre in Paris, has said, "The act of eating is very political. You buy from the right people, you support the right network of farmers and suppliers who care about the land and what they put in the food. If we don't preserve the natural resources, you aren't going to have a sustainable society."

However, the U.S. government has been resisting attempts to label GEFs. Despite the supposed environmentalist and consumer sympathies of the Clinton-Gore administration, the government believes nothing should impede the profitability of biotech as a mainstay to the future U.S. economy.

The administration's hostility to labeling may also be coupled to political contributions made to it by the interested industries.

Regulation and Free Speech

The government is constrained by the First Amendment from limiting or regulating the content of labels except for the historic functions of protecting health and safety and eliminating fraud or misrepresentation.

The American Civil Liberties Union has noted that "a simple distinction between noncommercial and commercial speech does not determine the extent to which the guarantees of the First Amendment apply to advertising and similar communications relating to the sale or other disposition of goods and services."

Supreme Court decisions have warned against attaching "more importance to the distinction between commercial and noncommercial speech than our cases warrant." Can the government prohibit certain commercial speech, such as barring a label saying "this product does not contain genetically engineered components"?

In several recent cases, the Court has restricted government regulation of commercial speech, in effect allowing more communication. The First Amendment directs us to be skeptical of regulations that seek to keep people in the dark for what the government perceives to be their own good. Thus, it would be hard to sustain the government if it tried to prohibit labeling foods as "free from genetically engineered products," if the statement were true.

In 1995, the FDA's Maryanski took the position that "the FDA is not saying that people don't have a right to know how their food is produced. But the food label is not always the most appropriate method for conveying that information." Is it acceptable for a government bureaucrat to make decisions about what are appropriate methods of information exchange among citizens?

The government and the industry suggest that labels on GEFs might amount to "misrepresentation" by implying that there is a difference between the genetically engineered and nongenetically engineered foods. It is hard, however, to understand how a truthful statement can ever amount to a "misrepresentation." (And of course, they are different, by definition.)

The first food product bearing a label "No GE Ingredients," a brand of corn chips, made its appearance this summer.

Some states have laws creating a civil cause of action against anyone who "disparages" an agricultural product unless the defendant can prove the statements were based on "reasonable and reliable scientific" evidence.

A Harvard analysis suggests that "at stake in the dispute about food-safety claims is scientific uncertainty in an uncertain and unpredictable world. Agricultural disparagement statutes are supposed to regulate the exchange of ideas in that gray area between science and the public good. The underlying approach of these statutes is to regulate speech by encouraging certain kinds of exchanges and punishing others. . . ."

According to the ACLU, "these so-called 'veggie libel' laws raise obvious First Amendment problems and threaten to chill speech on important issues of public concern." Consumers Union argues that "such laws, we believe, give the food and agriculture industry the power to choke off concerns and criticism about food quality and safety."

Such enactments did not prevail in the suit by Texas cattle ranchers against Oprah Winfrey and her guest Howard Lyman (of the Humane Society) for their on-air conversations about "mad-cow disease" possibilities in the United States. The lawsuit was widely seen as a test of the First Amendment constitutionality of such state statutes, although the case was actually resolved on much narrower grounds.

Consequences of Regulation

As Prince Charles noted in his essay, "we cannot put our principles into practice until there is effective segregation and labeling of genetically modified products. Arguments that this is either impossible or irrelevant are simply not credible."

Nonetheless, the biotech industry (and many governments, including our own) make the argument that it is impossible to keep genetically engineered foodstuffs separate from naturally produced ones. However, the same industries actually require rigorous segregation (for example, of seeds) when they are protecting their monopolies on patented food items.

Although it undoubtedly has related costs, the segregation of kosher food products from non-kosher ones, for example, has been routine in this country for decades. The only difference for GEFs appears to be one of scale, not technique, in monitoring the flow of foodstuffs, spot-testing and labeling them appropriately.

In Support of Mandatory Labeling

Can the government mandate commercial speech—for example, requiring GEFs to bear a label proclaiming their identity?

The government does require some label information which goes beyond consumer health effects; not every consumer must need mandated information in order for it to be required by law. These requirements have never been judged an infringement of producers' constitutional rights. For example:

- Very few consumers are sensitive to sulfites, although all wine must be labeled.
- The burden is put on tobacco manufacturers to carry the surgeon general's warning, even though the majority of cigarette smokers will not develop lung cancer and an intended effect of the label is to reinforce the resolve of nonconsumers to refrain from smoking.
- Labeling every processed food with its fat and calorie analysis is mandated, even though vast numbers of Americans are not overweight or suffering from heart disease.
- Irradiated foods (other than spices) must carry a specific logo.
- Finally, the source of hydrolyzed proteins in foods must be on a label to accommodate vegetarian cultural practices and certain religious beliefs.

These legal requirements are in place because many citizens want such information, and a specific fraction need it. An identifiable fraction of consumers actually need information about genetic modification—for example, as regards allergenicity—as the FDA itself has recognized in the Federal Register, and almost all want it.

Foods which are comprised, to any but a trace extent, of genetically altered components or products should be required to be labeled. This can be justified in some instances on scientific and health grounds, and for other foods on the social, cultural, religious and political interest consumers may have in the processes by which their food is produced.

Consumers' right to know is an expression of an ethical position which acknowledges individual autonomy; it is also a social approach which helps to rectify the substantial imbalance of power which exists in a modern society where commercial transactions occur between highly integrated and well-to-do corporations, on the one hand, and atomized consumers on the other.

We should let labeled GEFs run the test of the marketplace.

Joseph A. Levitt  **NO**

Statement of Joseph A. Levitt

Introduction

Mr. Chairman and members of the Committee, thank you for giving the Food and Drug Administration (FDA or the Agency) the opportunity to testify today on its regulatory program for foods derived from plants using the tools of modern biotechnology—also known as genetically engineered, or bioengineered, foods. I am Joseph A. Levitt, Director of FDA's Center for Food Safety and Applied Nutrition (CFSAN). Within FDA, CFSAN oversees bioengineered plant products or ingredients intended for human consumption. Our Center for Veterinary Medicine oversees bioengineered plant products used as or in animal feed, as well as bioengineered products used to improve the health or productivity of animals (including fish).

We believe it is very important for the public to understand how FDA is regulating the new bioengineered foods being introduced into the marketplace and to have confidence in that process. To that end, I appreciate this opportunity to describe our policies and procedures to the Committee and to the public.

First, let me state that FDA is confident that the bioengineered plant foods on the U.S. market today are as safe as their conventionally bred counterparts. This conclusion was echoed by a report by the National Resource Council of the National Academy of Sciences which stated, "The committee is not aware of any evidence that foods on the market are unsafe to eat as a result of genetic modification." Since FDA's 1994 evaluation of the Flavr Savr tomato, the first genetically-engineered plant food to reach the U.S. market, FDA has reviewed the data on more than 45 other products, ranging from herbicide resistant soybeans to a canola plant with modified oil content. To date, there is no evidence that these plants are significantly different in terms of food safety from crops produced through traditional breeding techniques.

The topic of bioengineering has generated much controversy, particularly about whether these foods should be labeled or not. As I discuss in more detail later in my testimony, FDA held three public meetings on bioengineered foods late last year, the second one of which I chaired. We wanted to hear the views from all, and importantly, we wanted to discuss and obtain feedback on ways in which information on bioengineered foods could be most appropriately and helpfully conveyed.

U.S. Senate, September 26, 2000.

Partly in response to information gained from the public meetings and comments received by the Agency, FDA announced on May 3, 2000, that it will be taking steps to modify our current voluntary process for bioengineered foods to establish mandatory premarket notification and make the process more transparent. Further, we will be developing guidance for food manufacturers who wish voluntarily to label their products regarding whether or not they contain bioengineered ingredients. To ensure that the Agency has the best scientific advice, we also are adding experts in this field to our foods and veterinary medicine advisory committees. FDA is taking these steps to help provide consumers with continued confidence in the safety of the U.S. food supply and to ensure that the Agency's oversight procedures will meet the challenges of the future. The proposed notification rule and draft guidance are currently under development. . . .

Legal and Regulatory Issues

FDA regulates bioengineered plant food in conjunction with the United States Department of Agriculture (USDA) and the Environmental Protection Agency (EPA). FDA has authority under the Federal Food, Drug, and Cosmetic (FD&C) Act to ensure the safety of all domestic and imported foods for man or other animals in the United States market, except meat, poultry and egg products which are regulated by USDA. (Note that the safety of animal drug residues in meat and poultry is regulated by FDA's Center for Veterinary Medicine.) Pesticides are regulated primarily by EPA, which reviews safety and sets tolerances (or establishes exemptions from tolerance) for pesticides. FDA enforces the pesticide tolerances set by EPA. USDA's Animal & Plant Health Inspection Service (APHIS) oversees the agricultural and environmental safety of planting and field testing of bioengineered plants.

Bioengineered foods and food ingredients must adhere to the same standards of safety under the FD&C Act that apply to their conventionally-bred counterparts. This means that these products must be as safe as the traditional foods in the market. FDA has broad authority to initiate regulatory action if a product fails to meet the standards of the FD&C Act.

FDA relies primarily on two sections of the FD&C Act to ensure the safety of foods and food ingredients:

1. The adulteration provisions of section 402(a)(1). Under this postmarket authority, FDA has the power to remove a food from the market (or sanction those marketing the food) if the food poses a risk to public health. It is important to note that the FD&C Act places a legal duty on developers to ensure that the foods they market to consumers are safe and comply with all legal requirements.
2. The food additive provisions (section 409). Under this section, a substance that is intentionally added to food is a food additive, unless the substance is generally recognized as safe (GRAS) or is otherwise exempt (e.g., a pesticide, the safety of which is overseen by EPA).

The FD&C Act requires premarket approval of any food additive—regardless of the technique used to add it to food. Thus, substances introduced into food are either (1) new food additives that require premarket approval by FDA or (2) GRAS, and are exempt from the requirement for premarket review (for example, if there is a long history of safe use in food). Generally, foods such as fruits, vegetables, and grains, are not subject to premarket approval because they have been safely consumed over many years. Other than the food additive system, there are no premarket approval requirements for foods generally.

In 1992, knowing that bioengineered products were on the horizon, FDA published a policy explaining how existing legal requirements would apply to products developed using the tools of biotechnology (57 FR 22984; May 29, 1992; "Statement of Policy: Foods Derived from New Plant Varieties"). The 1992 policy was designed to answer developers' questions about these products prior to marketing to assist them in meeting their legal duty to provide safe and wholesome foods to consumers. The basic principle of the 1992 policy is that the traits and characteristics of the foods should be the focus of safety assessment for all new varieties of food crops, no matter which techniques are used to develop them.

Under FDA policy, a substance that would be a food additive if it were added during traditional food manufacturing is also treated as a food additive if it is introduced into food through bioengineering of a food crop. Our authority under section 409 permits us to require premarket approval of any food additive and thus, to require premarket review of any substance intentionally introduced via bioengineering that is not generally recognized as safe.

Generally, substances intentionally introduced into food that would be reviewed as food additives include those that have unusual chemical functions, have unknown toxicity, or would be new major dietary components of the food. For example, a novel sweetener bioengineered into food would likely require premarket approval. In our experience with bioengineered food to date, however, we have reviewed only one substance under the food additive provisions, an enzyme produced by an antibiotic resistance gene, and we approved that one. In general, substances intentionally added to food via biotechnology to date have been well-characterized proteins and fats, and are functionally very similar to other proteins and fats that are commonly and safely consumed in the diet and thus are presumptively GRAS.

In 1994, for the first bioengineered product planned for introduction into the market, FDA moved deliberately, following the 1992 policy. We conducted a comprehensive scientific review of Calgene's data on the Flavr Savr™ tomato and the use of the kanamycin resistance marker gene. FDA also held a public meeting of our Food Advisory Committee (the Committee) to examine applicability of the 1992 policy to products such as the Flavr Savr™ tomato. The Committee members agreed with FDA that the scientific approach presented in the 1992 policy was sound and that questions regarding the Flavr Savr™ had been addressed. The Committee members also suggested that we remove unnecessary reviews to provide an expedited decision process on the marketing of bioengineered foods that do not raise substantive scientific issues.

In response, that same year, FDA established a consultative process to help companies comply with the FD&C Act's requirements for any new food, including a bioengineered food, that they intend to market. Since that time, companies have used the consultative process more than 45 times as they sought to introduce genetically altered plants representing ten different crops into the U.S. market. We are not aware of any bioengineered food product on the market under FDA's jurisdiction that has not been evaluated by FDA through the current consultation process.

Typically, the consultation begins early in the product development stage, before it is ready for market. Company scientists and other officials will meet with FDA scientists to describe the product they are developing. In response, the Agency advises the company on what tests would be appropriate for the company to assess the safety of the new food.

After the studies are completed, the data and information on the safety and nutritional assessment are provided voluntarily to FDA for review. The Agency evaluates the information for all of the known hazards and also for potential unintended effects on plant composition and nutritional properties, since plants may undergo changes other than those intended by the breeders. Specifically, FDA scientists are looking to assure that the newly expressed compounds are safe for food consumption, there are no allergens new to the food, no increased levels of natural toxicants, and no reduction of important nutrients. They are also looking to see whether the food has been changed in any substantive way such that the food would need to be specially labeled to reveal the nature of the change to consumers.

Some examples of the information reviewed by FDA include: the name of the food and the crop from which it is derived; the uses of the food, including both human food and animal feed uses; the sources, identities, and functions of introduced genetic material and its stability in the plant; the purpose or intended technical effect of the modification and its expected effect on the composition or characteristic properties of the food or feed; the identity and function of any new products encoded by the introduced genetic material, including an estimate of its concentration; comparison of the composition or characteristics of the bioengineered food to that of food derived from the parental variety or other commonly consumed varieties with special emphasis on important nutrients, anti-nutrients, and toxicants that occur naturally in the food; information on whether the genetic modification altered the potential for the bioengineered food to induce an allergic response; and, other information relevant to the safety and nutritional assessment of the bioengineered food.

It should be noted that if a plant developer used a gene from a plant whose food is commonly allergenic, FDA would presume that the modified food may be allergenic unless the developer could demonstrate that the food would not cause allergic reactions in people allergic to food from the source plant. If FDA scientists have more questions about the safety data, the company either provides more detailed answers or conducts additional studies. Our experience has been that no bioengineered product has gone on the market until FDA's questions about the product have been answered.

Labeling

Labeling, either mandatory or voluntary, of bioengineered foods is a controversial issue. Section 403 of the FD&C Act sets labeling requirements for all foods. All foods, whether derived using bioengineering or not, are subject to these labeling requirements.

Under section 403(a)(1) of the FD&C Act, a food is misbranded if its labeling is false or misleading in any particular way. Section 201(n) of the FD&C Act provides additional guidance on how labeling may be misleading. It states that labeling is misleading if it fails to reveal all facts that are "material in light of such representations (made or suggested in the labeling) or material with respect to consequences which may result from the use of the article to which the labeling or advertising relates under the conditions of use prescribed in the labeling or advertising thereof or under such conditions of use as are customary or usual."

While the legislative history of section 201(n) contains little discussion of the word "material," there is precedent to guide the Agency in its decision regarding whether information on a food is in fact material within the meaning of 201(n). Historically, the Agency has generally limited the scope of the materiality concept to information about the attributes of the food itself. FDA has required special labeling on the basis of it being "material" information in cases where the absence of such information may: 1) pose special health or environmental risks (e.g., warning statement on certain protein diet products); 2) mislead the consumer in light of other statements made on the label (e.g., requirement for quantitative nutrient information when certain nutrient content claims are made about a product); or 3) in cases where a consumer may assume that a food, because of its similarity to another food, has nutritional, organoleptic, or functional characteristics of the food it resembles when in fact it does not (e.g., reduced fat margarine not suitable for frying).

FDA does not require labeling to indicate whether or not a food or food ingredient is a bioengineered product, just as it does not require labeling to indicate which breeding technique was used in developing a food plant. Rather, any significant differences in the food itself have to be disclosed in labeling. If genetic modifications do materially change the composition of a food product, these changes must be reflected in the food's labeling. This would include its nutritional content (for example, more folic acid or greater iron content) or requirements for storage, preparation, or cooking, which might impact the food's safety characteristics or nutritional qualities. For example, one soybean variety was modified to alter the levels of oleic acid in the beans; because the oil from this soybean is significantly different when compared to conventional soybean oil, we advised the company to adopt a new name for that oil, a name that reflects the intended change.

If a bioengineered food were to contain an allergen not previously found in that food, information about the presence of the allergen would be material as to the potential consequences of consumption of the food. If FDA determined that labeling would be sufficient to enable the food to be safely marketed, the Agency would require that the food be labeled to indicate the presence of the allergen.

FDA has received comments suggesting that foods developed through modern biotechnology should bear a label informing consumers that the food was produced using bioengineering. While we have given careful consideration to these comments, we do not have data or other information that would form a basis for concluding under the FD&C Act that the fact that a food or its ingredients was produced using bioengineering is material within the meaning of 201(n) and thus, is a fact that must be disclosed in labeling. Hence, we believe that we have neither a scientific nor legal basis to require such labeling. We are developing, however, draft guidance for those that wish voluntarily to label either the presence or absence of bioengineered food in food products.

Public Outreach

Although FDA is confident that its current science-based approach to regulating bioengineered foods is protecting the public health, we realized we had been quietly looking at and reviewing these products and making decisions related to their safety while the public was largely unaware of what we were doing. When trade issues erupted last summer with Europe—and in the World Trade Organization meetings in Seattle—it raised public concern that there might be safety issues with these foods.

New technologies typically raise complex questions—scientific, policy, and even ethical. In light of the newness of this technology and the apparent concern, FDA held the three public meetings I previously mentioned. The public meetings had three purposes: to determine whether there were any new scientific or labeling issues that the Agency should consider; to help the public understand FDA's current policy and become familiar with what we are already doing; and to explore the ways in which information on bioengineered foods could be most appropriately and helpfully conveyed.

FDA asked specific questions on both scientific and safety issues as well as about public information issues. We heard from 35 panelists and over 250 additional speakers in the three meetings. More than 50,000 written comments have been submitted.

What did we learn at these meetings?

First and foremost, no information was presented that indicates there is a safety problem with any bioengineereed food or feed now in the marketplace.

In general, we heard support for strengthening FDA's premarket review process for bioengineered foods, in varying degrees. Views on labeling were very strong and much more polarized. Overall, we heard from many points of view that FDA needs to take additional steps to increase consumer confidence in these products.

As to specific concerns, there were four basic points of view:

1. One group was concerned primarily with anything that could possibly harm the environment, with food safety being a secondary concern.
2. A second group was concerned about the possibility that there might be unknown long-term food safety problems, despite the absence of any scientific information that would support the existence of such problems.

3. A third group said they were not so concerned about food safety—
   they would eat bioengineered foods—but still wanted to know what
   technologies and ingredients were involved in producing their food.
4. A fourth group speaking for developing countries, said they need this
   technology and do not want it limited or taken away.

New Initiatives

As I mentioned, FDA announced on May 3, as part of an Administration initiative, that we will be taking steps to strengthen the premarket notification
program for bioengineered foods. We also intend to provide guidance to food
manufacturers who wish voluntarily to label their products regarding whether
or not they contain bioengineered ingredients. Our goal is to enhance public
confidence in the way in which FDA is regulating bioengineered foods. We
want the public to know, loud and clear, that FDA stands behind the safety of
these products.

As part of this initiative, we will be proposing regulations to make it
mandatory that developers of bioengineered plant varieties notify FDA at least
120 days before they intend to market such products. FDA will require that
specific information be submitted to help determine whether the foods pose
any safety or labeling concerns. The Agency will be providing further guidance to industry on the scientific data needed to ensure that foods developed
through bioengineering are safe for human consumption. To help make the
process more transparent, the Agency has made a commitment to ensuring
that, consistent with information disclosure laws, consumers have access to
information submitted to FDA as part of the notification process and to FDA's
responses in a timely fashion.

The proposed rule on premarket notification and the draft labeling guidance are both high priorities for the Agency, and we intend to publish each of
these later this fall. Both will provide a full opportunity for public comment
before final policies are established. Let me assure you that when we come to
a decision regarding these matters, FDA will operate in an open, transparent
manner so that the public can understand our regulatory approach and continue to provide us with feedback about its impact. As a scientific organization
we are comfortable with debate over complex scientific issues, and welcome
the discussions that have occurred at public meetings to date. It is important
that the public, including the scientific community, clearly understand FDA's
policy on bioengineered foods.

Additional Activities

Before closing, let me briefly describe a few other activities of Agency involvement in the food biotechnology subject area. In our May 3 announcement,
FDA stated our intention to augment our food and veterinary medicine advisory committees by adding scientists with agricultural biotechnology expertise. FDA will use these committees to address over-arching scientific questions
pertaining to bioengineered foods and animal feed. More specifically, I am

restructuring the Food Advisory Committee so that it will contain several special focus subcommittees. One of those subcommittees will have scientists with expertise in bioengineering, and will focus on issues pertaining to food biotechnology.

As I am sure you are aware, the National Academy of Sciences has formed a new standing Committee on Agricultural Biotechnology. FDA has participated in several of its meetings, including one just last week, on September 18, in which two FDA experts made presentations. We think the work of this committee is very important. We are formalizing our relationship with it, particularly with regard to exploring what the potential is for any unknown long-term health effects to result from consumption of bioengineered food.

FDA is actively participating in the work of the U.S. Codex Committee on food labeling, which is considering issues on policies for possible labeling of foods derived using bioengineering. In addition, FDA is participating in the newly formed "Ad Hoc Committee on Foods Derived from Biotechnology." This committee is especially important because its initial focus is to develop principles and guidelines for the evaluation of the safety of bioengineered foods. FDA is providing an international leadership role in this committee to develop harmonized policies for assessing the safety of bioengineered food.

Let me comment briefly on the recall announced by Kraft Foods this past Friday. FDA commends Kraft Foods for acting responsibly in light of testing showing the possibility that the products contained a bioengineered protein that had not been approved for human consumption. This reinforces the importance of FDA, EPA and other interested parties to be vigilant in assuring that the rules pertaining to bioengineered foods are being fully adhered to. FDA's investigation is continuing in this case.

Mr. Chairman, thank you again for the opportunity to address these issues. I am happy to answer any questions you might have.

POSTSCRIPT

Should We Require Labeling for Genetically Modified Food?

William Safire, a journalist often amused by popular trends in the use of the English language, at one point titled his weekly essay "Franken-: A Terrifying New Prefix is Stalking Europe." His point was not that many European nations, acting in fear, had banned or restricted the import of genetically modified foods, but that language had evolved to express that fear. "Franken-," from Mary Godwin Shelley's nineteenth-century book *Frankenstein*, has come to characterize the product of any human "tampering" with nature that displeases the speaker. The fact that we have modified breeds of plants and animals for centuries, in fact millennia, through selective breeding or other methods of assisting evolution, tends to get lost in the scuffle. The language helps the scuffling.

Labeling is another way to use language to affect policy. It simply is not politically neutral to attach a label to something, especially when on our usual understandings, it should not need one. Every required addition to the labels on our food has been made in response to a public agenda, usually concerning public health, but occasionally (as in the case of the tuna and the pastrami) concerning public causes that have nothing to do with the quality of the food. Do we want genetically engineered products to follow that route?

Suggested Reading

If you would like to think further on this topic, you may profit from the following:

Center for Food Safety, International Food Information Council, Greenpeace: Biotechnology and Better Foods and Industry Web site.

Kristi Coale, "Mutant Food," *Salon* (January 12, 2000). This article looks at how a lawsuit filed against the Food and Drug Administration reveals FDA internal doubts of genetic engineering safety.

Food and Drug Administration Biotechnology Home Page. This FDA site explains federal policies on bioengineered foods.

Michael Fumento, "Crop Busters," *Reason* (January 2000). This article criticizes opponents of genetically engineered foods.

Frederic Golden, "Who's Afraid of Frankenfood?" *Time* (November 29, 1999).

Jon Luoma, "Pandora's Pantry," *Mother Jones* (January/February 2000).

U. S. Department of Agriculture (USDA) Biotechnology home page. This site answers frequently asked questions about biotechnology and provides information on regulatory oversight of biotechnology.

Internet References . . .

U.S. Business Cycle Indicators Data

This site leads to the 256 data series known as the U.S. Business Cycle Indicators, which are used to track and predict U.S. business activity. The subjects of the data groups are clearly listed.

http://www.economagic.com/bci-97.htm

Voice of the Shuttle: Postindustrial Business Theory Page

This site links to a variety of resources on many subjects related to business theory, including restructuring, reengineering, downsizing, flattening, the team concept, outsourcing, business and globalism, human resources management, labor relations, statistics, and history, as well as information and resources on job searches, careers, working from home, and business start-ups.

http://vos.ucsb.edu/browse.asp?id=2727

Society, Religion, and Technology Project

This is the home page on patenting living organisms of the Society, Religion, and Technology Project (SRT) of the Church of Scotland. It provides a simple introduction to the issues involved, other SRT pages on patenting, and links to related pages.

http://www.srtp.org.uk.patent.shtml

Global Objectives

*O*ur business is increasingly carried on in distant waters and foreign villages. The corporation of the future is a global enterprise, difficult to track, avoiding the jurisdiction of any national government. What sorts of ethical obligations attend their operations? Are there products we should not buy because of the way they were manufactured? Are there products we should not sell because of their potential to cause harm to the citizens of other lands (who willingly buy them)?

- Are Multinational Corporations Free from Moral Obligation?
- Are Sweatshops an Inhumane Business Practice?
- Should Patenting Genes Be Understood as Unethical?

ISSUE 17

Are Multinational Corporations Free from Moral Obligation?

YES: **Manuel Velasquez**, from "International Business, Morality, and the Common Good," *Business Ethics Quarterly* (January 1992)

NO: **John E. Fleming**, from "Alternative Approaches and Assumptions: Comments on Manuel Velasquez," *Business Ethics Quarterly* (January 1992)

ISSUE SUMMARY

YES: In the absence of accepted enforcement agencies, there is little probability that any multinational corporation will suffer for violation of rules restricting business for the sake of the common good. Since any business that tried to conform to moral rules in the absence of enforcement would unjustifiably cease to be competitive, it must be the case, Velasquez argues, that moral strictures are not binding on such companies.

NO: Velasquez's logic is impressive, replies Fleming, but conditions on the ground in the multinational corporation are not as he describes. Real corporations tend to deal with long-term customers and suppliers in the goldfish bowl of international media exposure and must adhere to moral standards or lose business.

$\mathbf{I}$n three ways, this issue is not what it seems.

First, to hear Velasquez tell it, it seems to be an issue between the hardheaded realists of Hobbesian persuasion—those who realize that business is business and the bottom line is all that really counts—and the liberal idealists, who'd like to think that high moral thoughts really influence world affairs. Velasquez concludes, very regretfully, that a Hobbesian realist, knowing all the worst about human nature, must acknowledge that moral obligations simply do not apply in the absence of moral community. Yet Fleming does not answer in the tone of lofty idealism, but in that of the practitioner who has to keep an enterprise afloat from day to day. Realism and hardheadedness seem to have switched sides in the course of the debate, apparently; realistically, the only way to serve the bottom line is by (tolerably) moral behavior. Velasquez, it now appears, is the lofty idealist, sacrificing moral principles at the altar of an abstract egoism that could never be put into practice on the multinational scene.

Second, to hear Velasquez tell it, right action is on trial: Can morality justify itself with regard to profit? Can we show that acting for the common good will not damage the profit picture or detract from the increase in shareholder wealth? For if not, we will have to forgo morality. Fleming appears to answer Velasquez's question in the affirmative: Yes, we can show that right action is compatible with (in fact necessary for) the health of the bottom line and the corporate enterprise in general. But in reality, his answer goes much further than that. It is not the behavior that is in question but the theory—not the conclusions of the syllogism but the major premise. For if Fleming is right, the major premise of Hobbesian capitalism—that the sole social responsibility of business is to increase its profits, as Milton Friedman put it so succinctly—is simply incorrect, or unworkable. For any activity that might be expected to follow from the injunction to serve the bottom line and increase profits, activity in total disregard of the moral persuasions of all others in your society, is not only morally wrong on some eternal scale but also self-defeating: Business will plunge and the shareholders will be left with valueless promises. So the theory—not, in this reading, a normative theory, but an empirical generalization about the way things happen in fact—fails to predict the data. It is a flawed theory, and needs, based on this reading, to be replaced.

Third, to hear both Velasquez and Fleming tell it, the dispute is over human behavior—both about the way humans *will* behave and the way they *should* behave—in business situations. But both of them condition their predictions and advice on the nature of the international business community. Fleming is claiming centrally that the international business scene is not at all as Velasquez thinks it is—strangers interacting in strange lands, on a one-time basis only—but is a place of custom, regular habits, and familiar people, where memories are long, word gets around, and tolerance for being taken advantage of is very short. It sounds like a small town. And indeed, that is what the world is coming to be.

Ask yourself, as you read these selections, how international dealings differ from domestic dealings. Does it stretch the imagination to consider folks abroad rather like the folks at home, after getting used to time zone changes and differences in manners? What are the real controls on human behavior—enforcement of laws or the simple social expectations of peers and colleagues?

YES

Manuel Velasquez

International Business, Morality, and the Common Good

During the last few years an increasing number of voices have urged that we pay more attention to ethics in international business, on the grounds that not only are all large corporations now internationally structured and thus engaging in international transactions, but that even the smallest domestic firm is increasingly buffeted by the pressures of international competition. . . .

Can we say that businesses operating in a competitive international environment have any moral obligations to contribute to the international common good, particularly in light of realist objections? Unfortunately, my answer to this question will be in the negative. . . .

International Business

. . . When speaking of international business, I have in mind a particular kind of organization: the multinational corporation. Multinational corporations have a number of well known features, but let me briefly summarize a few of them. First, multinational corporations are businesses and as such they are organized primarily to increase their profits within a competitive environment. Virtually all of the activities of a multinational corporation can be explained as more or less rational attempts to achieve this dominant end. Secondly, multinational corporations are bureaucratic organizations. The implication of this is that the identity, the fundamental structure, and the dominant objectives of the corporation endure while the many individual human beings who fill the various offices and positions within the corporation come and go. As a consequence, the particular values and aspirations of individual members of the corporation have a relatively minimal and transitory impact on the organization as a whole. Thirdly, and most characteristically, multinational corporations operate in several nations. This has several implications. First, because the multinational is not confined to a single nation, it can easily escape the reach of the laws of any particular nation by simply moving its resources or operations out of one nation and transferring them to another nation. Second, because the multinational is not confined to a single nation, its interests are not aligned

From *Business Ethics Quarterly*, vol. 2, no. 1, January 1992, pp. 41–43. Copyright © 1992 by Business Ethics Quarterly. Reprinted by permission of The Philosophy Documentation Center, publisher of Business Ethics Quarterly. References omitted.

with the interests of any single nation. The ability of the multinational to achieve its profit objectives does not depend upon the ability of any particular nation to achieve its own domestic objectives. . . .

The Traditional Realist Objection in Hobbes

The realist objection, of course, is the standard objection to the view that agents—whether corporations, governments, or individuals—have moral obligations on the international level. Generally, the realist holds that it is a mistake to apply moral concepts to international activities: morality has no place in international affairs. The classical statement of this view, which I am calling the "traditional" version of realism, is generally attributed to Thomas Hobbes. . . .

In its Hobbsian form, as traditionally interpreted, the realist objection holds that moral concepts have no meaning in the absence of an agency powerful enough to guarantee that other agents generally adhere to the tenets of morality. Hobbes held, first, that in the absence of a sovereign power capable of forcing men to behave civilly with each other, men are in "the state of nature," a state he characterizes as a "war . . . of every man, against every man." Secondly, Hobbes claimed, in such a state of war, moral concepts have no meaning:

> To this war of every man against every man, this also is consequent; that nothing can be unjust. The notions of right and wrong, justice and injustice have there no place. Where there is no common power, there is no law: where no law, no injustice.

Moral concepts are meaningless, then, when applied to state of nature situations. And, Hobbes held, the international arena is a state of nature, since there is no international sovereign that can force agents to adhere to the tenets of morality.

The Hobbsian objection to talking about morality in international affairs, then, is based on two premises: (1) an ethical premise about the applicability of moral terms and (2) an apparently empirical premise about how agents behave under certain conditions. The ethical premise, at least in its Hobbsian form, holds that there is a connection between the meaningfulness of moral terms and the extent to which agents adhere to the tenets of morality: If in a given situation agents do not adhere to the tenets of morality, then in that situation moral terms have no meaning. The apparently empirical premise holds that in the absence of a sovereign, agents will not adhere to the tenets of morality: they will be in a state of war. This appears to be an empirical generalization about the extent to which agents adhere to the tenets of morality in the absence of a third-party enforcer. Taken together, the two premises imply that in situations that lack a sovereign authority, such as one finds in many international exchanges, moral terms have no meaning and so moral obligations are nonexistent. . . .

Revising the Realist Objection: The First Premise

. . . The neo-Hobbsian or realist . . . might want to propose this premise: When one is in a situation in which others do not adhere to certain tenets of morality, and when adhering to those tenets of morality will put one at a significant competitive disadvantage, then it is not immoral for one to like-wise fail to adhere to them. The realist might want to argue for this claim, first, by pointing out that in a world in which all are competing to secure significant benefits and avoid significant costs, and in which others do not adhere to the ordinary tenets of morality, one risks significant harm to one's interests if one continues to adhere to those tenets of morality. But no one can be morally required to take on major risks of harm to oneself. Consequently, in a competitive world in which others disregard moral constraints and take any means to advance their self-interests, no one can be morally required to take on major risks of injury by adopting the restraints of ordinary morality.

A second argument the realist might want to advance would go as follows. When one is in a situation in which others do not adhere to the ordinary tenets of morality, one is under heavy competitive pressures to do the same. And, when one is under such pressures, one cannot be blamed—i.e., one is excused—for also failing to adhere to the ordinary tenets of morality. One is excused because heavy pressures take away one's ability to control oneself, and thereby diminish one's moral culpability.

Yet a third argument advanced by the realist might go as follows. When one is in a situation in which others do not adhere to the ordinary tenets of morality it is not fair to require one to continue to adhere to those tenets, especially if doing so puts one at a significant competitive disadvantage. It is not fair because then one is laying a burden on one party that the other parties refuse to carry.

Thus, there are a number of arguments that can be given in defense of the revised Hobbsian ethical premise that when others do not adhere to the tenets of morality, it is not immoral for one to do likewise. . . .

Revising the Realist Objection: The Second Premise

Let us turn to the other premise in the Hobbsian argument, the assertion that in the absence of a sovereign, agents will be in a state of war. As I mentioned, this is an apparently empirical claim about the extent to which agents will adhere to the tenets of morality in the absence of a third-party enforcer.

Hobbes gives a little bit of empirical evidence for this claim. He cites several examples of situations in which there is no third party to enforce civility and where, as a result, individuals are in a "state of war." Generalizing from these few examples, he reaches the conclusion that in the absence of a third-party enforcer, agents will always be in a "condition of war." . . .

Recently, the Hobbsian claim . . . has been defended on the basis of some of the theoretical claims of game theory, particularly of the prisoner's dilemma. Hobbes' state of nature, the defense goes, is an instance of a prisoner's dilemma, and *rational* agents in a Prisoner's Dilemma necessarily would choose not to adhere to a set of moral norms. . . .

A Prisoner's Dilemma is a situation involving at least two individuals. Each individual is faced with two choices: he can cooperate with the other individual or he can choose not to cooperate. If he cooperates and the other individual also cooperates, then he gets a certain payoff. If, however, he chooses not to cooperate, while the other individual trustingly cooperates, the noncooperator gets a larger payoff while the cooperator suffers a loss. And if both choose not to cooperate, then both get nothing.

It is a commonplace now that in a Prisoner's Dilemma situation, the most rational strategy for a participant is to choose not to cooperate. For the other party will either cooperate or not cooperate. If the other party cooperates, then it is better for one not to cooperate and thereby get the larger payoff. On the other hand, if the other party does not cooperate, then it is also better for one not to cooperate and thereby avoid a loss. In either case, it is better for one to not cooperate.

. . . In Hobbes' state of nature each individual must choose either to cooperate with others by adhering to the rules of morality (like the rule against theft), or to not cooperate by disregarding the rules of morality and attempting to take advantage of those who are adhering to the rules (e.g., by stealing from them). In such a situation it is more rational . . . to choose not to cooperate. For the other party will either cooperate or not cooperate. If the other party does not cooperate, then one puts oneself at a competitive disadvantage if one adheres to morality while the other party does not. On the other hand, if the other party chooses to cooperate, then one can take advantage of the other party by breaking the rules of morality at his expense. In either case, it is morally rational to not cooperate.

Thus, the realist can argue that in a state of nature, where there is no one to enforce compliance with the rules of morality, it is more rational from the individual's point of view to choose not to comply with morality than to choose to comply. Assuming—and this is obviously a critical assumption—that agents behave rationally, then we can conclude that agents in a state of nature will choose not to comply with the tenets of ordinary morality. . . .

Can we claim that it is clear that multinationals have a moral obligation to pursue the global common good in spite of the objections of the realist?

I do not believe that this claim can be made. We can conclude from the discussion of the realist objection that the Hobbsian claim about the pervasiveness of amorality in the international sphere is false when (1) interactions among international agents are repetitive in such a way that agents can retaliate against those who fail to cooperate, and (2) agents can determine the trustworthiness of other international agents.

But unfortunately, multinational activities often take place in a highly competitive arena in which these two conditions do not obtain. Moreover, these conditions are noticeably absent in the arena of activities that concern the global common good.

First, as I have noted, the common good consists of goods that are indivisible and accessible to all. This means that such goods are susceptible to the free rider problems. Everyone has access to such goods whether or not they do their part in maintaining such goods, so everyone is tempted to free ride on the generosity of others. Now governments can force domestic companies to do their part to maintain the national common good. Indeed, it is one of the functions of government to solve the free rider problem by forcing all to contribute to the domestic common good to which all have access. Moreover, all companies have to interact repeatedly with their host governments, and this leads them to adopt a cooperative stance toward their host government's objective of achieving the domestic common good.

But it is not clear that governments can or will do anything effective to force multinationals to do their part to maintain the global common good. For the governments of individual nations can themselves be free riders, and can join forces with willing multinationals seeking competitive advantages over others. Let me suggest an example. It is clear that a livable global environment is part of the global common good, and it is clear that the manufacture and use of chlorofluorocarbons is destroying that good. Some nations have responded by requiring their domestic companies to cease manufacturing or using chlorofluorocarbons. But other nations have refused to do the same, since they will share in any benefits that accrue from the restraint others practice, and they can also reap the benefits of continuing to manufacture and use chlorofluorocarbons. Less developed nations, in particular, have advanced the position that since their development depends heavily on exploiting the industrial benefits of chlorofluorocarbons, they cannot afford to curtail their use of these substances. Given this situation, it is open to multinationals to shift their operations to those countries that continue to allow the manufacture and use of chlorofluorocarbons. For multinationals, too, will reason that they will share in any benefits that accrue from the restraint others practice, and that they can meanwhile reap the profits of continuing to manufacture and use chlorofluorocarbons in a world where other companies are forced to use more expensive technologies. Moreover, those nations that practice restraint cannot force all such multinationals to discontinue the manufacture or use of chlorofluorocarbons because many multinationals can escape the reach of their laws. An exactly parallel, but perhaps even more compelling, set of considerations can be advanced to show that at least some multinationals will join forces with some developing countries to circumvent any global efforts made to control the global warming trends (the so-called "greenhouse effect") caused by the heavy use of fossil fuels.

The realist will conclude, of course, that in such situations, at least some multinationals will seek to gain competitive advantages by failing to contribute to the global common good (such as the good of a hospitable global environment). For multinationals are rational agents, i.e., agents bureaucratically structured to take rational means toward achieving their dominant end of increasing their profits. And in a competitive environment, contributing to the common good while others do not, will fail to achieve this dominant end. Joining this conclusion to the ethical premise that when others do not adhere to the requirements of morality it is not immoral for one to do likewise, the realist can conclude that multinationals are not morally obligated to contribute to such global common goods (such as environmental goods).

Moreover, global common goods often create interactions that are not iterated. This is particularly the case where the global environment is concerned. As I have already noted, preservation of a favorable global climate is clearly part of the global common good. Now the failure of the global climate will be a one-time affair. The breakdown of the ozone layer, for example, will happen once, with catastrophic consequences for us all; and the heating up of the global climate as a result of the infusion of carbon dioxide will happen once, with catastrophic consequences for us all. Because these environmental disasters are a one-time affair, they represent a non-iterated prisoner's dilemma for multinationals. It is irrational from an individual point of view for a multinational to choose to refrain from polluting the environment in such cases. Either others will refrain, and then one can enjoy the benefits of their refraining; or others will not refrain, and then it will be better to have also not refrained since refraining would have made little difference and would have entailed heavy losses.

Finally, we must also note that although natural persons may signal their reliability to other natural persons, it is not at all obvious that multinationals can do the same. As noted above, multinationals are bureaucratic organizations whose members are continually changing and shifting. The natural persons who make up an organization can signal their reliability to others, but such persons are soon replaced by others, and they in turn are replaced by others. What endures is each organization's single-minded pursuit of increasing its profits in a competitive environment. And an enduring commitment to the pursuit of profit in a competitive environment is not a signal of an enduring commitment to morality.

John E. Fleming

NO

Alternative Approaches and Assumptions: Comments on Manuel Velasquez

Introduction

I feel that Professor Velasquez has written a very interesting and thought-provoking paper on an important topic. His initial identification with a "strong notion of the common good" raises the level of analysis to a high but very complex plane. The author introduces the interesting and, from my view, unusual *realist objection* in the Hobbsian form. After a rigorous analysis of this concept Professor Velasquez reaches what I find to be a disturbing conclusion: "It is not obvious that we can say that multinationals have an obligation to contribute to the global common good. . . ." He then finishes the paper with a strong plea for the establishment of "an international authority capable of forcing everyone to contribute toward the global good."

It would be presumptuous of me to question the fine ethical reasoning that appears in the paper. I am impressed with its elegance. However, in a topic of this complexity I would like to think that there might be alternative approaches and assumptions that would lead us to a different conclusion. The presentation of such alternatives will be the path that I will take, examining the conceptual and empirical underpinnings of the argument from a management viewpoint.

The Model of a Multinational Corporation

The profit-maximizing, rational model of a multinational corporation presented in the paper is consistent with traditional economics and serves as a useful approximation of the firm from a theoretical viewpoint. But it falls somewhat short in less than purely competitive environments and was never intended to describe the decision processes of actual managers. Empirical studies of firms can lead to a profit-sacrificing, bounded rational model. The importance of profit is still there, but the stockholder does not get all the benefits. Other stakeholders are considered and rewarded. Out of all this can come the important concept of corporate social responsibility, which can include such topics as concerns for the environment and for host country governments.

I also find the faceless and interchangeable bureaucrat a poor model for business executives, particularly the chief executive officers of large corporations. Many of these individuals have a personal impact on the organization, including such areas as business ethics and corporate responsibility. There are also important behavioral aspects of management, such as pride in the firm and corporate culture, that are fertile soil for the nurture of ethics.

Most large American multinational corporations have codes of ethics and some have well-developed programs concerned with ethical behavior worldwide. A number of these firms emphasize that their one code of conduct applies everywhere that they do business. At the GTE Corporation its vision and values statements have been translated into nine different languages and distributed to all its employees to ensure this world-wide understanding of how it conducts its business. This is a far cry from the situational ethics described in the model used by Professor Velasquez.

Model of the International Business Climate

The planning and decision environment of the managers conducting international business is different from that described in the paper. There is the very real problem of a lack of an overarching global government and enforceable laws for the international arena. Nevertheless, there are other very strong restraining forces on companies that prevent the "state of nature" (or law of the jungle) described in the paper. For example, the national governments that do exist influence the ethical behavior of companies acting within their boundaries and beyond. The Foreign Corrupt Practices Act of the United States has set a new standard of behavior in the area of bribery that dictates how American companies will behave worldwide. The financial practices of large banks and securities markets have added major constraints to global corporate behavior. There are also a number of regional and functional organizations in the areas of trade and monetary issues that provide limitations to managerial decision making.

The decisions of multinational executives are also constrained by such factors as public opinion and the pressures of special interest groups. In this area the media also plays a strong role. Examples of these forces are the actions of interest groups that forced marketing changes on infant formula manufacturers and the strong "green" movement that is affecting business decisions throughout many parts of the world. My own view is that considerable progress has been made in the area of limiting the manufacture and release of chlorofluorocarbons. This is a very complex issue involving tremendous social and economic changes that are far more critical, widespread and controlling than the profits of the producing companies. Even with the existence of an enforcing government there is no guarantee that the problem would be solved speedily. An example in point is the acid rain problem of the United States.

Model of the Prisoner's Dilemma

From the standpoint of managerial decision making the Prisoner's Dilemma model does not simulate a situation that is frequently found in international business. An executive generally would not be negotiating or making mutually beneficial decisions with competitors. I would see the greatest amount of effort of multinational decision makers devoted to the development of repeat customers. Such an accomplishment comes about through solving customer problems with better product/service at a lower cost. An emphasis on efficiency and excellence is a far more effective use of executive time than questionable negotiations with a competitor. I believe that the weakness Professor Velasquez identifies in the Prisoner's Dilemma model as a one-time event with competitors applies even more to negotiations with customers.

The author also points out a major weakness of the model in the signaling of intent that goes on between individuals. He then states that this same signaling is not found to any great extent between companies. I would disagree with this thought. An important part of corporate strategic planning is analyzing market signals. United States antitrust forbids direct contact between competitors on issues relating to the market. But there is no limitation on independent analysis of competitive actions and the interpretation of actions by competitors. When Kodak introduced its instant camera, both Kodak and Polaroid watched the other's actions to determine whether it signaled detente or fight.

Conclusion

For the reasons enumerated above I tend to question the models and assumptions that Professor Velasquez has used in his ethical analysis. And, with these underpinnings in jeopardy, I also tend to question the tentative conclusion of his moral reasoning as it relates to the managerial aspects of international business. I feel that multinationals *do* have a strong obligation to contribute to the global common good.

POSTSCRIPT

Are Multinational Corporations Free from Moral Obligation?

As we write, international business has sunk into a sea of troubles: The once-booming Asian economies seem to have gone into self-destruct mode, movie stars and athletes spend air time defending their products from accusations of exploitation and sweatshop abuses, trade in securities has gone global and gone wild. What are the possibilities for the comprehensive set of international laws, guidelines, and the committees to enforce them, as suggested by Velasquez?

Is national sovereignty an idea whose time has come, gone, and gone south? While boundaries between peoples—which may or may not correspond to anyone's idea of settled "national" boundaries—are the subject of violent disputes worldwide, while the economy goes global with blinding speed, unable to recognize any national boundaries at all, can we say that national boundaries make any sense at all? But then, how would we know what each central government controls? What is the reason for the centrality of national sovereignty?

We have, as Velasquez mentions, international conventions on certain subjects—ozone-depleting substances, for example. But on more immediate, and expensive, environmental issues, agreement is hard to reach and harder to monitor (witness the global warming conference in Kyoto).

Suggested Reading

For further exploration of this issue, read any of the following:

Nader Asgary and Mark C. Mitschow, "Toward a Model for International Business Ethics," *Journal of Business Ethics* (vol. 36, no. 3, March 2002).

Thomas Friedman, *The Lexus and the Olive Tree* (Revised and Updated Ed. Farrar, Straus and Giroux, 2000).

Muel Kaptein, "Business Codes of Multinational Firms: What Do They Say?" *Journal of Business Ethics* (vol. 50, no. 1, March 2004).

ISSUE 18

Are Sweatshops an Inhumane Business Practice?

YES: Denis G. Arnold and Norman E. Bowie, from "Respect for Workers in Global Supply Chains: Advancing the Debate over Sweatshops," *Business Ethics Quarterly* (January 2007)

NO: Gordon G. Sollars and Fred Englander, from "Sweatshops: Kant and Consequences," *Business Ethics Quarterly* (January 2007)

ISSUE SUMMARY

YES: Philosophers Arnold and Bowie argue that managers of multinational enterprises have a duty to ensure that workers in their supply chains are treated with dignity and respect, which includes paying a living wage to those who work in factories with which they contract.

NO: Sollars and Englander contend that this work is needed for the very survival of individuals, and the multinational enterprises are not participating directly in the coercion of the workers in sweatshops.

$\mathbf{A}$ccording to the World Bank, about one-fifth of the world's population lives below the international poverty line. Economic success in China and India has decreased world poverty, but economic inequality is still extremely high. There are still many individuals in Third World countries receiving very low wages from either multinational companies themselves or subcontractors for those companies. This creates ethical problems for the parent company, the consumer, the supplier, and the worker. Critics hold that workers should have basic rights of dignity and safety, as well as a living wage in a job. What if these conditions are not met? Should we do away with the jobs because of these poor working conditions? Are bad jobs preferable to no jobs at all?

Creative approaches are needed if workers' rights are to be respected and commercial success and survival are to be fostered at the same time. Often, today's sweatshops violate the very tenets of business ethics and yet they continue to flourish. This is the case because companies and corporations have not settled on criteria that would condemn sweatshops. These criteria should be used to examine the impoverished and underdeveloped living conditions in regions where the companies locate their factories/sweatshops.

From a Kantian perspective, should multinational corporations do more to promote the dignity of the individuals they employ or rely upon? Top-brand manufacturers have been embarrassed by their sweatshop practices or by the practices of a subcontractor. Some corporations claim to have made changes to address these problems, but that has sometimes meant pulling their factories out of impoverished countries altogether rather than changing the working conditions there. They then trumpet that their products are sweatshop-free. The impoverished workers, meanwhile, are unemployed and may not find another job to sustain their meager quality of life—thus they become worse off than they were working in the substandard conditions in the first place. Other multinational corporations remain in the impoverished countries and claim to have changed their practices, but allegedly their subcontractors still use poor workers in sweatshop conditions.

YES

Denis G. Arnold and
Norman E. Bowie

Respect for Workers in Global Supply Chains: Advancing the Debate over Sweatshops

One of the principal human rights victories in recent years has been the transformation of the factories of many large multinational enterprises (MNEs) from sweatshops into safe and healthy places to work. Prompted by public outrage over the widespread abuse of worker rights in these factories, MNEs such as Nike, Adidas-Salamon, Mattel, and The Gap have implemented numerous measures to help ensure that the workers who manufacturer goods in their supply chains are treated with dignity and respect. In so doing, they have joined companies with longstanding policies of respect for workers in their supply chains, such as Levi Strauss and Motorola. In both their own factories, and in those of their contractors, these MNEs have enhanced compliance with local labor laws, implemented new and improved health and safety standards, improved wages, and created a variety of additional benefits such as after-hours educational opportunities and microenterprise loan programs.

For the past several years we have argued that MNEs' managers have duties, both in their own factories and in their contract factories, to ensure that the dignity of workers is respected. In "Sweatshops and Respect for Persons" we argued that these duties include the following: to adhere to local labor laws, to refrain from coercion, to meet minimum health and safety standards, and to pay workers a living wage. We are gratified that many MNEs, especially those in the apparel and footwear sector, are now meeting these duties (though we claim no responsibility for these changes). In their commentary on our paper, Gordon Sollars and Fred Englander challenge some of our conclusions. In what follows we argue that several of their criticisms are based on an inaccurate reading of our paper, and that none of their remaining criticisms successfully challenges our main arguments.

I. The Obligations of MNEs Regarding Subcontractors

In many cases, MNEs do not directly employ some or all of the workers who manufacture the goods that they design, market, and sell. For example, none of the 10,000 workers in the Tae Kwang Vina factory—discussed in "Sweatshops

From *Business Ethics Quarterly*, vol. 17, issue 1, 2007, pp. 135–145. Copyright © 2007 by *Business Ethics Quarterly*. Reprinted by permission of The Philosophy Documentation Center, publisher of Business Ethics Quarterly. References omitted.

and Respect for Persons"—work for Nike, although Nike is the only MNE that the factory supplies. In our paper we argued that MNEs have a duty to ensure that the dignity of such workers is respected. Sollars and Englander dispute this conclusion, but they misunderstand our line of argument. We began by endorsing Michael Santoro's claim that the moral duty of MNEs in this regard is similar to the legal doctrine of *respondeat superior*. We then argued that this duty has a two-fold justification. First, we argued that MNE managers are constrained by the categorical imperative in general, and the doctrine of respect for persons in particular. Second, we argued that individuals have unique duties as a result of their unique circumstances.

In reply to our first argument, Sollars and Englander rightly point out that much depends on the implications of respecting others. We addressed that issued in some detail in "Sweatshops and Respect for Persons." In that essay, after quoting Kant on human dignity, we summarized an argument by Hill regarding the implications of this, and then provided our own elaboration of the issue as based on Kant's *Metaphysics of Morals*:

> Thomas Hill Jr. has discussed the implication of Kant's arguments concerning human dignity at length. Hill argues that treating persons as ends in themselves requires supporting and developing certain human capacities, including the capacity to act on reason; the capacity to act on the basis of prudence or efficiency; the capacity to set goals; the capacity to accept categorical imperatives; and the capacity to understand the world and reason abstractly. *Based on Kant's writings in the* Metaphysics of Morals, *we would make several additions to the list. There Kant argues that respecting people means that we cannot be indifferent to them. Indifference is a denial of respect. He also argues that we have an obligation to be concerned with the physical welfare of people and their moral well being. Adversity, pain, and want are temptations to vice and inhibit the ability of individuals to develop their rational and moral capacities. It is these rational and moral capacities that distinguish people from mere animals. People who are not free to develop these capacities may end up leading lives that are closer to animals than to moral beings. Freedom from externally imposed adversity, pain, and want facilitate the cultivation of one's rational capacities and virtuous character. Thus, treating people as ends in themselves means ensuring their physical well being and supporting and developing their rational and moral capacities.*

Sollars and Englander's criticism of our interpretation of Kantian respect for persons is constituted mainly by a long exegesis of the passage from Hill, together with the claim that the passage from Hill does not support our position. They ignore our discussion of the *Metaphysics of Morals* (partially quoted above in italics) and Bowie's discussion of the issue in *Business Ethics: A Kantian Perspective*. Since we do not believe Sollars and Englander engage the first part of our argument in a substantive manner, we will put aside their remarks on that part of argument and instead turn our attention to their comments on the second part of our argument.

We argued that MNEs have distinct duties regarding the employees of their contract factories because of the power they have over the owners and managers of such factories, and because of the substantial resources at their disposal. MNEs typically dictate to their contractors such terms as price, quality, quantity, and date of delivery. This imbalance in power means that they have the ability to either hinder or enhance the ability of contract factory managers to respect employees. For example, if MNE supply chain managers know, or have reason to know, that the factory cannot meet the terms of the contract while adhering to local labor laws, providing safe working conditions, or paying a living wage, then they are properly regarded as partially responsibe for those disrespectful practices. Sollars and Englander's main criticism of this position is stated as follows:

> Our point is that the subcontractor or supplier has done *something* via the bargain to reduce pain, adversity, or poverty, while other actors may have done *nothing*. It is unreasonable to expect any bargain struck between two parties to redress every issue of fairness or desert that may apply to one party. MNEs are in some sense "taking advantage" of background conditions in the Third World when they outsource their production, but this alone does not make them responsible for the poverty that makes their sourcing decisions profitable.

So, because the subcontractor has improved the situation of employees by employing them via their contract with the MNE, and because the contract between the supplier and the MNE cannot reasonably be expected to "redress every issue of fairness or desert" that may apply to one party, MNEs have no distinctive duties regarding subcontractors of their employees. Note that on this account, if an MNE's management knew that the terms of the contract made it impossible for an employer to pay even the legally mandated wages and benefits of workers while fulfilling the contract, the MNE would not be responsible, partly or entirely, for the failure to pay such wages and benefits, nor would the MNE or its managers have violated any duties. The only justification that Sollars and Englander provide for this claim is the implicit reference to a reasonable person standard in the passage quoted above—a standard that we find unreasonable. By contrast, in our view, any ethically justifiable contract between two parties must be consistent with respect for the dignity of the two parties and those they represent. We acknowledge that this is a *prima facie* moral standard, one that could be superseded under special circumstances, or with the genuine consent of relevant parties. However, Sollars and Englander have provided no reason for thinking that this standard ought not apply when MNEs negotiate contracts with their suppliers.

Nonetheless, we do think that there are good objections to the brief argument regarding the duties of MNEs to subcontractors that we provided in "Sweatshops and Respect for Persons." But these are not Sollars and Englander's arguments. For example, some companies are too small to contract for use of all of a subcontractor's capacity, but must instead place orders that represent a small percentage of a supplier's capacity. In such cases, it is unreasonable to believe that the company can exert the sort of influence over the subcontractor that we assume above. This is especially true if the subcontractor is dealing with multiple companies at the same time, each with somewhat different standards or codes for the treatment of workers. Our response to such an objection would be to point out that companies genuinely interested in ensuring that workers in their supply chains are treated with dignity at work can collaborate with one another in order to ensure that uniform standards are adapted and implemented. Indeed, such collaborative efforts have been in place for several years.

Universalizability

At the conclusion of their discussion of the obligations of MNEs regarding subcontractors. Sonars and Englander attempt to undermine our Kantian analysis of MNEs' obligations regarding subcontractors by deploying Korsgaard's interpretation of the conceptual contradiction test of the first formulation of the categorical imperative. This interpretation holds that conceptual contradictions are best understood "by imagining, in effect, that the action you propose to perform in order to carry out your purpose is the standard procedure for carrying out that purpose." Their argument, in essence, is that demonstrating respect for workers by providing them with a living wage constitutes a conceptual contradiction. It does so, in their view, because living wages always increase unemployment, thus harming the class of persons that living wages are intended to benefit. First, we note that Korsgaard's interpretation of the categorical imperative has been persuasively criticized by Barbara Herman, but for present purposes we will ignore this. Second, in developing this argument, Sollars and Englander do not accurately characterize the position we defend in "Sweatshops and Respect for Persons." This is evident when they describe the maxim necessary for their position: "The maxim of paying a subsistence wage could have the purpose of helping persons, whose lot is among the very worst, have some means to use their rationality to achieve 'moral perfection.'" In "Sweatshops and Respect for Persons" we argued that MNE managers have duties regarding adherence to local laws, coercion, health and safety standards, and wages. However, in seeking to undermine our position Sollars and Englander focus only on the wage issue. Our position regarding wages is as follows:

> It is our contention that, at a minimum, respect for employees entails that MNEs and their suppliers have a moral obligation to ensure that employees do not live under conditions of overall poverty by providing adequate wages for a forty-eight hour work week to satisfy both basic food needs and basic non-food needs. Doing so helps to ensure the physical well-being and independence of employees, contributes to the development of their rational capacities, and provides them with opportunities for moral development. This in turn allows for the cultivation of self-esteem.

We argued further that employers should voluntarily raise wages to this level, and that they should do so without laying-off employees, seeking instead to cover any increased costs in other ways:

> Our contention is that it is economically feasible for MNEs to voluntarily raise wages in factories in developing economics without causing increases in unemployment. MNEs may choose to raise wages while maintaining existing employment levels. Increased labor costs that are

not offset by greater productivity may be passed on to consumers, or, if necessary, absorbed through internal cost cutting measures such as reductions in executive compensation.

A maxim that would correspond to our position is as follows.

> In order to satisfy the basic food needs and basic non-food needs of employees and provide them with opportunities for the development of their rational capacities and moral development, we will ensure that all employees are paid the following wage for a forty-eight-hour work week (whichever is greater): The minimum wage required by law, or the wage necessary to allow them to live above the overall poverty line, for a forty-eight-hour work week, covering any additional costs by means other than employee layoffs.

Sollars and Englander provide no reason for thinking that such a maxim is not universalizable. Indeed, their *only* basis for challenging the universalizability of such a maxim is the stipulation that improving employee wages *must* cause increased unemployment. While they never take up a maxim that corresponds precisely to our view, even their truncated version of a maxim regarding wages is consistent with Korsgaard's interpretation of the conceptual contradiction test of the categorical imperative if one allows that voluntarily raising wages while maintaining existing employment levels does not lead to greater unemployment. Their retort at this stage must be that one cannot raise wages without increasing unemployment, but as we shall argue below, such a view is untenable.

In concluding this section it is worth noting that in seeking to undermine our position regarding wages, Sollars and Englander ignore our arguments in "Sweatshops and Respect for Persons" regarding the rule of law and health and safety conditions. However, since adhering to local labor laws and ensuring decent health and safety conditions can be costly, we find their implicit acceptance of our defense of the duties of MNEs regarding the rule of law and decent health and safety standards puzzling. In other words, if, as they suppose, raising wages will cause inevitable increases in unemployment, isn't the same true of adhering to local labor laws and improving working conditions? Why focus on the wage issue alone? A more consistent view would seem to be that MNE managers have duties to ignore local labor laws, ignore working conditions, and pay the lowest possible wages, so long as none of these practices deterred employees from working in MNE factories. We have argued that such a view is indefensible on Kantian grounds.

II. Coercion

In "Sweatshops and Respect for Persons" we argued that MNE managers have a moral obligation to prevent the use of coercion for certain purposes within factories. In particular, we argued that "[u]sing coercion as a means of compelling employees to work overtime, to meet production quotas despite injury, or to remain at work while in need of medical attention, is incompatible with respect for persons because the coercers treat their victims as mere tools." On our account, psychological coercion is properly understood to take place when three conditions hold:

First, the coercer must have a desire about the will of his or her victim. However, this is a desire of a particular kind because it can only be fulfilled through the will of another person. Second, the coercer must have an effective desire to compel his or her victim to act in a manner that makes efficacious the coercer's other regarding desire. The distinction between an other regarding desire and a coercive will is important because it provides a basis for delineating between cases of coercion and, for example, cases of rational persuasion. In both instances a person may have an other regarding desire, but in the case of coercion that desire will be supplemented by an effective first-order desire which seeks to enforce that desire on the person, and in cases of rational persuasion it will not. What is of most importance in such cases is that P intentionally attempts to compel Q to comply with an other regarding desire of P's own. These are necessary, but not sufficient conditions of coercion. In order for coercion to take place, the coercer must be successful in getting his or her victim to conform to his or her other regarding desire. In all cases of coercion P attempts to violate the autonomy of Q. When Q successfully resists P's attempted coercion, Q retains his or her autonomy. In such cases P retains a coercive will.

Sollars and Englander accept this account of psychological coercion, but deny that we have provided a clear example of coercion. In their view, what we described as coercion is merely a case of an employer enforcing a job requirement. They claim that "In the case of a routine job practice X, the supervisor need not have a desire to compel a worker to do X, although the supervisor might well prefer that the worker do X to save the expense of finding a new worker. The desire of the supervisor may simply be that some worker or other do X." It is unclear what further point they are attempting to make about coercion or sweatshops, but one might read them as maintaining that coercion seldom, if ever, takes place in sweatshops.

In making their case, Sollars and Englander refer to only one of the three examples of coercion that we offered (example one, below). Since the explicit point of their discussion of coercion is to deny that we provided a persuasive example of coercion in sweatshops, we think it reasonable to consider each of the three examples of coercion that we provided.

[1] Bangladesh, El Salvador, and other developing economies lack the social welfare programs that workers in North America and Europe take for granted. If workers lose their jobs, they may end up without any source of income. Thus, workers are understandably fearful of being fired for noncompliance with demands to work long overtime hours. When a worker is threatened with being fired by a supervisor unless she agrees to work overtime, and when the supervisor's intention in making the threat is to ensure compliance, then the supervisor's actions are properly understood as coervive.

[2] Similar threats are used to ensure that workers meet production quotas, even in the face of personal injury. . . .
     We do not claim that production quotas are inherently coercive. Given a reasonable quota, employees can choose whether or not to

work diligently to fill that quota. Employees who choose idleness over industriousness and are terminated as a result are not coerced. However, when a supervisor threatens workers who are ill or injured with termination unless they meet a production quota that either cannot physically be achieved by the employees, or can only be achieved at the cost or further injury to the employee, the threat is properly understood as coercive. In such cases the employee will inevitably feel compelled to meet the quota.

[3] [W]orkers report being threatened with termination if they seek medical attention. For example, when a worker in El Salvador who was three months pregnant began hemorrhaging she was not allowed to leave the factory to receive medical attention. She subsequently miscarried while in the factory, completed her long work day, and took her fetus home for burial. Other workers have died because they were not allowed to leave the factory to receive medical attention. In cases where workers suffer miscarriages or death, rather than risk termination, we believe that it [is] reasonable to conclude that the workers are coerced into remaining at work.

We think these examples illustrate well our account of coercion, and nothing Sollars and Englander have written undermines that judgment. It may well be that the practices described in each of these examples are routinely found in sweatshops. However, such a claim by itself does not constitute an objection to our view, for coercion may well be routine. What Sollars and Englander seem to be claiming is that overtime (i.e., hours worked beyond the forty-eight-hour work week we specify in our essay), quotas, and a strict attendance policy (one banning absence for medical reasons) are conditions of employment that employees may accept or reject, rather than informal practices coercively enforced by callous supervisors.

There are numerous problems with such a view. First, Sollars and Englander provide no reasons that would lead one to believe that coercion is not routinely used by supervisors in the ways that we describe. Indeed, all that need be the case is that the supervisors intend to compel the worker to, e.g., remain at work longer than forty-eight hours in a week and that the worker acquiesce to the supervisors' threat. One can easily imagine a scenario in which an employee who thought she was signing on for a forty-eight-hour work week freely chooses to work many additional hours in order to improve her earnings. However, one can also easily imagine a working mother declining to work overtime so that she can care for her children, and a supervisor coercing her into working overtime. It is equally easy to imagine scenarios in which quotas are met despite the exacerbation of an employee's work related disability, or in which an employee attends work despite a grave illness, only because they are coerced into doing so.

Second, Sollars and Englander seem to regard coercion as morally unjustified in all circumstances. This is why, one suspects, they object to the idea that employees can be coerced into working overtime. In their view, overtime of any length and duration appears to be a reasonable expectation of factory owners and managers, especially when the worker is fortunate to have the job at all. However, coercion is only *prima facie* objectionable. For example, if a supervisor threatens an employee with termination unless he stops sexually harassing fellow employees, the supervisor is coercing the harasser. However, such coercion is morally justified insofar as the supervisor is seeking to stop one employee from disrespecting other employees in an especially harmful manner. A claim that might be more consistent with the view of Sollars and Englander is that supervisors coerce employees into working overtime, meeting production quotas, and attending work despite serious illnesses, but that such coercion is justifiable. In "Sweatshops and Respect for Persons" we argued that such coercion is *not* morally justifiable on Kantian grounds. It remains up to Sollars and Englander to argue the contrary thesis. Without such an argument, their position is untenable insofar as those types of coercion occur in the workplace.

III. Wages and the Inadequacy of Mere Economic Analysis

In "Sweatshops and Respect for Persons" we advanced the thesis that employers have a duty to pay workers the minimum wage required by law, or the wage necessary to allow them to live above the overall poverty line, for a forty-eight-hour work week, covering any additional costs by means other than employee layoffs. We did not take a position on whether or not such a duty should be enforced via legislation. Instead, we argue that such a duty should be voluntarily embraced by MNEs and their contractors. In reply to this thesis, Sollars and Englander argue that the body of empirical research in economics supports the following conclusions: (1) that there is significant controversy over whether or not legally mandated minimum wages cause increases in unemployment; and (2) that the effect of efficiency wages on worker productivity is indeterminate. For the sake of argument, we grant these conclusions. Neither claim undermines our main thesis regarding wages. Sollars and Englander's fundamental mistake is their failure to distinguish between legally mandated wages and the voluntary fulfillment of duties regarding wages. In particular, they fail to link their discussion of the literature on minimum wages, and the controversy among economists on that issue, to the claim that MNE managers have an obligation to pay a living wage without covering additional costs via layoffs. Furthermore, they ignore our claim that if enhanced efficiency alone cannot compensate for increased labor costs, other strategies can and should be utilized.

We suspect that Sollars and Englander would respond by arguing that even if living wages were implemented via voluntary actions on the part of MNE managers, rather than via minimum wage legislation, the result would still be increased unemployment. While we recognize the relevance of economic analysis to this debate, their analysis of wages appears to be grounded in the attribution of a purely instrumental account of practical reasoning to MNEs managers. In their discussion of wages, at least, they seem to view managers as subject to overwhelming economic forces such that if wages are increased, employees must be laid off in order to compensate for increased costs. However, once it is acknowledged that MNE managers are capable of acting on their duties to a variety of stakeholders, it is not difficult to see how competent managers could meet their duties to workers by voluntarily raising wages without laying off employees. Indeed, one recent study found that when wages were voluntarily increased in the Indonesian apparel and footwear sector as a result of anti-sweatshop campaigns, employment levels actually *increased* resulting in a "win-win" situation. The increased wage costs for MNEs were so small that they appear to simply have been absorbed as operating expenses. In cases where such increased costs cannot be easily absorbed as operating expenses, and where increased productivity and loyalty do not completely offset increased labor costs, available evidence demonstrates that these costs may be passed on to consumers. If cases arise where this is not possible, internal cost-cutting measures, such as reductions in executive compensation and perks, are an attractive means of compensating for the cost of treating workers with dignity. In our view, the costs of respecting workers must be regarded as a necessary condition of doing business.

IV. Conclusion

In "Sweatshops, and Respect for Persons" we argued that MNEs have duties to adhere to local labor laws, to refrain from coercion, to meet minimum health and safety standards, and to pay workers a living wage. All, or nearly all, of these duties are now being fulfilled by many MNEs. Sollar and Englander have, in our judgment, failed to undermine any of our main theses. We acknowledge that much work yet remains to be done in order to advance theoretical discussion of the "sweatshop" problem. We hope that by demonstrating the shortcomings of the arguments discussed above, we have made modest progress toward that goal.

Gordon G. Sollars and
Fred Englander

 **NO**

Sweatshops:
Kant and Consequences

Introduction

Arnold and Bowie (2003) attempt to derive ethical constraints on the actions
of the managers of multinational enterprises (MNEs) or the MNEs themselves
from a Kantian perspective. In particular, they adopt the Formula of Humanity version of Kant's categorical imperative, which they interpret in terms of
respect for persons. Arnold and Bowie use other elements from Kant's system
of ethics, but state that even "sympathetic readers" (Arnold & Bowie 2003: 222)
who do not accept Kant's full system should be responsive to Kant's argument
for the Formula of Humanity. From this starting point, Arnold and Bowie
claim to reach the conclusions that MNEs or their managers have duties not to
tolerate or encourage violations of the rule of law,[1] use coercion, allow unsafe
working conditions, or pay wages that are below subsistence levels.

  We contest Arnold and Bowie's claims, in particular, that they have established that MNEs have a duty to pay a subsistence wage above market levels.[2]
Although we try to be sympathetic readers, we conclude that even within Arnold
and Bowie's Kantian framework such a duty does not emerge. Regarding coercion, we agree with Arnold and Bowie that coercion is wrong on Kantian (and,
of course, other) grounds. No doubt instances of coercion exist, but we disagree
that Arnold and Bowie's example of a requirement to work overtime constitutes
an example of coercion even by their own definition. Thus, a supposed paradigm
case regarding sweatshops and overtime hours fails.

  Finally, although we applaud Arnold and Bowie for addressing economic
issues in an attempt to establish the feasibility of their subsistence-wage duty
within a Kantian framework, we find that the weight of economic argument goes
against them. As we discuss below, the best reading of current economic literature
is that the raising of wages above market levels should be expected to increase
unemployment, and, in particular, unemployment among the least skilled workers. Thus, if Kantian arguments actually could establish a subsistence-wage duty,
concern for the well-being of the least-advantaged should be expected to lead to
the classic tension between deontological and consequentialist concerns. Perhaps a strict Kantian perspective clearly favors the duty, trumping issues of consequences. However, Arnold and Bowie have broadened their audience beyond

From *Business Ethics Quarterly*, vol. 17, issue 1, 2007, pp. 115–133. Copyright © 2007 by Business Ethics Quarterly. Reprinted by permission of The Philosophy Documentation Center,
publisher of Business Ethics Quarterly. References omitted.

strict Kantians, by arguing that any persons sympathetic to the Formula of Humanity should accept the subsistence-wage duty. A pluralist view could both have such sympathy and be concerned about well being. Arnold and Bowie's argument does not address how conflicts between these perspectives should be resolved.

1. Subcontractors and Suppliers

Typically, MNEs do not employ workers under sweatshop conditions; rather the sweatshop workers are employed by subcontractors or suppliers of an MNE. This has led sweatshop critics to argue that such MNEs inherit responsibility for the actions of these other entities. Arnold and Bowie (2003: 226) present three arguments in favor of the idea that MNEs are responsible for the practices of their subcontractors or suppliers.

The first argument is actually quoted from Santoro (2000: 161). Santoro asserts that the standard for judging MNE responsibility for the treatment of sweatshop workers by subcontractor or supplier companies "is similar" to the legal doctrine of *respondeat superior*. First, we note that neither Santoro nor Arnold and Bowie give an argument that provides a moral justification for this legal doctrine, which is part of the law dealing with master-servant relationships. In particular, Arnold and Bowie do not attempt to derive it from the Formula of Humanity, which is their acknowledged Kantian touchstone. However, illustrating the usefulness of a Kantian perspective is only one of Arnold and Bowie's goals, and so for the sake of the argument we will assume the moral legitimacy of *respondeat superior*. The law distinguishes between a "servant," for whose actions the master may be liable under *respondeat superior*, and an "independent contractor," for whose actions the master is not liable. We claim that for an argument to be "similar" to *respondeat superior*, the argument should retain the distinction between servant and independent contractor. Thus, the question becomes whether subcontractors and suppliers are properly construed as servants rather than contractors.

Gifis defines a "contractor" as "one who makes an agreement with another to do a piece of work, retaining for himself the control of the means, method and manner of producing the result to be accomplished, neither party having the right to terminate the contract at will" (Gifis 1984: 97). The same source defines a "servant" as a person who "with respect to the physical conduct in the performance of the services is subject to" the control of another (Gifis 1984: 438). The commonsense meanings of "subcontractor" and "supplier" clearly favor the first definition over the second; indeed, a "subcontractor" is a kind of contractor, and thus not a servant. Further, as a factual matter, we claim that subcontractors and suppliers are not typically subject to the control of MNEs in their "physical conduct." Finally, the Restatement of Agency (2d) states that "service under an agreement to use care and skill in accomplishing results" marks an independent contractor.[3] Such service is the essence of the outsourcing relationships that MNEs have with subcontractors.

It might be said in defense of Arnold and Bowie's gesturing at *respondeat superior* that they simply mean to claim that subcontractors or suppliers are agents of MNEs, and that this agency confers responsibility on the MNEs.[4] We do not wish to deny that it is logically possible for such responsibility to be conferred on MNEs in some fashion, in some circumstances. However, the *respondeat superior* doctrine is all that Arnold and Bowie offer in this regard, and this very doctrine clearly illustrates that the principal/agent relationship does not necessarily confer responsibility for an agent's action on the principal. Indeed, it seems designed to exclude the very agents at issue in the sweatshop debate. The blanket statement that MNEs are responsible for the actions of their subcontractors and suppliers might be true, but it is simply not supported by the invocation of *respondeat superior*.

The second argument is that managers of MNEs are simply individuals who are constrained to show respect to others, including the employees of subcontractors or suppliers, as required by the categorical imperative in its Formula of Humanity interpretation. The challenge here is to unpack what is meant by "respect." Arnold and Bowie begin with the straightforward Kantian claim that showing respect means treating persons as ends in themselves. Next, they approvingly cite Hill (1992) regarding the implication of Kant's arguments concerning the treatment of persons as ends. According to Arnold and Bowie, Hill argues that treating persons as ends in themselves requires "supporting and developing certain human capabilities" (Arnold & Bowie 2003: 223). They add that Kant also argues that mere indifference fails to show respect, and that there is "an obligation to be concerned with the physical welfare of people and their moral well-being" (Arnold & Bowie 2003: 223). Finally, Arnold and Bowie's second argument incorporates by reference the argument in Bowie (1999).[5] All of this is in preparation for Arnold and Bowie's claim that, with regard to wages, respect for persons requires a forty-eight hour per week wage level that is sufficient to satisfy basic food and non-food needs:

> Doing so helps to ensure the physical well-being and independence of employees, contributes to the development of their rational capabilities, and provides them with opportunities for moral development. (Arnold & Bowie 2003: 234)

We find a number of difficulties with this argument. First, we simply do not read Hill's discussion of human capabilities as making the claim that these capabilities require development and support. The references given in both Arnold and Bowie (2003) and Bowie (1999) to Hill's capability discussion are to a description of the capabilities that Kant includes in the notion of "humanity": acting on principles; following hypothetical imperatives; setting goals; accepting categorical imperatives independently of reward or punishment; and some ability to understand the world and reason abstractly (Hill 1992: 40–41). Hill himself says nothing about a requirement to "develop and support" these capabilities in that discussion, and he makes it clear that Kant believed that this degree of humanity belongs to even "the most foolish and depraved persons" (Hill 1992: 41). These are capabilities that ordinary human beings possess as a matter of course.

Second, Hill's own discussion demonstrates that it is not an easy matter to be sure what Kant meant by "always treating humanity as an end."

Hill reviews a number of things that Kant says about ends, in particular, that objective ends are to be "conceived only negatively—that is, as an end against which we should never act" (Hill 1992: 44), The straightforward reading of this, Hill allows, is that treating humanity as an end can be achieved simply by restraint—no positive effort to help others by "development and support" is required. In light of Kant's various other remarks, Hill himself finds this statement about ends "puzzling" (Hill 1992: 44). In an attempt to resolve this puzzle (and other difficulties), Hill turns to Kant's distinction between personal ends—which only have a price—and ends in themselves—which have a dignity, that is, an "unconditional and incomparable worth" (Hill 1992: 47). It is at this point that Hill begins to prescribe what respect for persons entails, rather than simply describe the constituent capabilities of humanity possessed by any ordinary person. He lists seven items:

1. refusing to damage a person's rational capacities (*e.g.,* via drugs or lobotomy);
2. refusing to destroy a person;
3. attempting to develop and improve rational capabilities;
4. attempting to exercise these capabilities as far as possible;
5. appealing to reason rather than use manipulation;
6. leaving freedom for others to pursue their (rational) ends; and
7. requiring that humanity should be honored or at least not "mocked, dishonored, or degraded" (Hill 1992: 50–51).

We note that the first, second, sixth, and seventh items are consistent with the idea that only restraint, not any positive "developing" or "supporting" action, is required. Indeed, if we identify, as seems plausible here, "manipulation" with "coercion," then item five can be viewed in the same way.[6] Now it is clear on Kantian grounds that workers ought not to be coerced.[7] From the discussion of *respondeat superior* above, we do not see how managers of MNEs are responsible for such coercion of workers as might occur, initiated by subcontractor or supplier companies. However, while the status of subcontractors and suppliers as independent contractors insulates MNEs from responsibility for coercion, MNEs certainly ought not endorse or acquiesce in the use of coercion by their subcontractors or suppliers. Our concern is with imperfect duties, not the violation of perfect ones.

Items three and four deal with rational capacities. With regard to item three, the development of rational capacities, Kant, perhaps surprisingly, does not hold that we have a duty to develop the rational capabilities of others (Hill 1992: 52; Kant 1964: 44). Hill does note that Kant was, nevertheless, "in his own life" committed to the idea that "one should at least provide opportunities for others' rational development" (Hill 1992: 53). This brings us to item four, which deals with each person's own exercise of these capacities. Here, Hill points out that reason is to be exercised in order to attain "moral perfection," not happiness, either one's own or others. Standing in the way of such perfection is pain, adversity, and poverty, since these are temptations to vice (Hill 1992: 53). However, assuming that coercion and deception are not present, the bargain between employer and employee improves the situation of the employee from her own perspective, that is, in terms of her own plans and projects. The bargain acts to lessen the pain, adversity, or poverty present in a pre-existing situation. To the extent that MNEs contracting with various companies that employ sweatshop workers create jobs for workers, MNEs are assisting in the exercise of reasoning by workers. Thus, they contribute to the provision of item three, even though Kant, at least, did not consider it a duty to do so.

Now, Arnold and Bowie might argue that managers of MNEs could do more for the employees of their subcontractors and suppliers. This is true, but then so could anyone. We must be careful not to implicitly turn the ethical principle that "ought implies can" into "can implies ought."[8] There is any number of things that could be done to remove pain, adversity, or poverty. The bargain (excluding coercion or fraud) between employer and employee is one of those things, and it is perverse to fault it in particular because it might have done more for one party. Note that we do not imply here that a sweatshop worker has no moral grounds for complaint against *some party or other* simply because she makes a bargain with a subcontractor or supplier of an MNE. Rather, our point is that the subcontractor or supplier has done *something* via the bargain to reduce pain, adversity, or poverty, while other actors may have done *nothing.* It is unreasonable to expect any bargain struck between two parties to redress every issue of fairness or desert that may apply to one party. MNEs are in some sense "taking advantage" of background conditions in the Third World when they outsource their production, but this alone does not make them responsible for the poverty that makes their sourcing decisions profitable. It would be a different matter if, for example, particular MNEs conspired with host governments to keep sweatshop workers impoverished. However, Arnold and Bowie provide no examples of this. With regard to MNEs taken as a group, considerable evidence of their salutary effect on Third World poverty comes from a wide variety of sources such as those cited in Maitland (2001) and Brown, Deardorff, and Stern (2004).

Arnold and Bowie point out that Kant argued that a rich person has a duty of charity that a poor person lacks, and that Kant acknowledged that individuals have particular duties as a result of particular circumstances.[9] However, they do not attempt to derive either of these claims from the Formula of Humanity interpretation of the categorical imperative, so it is not clear how central a position these claims hold in their approach.[10] In any event, the duty of charity is a "wide" or "imperfect" duty. Thus, according to Hill's analysis, there is not only freedom to choose to do or not do some act of charity on some occasion, but also latitude for judgment in deciding if a given principle is relevant to a particular situation and freedom to choose various ways of satisfying a principle (Hill 1992: 155). The decision to increase wages is precisely a matter of such judgment. The effect of such a decision could well be to increase unemployment, which would presumably increase pain, adversity, or poverty for those unemployed. Further, the employer could have other duties, in particular a duty to investors or other stakeholders that, given these freedoms of judgment, may mitigate any duty to ameliorate pain, adversity, or poverty beyond the contribution the bargain already makes.

We are not directly challenging the Kantian framework. Rather, we are pointing out that the framework itself does not provide support for the selection of a wage level (or working hours) apart from the knowledge of a myriad of factors that are purely contingent. Indeed, Hayek has argued that market institutions are the best we have for dealing with the severe constraints that human beings face in bringing our necessarily fragmented knowledge to bear in a way that will improve our welfare (Hayek 1945). A market wage, even one that is insufficient for meeting basic food and non-food needs, can still be the best alternative to unemployment. As a result of this item-by-item examination of Hill's claims, we conclude that a reliance on market-determined wages—absent coercion or deception—is fully consistent with the Kantian duties of individuals.

Arnold and Bowie's third argument has already been touched on: the claim that individuals can have unique duties as a result of unique circumstances.[11] We have previously raised the question of how this principle might be tied to the categorical imperative. However, we prefer not to propose and then critique such attempted ties ourselves. Rather, we will point out that Arnold and Bowie have switched the focus from persons as moral agents to MNEs as moral agents. Arnold and Bowie stress the resources that MNEs have to "ensure that the employees of its business partners are respected" (Arnold & Bowie 2003: 227). However, the resources of MNEs are not the same as the resources freely available to any person who might be an MNE manager. We have dealt with the case of individuals above. Arnold and Bowie make a separate point about MNEs with their third argument only to the extent that MNEs, as opposed to the individuals that comprise them, can have duties.

We favor the view that organizations are not moral agents, but this contentious issue need not be explored here. Within a Kantian approach, viewing the corporation as a moral agent has the radical consequence that the corporation has a dignity, not a price. Thus, it would be wrong to buy or sell corporations or shares in corporations. Such a view would completely invalidate any present form of capitalism, and Arnold and Bowie give no indication that they endorse such a view. Given the obvious problem with viewing the corporation as a moral agent from a Kantian perspective, we do not find that Arnold and Bowie provide sufficient detail for us to be confident that we understand exactly what they are claiming in their third argument. In any event, we do not see how to make sense of a claim that an organization has a duty to do some action X without also claiming that at least some individual in the organization has a duty to do some action Y. We have argued above that individuals do not have a duty to do such things Y as Arnold and Bowie suggest would discharge such purported Kantian obligations. As such, MNEs (or their managers) cannot be faulted for the wage levels of their subcontractors or suppliers.

This completes our critique of Arnold and Bowie's attempt to derive a subsistence-wage duty from the Formula of Humanity. We believe that the attempt fails. However, Kantian arguments are famously recondite, and we do not wish to express overconfidence in our rebuttal. Kant states that the various interpretations he gives for the categorical imperative are equivalent (Kant 1997: 43); therefore, each interpretation should yield the same answer regarding a putative duty. As an alternative check of our conclusion, we offer some additional analysis using the Formula of Universal Law interpretation of the categorical imperative:

> act only in accordance with that maxim through which you can at the same time will that it become a universal law. (Kant 1997: 31)

This is to be understood in terms of what can be willed without contradiction, and Kant explains that there are two ways in which contradictions can arise. The first is that some actions have as their maxim something that could not even be conceived as a universal law without contradiction in the conception; the second is that some actions have as their maxim something that, although conceivable, could not be willed without that will contradicting itself. Korsgaard notes that there have been at least three different interpretations of what Kant meant by "contradiction" in the literature (Korsgaard 1996: 78). We cannot hope to do better than to follow the one favored by Korsgaard herself, the Practical Contradiction Interpretation.

Korsgaard states:

> [T]he contradiction that is involved in the universalization of an immoral maxim is that the agent would be unable to act on the maxim in a world in which it were universalized so as to achieve his own purpose—that is the purpose that is specified in the maxim. Since he wills to act on his maxim, this means that his purpose will be frustrated. If this interpretation is correct, then it is essential that in testing maxims of actions the purpose always be included in the formulation of the maxim. (Korsgaard 1996: 92)

The maxim of paying a subsistence wage could have the purpose of helping persons, whose lot is among the very worst, have some means to use their rationality to achieve "moral perfection" (as discussed above). (Other purposes might also be plausible, but any such purpose would seem to be directed at assisting these persons in some way.) Will this very purpose be frustrated by the universalization of the maxim to pay a subsistence wage?

There are three cases to consider: the subsistence wage is below, equal to, or above the market-determined wage. In the first two cases, the purpose can be met by universalizing the maxim, but acting on the maxim has no independent effect. The wage arrived at by the market is already meeting the purpose. The only interesting case is when the subsistence wage is above market levels. When a minimum or subsistence wage is set above the market wage, we argue below (section 4) that the best understanding of the economic literature is that some increased amount of unemployment will result. Assuming, then, that some unemployment will result when a wage above the market level is paid, persons who are unemployed will have even fewer means provided to them under the maxim than they would if they were employed at the market wage. Thus, the maxim contradicts its own purpose, at least with regard to those who remain or become unemployed. It is open to Arnold and Bowie to argue that the maxim should apply only to those who do manage to get employment under it, but we see no reason why those who cannot find work or who lose their jobs should be excluded from consideration.

To conclude this section we note that the concept of respect can be explicated in a variety of ways, and there is no obvious limit on the number of ways that respect can be given or withheld. Arnold and Bowie argue for an expansive concept of respect; however, persons also show respect when they decide to rely upon agreements to further their life plans and projects rather than on the use of force, and when they reach agreements without deception. Since this minimalist concept of respect is consistent with Hill's arguments, it should be both plausible and attractive to Arnold and Bowie's "sympathetic readers" as an alternative. Further, adopting this view of respect keeps the conclusions drawn from the Formula of Humanity consistent with those drawn from the Formula of Universal Law.

2. Coercion

Arnold and Bowie distinguish between physical and psychological coercion, and they report evidence of both in sweatshop environments. Physical coercion need not detain us. We agree with Arnold and Bowie that workers should not be physically coerced on Kantian (or, for that matter, various other) grounds. MNEs and their subcontractors and suppliers should not use physical coercion; and we accept that there are Kantian reasons for MNEs not to contract under circumstances in which the employees of their subcontractors and suppliers are physically coerced. Regarding psychological coercion, Arnold and Bowie give three conditions as definitional: (1) the coercer must have a desire about the will of the victim; (2) the coercer must have a desire to compel the victim to act in a way that makes the coercer's first desire efficacious; and (3) the coercer must be successful in getting the victim to conform (Arnold & Bowie 2003: 229). They make clear that a person who simply makes a choice that is not very desirable is not coerced by the lack of good options. Thus choosing to work in a sweatshop because the only alternatives are worse does not, by itself, on Arnold and Bowie's account constitute psychological coercion. However, Arnold and Bowie hold that psychological coercion does occur when:

> a worker is threatened with being fired by a supervisor unless she agrees to work overtime, and when the supervisor's intention in making the threat is to ensure compliance. (Arnold & Bowie 2003: 230)

We will accept this account of psychological coercion (if only for the sake of the argument), but not that Arnold and Bowie have given a clear example of such coercion. For some action X, it could well be the case that a supervisor making such a threat is acting coercively, but this does not fit well when X is replaced by "overtime" (or even "extensive overtime") in the context of sweatshops. We assume that the practice of overtime is understood by prospective workers; they might prefer not to work overtime and especially not the overtime that is actually demanded of them. However, this simply makes their choice of a sweatshop that requires overtime less desirable than it might otherwise be. To the extent that overtime is routine, the supervisor's request is not a threat, but simply a statement of the conditions of employment. Workers who are acceptable to management are those who will work overtime, and unacceptable workers may be fired (or are never hired in the first place). Failure to observe this distinction would collapse Arnold and Bowie's account of coercion into a "bad-alternatives" account, which they seem to reject.

In the case of a routine job practice X, the supervisor need not have a desire to compel a worker to do X, although the supervisor might well prefer that the worker do X to save the expense of finding a new worker. The desire of the supervisor may simply be that some worker or other do X. Now, a particular—less ethical—supervisor might find more satisfaction or enjoyment in a situation in which overtime was routine than one in which it was not. Perhaps such a supervisor satisfies Arnold and Bowie's conditions for psychological coercion—we are not sure. However, in the case of a routine practice, this would simply mean that their definition of psychological coercion was at odds with their claim not to accept a "bad-alternatives" account of coercion.

Conclusion

We have explored Arnold and Bowie's claim regarding a duty of MNEs or their managers to ensure the payment of subsistence wages by their subcontractors and suppliers, and concerning the use of coercion by these same groups. With the exception of physical coercion, we find that their rationale, based on the Formula of Humanity, is insufficient to establish the duty they state. In particular, a duty to pay above-market wages does not follow from the arguments they present. Nor, even if it did, should the reader, based on current economic research, be unconcerned that such a duty would not work to worsen the situation of the least advantaged workers.

Notes

1. We do not contest this claim.
2. We will not treat working conditions separate from wages. Our justification, apart from space limitations, is that many attempts to improve working conditions would increase costs of labor, and so have much the same effects as raising wage levels. However, we have no intention to argue that working conditions should not be improved if this can be done at no cost or at a net economic benefit.
3. The Restatement of Agency (2d) lists ten conditions to be considered when determining if an agent is a servant or an independent contractor. We believe that these conditions clearly mark subcontractors and suppliers of MNEs as independent contractors, but since Arnold & Bowie do not attempt to support their claim regarding *respondeat superior* in any detail, we spare the reader an item by item examination of the conditions in favor of the commonsense argument in the text. See American Law Institute (1958).
4. This point was suggested by an anonymous reviewer.

5. See especially chapter two. We will not treat the argument in Bowie (1999) separately. We find it most persuasive in dealing with the prohibitions on coercion and deception, which can be observed negatively. Bowie's argument for duties to take some positive action is on a par with the one we discuss below.

6. We will discuss "psychological" coercion, another element of Arnold and Bowie's argument, below.

7. See the "Coercion" section below.

8. Arnold and Bowie's concern with consequences at the end of their paper could perhaps be viewed as intended to rebut a claim that the principle "ought implies can" would be violated by their conclusions regarding duties. However, at this stage in their argument, the duties (oughts) they call for have not yet been established.

9. This claim actually constitutes their third argument, which we handle here in terms of individuals. The implications for companies are treated below.

10. Since Arnold and Bowie are not urging that we adopt Kant's complete system of philosophy, but only drawing out what they take to be implications of the Formula of Humanity, their argument is convincing only to the extent that any ethical elements they introduce are linked to this formulation.

11. We do not contest that persons can have special obligations as the result of voluntary choice, such as the choice to make a promise. Employers should of course keep their promises; many reasons, Kantian and non-Kantian, can be given for this. The challenge is to show that simply being in a certain (unchosen) circumstance can create a duty. Even here, we do not necessarily claim that there are no such duties, but only that Arnold and Bowie owe the reader an explanation of how such duties follow from the Formula of Humanity.

References

American Law Institute. 1958. Restatement of Agency (2d). St. Paul, MN: American Law Institute Publishers.

Arnold, D. G., & Bowie, N. E. 2003. Sweatshops and respect for persons. *Business Ethics Quarterly*, 13: pp. 221–42.

Baker, M., Benjamin, D., & Stranger, S. 1999. The highs and lows of the minimum wage effect: A time-series cross-section study of the Canadian law. *Journal of Labor Economics*, 17 (2): pp. 318–50.

Bellante, D., & Picone, G. 1999. Fast food and unnatural experiments: Another perspective on the New Jersey minimum wage. *Journal of Labor Research*, 20 (4): pp. 463–77.

Bliss, C., & Stern, N. H. 1978. Productivity, wages and nutrition, parts i and ii. *Journal of Development Economics*, 5: pp. 331–98.

Borjas, G. J. 2005. Labor economics. New York: McGraw-Hill.

Bowie, N. E. 1999. Business ethics: A Kantian perspective. Oxford: Blackwell Publishers Inc.

Brown, D. K., Deardorff, A. V., & Stern, R. M. 2004. The effects of multinational production on wages and working conditions in developing countries. In R. E. Baldwin & L. A. Winters (Eds.), *Challenges to globalization: Analyzing the economics*. Chicago: The University of Chicago Press.

Burkhauser, R. V., Couch, K. A., & Wittenburg, D. C. 2000a. A reassessment of the new economics of the minimum wage literature with monthly data from the current population survey. *Journal of Labor Economics,* 18 (4): pp. 653–701.

———. 2000b. Who minimum wage increases bite: an analysis using monthly data from the sipp and the cps. *Southern Economic Journal,* 67 (1): pp. 16–40.

Campbell, C. M., III. 1993. Pay efficiency wages? Evidence with data at the firm level. *Journal of Labor Economics,* 11 (3): pp. 442–70.

Cappelli, P., & Chauvin, K. 1991. An interplant test of the efficiency wage hypothesis. *The Quarterly Journal of Economics,* 106 (3): pp. 769–87.

Card, D., & Krueger, A. B. 1994. Minimum wages and employment: A case study of the fast-food industry in New Jersey and Pennsylvania. *The American Review,* 84 (4): pp. 772–93.

———. 1995. Myth and measurement: The economics of the minimum wage. Princeton, NJ: Princeton University Press.

Castillo-Freeman, A. J., & Freeman, R. B. 1992. When the minimum wage really bites: The effect of the U.S.-level minimum wage on Puerto Rico. In G. J. Borjas & R. B. Freeman (Eds.), *Immigration and the work force: Economic consequences for the United States and source areas:* pp. 177–211. Chicago: University of Chicago Press.

Ehrenberg, R. G., & Smith, R. S. 2003. Labor economics: Theory and public policy (8th ed.). Boston: Addison Wesley, Inc.

Freeman, R. B. 1997. Honor of David Card: Winner of the John Bates Clark medal. *Journal of Economic Perspectives,* 11 (2): pp. 161–78.

Gera, S., & Grenier, G. 1994. Interindustry wage differentials and efficiency wages: Some Canadian evidence. *Canadian Journal of Economics,* 27 (1): pp. 81–100.

Gifis, S. H. 1984. Law dictionary (2nd ed.). New York: Barron's Educational Series.

Hayek, F. A. 1945. The use of knowledge in society. *The American Economic Review,* 35 (4).

Hill, T. E., Jr. 1992. Dignity and practical reasoning in Kant's moral theory. Ithaca, NY: Cornell University Press.

Huang, T.-L., Hallam, A., Orazem, P. F., & Paterno, E. M. 1998. Empirical tests of efficiency wage models. *Economica,* 65: pp. 125–43.

Kant, I. 1964. The metaphysical principles of virtue (J. Ellington, Trans.). Indianapolis: The Bobbs-Merrill Company, Inc.

———. 1997. Groundwork of the metaphysics of morals (M. Gregor, Trans.). Cambridge: Cambridge University Press.

Karz, L. F., & Krueger, A. B. 1992. The effects of the minimum wage on the fast-food industry. *Industrial and Labour Relations Review,* 46 (1): pp. 6–21.

Keane, M. P. 1993. Individual heterogeneity and interindustry wage differentials. *Journal of Human Resources,* 28 (1): pp. 134–61.

Korsgaard, C. M. 1996. Creating the kingdom of ends. Cambridge: Cambridge University Press.

Krueger, A. B. 1991. Ownership, agency, and wages: An examination of franchising in the fast food industry. *The Quarterly Journal of Economics*, 106 (1): pp. 75–101.

Leonard, J. S. 1987. Carrots and Sticks: Pay, supervision and turnover. *Journal of Labor Economics*, 5 (4): pp. S136–S151.

Maitland, I. 2001. The great non-debate over international sweatshops. In T. L. Beauchamp, & N. E. Bowie (Eds.), *Ethical theory and business,* 6th ed. Englewood Cliffs, NJ: Prentice Hall.

Maloney, W. F., & Mendez, J. N. 2003. Measuring the impact of minimum wages: Evidence from Latin America, *NBER Working Papers 9800:* National Bureau of Economic Research.

Michl, T. 2000. Can rescheduling explain the New Jersey minimum wage studies? *Eastern Economic Journal*, 26 (3): pp. 265–76.

Neumark, D., & Wascher, W. 1995. Minimum wage effects on school and work transitions of teenagers. *American Economic Review*, 85 (2): pp. 244–49.

_____. 2004. Minimum wages, labor market institutions, and youth employment: A cross-national analysis. *Industrial and Labor Relations Review*, 57 (2): pp. 223–48.

Partridge, M. D., & Partridge, J. S. 1999a. Do minimum wage hikes raise US long term unemployment? Evidence using state minimum wage rates. *Regional Studies*, 33 (8): pp. 713–26.

_____. 1999b. Do minimum wage hikes reduce employment? State-level evidence from the low-wage retail sector. *Journal of Labor Research*, 20 (3): pp. 393–414.

Republic of El Salvador. 2000. Monitoring report on maguilas and bonded areas: Ministry of Labor, Monitoring and Labor Relations Unit.

Ressler, R. W., Watson, J. K., & Mixon, F. 1996. Full wages, part-time employment, and the minimum wage. *Applied Economics*, 28 (11): pp. 1415–19.

Santoro, M. A. 2000. Profits and Principles: Global capitalism and human rights in China. Ithaca, NY: Cornell University Press.

Spriggs, W., & Schmitt, J. 1996. The minimum wage. In T. Schafer & J. Faux (Eds.), *Reclaiming Prosperity: A blueprint for progressive economic reform:* pp. 166–73. Armonk, NY: M. E. Sharpe.

Strauss, J., & Thomas, D. 1998. Health, nutrition, and economic development. *Journal of Economic Literature*, 36 (2): pp. 766–817.

Walsh, F. 1999. A multisector model of efficiency wages. *Journal of Labor Economics*, 17 (2): pp. 351–75.

Zavodny, M. 2000. Effect of the minimum wage on employment and hours. *Labour Economics*, 7 (6): pp. 729–50.

POSTSCRIPT

Are Sweatshops an Inhumane Business Practice?

Consumers are thinking about the people who make the products they purchase and the conditions in which they work. American retailers and name brands have produced clothing, shoes, toys, and more. Store shelves are filled with merchandise made in sweatshops, where the workers often conduct their labor in unsafe conditions with little pay. Many of these retailers say that they are following strict codes of conduct and performing on-site monitoring. However, business ethicists believe that some factories have found ways to conceal abuses and to keep double sets of books to fool auditors. At some factories, individuals are tutored with a script to recite to auditors, but this script does not accurately reflect the real conditions at the sweatshop. What can Americans ethically believe about what they wear and use? Is a Kantian ideal being followed in the production of these goods? Should it be?

Suggested Readings

Ronald J. Adams, "Retail Profitability and Sweatshops: A Global Dilemma," *Journal of Retailing and Consumer Services* (vol. 9, no. 3, 2002).

Denis G. Arnold and Laura P. Hartman, "Beyond Sweatshops: Positive Deviancy and Global Labour Practices," *Business Ethics: A European Review* (vol. 14, no. 3, 2005), pp. 206–222.

John Miller, "Why Economists Are Wrong About Sweatshops and the Anti-sweatshop Movement," *Challenge* (vol. 46, no. 1, 2003).

Tara J. Radin and Martin Calkins, "The Struggle Against Sweatshops: Moving Toward Responsible Global Business," *Journal of Business Ethics* (vol. 66, no. 2–3, 2006), pp. 261–272.

Ellen Israel Rosen, *Making Sweatshops: The Globalization of the U.S. Apparel Industry* (Berkeley: University of California Press, 2002).

Robert J. S. Ross, *Slaves to Fashion: Poverty and Abuse in the New Sweatshops* (Ann Arbor: University of Michigan Press, 2004).

Matt Zwolinski, "Sweatshops, Choice, and Exploitation," *Business Ethics Quarterly* (vol. 17, no. 4, 2007), pp. 689–727.

ISSUE 19

Should Patenting Genes Be Understood as Unethical?

YES: Miriam Schulman, from "Of SNPS, TRIPS, and Human Dignity: Ethics and Gene Patenting," *BioProcess International* (January 2003)

NO: Annabelle Lever, from "Ethics and the Patenting of Human Genes," *The Journal of Philosophy, Science and Law* (vol. 1, November 2001)

ISSUE SUMMARY

YES: Schulman holds that the human genome is a different business enterprise than other patent applications. The genome stands for essential building blocks of the human species and as such questions of ethics and human dignity should be studied.

NO: Lever explains that the U.S. Patent Office has issued thousands of patents on genes and believes the legality of this is established. She also believes the moral concerns have been answered on patents, mainly because the genes have been isolated and altered significantly and are part of a scientific bank of genes for overall research.

Within the issue of gene patenting, we find two of the most important concerns of the Enlightenment brought into focus and set in opposition. In the interests of science, we ought to encourage all the research into the human genome that we can, and if the practice of placing genes under patent, to protect the researcher's interests, advances that goal, then we ought to allow and encourage such a practice. In the interests of the public good, we ought to make sure that private interests do not place obstacles to the rapid dissemination of knowledge for the advancement of the public health. Our Enlightenment forebears insisted that the resolution of such conflicts should proceed from the informed judgment of the sovereign people. This is reflected in the American Constitution through the Fourth Amendment, which protects citizens from search and seizure of property without due process of law; a patent is property and what right do we have to take intellectual property from its inventor? The founders of the country were certainly speaking of material belongings, as they could not have possibly imagined a realm like the Internet or sequencer for DNA. John Locke emphasized the right of the individual to own property. How do we limit that right? Should sharing all knowledge about the human body be a right for all scientists? Annabelle Lever explains that it is important for patents to continue on the human genome. She states human genes are removed from human bodies and scientifically isolated and manipulated in a laboratory. This process takes any ownership of the gene from any individual, and makes it intellectual property. Intellectually working through this process, Lever believes, allays claims of philosophical or legal impropriety.

Some research scientists who work in public institutions often are troubled by the concept of intellectual property because their norms tell them that science will advance more rapidly if researchers enjoy free access to knowledge. By contrast, the law of intellectual property rests on an assumption that, without exclusive rights, no one will be willing to invest in research and development (R&D). When a biotechnology patent involving an altered product of nature is issued, the patent holder is required to deposit a sample of the new invention into one of the 26 worldwide culture depositories. Currently over three million genome-related patent applications have been filed in the United States, Europe, and Japan. Patenting provides a strategy for protecting inventions without secrecy. However, the patent grants the right to exclude others from making, using, and selling the invention for a limited term, 20 years from application filing date in most parts of the world.

Science also poses questions of "how to" rather than "whether to." Are there certain limits we as humans must respect? If so, where do they come from? Where do we draw those lines and limits? "Where do we set the bar?" Miriam Schulman explains that the human genome is different from other subjects of patent application. She says much of this difference is what it means, essentially, to be a human being. She affirms human dignity and believes that the building blocks of human life should not be exploited. The common good needs to be protected of the human genome as well.

Robert Cook-Deegan explains that academic institutions own most of the exclusive licenses to gene patents. The patents are based on taxpayer-funded research. He contends that the business model in gene patenting is incorrect because it does more to block competition in the gene testing market than to spur the development of new technologies for gauging disease risk. A study completed by Cook-Deegan and other Duke researchers concludes that a large ethical problem is combining overly broad patents that are exclusively licensed to single companies. Particularly under the spotlight are firms such as Myriad Genetics, which is associated with the University of Utah research foundation. Myriad Genetics holds a monopoly on the market for BRCA genes. Because of its broad patent claims, it is nearly impossible to pursue alternative ways to test clinically for BRCA genes without the risk of patent infringement.

YES

Miriam Schulman

Of SNPS, TRIPS, and Human Dignity: Ethics and Gene Patenting

If you bring up the topic of gene patenting with a group of scientists, they are likely to talk about what impact limiting access to DNA sequences will have on research. A similar conversation with lawyers may provoke debate about the utility or inventiveness of particular patent applications. But raise the question of granting intellectual property rights over pieces of the human genome in any gathering of regular folks, and the initial response is probably going to be, "Yuck."

Intellectual property attorney William L. Anthony Jr., a partner at Orrick, Herrington & Sutcliffe LLP, frequently discusses these issues with jury focus groups. At a recent conference, "Patenting Human Life," held at Santa Clara University, Anthony described his experience: "Almost invariably, if I talk about patenting something that has to do with human beings, the first reaction is revulsion."

While it may be tempting for people in the biotechnology field to dismiss this response as untutored, it points to a significant ethical issue that should be of concern to people at all levels of scientific and legal understanding: There is something about the human genome that is different from other subjects of patent application, and the difference is encapsulated in the adjective. Human DNA symbolizes something essential about humans themselves, and, as such, raises the issue of human dignity. While we may be able to respect that dignity and still offer the intellectual property protections crucial to drug development, it is unwise to ignore widespread public concern about how we deal with the building blocks of human life.

Dignity was just one of the ethical issues raised at the "Patenting Human Life" conference, sponsored by SCU's High Tech Law Institute and Markkula Center for Applied Ethics and the Bay Area Bioscience Center. Other ethical questions included: What system of intellectual property protection would produce the best therapeutics and so improve human well-being? And what system would come closest to ensuring that these discoveries are accessible to all who need them?

From *BioProcess International*, January 2003, pp. 1–6. Copyright © 2003 by BioProcess International. Reprinted by permission.

Dignity

When the average person expresses reservations about patenting DNA, they are often reacting to the idea of owning something fundamental to human personhood. A lawyer would probably respond that a patent doesn't confer ownership. John Barton, professor of law at Stanford University, described intellectual property protections as "a set of statutory exclusion rights." In other words, the holder of a DNA patent does not own the gene sequence; he or she simply has the right, for a limited period of time, to prevent others from using it.

True, but not enough to entirely moot the concern over dignity. Patenting DNA still suggests to many that human genes are commodities. It's an equation that troubled Suzanne Holland, associate professor of religion at University of Puget Sound and affiliate associate professor in medical history and ethics at the University of Washington School of Medicine. "Biotechnology products are not widgets," she said. Holland worried that patenting genes may "erode our dignity, as the process results in increasing acceptance that it's okay to buy and sell things that speak to us of our humanity."

Of course, there are those who believe that humans don't deserve any specially protected status and that such dignity concerns reveal a sort of hubris. In his conference keynote, Rigel Pharmaceuticals President Brian Cunningham sounded this note: "It seems to be okay to patent every animal in the zoo but us, a reflection of our need to believe that we are special—not part of the continuum of nature."

Margaret R. McLean, director of biotechnology and health care ethics at the Markkula Center for Applied Ethics, took a middle view. While accepting the basic notion that humans "ought not to be used," she allowed that patenting DNA "doesn't necessarily imply commodification of human persons." The trick, McLean argued, is to distinguish between genetic identity and personal identity. "A human is more than the sum of his or her genes," she said. In discussing the patent issue, we must be careful not to suggest that humans can be reduced to a piece of code, she continued, which would indeed be an assault on dignity.

Promoting Human Health

While patenting DNA runs the risk of diminishing respect for human dignity, some risk might be acceptable if the end result were an increase in human well-being. Most people in the biotechnology industry start with this understanding and proceed to the instrumental ethical question: If the goal is to improve human health by the creation of diagnostics and therapeutics, does the patent system help to achieve that goal?

There was almost universal agreement among lawyers and biotech professionals at the conference that some form of intellectual property protection was necessary to encourage investment in the development of new drugs. Investors will not put money into a company without evidence that the firm has secured protection for its intellectual property, Sue Markland Day, president of the Bay Area Bioscience Center, argued. As an example, she cited the plunge in biotech stock prices when Former President Bill Clinton and British Prime Minister Tony Blair issued a joint statement March 14, 2000, which was interpreted to advocate limits on gene patenting. "Patents," Markland Day said, "are the lifeblood of biotechnology."

That does not mean that people in the biotech industry want to ignore the ethical dimension of gene patenting, simply that their ethical questions tend to be not "Whether to?" but "How to?" Thane Kreiner, vice president for corporate affairs at Affymetrix, posed the issue this way, "It's not a question of whether patents are right or wrong, but where to set the bar."

Kreiner was referring to the guidelines for patentability and how they are applied to biotechnology. There are three key criteria in this regard: novelty, inventiveness, and usefulness. As the United States and other signatories to the Agreement on Trade-Related Aspects of Intellectual Property Rights (TRIPS) evaluate whether to grant patents on gene sequences, they must decide whether to apply these standards stringently (that is, to set the bar high) or loosely (to set the bar low). A high bar might require, for example, that applicants state the specific utility of a sequence and include evidence that the gene actually does what the applicant claims. A low bar might allow applications to rest on the theoretical possibility that a gene might have a certain utility.

The issue is complicated by the fact that the science is in such rapid flux. The discovery of a sequence that might have represented considerable novelty and inventiveness in the 1990s—such as the connection of the BRCA1 gene with breast cancer—might be less impressive now that technology has made it much easier to identify disease susceptibility genes.

Another complication has to do with the scope of the patents. Many applications have been filed for fragments of genes—ESTs and SNPs—and it is unclear whether patents on these fragments extend to uses of the entire gene.

These were among the issues that troubled Stanford's Barton, who was a member of the roundtable that produced the Nuffield Council on Bioethics report on the ethics of patenting DNA. That roundtable concluded:

> In general, the law has, in our view, tended to be generous in granting patents in relation to DNA sequences. Not only are many of the patents broad in scope, but they have been granted when the criteria for inventiveness and utility were weakly applied. Many of these patents are broad because an inventor who successfully makes a claim in relation to a DNA sequence will, in effect, obtain broad protection on all uses of the DNA, and sometimes the proteins which the DNA produces.

What does all this have to do with ethics? If the bar for patentability is set too low, it will pervert the incentive structures of the patent system, which should reward new inventions that increase human well-being. Patent holders who may have contributed very little to the understanding of the gene or its function will have too much control over its use in research and development. Especially in the area of genetics, where more than one gene may control a disease process, a company that wants to develop therapeutics may need to buy licenses from multiple patent holders. That, Kreiner argued, could make research prohibitively expensive.

If the bar is set too high, on the other hand, pharmaceutical and biotechnology companies will not put the vast sums necessary into research because they will have no way of protecting their investment. "The patent system doesn't exist to pin a badge of appreciation on the inventor," Anthony said, "but to encourage ordinary people to invest in something that might do some good."

Accessibility

Proper setting of the bar may promote the creation of therapeutics that have the potential to improve human lives. But the ethical story does not end there. Sometimes, our patent policies produce good medicines that are simply too expensive to reach all of the people who need them.

Many who work in biotech agree this is a problem but argue it is not their problem. A company, they point out, is not a philanthropic institution. It exists to make profits. But to raise the issue of accessibility is not to suggest that industry should solve the problem on its own. Industry, however, needs to be part of the discussion, which might begin with an exploration of distributive justice: How can benefits—in this context, therapeutics—be allocated fairly.

One criterion of fairness says that those who have contributed to the creation of the benefit should have a share in it. Usually, there has been some public contribution to successful drug discovery. Of the 50 best-selling drugs in this country, 48 benefited from public money, according to Holland. In the case of genes, the public has certainly contributed to the knowledge base that is producing innovations through government funding of the Human Genome Project and other scientific endeavors. By that measure, the public is entitled to expect some access to the fruits of genetic research.

Can the patent system be adjusted to spread the fruits more widely? Not without tradeoffs, said June Carbone, Presidential Professor of Ethics and the Common Good at SCU and one of the conference organizers.

The real public policy question is whether we want:

a. the existing system, which places a premium on the development of life-saving drugs, even if they are so costly they cannot realistically be made available to everyone;
b. greater redirection of government-subsidized research toward products of more general utility or accessibility, even if that means the development of some life-saving drugs will be delayed or discouraged; or
c. dramatically higher overall public health expenditures.

These public health decisions have important implications for the common good. Physical well-being is not solely an individual matter. For example, we all rely on the public provision of clean water and sewage systems to protect our health. We handle serious infectious disease risks by offering vaccines to everyone because a policy that provided protection only for those who could afford it might eventually harm everyone.

Gene patenting needs to be seen within this common good context, McLean argued. If, as a society, we develop patent policies that direct research only to the development of expensive drugs, we may ultimately bankrupt the health care infrastructure on which we all rely.

Finally, as we think about patents and access, we must invoke the old-fashioned virtue of compassion. Do we really want to be the kind of people who restrict the access of the poor and the uninsured to life-saving therapies? Holland proposes this litmus test for patenting DNA: "What does it do for the most vulnerable members of society?"

These ethical issues might be addressed in any number of ways. We could support government programs that provide DNA-based therapeutics to the underserved. We could support industry efforts, such as the Genentech policy described by Brian Cunningham, through which the company put aside a portion of its profits from Human Growth Hormone to provide the therapy for any child whose family could not afford it. We could force companies to license patents so that research could be expanded and cheaper therapeutics developed.

The resolution of all these ethical dilemmas is limited only by our moral imagination. The only thing we can't do is [to] ignore the ethical dimension of patenting human life.

Annabelle Lever  **NO**

Ethics and the Patenting of Human Genes

Human gene patents are patents on human genes that have been removed from human bodies and scientifically isolated and manipulated in a laboratory. The U.S. Patent Office has issued thousands of patents on such genes and it is generally believed that their legality is well-established, although no court has yet ruled on the matter directly. The legality of such patents under the European Patent Convention [EPC] [is] yet to be determined. However, legal experts believe that there would be no legal objection to treating human genes as patentable inventions under the EPC either.

Legal and moral justification, however, are not identical, and it is possible for a legal decision to be immoral although consistent with legal precedent and procedure. Thus, it is not surprising that the emerging legal consensus on human gene patents has not significantly allayed doubts about their morality.[1] If anything, it is surprising to learn that there are those who believe that attention to the legal justification for human gene patents could remove the most serious moral objections to them. Yet that, precisely, is Pilar Ossorio's claim, and she is not alone in making it.[2] Like Ossorio, those who are well-versed in patent law often believe that confusion over some quite basic legal and scientific facts can account for the belief that human gene patents are immoral and, in particular, for the belief that they justify the ownership of one person by another.[3] Once these confusions are removed, they contend, we will see that there is nothing especially alarming about these patents, and no reason to believe that they are immoral.[4]

Legal Facts about Human Gene Patents

The idea that patents on human genes is immoral, because [it is] indistinguishable from the claim to own other people, rests on two confusions about patent law, according to Ossorio. The first is confusion over what is patented by a human gene patent; the second, there is confusion over what a patent enables one legally to do. Because patents on human genes do not, and legally cannot, apply to genes as they naturally occur in our bodies, Ossorio maintains that human gene patents constitute no threat to the bodily integrity of individuals, or to their use of their own genes in living and reproducing. Because

From "*Ethics and the Patenting of Human Genes*" in the Journal of Philosophy, Science & Law, Vol. 1, November 2001. Reprinted with permission of the Georgia Tech School of Public Policy, the University of Miami Ethics Programs and the author.

patent rights are different from ownership rights, and do not confer ownership on anything, she believes that patenting must be distinguished from owning, whether we are talking about patents on bicycles or on human genes.

Human genes can only be patented in the U.S.—or, indeed, anywhere— if they can be distinguished from genes as they naturally occur in human bodies.[5] To be patentable in the U.S. an object or process must count as an invention, not a discovery, in addition to meeting further legal tests such as those for novelty, non-obviousness, and usefulness. It is, therefore, a legal fact about patents that they do not apply to objects that occur naturally, unless these have been sufficiently altered by human effort as to count as "made by man" for legal purposes. Thus, human genes can only pass the threshold test that marks them as legally patentable, if they have been altered sufficiently to be legally distinguishable from naturally occurring genes, which cannot be patented.

Though the genes in your body are not patentable, the degree of manipulation and alteration that is required to isolate and identify a human gene scientifically means that genes so altered and manipulated can merit a legal patent. Or so the U.S. Patent Office has held, when granting patents on human genes. As Ossorio describes it, this is hardly surprising for human genes that are patentable to have scientific and commercial properties that distinguish them from naturally occurring genes. For example, Ossorio explains that while there are several methods of sequencing DNA, all of them require at least some of the following: isolating DNA, purifying DNA, removing a small segment of the DNA from its place in the genome and connecting it to bacterial DNA (apparently, doing this is called "cloning" DNA), chemically unwinding DNA, and constructing radioactive or florescent copies of the genomic DNA fragment.[6] She explains that "When a patent claims a particular DNA sequence, it must teach others how to 'make' that sequence—the patent must give enough information that another investigator can synthesize the sequence de novo or clone the sequence herself. Cloning or synthesizing DNA according to information in a patent generally results in DNA that resides in a very different biochemical environment than that of a human cell."[7]

In *Diamond v. Chakrabarty*,[8] the U.S. Supreme Court upheld a patent on oil-eating bacteria, arguing that such a patent was perfectly consistent with legal objections to patenting natural objects that have not been significantly altered by human endeavor. In *Parke–Davis and Co. v. H. K. Mulford and Co.*, a lower Court held that purified human adrenaline was patentable because, through purification, it became "for every practical purpose a new thing commercially and therapeutically."[9] Hence, given the work that goes into scientifically isolating and identifying a gene, and the changes in the properties of the gene that this involves treating human genes as patentable inventions does not, in and of itself, threaten the bodily integrity of human beings.

As Ossorio believes, these considerations should allay at least some significant doubts about the morality of patenting human genes. Perhaps patentable genes do not differ as greatly from naturally-occurring human genes as do oil-eating bacteria from naturally occurring bacteria—though this is not self-evident. However, it is clear that, legally, patents on human genes are on genes that are scientifically and legally distinguishable from the genes in our bodies, or from natural genes taken out of our bodies.

Moreover, Ossorio argues, the difficulty with the main moral objections to human gene patents is not simply that they confuse legally patentable genes with naturally occurring genes. In addition, they confuse patenting with owning.[10] Thus, they fail to see that whatever the complexity involved in legal ownership, a patent does not confer legal ownership of anything. One can have a legal patent on a bicycle without owning any bicycles. Indeed, one can have a legal patent on an invention, but lack any legal rights to use that invention, let alone to license others to use or manufacture it. This is because the only legal right conferred by a patent is the right to prevent others from using or possessing one's invention.[11] Because a patent does not confer the rights to use or possess, Ossorio maintains that patenting is quite distinct from owning. Hence, she concludes, a patent on a human gene does not confer ownership of that gene, let alone ownership of all genes made according to the patent.[12] A human gene patent, then, cannot be identified with legal ownership of human bodies, not simply because human gene patents confer no rights over naturally occurring genes, but because patent rights confer none of the positive rights to possess and use that are typically associated with ownership.

So, Ossorio is right to claim that attention to the legal facts about human gene patents removes the most serious doubts about their moral justification. We may, with Ossorio, be skeptical that these patents are necessary to promote research and investment in biotechnology, or in the prevention and cure of human suffering.[13] Nevertheless, doubts on this score hardly imply that human gene patents are intrinsically immoral, as they would be if they prevented people from using their genes to live or to reproduce.

Moreover, while these legal features of human gene patents do not alleviate the concern that patenting may exacerbate existing inequalities between rich and poor countries, or between rich and poor people in the same country,[14] they suggest that there is nothing about a legal patent that precludes government regulation of licensing agreements with these worries in mind. For example, governments might require patentholders to license the use and manufacture of human genes for some purposes (thereby implying that the right to exclude is not absolute),[15] prohibit their use for others, and limit how much they can charge for their use or manufacture by poor countries or poor people.[16] In these ways any morally objectionable consequences of human gene patents could be met, and even preempted, while acknowledging the legality of these patents. Yet this, too, would be impossible, were human gene patents the moral equivalent of slavery.

Why Moral Concerns Remain

However, if reflection on Ossorio's claims indeed suggests that there is nothing inherently wrong with these patents, the moral significance of the legal facts she cites is less conclusive than she thinks. Perhaps some confusion about what is patented by a human gene patent, or over the rights conferred by a patent, motivate the thought that these patents are intrinsically objectionable.

Nonetheless, patents on human genes pose a greater threat to human freedom, equality, and dignity than she acknowledges.[17] Indeed, I will argue that although ownership objections to human gene patents are not very helpful analytically, they need involve no confusion about relevant legal or scientific matters. On the contrary, they may simply reflect doubts about the moral justification of quite ordinary legal rights, and point to the conclusion that considerable moral, as well as legal, reflection may be necessary to resolve ethical controversy over gene patenting.[18]

For instance, take the claim that patenting is different from owning, because the patenting simply consists in the right to exclude, whereas the owning presupposes positive rights to use and possess.[19] How significant this difference is conceptually, morally, and politically depends on the background assumptions about people's rights and powers that one uses to assess it. The right to exclude—can be a very significant and controversial right, and may be sufficient to turn what, previously, would have been collective property into private property.

If, therefore, one supposes that, prior to patenting, human genes are collective property, one might be struck by the similarities between patent rights and other forms of private property, rather than by the differences between the right to exclude and the rights of exclusive use and possession that are distinctive of private ownership. Ossorio considers this possibility when assessing "common heritage" objections to patenting human genes.[20] She concludes that if one interprets people's rights to imply that the genome belongs equally to all, and that all should therefore have equal access to the derived knowledge or beneficial uses of research on the genome, then "it would be unjust to grant patents on the human genome." However, those who object to human gene patents on the grounds that they unjustifiably give one person property rights over may also believe that human genes are collective property, although people should have exclusive rights over the genes in their own bodies. Hence, Ossorio is wrong to suppose that ownership objections to patenting can be dismissed more easily than those based on the idea that genes are part of the common heritage of humankind. Similarly, if one assumed that human genes were unowned and unownable prior to patenting, one might be struck more by the fact that patenting creates a right to prevent others from using or possessing a gene—as would private ownership—and less by the thought that it creates only one of the many rights in which private ownership might consist.

Nor would such objections to patenting collapse in face of the thought that patentable genes are not spontaneous natural occurrences but the product of human effort and skill. After all, it is not self-evident that people lack rights to use or to possess something, such as land or medicine, that they did not create (although these may not be rights of exclusive use and possession), or that they cannot be harmed, or unjustly treated, if they are denied such rights by law. Indeed, the thought that this is a real possibility underpins objections to libertarian views about people's rights from a wide variety of philosophical perspectives.

Perhaps one has no right to the creation of a gene that can be scientifically manipulated and commercially manufactured in ways that are useful and medically beneficial. However, it does not follow that one therefore lacks rights to those genes once they have been invented. Indeed, if patenting rights are assumed to be absolute (as they might be on libertarian views of rights), so that patentholding can prevent the use or commercial development of inventions, however useful and desirable, there might be very strong moral objections to the idea that human genes are legally patentable.

These objections might be couched in the language of property rights and ownership, to highlight the idea that rights to use, possess, and exploit human genes are being wrongly denied to people, though these may no less merit the description "property rights" than the right to patent itself. But one need not couch the objection this way, even if one's objections to patenting human genes are based on concerns about private ownership.

For example, if one is worried about the consequences of patents for disparities in medical care, or in political and economic power between countries and individuals,[21] one might object to patents on human genes not because they prevent people from owning something that they ought to be able to own, or from buying, selling, or leasing services that they ought to be able to buy, sell or lease, but because one thinks that this is the wrong way to describe and think about people's rights to genes.[22] One might be perfectly open to the idea that people should pay for medical services in some form, and that reciprocity requires acknowledging and rewarding or compensating the efforts and skills of those who have benefited us. One would merely doubt that such recompense should take the form of exclusive rights to human genes, let alone absolute rights to prevent others from using or possessing them, even if only for a finite period of time.[23]

It is likely that people, who object morally to patents on human genes for reasons I have described, will find patents on other things objectionable too. Thus, they might suppose that medical or therapeutic inventions ought not to be patentable and that, therefore, there must be some other way to reward people who create and invest in medical research and technology. As I understand the matter, this is precisely the interpretation of patent law reflected in the European Patent Convention. Under that convention, medical and therapeutic devices and techniques are not patentable.[24] In this the EPC differs from U.S. law, where the patent right to exclude is thought to be consistent with the rights of researchers to use a patented invention for non-commercial purposes, and some use of a patented invention for personal, non-commercial enjoyment and entertainment by the general public.

If this distinction between U.S. and European law is as I've described it, this may, perhaps, reflect differences in the way that medical care and training are organized and funded in the U.S., as opposed to Europe. But I have some doubts on this score. If this were the case one would expect to see public and private doctors, hospitals, and medical facilities treated differently for the purposes of patent law in the U.S.—and to see these differences reflected in public debate on the ethics of patenting human genes. But one does not. Instead, the U.S. supposes that scientific research, though not medical treatment, constitutes grounds for an exception to the rights created by a patent—quite possibly with the result that people will have access to drugs as part of an experiment that they will be unable to afford as part of their regular care.

Thus far I've focused on concerns about the implications of gene patents for medicine. But the objections to patenting human genes that I've described have broader implications that need to be examined. Indeed, they seem either to imply that there are no other purposes—or, at any rate, no legitimate purposes—that human gene patents could serve, or that human genes are special in some way that makes the very idea of patenting them shocking.

It is not clear how sharply one can distinguish these two lines of thought, or how far they support the view that what is bad about patenting is that it gives one person unjustified forms of power and control over another, as ownership objections to patenting imply. Still, I think these two lines of thought can be distinguished and that, in some circumstances, the differences between them may prove theoretically and practically important. For the first view implies that there might, conceivably, be some legitimate uses of human genes that would justify patenting them, something which the latter view denies. If both would likely object to patenting if the non-medical uses of human genes were, say, to produce new forms of food, or new toys, they might nonetheless differ in their approach to these patents as the source of genetic tests for non-medical purposes.

Even in the absence of a cure, or a treatment, people may want to take a test that tells them whether they have, or are likely to have, a serious disease. Indeed, they might simply want to take such a test because they are curious about their genetic makeup.[25] While the former objection to patenting would reject patents on medical resources, because they give some people unacceptable forms of power and control over others—given the importance of life and health to all people—they may find the promotion of a wide array of safe, relatively cheap and accessible genetic tests, in the long term, an adequate justification for some patents on human genes in the short-term. They might be moved by the thought that some people could benefit from genetic testing, even if it serves no special medical purpose, and that patents on human genes for these reasons would be ethical.

People troubled by the patenting of genes for medical purposes will, very likely, want to ensure that genetic testing not be mandatory, and that it not threaten people's jobs, healthcare, civil and political rights, and so on.[26] They may also want to ensure, perhaps, that counseling is available for those who use the tests. But these problems with genetic testing will likely arise, and need to be dealt with, whether or not genes are patented. Patenting will likely exacerbate these problems, by creating more tests, and more opportunities for genetic testing, than there otherwise would be. However, excluding people who cannot afford such testing from satisfying their curiosity, or from more accurate estimates of their likely life-course, implies significantly less control over people's lives, and over basic resources, than does the ability to deny people needed medical care, or to make this unaffordable. Hence one might well find the one acceptable, although believing the other immoral.

So, it may be possible for some people who object to the patenting of human genes to distinguish amongst the uses to which a patentable gene might be put theoretically, and in practice. Thus one could allow—as, it seems, the EPC will allow—for a person to have a patent on a human gene, but deny them the right to prevent people from using the gene for purposes a, b, and c; perhaps require them to use it for purposes d, e, and f; and give them considerable leeway thereafter. Notice, however, that one could still say that patents *on particular human genes* are immoral, and that patents on human genes *for certain purposes* are always immoral, while granting that other gene patents might be morally justified. However, on this interpretation of objections to patenting, the difference between patenting and owning, stressed by Ossorio, would be relatively insignificant. Instead, what is critical for this first version of the ownership objection is whether or not the patent rights should be treated as absolute, for moral and legal purposes.

By contrast, those who think that human genes should never be patented may be moved by two rather different concerns with slavery. The first would be the concern about the illegitimate power and control of one person by another made possible by the right to exclude people from some important or necessary human good. The second would be the concern with the attitude toward people's needs, aspirations, and capacities implicit in the right to own slaves. Someone concerned as much with the attitude toward people implied by slavery, as with the power and control it brings, and the misuse of people that it licenses, may simply believe that no one can have exclusive rights over human genes and that there is something morally objectionable in thinking of them as property at all.[27]

What might motivate such objections? One possibility is that they may believe that our genetic endowment cannot be separated from our capacities for invention and, more generally, from reflective thought and action. They may, therefore, believe that the reasons to reject slavery, based on the attitude to human capacities that it involves, tell against treating human genes as though they were cars, which are patentable, or as great pieces of art, which are not. They may be willing to say that some reasons for patenting genes are better than others, and that some of the potential consequences of patenting raise concerns about slavery more acutely than do others. Nonetheless, they may think that all patents in human genes, and all efforts to turn human genes into property, confuse human beings, and their potential, with that of objects, however lovely, useful, and valuable.

Clearly, if considerations of this sort underpin "ownership" objections to patenting human genes, they do so in ways that are more radical and for reasons that are even more controversial than the reasons I have described. But just because they are controversial, and because their rejection of patents is so radical, it does not follow that they are confused about what is patented by a human gene patent, over the rights conferred by a patent, or about what is and is not immoral. Such objections to patenting need not imply that all biotechnology research is immoral, or that debts of gratitude and justice are not owed to those who benefit humankind through their efforts and ingenuity. Nor, importantly, need they depend on any confusion about scientific facts about genes.

For example, those who believe that there is something about human genes that makes patenting them immoral may be well aware of the fact that the human genome is very like the genome of worms, not to mention that of animals with whom we may identify more closely.[28] Just because humans do not differ all that much from other animals, it does not follow that we should be indifferent to the moral significance of whatever genetic or other differences that there are. Indeed, they might think, it would be as wrong to ignore the significance of these differences as to fixate on them at the cost of appreciating the moral significance of the similarities amongst living things.

An implication of this view might be that some patents on animal genes are immoral, just as some uses of animals are immoral and condemned by reflection on the evils of slavery and its indifference to human suffering, human hopes and human capacities. But whether this type of objection to patenting human genes extends to other biotechnology patents—or, indeed, to other patents generally—it need no more exaggerate the genetic differences between humans and other animals than need objections to rape or justifications for marriage exaggerate those between one person and another. Racist assumptions may underpin objections to rape and justifications for marriage, but they need not. Likewise, some arguments against patenting human genes may exaggerate the genetic and non-genetic differences between humans and other animals. But there is no compelling reason to suppose that this must be the case, anymore than it is inevitable that ethical objections to patenting human genes should be racist just because they could, conceivably, be.[29] Hence, I am unpersuaded by Tom Wilkie's claim that gene patenting poses no necessary threat to the privacy of individuals *because* individuals' genes are so similar. Our diaries, as well as our genes, may be very similar to those of other people, yet our privacy, as well as our property rights, can be violated when someone sells or publishes our diary without our consent. So, while Wilkie may be right that the risks to privacy from gene patenting are contingent and avoidable, rather than inherent and unavoidable, it cannot be for the reasons that he gives.

If one accepts these points, it looks as though one can also dismiss the charge that those who believe patenting to be immoral must, therefore, be genetic fundamentalists, or identify being human with having some particular set of genes, in ways that are unreasonable or, even, unethical. Given the current state of our knowledge, one might simply suppose that our genetic endowment constitutes an important part of the reason why humans have the morally significant capacities that they have, including the capacity for conscious reflection on the moral significance of their genetic attributes.[30]

For people who think this way, and so suppose that there is something morally wrong with treating genes as property—whether they couch their concerns in the language of ownership, or on analogy to slavery—their concerns about the way that people see and treat their genes may extend to the way that people treat their natural and social environment.[31] While some people tend to think that our genetic endowment is more closely connected to our sense of ourselves as moral agents than it is our environment, others do not. Rather, they think that our natural and social environment is at least as significant for our moral capacities, and our ability to recognize, develop, and exercise these, as are our genes. Consequently, their objections to patenting human genes may reflect their concerns about the destruction of some human habitats and ways of life, and to the ways that other human habitats and ways of life are fostered and insulated from criticism and change.

In short, I do not believe that one needs to draw untenable lines between nature and nurture, genes and environment, individual and society, or one species and another to believe that patenting human genes is immoral. Although one may have to make some controversial assumptions, or to reach some controversial conclusions if one believes that it is always wrong to patent human genes, neither the assumptions, nor the conclusions need be unreasonable, even if they are not the only reasonable ones that one might make. So, while it is possible that some ownership objections to the patenting of human genes may collapse when confronted with the legal facts to which Ossorio draws our attention, I do not see that they all must do so.

The Justification for Patenting

Indeed, it is not clear that objections to patenting, however interpreted, must be any less reasonable, or any more speculative, controversial, and sectarian than justifications for these particular patents, or for a patenting system in general. Once one considers that most justifications given for patents on human genes depend heavily on the thought that patenting in general is justified, it becomes clear how speculative, controversial, and morally problematic most arguments are for these particular patents.[32] For that reason, I will suggest, it erroneous to suppose that the burden of proof lies with those who would reject these patents as immoral, rather than with those who ask us to accept them, albeit provisionally, on the assumption that these patents are morally justified in and of themselves, or that they are a morally acceptable consequence of a practice (patenting) that is, itself, morally justified. Instead, the burden of proof rests equally on those would deny, and those who would affirm the morality of patenting human genes.

As Ossorio explains, the justification for a system of patent rights reflects a couple of rather different considerations.[33] On the one hand, there is the thought that patents are a solution to the problem of motivating people to invest their time, energy, and money in the creation and development of socially useful knowledge and products. On the other [hand], there is the thought that patents are a solution to the problem of rewarding people who successfully contribute to the public good, given that all of us have incentives to try to enjoy these benefits without acknowledging and rewarding those who made them. Neither reason by itself singles out patents, as opposed to other ways of rewarding and motivating people.[34] Taken together, however, patents appear to have attractive features that other ways of motivating and rewarding people will probably lack. For example, patents ensure the publication of useful knowledge, and not merely its creation. They establish rules that are relatively automatic, and capable of being fairly applied to the problem of deciding what counts as knowledge deserving of recognition and reward. They tailor the size and costs of rewards to inventors based on the preferences, beliefs, and interests of people in the invention, and so on. In short, patents seem to combine concerns for efficiency, reciprocity, freedom, and equality in a rather attractive way.

But appearances are, to some extent, deceptive here, as in other matters. Like other private property rights, it is unclear that patent rights actually reward merit, and they certainly do not seem to reward effort, *per se.*[35] The relationship between benefit and reward, created by patent rights, may be very loose, as is the relationship to the common good or public interest.[36] Moreover, such rewards as patents generate, and such success as they are likely to have in motivating people, depends on us assuming what Ossorio ignores when distinguishing patenting and owning: namely, that patent rights typically enable their holder to benefit financially from a patent. Hence, they either presuppose the existence of rights to use and possess the invention (if not by the patent-holder, by other people), or motivate the creation of such rights. In short, while it may well be true that one can have a patent on a bicycle without owning any bicycles,[37] it is typically the case that someone, if not the bicycle inventor, can legally own a bicycle. Once we recognize this, it is hard to know how well patents motivate the creation or publication of knowledge that, otherwise, would not be produced, or publicized. And it is very hard to know how far the legal, economic, and political benefits conferred by patent rights tailor reward to merit, or proportion it to benefits conferred. In short, as Ossorio concedes, the justification for a system of patent rights rests largely on speculation about human motivations, needs and interests.

Finally, there is, a further difficulty with patents, as compared to other ways of rewarding and motivating people, which moral objections to human gene patents highlight, even though they rarely raise them explicitly.[38] If patents look democratic when compared to the granting of titles of nobility, to inheritable personal powers to tax, and so on, they do not look especially democratic when contrasted with tax-breaks, election to public office, or to public honors.[39] If, from a democratic perspective, patenting is attractive because it involves specifying public criteria for rights, and then providing a relatively automatic procedure through which people can determine whether they are entitled to those rights, it also has considerable disadvantages. For the public may have no idea about the significance of the inventions that provide the claim to a patent or about the adequacy of the criteria used to distribute these rights.[40] This casts doubt on the idea that the benefits created by patentable inventions are sufficiently general or public to merit special reward. It also means that very significant changes in people's rights, expectations, and beliefs may occur without ever being publicly acknowledged, discussed or chosen. In a democracy, this should cause some concern.

Legislators can pay attention to the sorts of things are being patented and why.[41] And as Ossorio rightly stresses, patenting does not preclude considerable legislative oversight and regulation of inventions. Moreover, in any system that gives private individuals the power to alter their legal relationship to each other, as will bodies of private law, many changes in people's rights, powers and expectations, for good and bad, are likely to occur without public knowledge, representation, and control. Still, the moral objections to patenting point to the need to think more carefully about the place, content, and justification of a patenting system in a democratic society, and in particular, its implications for democratic forms of accountability, choice, and participation—not just efficiency. For some of the bitterness, mutual distrust, and incomprehension, evidenced by debates on genetic patenting, reflect the lack of open public debate on the issue, and the assumption that ordinary people have little knowledge about, or control over, legal rights, public policies, and scientific developments that may fundamentally affect their lives.[42]

Thus, proponents of patenting suppose that the general public is unlikely to know even quite basic and straightforward facts about patent rights, such as their justification, the sorts of things to which they apply, the way that they differ from other rights. Likewise, critics of patenting, especially in the U.S., clearly suppose that most people do not know that plants, animals and human genes can all be patented. This contrasts with the situation in Europe where efforts by groups like the Greens and Greenpeace to publicize these issues mean that people have been subjected to questionnaires, as well as a great deal of publicity about recent developments in the law and biotechnology. Yet it is evident that in the U.S., too, there is a public interest in, and demand to know more about, recent advances in biotechnology and their legal, scientific, moral, and political implications for people's lives. Thus, one can find articles about genetic testing, and its moral and medical implications in local, as well as national, newspapers; public interest in, and public sources of information on, the science of the genome project, as well as more sensational developments like the cloning of sheep. By contrast, it is rare to find discussions of the ethics or the economics of patenting human genes outside of relatively specialized and obscure journals and book presses.

Of course, given what one might consider to be the disastrous consequences of the politicization of abortion in the U.S., it would be foolish to assume that democratic discussion of patents on human genes—whatever one thinks that might mean or involve—would preclude confusion, mutual suspicion or promote the speedy and principled resolution of complex questions of ethics and public policy. But it would, at least, give people the chance to learn about, and to participate in, decisions that can fundamentally shape their life-prospects and those of future generations, even if it failed to promote other desirable things.

If, as seems likely, the patenting system has made such discussion and decision-making significantly less likely, despite considerable public interest in biotechnology and its consequences, there is reason to incorporate concerns for democracy into one's evaluation of human gene patents. This is partly because concerns about the justification for patents in general can, quite properly, affect our judgment about the merits of any particular patent that a patenting system creates. More fundamentally, though, it is likely that ethical objections to patenting human genes reflect doubts about the democratic credentials of the motivations, procedures, and criteria that have led to this event.

Conclusion

I conclude that Ossorio is right to believe that attention to legal facts and theory can illuminate the ethics of patenting human genes. However, she is wrong to assume that legal facts and theory are as morally conclusive as she thinks, when neither need reflect our considered judgments about morality. Moreover, I have argued that the rights that ownership consists in are hardly self-evident conceptually, morally, or legally. As Ossorio says, this tells against ownership objections to the patenting of human genes, and in favor of the effort to specify, as precisely as possible, what rights, values, powers, and liberties make the patenting of human genes unethical. But, I have argued, this objection tells as much against moral justifications of patenting that turn on sharp distinctions between patenting and owning, as it does against those who elide the two when opposing such patents. If patenting genes is ethical, therefore, we need to know what rights, values, powers, and liberties justify these particular patents, or those legal, scientific, economic, and political practices that have made the patenting of human genes seem natural, justified, and inevitable. We do not yet have the answers to such questions.

Finally, I conclude that our conception of, and commitment to, democracy has a place in resolving ethical debate about human gene patents though, so far, this has been largely ignored. The point is not just that our conceptions of, and faith in, democratic forms of choice, deliberation, and accountability likely influence our perspectives on ethical questions, and so need to be factored into these explicitly. Rather, as long as one wants legally binding resolutions of ethical disputes to be made democratically, it is necessary, and urgent, to decide what this would imply for the procedures through which, and the evidence upon which, ethical disputes about human gene patents are to be settled. Those disputes, I have shown, are not over the meanings of words alone, but over the justification of public policies and legally binding rights, powers and obligations. They require us to consider not only the justification of past practices and institutions, and of present actions and decisions, but of the terms on which, in future, people will have access to the knowledge, powers, and liberties that they need to live and to flourish.

What those terms will be is still largely open to influence, from a variety of quarters, but probably not for long. One of the merits of Ossorio's article is to highlight this fact, by stressing how little is settled, legally, morally, and politically, by treating human genes as legally patentable. However, the difficulties with her distinction between patenting and owning indicate how easily what is possible conceptually becomes practically unthinkable, and what that transformation may cost us in moral and political judgment.

Notes

1. For the main critical positions, see George J. Annas, "Life Forms, the Law and Profits," *The Hastings Center Report,* (Oct. 1998), pp. 21–22; Jeremy Rifkin, *The Biotech Century: Harnessing the Gene and Remaking the World,* (Putnam Books, New York, 1998) ch. 2; and the views of Isabell Meister, Jan Mertens, Steve Emmot and Daniel Alexander in Sigrid Sterckx, ed. *Biotechnology, Patents and Morality,* (Ashgate Publishing Ltd., Aldershot, England). The Sterckx volume is based on the proceedings of the International Workshop on "Biotechnology, Patents and Morality: Towards a Consensus," held in January 1996, by the Department of Philosophy and Moral Science and the Centre for Environmental Philosophy and

Bio-Ethics of the University of Ghent. It consists in a series of relatively short presentations, by legal experts, representatives of various environmental groups, and so on, and also provides a helpful introduction and concluding summary of the proceedings and debate.

2. Pilar Ossorio, "Legal and Ethical Issues in Patenting Human DNA", forthcoming in *A Companion to Genethics: Philosophy and the Genetic Revolution*, eds. Justine Burley and John Harris, (Blackwell's, Oxford, Jan 2002). (ISBN 0631206981). Page numbers to Ossorio's article are to the unpublished manuscript. Ossorio is the Director for the genetics section of the American Medical Association's Institute for Ethics.

3. It is hard to find a published source for this belief, but it occurs frequently enough in oral arguments about patenting to merit attention by Crespi, at p. 225, and for Ossorio to try to dismiss it as a red herring, at p. 6. However, Jeremy Rifkin claims that "genetically altered human embryos and fetuses as well as human genes, cell lines, tissues, and organs are potentially patentable, leaving open the possibility of patenting all of the separate parts, if not the whole, of a human being," Rifkin, supra, pp. 44–45.

4. Such claims seem especially surprising because the morality of an invention is, generally, supposed to have little role in decisions about whether or not the invention deserves a patent under US law. Though, the European Patent Convention's article 53 (a) prohibits patenting inventions, the publication or exploitation of which would be contrary to public order or morality, it turns out that this clause rarely justifies withholding a patent from an invention that otherwise meets legal criteria. Thus, although 320,000 patents have been granted by the EPO since its creation 18 years ago, this clause has never been used successfully to strike down a claim for a patent. Indeed, Ulrich Satz explains, "Poisons, explosives, extremely dangerous chemical substances, devices used in nuclear power stations, agro-chemicals, pesticides and many other things which can threaten human life or damage the environment have been patented, despite the existence of the public order and morality bar" in almost all European countries. See Schatz, pp. 159–160, and his interpretation of ART. 53 (a), at pp. 160–166.

5. See Ossorio, pp. 6–9; and Schatz, p. 169.

6. Ossorio, p. 7. She notes, (footnote 1, p. 18) that molecular cloning should not be confused with the kind of cloning that produces genetically near-identical animals.

7. Ossorio, p. 7.

8. *Diamond v. Chakrabarty*, 447 U.S. 303 (1980).

9. *Parke-Davis and Co. v. H.K. Mulford and Co.*, 189 F. 95, 102 (SDNY 1911), affd. 196 F. 496 (Second Cir. 1912). Quoted In Ossorio, p. 8.

10. Ossorio, pp. 5–6.

11. Hence, at p. 5, Ossorio states that "patents do not grant rights of use or possession, only rights to exclude." However, because people typically have rights to use, possess and exploit patentable inventions, it is common even for legal experts to define patents, as does Gerrtrui Van Overalle, as a "legal title granting its holder the exclusive right to exploit." See p. 139 ed. Stercx.

12. Ossorio, p. 10: "a person who held a human gene patent, and obtained the further right to make, use or sell DNA constructed according to that patent, would be trafficking in copies or representations of the DNA inside of another person's body."

13. Ossorio, p. 4. See also, Michael A. Heller and Rebecca S. Eisenberg, "Can Patents Deter Innovation? The Anticommons in Biomedical Research" in *Science,* 280, (5364), 1998. Available on the web at www.Sciencemag.org. Theirs is a response to an article by John J. Doll, "The Patenting of DNA," in the same issue of *Science,* also available on the web. Doll maintains that "A strong U.S. patent system is critical for the continued development and dissemination to the public of information on DNA sequence elements," and that "It is only with the patenting of DNA technology that some companies, particularly small ones, can raise sufficient venture capital to bring beneficial products to the marketplace or fund further research." These debates have their counterpart in disputes about the necessity or, indeed, the desirability, of patents in computer science and business. See, for instance, "Patently Absurd" by James Gleick, in the *New York Times Magazine,* Sun. March 12, 2000, Section 6, pp. 44–49.

14. For such concerns see Krishna R. Dronamraju, *Biological and Social Issues in Biotechnology Sharing,* (Ashgate Publishing Ltd. Aldershot, 1998), chs. 13 and 15; and "The Consequences of Modern Genetic Engineering: Patents, 'Nomads' and the 'Bio-Industrial Complex" by Ruth McNally and Peter Wheale in *The Social Management of Genetic Engineering,* ed. Wheale, von Schomberg and Glasner, (Ashgate, Aldershot, 1998), ch. 18. For a skeptical view, see Crespi, in ed. Sterckx, pp. 229–235.

15. However, as Seth Shulman notes, p. 7, "Compulsory licensing is anathema to many participants in the U.S. patent system." See Seth Shulman, "Patent Medicine," a special feature of *Technology Review,* 1995, available on the web at www.usis.usemb.se/sft.

16. See Ossorio, p. 15.

17. Ossorio, p. 10: "Making, using or selling the patented DNA would not interfere with the bodily integrity or functioning of the person from whom the patented sequence was derived. The 'ownership argument' against patenting would therefore rest on the claim that it would diminish us if one person can make, use, or sell copies of another's extracorporeal, nonparticularized body parts. Some may want to defend this claim; for me, it does not carry much persuasive force."

18. For example, Jan Mertens, suggests that, for The Greens, patents on human and other life-forms are politically significant because this is something that the Greens believe they can alter, although their ethical objections to patents reflect a broader moral and political critique of the ways that people see and treat both human and non-human nature. See p. 190 in ed. Sterckx.

19. Ossorio makes a similar use of the negative/positive distinction between rights to exclude and rights to use and possess at p. 12, when assessing the claim that patenting is immoral because it commodifies human genes. According to Ossorio, "Although patents may be integral to the process of creating commodities it is the affirmative rights, the actions of manufacturing and selling, which constitute commodification." However, as she

recognizes, at p. 13, the point of a patenting system is, in part, to facilitate the commercial application and development of knowledge, and so patents typically presume that people–if not, necessarily the inventor–will have, or be likely to have, the legal rights of use, possession and so on that, as she sees it, make for commodification.

20. Ossorio, p. 16.

21. Martens, p. 191, where he also notes the pressure placed on India to make its patent laws consistent with those in the U.S. and Europe.

22. Ossorio recognizes this possibility at pp. 15–16 when discussing "common heritage" objections to patenting.

23. See Heller and Eisenberg, supra, on the changing standards of rewards in academia.

24. See Larissa Gruszow in ed. Sterckx, p. 153. Article 52 (4) of the EPC "excludes from patentability therapeutic, diagnostic and surgical methods applied to the human and animal body." Quite what this means in practice, I must say, is unclear, if, as appears to be the case, the EPO initially granted a patent on a DNA fragment able to encode human relaxin, in April 1991, though it subsequently had to review the decision. See Grusow, p. 154. Schatz discusses article 52(4) at p. 167. He claims that "The reason [for the exclusions it defines] is that the patent system is a regulation of competition in industry and trade, whereas the medical art has to abide by medical deontology rather than by the rule of commercial competition. . . ." It is the profession that is exempted from the reign of patent law." At p. 172 R. Schapira expresses some doubts about the efficacy of this clause.

25. Additional uses might include the development of increasingly accurate and simple tests for the purposes of facilitating the identification and prosecution of those who are guilty of various crimes, and as tools for exonerating the innocent.

26. See Philip Kitcher, *The Lives to Come: The Genetic Revolution and Human Possibilities,* (Touchstone, New York, 1996), ch. 6.

27. For example, Isabelle Meister, a spokesperson for Greenpeace, seems troubled by the patenting of human genes and, indeed, those of life—forms more generally, because, she claims, this inappropriately confuses living things with industrial products.

28. Compare Ossorio, pp. 10–11: "Human-dignity arguments against patenting human DNA occasionally refer to the notion that our DNA is unique and uniquely involved in our identities. However, it is difficult to formulate a credible argument based on that premise . . . If we excluded from patentability only that part of the human genome which is unique to human beings, then only a tiny fraction would be unpatentable. If we excluded from patentability only gene sequences that were unique to a particular person, than any human gene or DNA would probably be patentable." See also Tom Wilkie, "Lords of Creation," in *Prospect,* no. 32, July 1998. Ossorio's interpretation of human dignity arguments tends to suppose that the threat to identity presented by human gene patenting must be a threat to personal identity, rather than to our collective identity as humans. This highly individualistic interpretation of our personal identity and dignity then leads her to conclude that while a concern to protect

personal identity tells against patenting the whole genome of a person, it does not ground a compelling objection to patenting in general. The key assumption here seems to be that only what differentiates us from others marks, and could therefore threaten, our personal identity. But if, as seems plausible, our personal identity includes ways in which we are similar, as well as different, from others (hence its' precise content can be affected, quite dramatically, by changes in our circumstances and those with whom we compare), it is at least as possible that our personal identity is threatened by patenting genes that we share with other humans (or even with animals), as by the patenting of genes that are unique to us. For some empirical evidence on how this might happen, see Philip Kitcher, pp. 130–131 and Eric T. Juengst's "Groups as Gatekeepers to Genomic Research: Conceptually Confusing, Morally Hazardous, and Practically Useless" in *Kennedy Institute of Ethics Journal,* 8.2. (1998). (Available through the Internet). It should be noted that Juengst's argument is against turning groups into gatekeepers with powers currently ascribed to individuals to enable or prohibit research via their consent. It presupposes that groups can be seriously harmed by genomic research, even research to which some group member consisted. What is strange is that Ossorio seems to concede the possibility of such harms at p. 15, when discussing common heritage arguments, although these have no place in her interpretation and assessment of either ownership or dignitarian objections to gene patenting.

29. Tom Wilkie, "The Lords of Creation," supra, p. 12.

30. An editor of this journal notes that there are important differences between a human infant and a human adult; as there are amongst different adults and different infants. Indeed, adult mammals of other species, such as apes, are more similar to adult humans in their abilities to think than are infants, and a full-grown horse or dog, so Bentham assures us, "is beyond comparison a more rational, as well as a more conversable animal, than an infant of a day, or a week, or even a month, old." However, the fact that human attributes, such as the capacity for self-reflection, do not develop all at once, nor to the same degree in everyone, is no reason to deny that they are morally significant. Nor, from the fact that the development of such attributes or skills depends on nurture, as well as nature, does it make sense to ignore the significance of the latter. Still, I would like to emphasise that I do not think that morally significant capacities are the sole prerogative of humans, even though I differ from Bentham in supposing that the morally significant capacities of humans are not limited to the capacity to feel pleasure and pain. For Bentham's views see the wonderful footnote 1, of his *Introduction to the Principles of Morals and Legislation,* ch. xvii, "of the limits of the penal branch of jurisprudence," pp. 310–11.

31. Mertens, p. 190 in ed. Sterckx implies that this is, indeed, the case for the Greens; and Meister implies that it is also true for Greenpeace. See ed. Sterckx, p. 185 Hence I do not see the clear differences that Ossorio appears to see amongst Ownership, Human Dignity and Commodification objections to human gene patenting, even though it can be helpful to distinguish amongst them.

32. See Ossorio, p. 3 "An underlying assumption of the patent system is that other, non-market incentives will not lead to as good or as much development of new and useful knowledge and products" and "The assumption

is that without patents the biotechnology industry could not compete effectively for private capital against other industries, such as the computer industry." Neither of these assumptions, of course, is self-evidently correct. Moreover, as Ossorio notes at p. 2 while "patent law can be described as serving a positivist, functionalist strategy: we choose the rule governing patentability to accomplish the goal of getting new and useful knowledge disseminated, and the rules are justified according to whether or not they accomplish this goal," her conclusion is that "In practice, this is an empirical determination which is quite difficult to make with any confidence."

33. Ossorio, p. 2.

34. Hence, David Resnik is wrong to suppose that a purely utilitarian justification of patents is possible, even if we suppose that such a utilitarian justification would operate against a background of moral and legal rights precluding such things as theft, forced labour, and so on. See David B. Resnik, "The Morality of Human Gene Patents" in *Kennedy Institute of Ethics Journal*, 7.1., (1997), p. 4 online version.

35. Re. Effort, see Ossorio, p. 2, and Resnik p. 4: "the law seems to reward results, not contributions and efforts."

36. See Ossorio, p. 4, concerning what may be a substantial difference between the socially optimal rate of invention and the maximal rate of invention.

37. Ossorio, pp. 5–6.

38. Some exceptions are Jan Mertens, pp. 189–90, Van Overwalle, p. 147, and Steve Emmott, pp. 192 and 194 in ed. Sterckx.

39. Grants are, here, understood as an alternative to patents, not as an addition to them. Hence, they do not raise the concerns about "doubledipping" usefully described by Ossorio, at p. 3.

40. See Seth Shulman, "Patent Medicine," supra. At p. 2 Shulman notes of the USPTO that "despite its size, age and pedigree, the agency must surely rank as one of the least-known agencies of the U.S. government." P. 2 also expresses common doubts about the ability of the USPTO to interpret its criteria for awarding patents, and gives the example of the patenting of Kirchoff's law, first expounded in 1845.

41. Resnik notes, at p. 1, that "In 1996 the US Congress considered a measure, the Ganske-Wyden Bill (9Hr1137) that would have prevented the PTO from awarding patents that do not involve a new machine or compound." This, so it seems, would have met some of the concerns about patents raised by Gleick in "Patently Absurd." However, this would have no obvious effect on what, so it seems, is the "capture" of the PTO by companies pursuing patents, on whom the Office frequently depends both for expertise and for revenues. Gleick notes at p. 41, "In 1991, the patent office was cut off from general tax revenues and required to subsist entirely on fees from its operating budget. The political argument was that customers should pay for government services. Thus, officials think of their fee-paying applicants as their customers: *the more the better*," (emphasis in the text). Gleick says, "It is virtually forgotten that government's customers also include the rest of the nation, the citizenry at large, whose fortunes depend on the agency's judgments and policies."

42. See Martens' complaint at pp. 198–90 in ed. Stercx.

POSTSCRIPT

Should Patenting Genes Be Understood as Unethical?

Is the patenting of genes in the best interest of health and patients? Lever explains that human genes can only pass the threshold test that marks them as legally patentable if they have been altered sufficiently to be legally distinguishable from naturally occurring genes, which cannot be patented. So, the genes in one's body can't be patented. However, manipulated genes can. Some scientists believe the gene patent system is able to exploit and utilize business models and economic self-interest. They question whether this science should be principally for generating profits rather than advancing science. For many, true science should be pursued with the goal of finding cures for diseases that will save lives. For ethicists such as Schulman, human genes are not commodities. If we can sell the very building blocks of what makes us human, it makes us wonder if a human is only the sum of his or her genes. Other ethicists agree with Schulman in maintaining that human dignity should not be reduced to a piece of code.

Suggested Readings

Beth E. Arnold and Ogeilska-Zei Eva, "Patenting Genes and Genetic Research Tools: Good or Bad for Innovation?" *Annual Review of Genomics & Human Genetics* (vol. 3, no. 1, 2002), p. 415.

Sam Kean, "The Human Genome (Patent) Project," *Science* (vol. 33, no. 6017, 2011), pp. 530–531.

David Koepsell, *Who Owns You: The Corporate Gold Rush to Patent Your Genes* (Malden: Wiley-Blackwell, 2009).

Dorothy Nelkin, "Patenting Genes and the Public Interest," *American Journal of Bioethics* (vol. 2, no. 3, 2002), pp. 13–15.

ISSUE 20

Should the World Continue to Rely on Oil as a Major Source of Energy?

YES: **Red Cavaney**, from "Global Oil Production about to Peak? A Recurring Myth," *World Watch* (January–February 2006)

NO: **James Howard Kunstler**, from *The Long Emergency* (Grove/Atlantic, 2005)

ISSUE SUMMARY

YES: Red Cavaney, president and chief executive officer of the American Petroleum Institute, argues that recent revolutionary advances in technology will yield sufficient quantities of available oil for the foreseeable future.

NO: James Howard Kunstler contends that the peak of oil production, Hubbert's Peak, was itself the important turning point in our species' relationship to petroleum. Unless strong conservation measures are put in place, the new scarcity will destroy much that we have come to expect in our lives.

W e might begin with the fact that the idea of an "oil crisis" has become part of our lives in the last half century. Suddenly gasoline prices are higher, there are lines at the gas stations, political commentators suddenly discover international affairs, and a mood of panic pervades the country. Resolutions are made, actions begun, but then the whole crisis seems to peter out. What's happening?

First, is oil "running out"? Since the 1930s, energy prognosticators have used a model called Hubbert's Curve (named for geologist M. King Hubbert, who first projected it) that predicted the end of oil as an available resource. As oil recovery technology has progressed, the curve has been lengthened; Red Cavaney's selection relies heavily on this fact. But the curve is still there, and even a major contraction in the oil supply will have a very significant effect on the way America continues to grow and develop; James Kunstler calls our attention to some of the changes we may expect.

There are two major dimensions to the "oil crisis," both of which affect the business community. The first is a management dilemma, stemming from the interaction of the U.S. economy and a global monopoly: how to control the impact of the decisions of international business consortia in the energy business. Business is all about supply and demand (see the selection by Adam Smith in Issue 1). In the case of petroleum, the lion's share of the supply is controlled by energy consortia that as Smith would approve, consider their own economic interests first, with the result that they rarely have the interests of the people of the United States as a priority. The logic of economic success for the industry, as all oil producers know, requires that the producers reduce the supply available for purchase, causing the price to rise, for an interval of time that will be limited by the customer's perception that he is spending too much for oil, and has recourse to other methods of obtaining energy—for instance, by developing solar energy as a source of power or placing restrictions on the amount of gasoline that automobiles sold in the United States can consume in a mile. At that point, production is raised dramatically, oil prices drop precipitously, and as a result, all investments in alternatives to oil consumption are abandoned. After that point, enough time is allowed to elapse so that investments will have been liquidated and the alternative workforce scattered; then the squeeze begins again. American consumers, on this understanding, are at the mercy of a foreign monopoly in complete control of the price of gasoline and heating oil, and would be well advised to use the periods of inexpensive oil to assemble the capital needed to solve the energy problem once and for all. That gathering of capital can only be done by heavy taxation of oil alone, or of all carbon, sufficient to keep the price of oil level for the consumer while the capital accumulates. The American public dislikes taxes in general, and the oil industry dislikes oil taxes even more.

The second dimension is an industry crisis caused by an environmental threat: how to adjust our automotive industry, traditionally the heart and pride of our manufacturing capacity, to minimize the damage done to the environment by the burning of all fossil fuels, especially the burning of gasoline in the use of automobiles and trucks for transportation. Our automotive industry is set up like all the others—to provide a healthy return to the shareholders by producing products that the consumers want and will buy and that yield a high profit margin. That requirement does not well describe small, fuel-efficient cars, but it does describe the large, low-fuel-mileage sport utility vehicles (SUVs) introduced in the 1990s and now flooding our highways. As the American public contemplates images of polar bears stranded on vanishing ice, hurricanes in the Caribbean, and expanding deserts in Africa, it becomes increasingly likely that each new administration will insist on conservation measures, starting with the all-too-visible SUVs. How should the automotive industry—and the advertisers, the oil companies, and the consumers—respond?

Bear in mind, as you read these selections, that global business will suffer major disruptions in any initiative to end oil dependence; what advantages might make the sacrifices worth their cost?

YES

Red Cavaney

Global Oil Production about to Peak? A Recurring Myth

Once again, we are hearing that world oil production is "peaking," and that we will face a steadily diminishing oil supply to fuel the global economy. These concerns have been expressed periodically over the years, but have always been at odds with energy and economic realities. Such is the case today.

Let's look at some history: In 1874, the chief geologist of Pennsylvania predicted we would run out of oil in four years—just using it for kerosene. Thirty years ago, groups such as the Club of Rome predicted an end of oil long before the current day. These forecasts were wrong because, nearly every year, we have found more oil than we have used, and oil reserves have continued to grow.

The world consumes approximately 80 million barrels of oil a day. By 2030, world oil demand is estimated to grow about 50 percent, to 121 million barrels a day, even allowing for significant improvements in energy efficiency. The International Energy Agency says there are sufficient oil resources to meet demand for at least the next 30 years.

The key factor here is technology. Revolutionary advances in technology in recent years have dramatically increased the ability of companies to find and extract oil—and, of particular importance, recover more oil from existing reservoirs. Rather than production peaking, existing fields are yielding markedly more oil than in the past. Advances in technology include the following:

Directional Drilling.   It used to be that wellbores were basically vertical holes. This made it necessary to drill virtually on top of a potential oil deposit. However, the advent of miniaturized computers and advanced sensors that can be attached to the drill bit now allows companies to drill directional holes with great accuracy because they can get real-time information on the subsurface location throughout the drilling process.

Horizontal Drilling.   Horizontal drilling is similar to directional drilling, but the well is designed to cut horizontally through the middle of the oil or natural gas deposit. Early horizontal wells penetrated only 500 to 800 feet of reservoir laterally, but technology advances recently allowed a North Slope operator to

From *World Watch*, January/February 2006, pp. 13–15. Copyright © 2006 by Worldwatch Institute. Reprinted by permission. www.worldwatch.org

penetrate 8,000 feet of reservoir horizontally. Moreover, horizontal wells can operate up to 10 times more productively than conventional wells.

3-D Seismic Technology. Substantial enhancements in computing power during the past two decades have allowed the industry to gain a much clearer picture of what lies beneath the surface. The ability to process huge amounts of data to produce three-dimensional seismic images has significantly improved the drilling success rate of the industry.

Primarily due to these advances, the U.S. Geological Survey (USGS), in its 2000 *World Petroleum Assessment,* increased by 20 percent its estimate of undiscovered, technically recoverable oil. USGS noted that, since oil became a major energy source about 100 years ago, 539 billion barrels of oil have been produced outside the United States. USGS estimates there are 649 billion barrels of undiscovered, technically recoverable oil outside the United States. But, importantly, USGS also estimates that there will be an *additional* 612 billion barrels from "reserve growth"—nearly equaling the undiscovered resources. Reserve growth results from a variety of sources, including technological advancement in exploration and production, increases over initially conservative estimates of reserves, and economic changes.

The USGS estimates reflected several factors:

- As drilling and production within discovered fields progresses, new pools or reservoirs are found that were not previously known.
- Advances in exploration technology make it possible to identify new targets within existing fields.
- Advances in drilling technology make it possible to recover oil and gas not previously considered recoverable in the initial reserve estimates.
- Enhanced oil recovery techniques increase the recovery factor for oil and thereby increase the reserves within existing fields.

Here in the United States, rather than "running out of oil," potentially vast oil and natural gas reserves remain to be developed. According to the latest published government estimates, there are more than 131 billion barrels of oil and more than 1,000 trillion cubic feet of natural gas remaining to be discovered in the United States. However, 78 percent of this oil and 62 percent of this gas are expected to be found beneath federal lands—much of which are non-park and non-wilderness lands—and coastal waters. While there is plenty of oil in the ground, oil companies need to be allowed to make major investments to find and produce it.

The U.S. Energy Information Administration has projected that fossil fuels will continue to dominate U.S. energy consumption, with oil and natural gas providing almost two-thirds of that consumption in the year 2025, even though energy efficiency and renewables will grow faster than their historical rates. However, renewables in particular start from a very small base; and the major shares provided by oil, natural gas, and coal in 2025 are projected to be nearly identical to those in 2003.

Those who block oil and natural gas development here in the United States and elsewhere only make it much more difficult to meet the demand for oil, natural gas, and petroleum products. Indeed, it is not surprising that some of the end-of-oil advocates are the same people who oppose oil and natural gas development everywhere.

Failure to develop the potentially vast oil and natural gas resources that remain in the world will have a high economic cost. We must recognize that we live in a global economy, and that there is a strong link between energy and economic growth. If we are to continue to grow economically, here in the United States, in Europe, and the developing world, we must be cost-competitive in our use of energy. We need *all* sources of energy. We do not have the luxury of limiting ourselves to one source to the exclusion of others. Nor can we afford to write off our leading source of energy before we have found cost-competitive and readily available alternatives.

Consider how oil enhances our quality of life—fueling growth and jobs in industry and commerce, cooling and warming our homes, and getting us where we need to go. Here in the United States, oil provides about 97 percent of transportation fuels, which power nearly all of the cars and trucks traveling on our nation's highways. And plastics, medicines, fertilizers, and countless other products that extend and enhance our quality of life are derived from oil.

In considering our future energy needs, we also need to understand that gasoline-powered automobiles have been the dominant mode of transport for the past century—and the overwhelming preference of hundreds of millions of people throughout the world. Regardless of fuel, the automobile—likely to be configured far differently from today—will remain the consumer's choice for personal transport for decades to come. The freedom of mobility and the independence it affords consumers is highly valued.

The United States—and the world—cannot afford to leave the Age of Oil before realistic substitutes are fully in place. It is important to remember that man left the Stone Age not because he ran out of stones—and we will not leave the Age of Oil because we will run out. Yes, someday oil will be replaced, but clearly not until substitutes are found—substitutes that are proven more reliable, more versatile, and more cost-competitive than oil. We can rely on the energy marketplace to determine what the most efficient substitutes will be.

As we plan for our energy future, we also cannot afford to ignore the lessons of recent history. In the early 1970s, many energy policymakers were sure that oil and natural gas would soon be exhausted, and government policy was explicitly aimed at "guiding" the market in a smooth transition away from these fuels to new, more sustainable alternatives. Price controls, allocation schemes, limitations on natural gas, massive subsidies to synthetic fuels, and other measures were funded heavily and implemented.

Unfortunately, the key premises on which these programs were based, namely that oil was nearing exhaustion and that government guidance was desirable to safely transition to new energy sources, are now recognized as having been clearly wrong—and to have resulted in enormously expensive mistakes.

Looking into the distant future, there will be a day when oil is no longer the world's dominant energy source. We can only speculate as to when and how that day will come about. For example, there is an even bigger hydrocarbon resource that can be developed to provide nearly endless amounts of energy: methane hydrates (methane frozen in ice crystals). The deposits of methane hydrates are so vast that when we develop the technology to bring them to market, we will have clean-burning energy for 2,000 years. It's just one of the exciting scenarios we may see in the far-off future. But we won't be getting there anytime soon, and until we do, the Age of Oil will continue.

James Howard Kunstler  **NO**

The Long Emergency

A few weeks ago, the price of oil ratcheted above fifty-five dollars a barrel, which is about twenty dollars a barrel more than a year ago. The next day, the oil story was buried on page six of the *New York Times* business section. Apparently, the price of oil is not considered significant news, even when it goes up five bucks a barrel in the span of ten days. That same day, the stock market shot up more than a hundred points because, CNN said, government data showed no signs of inflation. Note to clueless nation: Call planet Earth.

Carl Jung, one of the fathers of psychology, famously remarked that "people cannot stand too much reality." What you're about to read may challenge your assumptions about the kind of world we live in, and especially the kind of world into which events are propelling us. We are in for a rough ride through uncharted territory.

It has been very hard for Americans—lost in dark raptures of nonstop infotainment, recreational shopping and compulsive motoring—to make sense of the gathering forces that will fundamentally alter the terms of everyday life in our technological society. Even after the terrorist attacks of 9/11, America is still sleepwalking into the future. I call this coming time the Long Emergency.

Most immediately we face the end of the cheap-fossil-fuel era. It is no exaggeration to state that reliable supplies of cheap oil and natural gas underlie everything we identify as the necessities of modern life—not to mention all of its comforts and luxuries: central heating, air conditioning, cars, airplanes, electric lights, inexpensive clothing, recorded music, movies, hip-replacement surgery, national defense—you name it.

The few Americans who are even aware that there is a gathering global-energy predicament usually misunderstand the core of the argument. That argument states that we don't have to run out of oil to start having severe problems with industrial civilization and its dependent systems. We only have to slip over the all-time production peak and begin a slide down the arc of steady depletion.

The term "global oil-production peak" means that a turning point will come when the world produces the most oil it will ever produce in a given year and, after that, yearly production will inexorably decline. It is usually represented graphically in a bell curve. The peak is the top of the curve, the halfway point of the world's all-time total endowment, meaning half the world's oil will be left. That seems like a lot of oil, and it is, but there's a big catch: It's the half that is much more difficult to extract, far more costly to get, of much poorer quality and located mostly in places where the people hate us. A substantial amount of it will never be extracted.

The United States passed its own oil peak—about 11 million barrels a day—in 1970, and since then production has dropped steadily. In 2004 it ran just above 5 million barrels a day (we get a tad more from natural-gas condensates). Yet we consume roughly 20 million barrels a day now. That means we have to import about two-thirds of our oil, and the ratio will continue to worsen.

The U.S. peak in 1970 brought on a portentous change in geoeconomic power. Within a few years, foreign producers, chiefly OPEC, were setting the price of oil, and this in turn led to the oil crises of the 1970s. In response, frantic development of non-OPEC oil, especially the North Sea fields of England and Norway, essentially saved the West's ass for about two decades. Since 1999, these fields have entered depletion. Meanwhile, worldwide discovery of new oil has steadily declined to insignificant levels in 2003 and 2004.

Some "cornucopians" claim that the Earth has something like a creamy nougat center of "abiotic" oil that will naturally replenish the great oil fields of the world. The facts speak differently. There has been no replacement whatsoever of oil already extracted from the fields of America or any other place.

Now we are faced with the global oil-production peak. The best estimates of when this will actually happen have been somewhere between now and 2010. In 2004, however, after demand from burgeoning China and India shot up, and revelations that Shell Oil wildly misstated its reserves, and Saudi Arabia proved incapable of goosing up its production despite promises to do so, the most knowledgeable experts revised their predictions and now concur that 2005 is apt to be the year of all-time global peak production.

It will change everything about how we live.

To aggravate matters, American natural-gas production is also declining, at five percent a year, despite frenetic new drilling, and with the potential of much steeper declines ahead. Because of the oil crises of the 1970s, the nuclear plant disasters at Three Mile Island and Chernobyl and the acid-rain problem, the U.S. chose to make gas its first choice for electric-power generation. The result was that just about every power plant built after 1980 has to run on gas. Half the homes in America are heated with gas. To further complicate matters, gas isn't easy to import. Here in North America, it is distributed through a vast pipeline network. Gas imported from overseas would have to be compressed at minus-260 degrees Fahrenheit in pressurized tanker ships and unloaded (re-gasified) at special terminals, of which few exist in America. Moreover, the first attempts to site new terminals have met furious opposition because they are such ripe targets for terrorism.

Some other things about the global energy predicament are poorly understood by the public and even our leaders. This is going to be a permanent energy crisis, and these energy problems will synergize with the disruptions of climate change, epidemic disease and population overshoot to produce higher orders of trouble.

We will have to accommodate ourselves to fundamentally changed conditions.

No combination of alternative fuels will allow us to run American life the way we have been used to running it, or even a substantial fraction of it. The wonders of steady technological progress achieved through the reign of cheap oil have lulled us into a kind of Jiminy Cricket syndrome, leading many Americans to believe that anything we wish for hard enough will come true. These days, even people who ought to know better are wishing ardently for a seamless transition from fossil fuels to their putative replacements.

The widely touted "hydrogen economy" is a particularly cruel hoax. We are not going to replace the U.S. automobile and truck fleet with vehicles run on fuel cells. For one thing, the current generation of fuel cells is largely designed to run on hydrogen obtained from natural gas. The other way to get hydrogen in the quantities wished for would be electrolysis of water using power from hundreds of nuclear plants. Apart from the dim prospect of our building that many nuclear plants soon enough, there are also numerous severe problems with hydrogen's nature as an element that present forbidding obstacles to its use as a replacement for oil and gas, especially in storage and transport.

Wishful notions about rescuing our way of life with "renewables" are also unrealistic. Solar-electric systems and wind turbines face not only the enormous problem of scale but the fact that the components require substantial amounts of energy to manufacture and the probability that they can't be manufactured at all without the underlying support platform of a fossil-fuel economy. We will surely use solar and wind technology to generate some electricity for a period ahead but probably at a very local and small scale.

Virtually all "biomass" schemes for using plants to create liquid fuels cannot be scaled up to even a fraction of the level at which things are currently run. What's more, these schemes are predicated on using oil and gas "inputs" (fertilizers, weed-killers) to grow the biomass crops that would be converted into ethanol or bio-diesel fuels. This is a net energy loser—you might as well just burn the inputs and not bother with the biomass products. Proposals to distill trash and waste into oil by means of thermal depolymerization depend on the huge waste stream produced by a cheap oil and gas economy in the first place.

Coal is far less versatile than oil and gas, extant in less abundant supplies than many people assume and fraught with huge ecological drawbacks—as a contributor to greenhouse "global warming" gases and many health and toxicity issues ranging from widespread mercury poisoning to acid rain. You can make synthetic oil from coal, but the only time this was tried on a large scale was by the Nazis under wartime conditions, using impressive amounts of slave labor.

If we wish to keep the lights on in America after 2020, we may indeed have to resort to nuclear power, with all its practical problems and eco-conundrums. Under optimal conditions, it could take ten years to get a new generation of nuclear power plants into operation, and the price may be beyond our means. Uranium is also a resource in finite supply. We are no closer to the more difficult project of atomic fusion, by the way, than we were in the 1970s.

The Long Emergency is going to be a tremendous trauma for the human race. We will not believe that this is happening to us, that 200 years of modernity can be brought to its knees by a world-wide power shortage. The survivors will have to cultivate a religion of hope—that is, a deep and comprehensive belief that humanity is worth carrying on. If there is any positive side to stark changes coming our way, it may be in the benefits of close communal relations, of having to really work intimately (and physically) with our neighbors, to be part of an enterprise that really matters and to be fully engaged in meaningful social enactments instead of being merely entertained to avoid boredom. Years from now, when we hear singing at all, we will hear ourselves, and we will sing with our whole hearts.

POSTSCRIPT

Should the World Continue to Rely on Oil as a Major Source of Energy?

"Twixt the optimist and the pessimist, the difference is droll: the optimist sees the donut, and the pessimist sees the hole" (Anonymous). The selections you have just finished represent the optimistic and the pessimistic sides of the "oil reserves conflict" as we know it. There is more to this subject. We might ask the optimist if the availability of oil is really the heart of this question. Burning fossil fuels hurts the earth; should we cut back on our consumption of oil just to save the earth, now, even if oil supplies are abundant? But there is a question for the pessimist, too: Granted that our "lifestyles" this minute require lots of oil, does our happiness depend on it, too? What would it be like to live in a way that consumes lots less oil because it consumes lots less of any kind of energy? Outside of the field of business ethics (and sometimes inside it, too) explorations into the notions of "simplicity" and "the simple life" continue. The less consumption-oriented life suggested in these explorations does not seem to be significantly lower in quality than our own—in many ways, it seems better. Should some ambitious entrepreneurs be looking into these possibilities, as the wave of America's economic future? Think about it.

Suggested Reading

Hawken, Paul, Amory B. Lovins, and L. Hunter Lovins, *Natural Capitalism: Creating the Next Industrial Revolution* (New York: Little, Brown, 1999).

Newton, Lisa, *Ethics and Sustainability* (New York, NY: Prentice Hall, 2002).

Newton, Lisa, *Business Ethics and the Natural Environment* (Hoboken, NJ: Wiley, John and Sons, Incorporated, 2005).

Newton, Lisa, *Business Ethics and the Natural Environment* (Blackwood, NY: Blackwell Publishers, 2005).

Contributors to This Volume

EDITORS

ELAINE E. ENGLEHARDT is a distinguished professor of ethics and professor of philosophy at Utah Valley University (UVU). She has taught ethics, philosophy, and communication classes at UVU for the past 30 years. For the past 20 years, she has written and directed seven multiyear, national grants. Four large grants are in ethics across the curriculum from the Department of Education; and three are from the National Endowment for the Humanities. She is the author of five books and the coeditor of *Teaching Ethics*. She has also written numerous articles. She received her Ph.D. from the University of Utah.

LISA H. NEWTON is a professor of philosophy at Fairfield University. She joined the faculty in 1969 and teaches courses in ethics, applied ethics, environmental studies, health care ethics, and several other areas. She is the director of the Applied Ethics Center at Fairfield University. She is also the director of the program in environmental studies at Fairfield University. Dr. Newton received her Ph.D. in Philosophy from Columbia University in New York City. She is currently on the Executive Committee of the Association for Professional and Practical Ethics. She is the author of 15 books and articles. She received her Ph.D. from Columbia University.

MICHAEL S. PRITCHARD is Willard A. Brown professor of philosophy and codirector of the Center for the Study of Ethics in Society at Western Michigan University. He is coeditor of *Teaching Ethics*, the official journal of the Society for Ethics Across the Curriculum. He also serves on the Executive Committee of the Association for Practical and Professional Ethics. His areas of teaching include: ethical theory; practical ethics; ethics in engineering; and philosophy for children. He is the author of 10 books and numerous articles. He received his Ph.D. from the University of Wisconsin.

AUTHORS

DENIS G. ARNOLD received his Ph.D. in philosophy from the University of Minnesota in 1997 and is a past fellow of the National Endowment for the Humanities. His work in ethics and business ethics has appeared in *History of Philosophy Quarterly, American Philosophical Quarterly*, and other publications. Arnold is coeditor of *Rising above Sweatshops: Innovative Management Approaches to Global Labor Challenges* (New York: Praeger, 2004). He teaches philosophy and chairs the legal studies program at Pacific Lutheran University. His current research focuses on the ethical dimensions of global capitalism.

PATRICK BASHAM is currently an adjunct scholar with Cato's Center for Representative Government and the founding director of Washington think-tank, the Democracy Institute. His articles, spanning a wide range of topics, can be found in newspapers such as *The New York Times* and *The Washington Post*. Basham has also provided commentary on multiple television programs.

THOMAS A. BASS is the author of *The Eudaemonic Pie, Camping with the Prince, Reinventing the Future, Vietnamerica, The Predictors*, and *Spy Who Loved Us*. He has been cited by the Overseas Press Club for his foreign reporting. He is a frequent contributor to *The New Yorker, Wired, The New York Times*, and other publications. He is a professor of English and journalism at the State University of New York at Albany.

PHILIP L. BEREANO is a professor in the College of Engineering, Department of Technical Communication, University of Washington, Seattle. For over 30 years he has worked on issues regarding technologies and public policies and is widely published in these areas. He chairs the national Committee on Databases and Civil Liberties of the American Civil Liberties Union, and is a cofounder of the Council for Responsible Genetics. He participated in the development of the UN Cartagena Biosafety protocol. He is active in the American Civil Liberties Union, the Council for Responsible Genetics, and the Washington Biotechnology Action Council.

LLOYD C. BLANKFEIN has served as chairman of the board and CEO of Goldman Sachs Group, Inc. since June 2006. Having been with Goldman Sachs since 1994, previous to his appointment as CEO, Blankfein served as the company's president and COO, vice-chairman, co-president of the FICC Division, and co-president of Commodities Division.

JOHN C. BOGLE is the founder of the mutual fund organization, The Vanguard Group, Inc. and President of Vanguard's Bogle Financial Markets Research Center. Besides his work with Vanguard, Bogle is a best-selling author; his books include *Bogle on Mutual Funds: New Perspectives for the Intelligent Investor* (1993), *Common Sense on Mutual Funds: New Imperatives for the Intelligent Investor* (1999), *John Bogle on Investing: The First 50 Years* (2000), *Character Counts: The Creation and Building of the Vanguard Group* (2002), and *Battle for the Soul of Capitalism* (2005). He also serves as Chairman of the Board for the National Constitution Center and is active as a member in multiple other groups, such as The Conference Board's Commission on Public Trust and Private Enterprise, the American Philosophical Society, and the American Academy of Arts and Sciences.

SISSELA BOK is the author of several books and journal articles on ethics including *Lying: Moral Choice in Public and Private Life*; *Secrets: on the Ethics of Concealment and Revelation*; *A Strategy for Peace: Human Values and the Threat of War*; *Alva Myrdal: A Daughter's Memoir*; *Common Values*; and *Mayhem: Violence as Public Entertainment*. She received her B.A. and M.A. in psychology from George Washington University in 1957 and 1958, and her Ph.D. in philosophy from Harvard University in 1970. Formerly a professor of philosophy at Brandeis University, she is currently a senior visiting fellow at the Harvard Center for Population and Development Studies, Harvard School of Public Health.

NORMAN E. BOWIE was the Elmer L. Andersen Chair in Corporate Responsibility at the University of Minnesota, where he held a joint appointment in the departments of Philosophy and Strategic Management and Organization. He is a frequent contributor to scholarly journals in business ethics. His most recently edited book is *The Blackwell Guide to Business Ethics*. His coedited text *Ethical Theory and Business* is in its sixth edition. He has held a position as Dixon's Professor of Business Ethics and Social Responsibility at the London Business School and has been a fellow at Harvard's Program in Ethics and the Professions.

RED CAVANEY has served as president and chief executive officer of the American Petroleum Institute. He was president, chief executive officer and a director of the American Plastics Council from 1994 to 1997, immediately following service as president of the American Forest & Paper Association and president of its predecessor, the American Paper Institute. He is a past chairman of the American Society of Association Executives and the current chairman of the American Council on Capital Formation.

STEPHANIE CLIFFORD received her degree from Harvard University and has been working for *The New York Times* business desk, covering the retail industry, since 2008.

BARRY EICHENGREEN is currently a George C. Pardee and Helen N. Pardee Professor of Economics and Professor of Political Science at the University of California, Berkley and also holds multiple research fellowships. He received his M.A. in history and M.A. in economics, as well as an M.Phil. and Ph.D. in economics, all from Yale University. Recent work includes his book, *Exorbitant Privilege: The Rise and Fall of the Dollar and the Future of the International Monetary System* (2011), as well as multiple articles for such publications as the *Oxford Review of Economic Policy* and *The National Interest*. In addition to his work in academics, he served as the senior advisor for the International Monetary Fund from 1997 to 1998.

BRIAN ELZWEIG is an assistant professor of business law at Texas A&M—Corpus Christy. Elzweig received his J.D. from California Western School of Law and his LL.M. from the Georgetown University Law Center.

FRIEDRICH ENGELS (1820–1895), a German socialist, was the closest collaborator of Karl Marx in the foundation of modern communism. The official Marxism of the Soviet Union relied heavily on Engels's contribution to Marxist theory. After the death of Marx in 1883, Engels served as the foremost authority on Marx and Marxism, and he edited volumes 2 and 3 of *Das Kapital* on the basis of Marx's incomplete manuscripts and notes. Two major works by Engels are *Anti-Duhring* and *The Dialectics of Nature*.

FRED ENGLANDER is a professor of economics in the Economics and Finance Department at Farleigh Dickinson University at the Silberman College of Business. He holds M.A. and Ph.D. degrees from Rutgers University. His research includes, "the role of government in the economy, and "ethical dimensions of public policy issues."

RICHARD A. EPSTEIN is a James Parker Hall Professor of Law at the University of Chicago. He served as editor of the *Journal of Legal Studies* from 1981 to 1991, and of the *Journal of Law and Economics* from 1991 to 2001. At present he is a director of the John M. Olin Program in Law and Economics. His books include: *Antitrust Decrees in Theory and Practice: Why Less Is More* (2007); *Overdose: How Excessive Government Regulation Stifles Pharmaceutical Innovation* (2006); *How Progressives Rewrote the Constitution* (2006); *Cases and Materials on Torts* (Aspen Law & Business, 8th ed. 2004); *Skepticism and Freedom: A Modern Case for Classical Liberalism* (2003); *Torts* (1999); *Principles for a Free Society: Reconciling Individual Liberty with the Common Good* (1998); *Mortal Peril: Our Inalienable Rights to Health Care* (1997); *Simple Rules for a Complex World* (1995); *Bargaining with the State* (1993); *Forbidden Grounds: The Case against Employment Discrimination Laws* (1992); *Takings: Private Property and the Power of Eminent Domain* (1985); and *Modern Products Liability Law* (1980). He has written numerous articles on a wide range of legal and interdisciplinary subjects.

MILTON FRIEDMAN, a U.S. laissez-faire economist, emeritus professor at the University of Chicago, and senior research fellow at Hoover Institution, was one of the leading modern exponents of Liberalism in the nineteenth century European sense. He was the author of *Capitalism and Freedom* and coauthor of *A Monetary History of the United States* and *Free to Choose*. He was awarded the Nobel Prize for Economics in 1976.

GILBERT HARMAN is a Stuart Professor of Philosophy at Princeton University. He regularly co-teaches interdisciplinary courses in "The Philosophy and Psychology of Rationality" and "The Psychology and Philosophy of Ethics." He has been codirector of the Princeton University Cognitive Science Laboratory and is chair of the Faculty Committee for Cognitive Studies. He is author of *Explaining Value and Other Essays in Moral Philosophy* and *Reasoning, Meaning and Mind*, both published by Oxford University Press.

DAVID S. HASLER is currently the senior director of Finance & Treasury, Investor Relations at Walmart, but has served the company in various other positions since 2006. Hasler received his MBA from Xavier University.

SIMON JOHNSON is a Ronald A. Kurtz professor of entrepreneurship at the Massachusetts Institute of Technology's Sloan School of Management and a senior fellow at the Peterson Institute for International Economics. He is also a cofounder of BaselineScenario.com, a popular Web site about the global economy and has coauthored a book with James Kwak, *13 Bankers: The Wall Street Takeover and the Next Financial Meltdown* (2010).

IRA T. KAY is the director of Watson Wyatt's compensation practice. He works closely with U.S., public, international, and private companies on long-term incentive plans to increase shareholder value. He conducts research on stock option overhang, executive pay and performance, and CEO stock ownership. He is a coauthor of *The Human Capital Edge, CEO Pay and Shareholder Value: Helping the U.S. Win the Global Economic War;* and *Value at the Top: Solutions to the Executive Compensation Crisis*. He holds a Ph.D. in economics from Wayne State University.

MARK R. KRAMER received his master's degree from the Wharton School at the University of Pennsylvania and his J.D. from the University of Pennsylvania Law School. He is the founder and managing director of the social impact consulting group, FSG and a senior fellow for the CSR Initiative with the Mossavar-Rahmani Center for Business in Government at the Harvard Kennedy School of Government. Kramer has had multiple articles published in *The Harvard Business Review* and *The Stanford Social Innovation Review*.

ERIC KRELL is a freelance writer, working with topics such as "corporate finance, corporate governance and compliance, business continuity management, the management consulting sector, human capital management, enterprise technology ROI, healthy living and personal fulfillment." His articles can be found in a wide variety of publications, from *Men's Fitness* to *Cooking Light* to *Baylor Business Review*. Krell received his education at the College of William and Mary and holds a B.A. from this institution.

JAMES HOWARD KUNSTLER is best known for his books *The Geography of Nowhere* (1994), a history of American suburbia and urban development, and the more recent *The Long Emergency* (2005). He has written a science fiction novel describing a future culture, *World Made by Hand* (2008). He is a leading proponent of the movement known as "New Urbanism." He has also written *Home from Nowhere* and *The City in Mind*.

JAMES KWAK received his J.D. from Yale Law School in 2011 and holds a Ph.D. in History from the University of California, Berkley. Kwak coauthored the book *13 Bankers: The Wall Street Takeover and the Next Financial Meltdown* (2010) with Simon Johnson, with whom he has coauthored many articles and also cofounded the popular Web site BaslineScenario.com.

ANNABELLE LEVER is currently a research fellow in interdisciplinary bioethics for the Institute of Science, Ethics and Innovation at the University of Manchester School of Law, as well as a Hoover Fellow in Economics and Social Ethics at The Catholic University in Belgium. Her areas of research include privacy, democracy, equality, intellectual property, and security.

Publications include her upcoming books, *On Privacy* and *Contemporary Democratic Theory: A Critical Introduction*, as well as multiple journal articles. Lever received her Ph.D. in political science from the Massachusetts Institute of Technology.

JOSEPH A. LEVITT, Esq. is the director, Center for Food Safety and Applied Nutrition, Food and Drug Administration, Department of Health and Human Services, Washington, DC.

ROGER LOWENSTEIN is a financial journalist and author. He worked for *The Wall Street Journal* for over a decade and continues to write for such publications as *SmartMoney* magazine and *The New York Times Magazine*. He has authored five books, including two best sellers, *Buffet: The Making of an American Capitalist* (1995) and *When Genius Failed: The Rise and Fall of Long-Term Capital Management* (2000). Lowenstein also serves as a director of the Sequoia Fund.

JOHN LUIK is a senior fellow with Washington think-tank, the Democracy Institute. Works by Luik include his book, *Unintended Consequences of Health Facism* (2011), and coauthored works *Diet Nation: Exposing the Obesity Crusade* (2006) and *Passive Smoke: The SPA's Betrayal of Science and Policy* (1999), as well as various journal articles regarding government involvement in obesity and the tobacco industry.

KARL MARX was born on May 5, 1818 in Trier, Germany. He studied jurisprudence at Bonn and later in Berlin. His preoccupation with philosophy turned him away from the law. Marx was expelled from several countries for his writings. Around 1844 while in Paris he became a close friend of Friedrich Engels. Together the two of them wrote fundamental economic and political theories in journal articles, newspapers, and numerous books. Some of these include *Communism and the Augsburg Allgemeine Zeitung* (Marx 1843): *Letters to Arnold Ruge* (Marx 1844), *Contribution to the Critique of Hegel's Philosophy of Right* (Marx 1844); *On The Jewish Question* (Marx 1844); *Critical Notes on "The King of Prussia"* (Marx 1845); *Theses on Feuerbach* (Marx 1847); *Communist League* (Marx 1847); *The Poverty of Philosophy* (Marx 1848) *The Communist Manifesto* (Marx/Engels 1848); *Communism, Revolution, and a Free Poland* (Marx 1848); *On the Question of Free Trade* (Marx/Engels 1849); *Wage-Labor and Das Capital* (Marx 1850); *England's Seventeenth-Century Revolution* (Marx/Engels 1852); *The Eighteenth Brumaire of Louis Napoleon* (Marx 1853); *Capital* (Marx 1867); *Landed Property* (Marx 1871); *Strategy and Tactics of the Class Struggle* (Marx/Engels 1879).

JOHN J. McCALL is a professor in the departments of philosophy and management at St. Joseph's University. He has also taught at Georgetown University's McDonough School of Business and at the Wharton School of the University of Pennsylvania. He is a coeditor (with Joe DesJardins) of *Contemporary Issues in Business Ethics,* now in its fourth edition. He has published works on welfare reform, corporate responsibility, product liability, and especially on employee rights issues.

RICK MORAN is a conservative freelance writer and "has worked for a number of business trade associations running programs that teach local businessmen how to become active in the political process." He is also the administrator of the Web site rightwingnutjob.com.

DONNA K. PEEPLES is an associate professor of Management at Texas A&M, Corpus Christie. Peeples received her MBA from Texas A&M and her Ph.D. from Texas A&M, Corpus Christie.

MICHAEL E. PORTER is an expert in the areas of competitive strategy, the competitiveness and economic development of nations, states, and regions, and the application of competitive principles to social problems (health care, the environment, social responsibility, etc.). He received his Ph.D. in business economics from Harvard University and is currently a Bishop William Lawrence University Professor at Harvard Business School. Apart from his work in academics, he developed and chairs the New CEO Workshop in conjunction with the Harvard Business School.

ROBERT J. SAMUELSON is a contributing editor for both *Newsweek* and *The Washington Post*, writing on economics and business. In addition to his career in journalism, Samuelson has authored multiple books, including *The Good Life and Its Discontents: The American Dream in the Age of Entitlement* (1995), *Untruth: Why the Conventional Wisdom Is (Almost Always) Wrong* (2001), and *The Great Inflation and Its Aftermath: The Past and Future of American Affluence* (2008).

MIRIAM SCHULMAN is the director of communications and administration for the Markkula Center for Applied Ethics at Santa Clara University. She received master's degrees in journalism from Columbia University and creative writing from Stanford University.

ADAM SMITH (1723–1790) was a Scottish moral philosopher and a pioneer of political economy. Smith was one of the key figures of the Scottish Enlightenment. He is the author of the *Theory of Moral Sentiments* (1759). It provided the ethical, philosophical, psychological, and methodological underpinnings of his later writings, including *An Inquiry Into the Nature and Causes of the Wealth of Nations* (1776), *A Treatise on Public Opulence* (1764) (first published in 1937), *Essays on Philosophical Subjects* (1795), *Lectures on Justice, Police, Revenue, and Arms* (1763) (first published in 1896), and *Lectures on Rhetoric and Belles Lettres*. Many economists believe that *The Wealth of Nations* is the first modern work of economics. He is often cited as the father of modern economics. Smith studied moral philosophy at the University of Glasgow and Oxford University. Smith obtained a professorship at Glasgow teaching moral philosophy.

JEREMY SNYDER has written several journal articles on price gouging, illegal organ transplantations, ethical problems with health workers, and caring within the "hospitalist model." He is an assistant professor at Simon Fraser University. He received his Ph.D. from Georgetown University.

GORDON G. SOLLARS is an associate professor of management at Farleigh Dickinson University at the Silberman College of Business. He has an MBA from the Wharton School, University of Pennsylvania, and a Ph.D. from the University of Virginia.

ROBERT C. SOLOMON was Quincy Lee Centennial Professor of Business and Philosophy and distinguished teaching professor at the University of Texas at Austin. He is the author of more than 40 books, 6 in business ethics: *Above the Bottom Line, It's Good Business, Ethics and Excellence, New World of Business, A Better Way to Think About Business,* and *Building Trust* (with Fernando Flores). He has written many articles, essays, and songs. He lectured and consulted worldwide for a variety of institutions and corporations. He died in 2007.

JUSTIN WELBY was ordained in the Church of England in 1992, before which he worked at a senior level in the oil industry in France and the UK. He is currently Sub Dean & Canon for Reconciliation Ministry at Coventry Cathedral, working on interfaith relations, reconciliation, and conflict resolution in the UK, Africa, and the Middle East. He is an ethical advisor at the UK Association of Corporate Treasurers. He has also chaired an NHS general hospital trust and two school boards.

EDGAR S. WOOLARD, JR. is a member of the Board of Telex Communications, Inc. He is a former director of the New York Stock Exchange, Inc., Citigroup Inc., IBM, Apple Computer, Inc., and Bell Atlantic Delaware. He is also a former chairman of the Business Council. He is a member of the Board of Trustees of the Christiana Care Health System and the North Carolina Textile Foundation, Inc., and a member of the National Academy of Engineering and the American Philosophical Society.

GREG YOUNG is an associate professor in the College of Management as well as the faculty fellow of the Enterprise Risk Management Initiative at North Carolina State University. Young also serves on the Editorial Board of the *Encyclopedia of Business Ethics and Society.* His areas of research include industry structure, organizational resources, strategic activity, decision making, and competitive advantage. His papers on these topics have been published in journals such as the *Strategic Management Journal* and *Journal of Business Research.*

MATT ZWOLINSKI has researched extensively in the area of the nature and moral significance of exploitation for individual ethics and political institutions. Other research includes work on the normative status of liberty and political liberalism. He recently published a textbook, *Arguing about Political Philosophy.* He is an assistant professor of philosophy at the University of San Diego, and a codirector of USD's Institute for Law and Philosophy.